FORENSICS IN LAW ENFORCEMENT

FORENSICS IN LAW ENFORCEMENT

MARIA V. SHOESTER
EDITOR

Nova Science Publishers, Inc.
New York

For permission to use material from this book please contact us:
Telephone 631-231-7269; Fax 631-231-8175
Web Site: http://www.novapublishers.com

Library of Congress Cataloging-in-Publication Data:
Forensics in law enforcement / Maria V. Shoester (editor).
p. cm.
Includes index.
ISBN 1-60021-164-X
1. Forensic genetics. 2. DNA fingerprinting. 3. Law enforcement. 4. Criminal investigation. 5. Evidence, Expert. 6. Forensic sciences. I. Shoester, Maria V.
RA1057.5.F67 2006
614'.1--dc22 2006010281

Published by Nova Science Publishers, Inc. ✢ New York

CONTENTS

PREFACE

In recent years forensic DNA evidence has been used by agencies and actors in the criminal justice system more and more frequently to both convict the guilty and exonerate the innocent. Cases that previously may have been unsolvable have been transformed into solvable cases where viable suspects can be identified and arrested or removed from suspect lists. This book presents examinations of how DNA, and some other forensic methods, are being used by our justice system and the issues that surround these uses.

In: Forensics in Law Enforcement
Editor: M. V. Shoester, pp. 1-63
ISBN 1-60021-164-X

Chapter 1

NATIONAL FORENSIC DNA STUDY REPORT*

***Nicholas P. Lovrich*[1], *Michael J. Gaffney*[1], *Travis C. Pratt*[1], *Charles L. Johnson*[1], *Smith Alling Lane, Christopher H. Asplen*[2], *Lisa H. Hurst*[3] *and Timothy M. Schellberg*[4]**

[1] 701 Johnson Tower; Washington State University; Pullman, Washington 99164;
[2] 1102 Broadway Plaza, Suite 403 Tacoma, Washington 98402 ;
[3] 927 – 15th Street NW, Suite 1200 Washington, District of Columbia 20005;
[4] 47 Marlborough Crescent London, England W4 1HG; December 12, 2003

EXECUTIVE SUMMARY

This report was prepared by Smith Alling Lane in partnership with Washington State University through the support of a grant awarded by the National Institute of Justice, Office of Justice Programs, U.S. Department of Justice (Grant 2002-LT-BX-K 003). Points of view or opinions in this document are those of the authors and do not necessarily represent the official position or policies of the United States Department of Justice.

In recent years forensic DNA evidence has been used by agencies and actors in the criminal justice system more and more frequently to both convict the guilty and exonerate the innocent. Cases that previously may have been unsolvable have been transformed into solvable cases where viable suspects can be identified and arrested or removed from suspect lists. While this new technology enhances the opportunity for the criminal justice system to "do justice" in more cases of suspected wrongdoing, it also creates an added need for law enforcement agencies to review old cases for potential biological evidence that should be sent to a crime laboratory for testing. Many policy makers are interested in discussing solutions to this problem of an added burden on law enforcement and crime laboratories, but they need to have a more complete understanding of the major dimensions of the problem – How big is the case backlog? How did it grow so large? What is the capacity of the evidence collection, storage, analysis and retrieval system to reduce that backlog and provide timely information for the criminal justice system?

---

* Excerpted from www.ncjrs.gov/pdffiles1/nij/grants/203970.pdf

This Report relied largely on a nation-wide mail assessment of local and state forensics laboratories and local law enforcement agencies, as well as extensive interviews of prosecutors, investigators and laboratory administrators to arrive at answers to the questions posed above. While it is generally acknowledged that there is likely a significant backlog of criminal cases that might benefit from DNA analysis, no effort had been made to quantify this number. This study arrives at estimates for the numbers of unsolved criminal cases in the U.S. which might benefit from DNA analysis, assesses both law enforcement and laboratory capacities for dealing with cases involving DNA, and identifies significant issues relating to the expansion of the use of DNA forensic analysis in criminal cases.

SUMMARY OF REPORT FINDINGS

Backlogs and Capacity

The Backlog of Unsolved Rapes and Homicides in the U.S. is Massive

Through the data collected from a large, representative sampling of local law enforcement agencies in the United States, the study arrives at the following pertinent estimates:

- The number of rape and homicide cases with possible biological evidence which local law enforcement agencies have not submitted to a laboratory for analysis is over 221,000.

    - Homicide cases – 52,000 (approximate)
    - Rape cases – 169,000 (approximate)

- The number of property crime cases with possible biological evidence which local law enforcement agencies have not submitted to a laboratory for analysis is over 264,000.
- The number of unanalyzed DNA cases reported by State and local crime laboratories is more than 57,000.

    - State laboratories – 34,700 cases (approximate)
    - Local laboratories – 22,600 cases (approximate)

- Total crime cases with possible biological evidence either still in the possession of local law enforcement, or backlogged at forensic laboratories is over one half million (542,700).

A Significant Proportion of Law Enforcement Agencies Continue to Misunderstand the Potential Benefits of DNA Testing

While these figures address the first question as to the approximate size of the case backlog, the second question remains regarding how the backlog came to grow so large. The answer to this question is quite complicated, and the phenomenon of a substantial growth in criminal case backlogs involves a variety of factors – some of which are vexing and difficult to manage. However, a series of questions posed to local law enforcement agencies and forensic laboratories reveal several interesting patterns of response which, when considered collectively, begin to provide an accurate picture of how the backlogs tend to develop and why they continue to exist. The following provides some of these responses:

Reasons why cases with DNA evidence have not been submitted to the laboratory:

- 50.8 percent of responding local law enforcement agencies indicated that forensic DNA was not considered a tool for crime investigations.
    - 31.4 percent responded that no suspect had been identified
    - 9.2 percent indicated that the prosecution had not requested testing
    - 10.2 percent responded that a suspect had been identified, but not yet charged
- 23.6 percent of responding agencies suggested that DNA evidence from unsolved cases was not submitted for reasons relating to poor funding.
    - 9.4 percent indicate a lack of funding for DNA analysis
    - 10.4 percent indicate inability of laboratories to produce timely results
    - 3.8 percent indicate crime laboratory is not processing requests for DNA testing

Both State and Local Crime Laboratories Are Overworked, Understaffed, and Insufficiently Funded

Processing times at crime laboratories pose significant delays in many jurisdictions. State laboratories take an average of 23.9 weeks to process an unnamed suspect rape kit, and local laboratories average 30.0 weeks for such tests. The cost for testing these rape kits was estimated at $1,100 per case, and does not account for many overhead costs. Both state and local laboratories indicated that personnel needs were among the most significant concerns for their DNA programs. Specifically, most crime laboratories expressed the need for supplemental funding for additional DNA staff; several laboratories indicated that their priority concern was for additional funding to augment current salaries to avoid the loss of skilled personnel to other prospective employers. A strong need was also reported for reagents (chemicals used in DNA analysis) and for technical equipment used for DNA analysis.

While the need for the expansion of mitochondrial DNA testing is substantial, the need for the more common nuclear DNA testing is even more pressing. Forensic laboratories reported nearly three thousand (2,999) cases over the last twelve-month period that could have benefited from mitochondrial testing.

The Role of the Federal Government in Funding Forensic DNA Analysis Has Been, Up to this Point, Important but Rather Minimal

Finally, most laboratories also reported that while federal funding has played an important role in assisting with backlogged DNA cases, the proportion of their overall DNA budgets funded through federal sources is minimal. Only 20.5 percent of state crime laboratories receive 50 percent or more of their funding from federal sources; that figure is only 4.5 percent for the local laboratories.

Benefits from DNA Analysis

Armed with a better understanding of the problem, policy makers subsequently ask for a definition of the expected benefits of devoting limited resources to the solution. Although this Report does not attempt a comprehensive, econometrically-derived cost-benefit analysis, the Report includes case studies on "preventable" crimes through strong DNA programs, along with an overview of DNA database successes.

Forensic DNA Databases are Important Tools in Solving a Variety of Crimes, Committed by a Variety of Criminals

The analysis of DNA database hits presented in the Report provides a breakdown of 4,092 DNA database hits in 38 states. The majority of database hits have linked repeat offenders to violent crimes. In fact, for several years the Virginia Division of Forensic Science has reported that more than 80% of the hits on the state's DNA database would have been missed if the database had been limited to only violent offenders. Most states, however, have only recently begun to require DNA testing for non-violent offenders for placement on their DNA database. Similarly, several laboratories will not process DNA evidence from property crimes if it is sent to the laboratory for analysis.

There are Numerous Crimes that are Potentially Preventable Through Better, More Efficient Use of Forensic DNA Analysis

A review of specific cases in nineteen states reveals over 100 serious crimes that could have been prevented through either the inclusion of all convicted felons in the database or shorter DNA analysis processing times. The early identification of repeat offenders is possible with comprehensive DNA databases, and just how that identification would be made is highlighted in each actual case.

The Cost and the Offsetting Benefits Associated with DNA Testing Present Several Questions Relating to Return on Investment which Merit Further Study

Finally, there are many additional benefits, and indeed costs, that are derived from expanded utilization of forensic DNA analysis. Although this Report discusses some of those benefits resulting from DNA database hits and preventable crimes, there are several additional areas for further study which may give policy makers a more vivid picture of how forensic DNA issues impact their communities.

I. Introduction

This Report summarizes the findings of an in-depth Forensic DNA Assessment project undertaken by Smith Alling Lane in partnership with the Division of Governmental Studies and Services at Washington State University. The study employed multiple data collection approaches, including a nation-wide mail assessment of local and state forensics laboratories and law enforcement agencies, as well as extensive interviews of prosecutors, investigators and laboratory administrators. The findings detailed herein are based upon data obtained through this process from significant numbers of law enforcement agencies, local forensics laboratories, state forensics laboratories, and dedicated individuals in every U.S. state. This study brings to bear scientific quantitative methodology and rigorous qualitative analysis on a question that has increasingly occupied public debate in both law enforcement and public policy circles. Recent newsworthy developments have fueled this broad interest – ranging from the activities of the *Innocence Project* in applying DNA analysis in pursuit of the release of those wrongfully convicted, to cases in which DNA has been used to solve long-unresolved cases and obtain convictions in extended serial cases. Heretofore *not* well addressed, however, have been the related questions of capacity and backlog at local law enforcement agencies and the corresponding impact, or potential for impact, at crime laboratories. While popular wisdom has acknowledged the existence of a backlog of cases that might benefit from the application of forensic DNA analysis, no clear insight into the extent of any such backlog has previously been available. Using the data compiled from this study, it is possible to make scientifically supportable estimates of the numbers of unsolved criminal cases in the U.S. which might benefit from DNA analysis, to assess both law enforcement and laboratory capacities for dealing with cases involving DNA, and to identify significant issues relating to the expansion of the use of DNA forensic analysis in criminal cases. Given this general background, this Report addresses a number of key issues for the continued development of comprehensive statistical data on the effectiveness of forensic DNA in both solving and preventing crime. In doing so, Section II describes the methods used in administering the assessment tool to law enforcement agencies, local crime laboratories and state crime laboratories. Section III presents the analyses results that estimate the backlog of unsolved homicide and rape cases in the U.S. Section IV then provides an overview of a number of issues associated with the capacity of these various agencies to collect and process forensic DNA evidence. The issue of unsolved case "hits" (based on CODIS data) is then addressed in Section V; Section VI considers the issue of DNA testing and crime prevention; and a discussion of cost-benefit analysis issues is in Section VII. The Report concludes in Section VIII with a review of the major findings derived from the study and the resulting implications for public policy development.

II. METHODOLOGY

As noted above, this study applies several distinct data collection methods. Section VI, for example, relies entirely on information collected using telephone interviews of local crime investigators and prosecutors. Sections III, IV, and V, on the other hand, report analysis of data collected through a series of self-administered assessment tools. The methodology developed for this portion of the study involves an application of Don Dillman's *Total Design Method* to a self-administered mail survey of law enforcement agencies and forensics laboratories. The ultimate goal of the study was to arrive at defensible estimates of the numbers of unsolved cases (homicides, rapes, and property crimes) extant in the U.S., of the backlog pressure that might be anticipated if DNA testing were applied to those cases, and of the impact which such testing might have upon agency (e.g., law enforcement and crime laboratory) capacity. To accomplish this goal a sampling protocol was constructed to allow for the assessment of a representative sample of law enforcement agencies, as well as nearly all state and local crime laboratories.

All state and local forensic DNA laboratories were thus assessed. (For the purposes of this study, the term "local" laboratory(ies) is defined to include those laboratories serving city, county or regional jurisdictions.) Responses were obtained from 50 state laboratories and 70 local laboratories across the country. This level of response provides an overwhelming confidence in the analysis conducted using the data provided by these laboratories. Because of the large number of local law enforcement agencies in this country (between 15,000, and 18,000 – depending upon the inclusion or exclusion of "special police" agencies such as the U.S. Border Patrol, airport police, etc.), the study design called for the development of a law enforcement agency sampling protocol. This protocol allowed for the selection of agencies from within twelve basic selection strata. Working from up-to-date national mailing lists, both Sheriff offices and municipal police departments were divided into strata on the basis of the number of commissioned officers employed by a law enforcement agency. All police agencies with over 100 commissioned officers (both Sheriff and municipal police agencies) were included. Random samples ranging from 500 to 1000 were taken from the remaining sampling frames thus identified (Unspecified size, Under 25 Officers, 25-50 Officers, 50-100 Officers) to which all tribal law enforcement agencies were added to arrive at a final mail sample list of approximately 3,400 law enforcement agencies. As discussed below, a significant number of agencies, particularly the larger organizations, completed the forensic DNA assessment questionnaire. Again, this relatively high level of response provides significant confidence in the results reported here. Local law enforcement agencies from every state, and representing approximately 154,467,000 citizens of the United States, responded to this assessment. Based upon the broadly representative nature of the many responding agencies, and based upon the overall response rate, the authors have a high level of confidence that the conclusions drawn from the analysis of the responses to the mail assessments are methodologically supportable and representative of law enforcement in the nation as a whole. Working from the list of law enforcement agencies developed through the sampling protocol, and similar current lists for state and local forensic laboratories, a three-wave mailing process was administered, with each non-responding agency ultimately receiving three separate mailings of the assessment tool and a letter encouraging completion of the form. Once the mail process was concluded, select non-responding laboratories and agencies were contacted by telephone in order to check for any bias related to non-response error in the survey process. The number of final responses (1,692 law enforcement agencies, 70 local laboratories, 50 state laboratories) provides significant confidence for the observations and conclusions contained in this article. Response rates for each size and type of entity are set forth in the table below. These rates of response compare favorably to the anticipated 40 percent minimum response rate set at the outset for this study, with higher response rates from the laboratories and larger law enforcement organizations increasing confidence in findings relating to those entities.

	State Forensics Laboratories	Local/Forensics Laboratories	Large LE Agencies	LE Agencies 50-100	LE Agencies 25-50	LE Agencies < 25	LE Agencies Unspecified
Responses	50[1]	70	586	287	476	170	98
Percent	100%	100%	59%	52%	47.6%	34%	19.8%

194 Tribal law enforcement agencies were mailed assessment forms. However, with a response rate of approximately 27.8 percent (54 responses) the data did not generate statistically reliable information.

Analysis of the responses obtained from this mail-out assessment collection process indicates that the final assessment dataset derived from the data collection effort is broadly representative of the local law enforcement agency community nationally. The law enforcement agency responses are (in a geographic sense) proportionately spread across the agency size strata identified above, and they represent local police agencies from each of the fifty states. In this analysis, only tribal agencies and those of unspecified size are under-represented among participating agencies. In many instances the tribal agencies did not have access to the data sought by the assessment since the federal government (Bureau of Indian Affairs) typically handles these types of cases on reservations. One issue does arise from the consideration of the level of response achieved in the study. The smaller agencies did not respond at as high a rate as did the large agencies, and those agencies of unspecified size responded at a rather low rate. This unfortunate fact influenced both our analyses and some of the conclusions drawn; in light of this limitation, particularly conservative approaches to the analysis of central tendencies and in the estimation of backlogs were employed. Researchers compensated for this reduced confidence regarding the smaller agencies when dealing with total numbers or issues specific to these classes of law enforcement agencies. In follow-up questioning with those non-responding agencies, a lack of resources was the primary reason given for failure to complete the assessment. In many jurisdictions, case management systems are either non-existant or so antiquated as to not be of much utility in developing the numbers requested in the assessment. Moreover, local jurisdictions did not have the manpower to devote scarce personnel resources to manually reviewing old case files for open cases that may contain DNA evidence.

While due care was taken to develop conservative estimates, it should be noted that the analysis confirms the anticipated utility of the assessment process and the data obtained from the effort. For instance, relatively few agencies report difficulty in responding to the questionnaires (e.g., only 10.9 percent of large agencies report being unable to formulate an educated guess in response to a question about rape cases with potential DNA evidence). In short, sufficient data of good quality have been received as a consequence of the mail assessment collection process to allow estimation of national totals with considerable confidence, especially given the cautionary note above and the conservative estimation approach applied as a result.

III. Casework Backlogs

One of the single most troublesome obstacles to generating accurate figures from the local law enforcement assessment is that a significant portion of respondents (particularly from the larger jurisdictions) indicate that an educated guess on issues of unsolved rapes and homicides is not possible without a time-consuming comprehensive review of case records. Many jurisdictions are not able, or possibly were not willing, to venture a guess as to how many cases are still open—much less speculate as to whether or not there may be biological evidence associated with such criminal offenses. In order to generate the most accurate estimates possible, project researchers worked directly with these jurisdictions over the telephone and through e-mail communications to encourage supportable "educated guesses" for these few agencies. The researchers did not suggest to the agencies methodologies for developing numbers, but rather spoke with various departments within agencies (such as homicide units, sexual assault units and property rooms) to encourage coordination and completion of the assessment. With a combination of assessment instrument-based evidence and these "refined guesses" for a small number of law enforcement agencies, it was possible to generate figures for consideration which provide some needed perspective on the likely scale of the current forensic DNA analysis backlog issue in this country. It is possible to apply multiple methods to the estimation of backlogs of cases involving forensic DNA evidence. Federal Bureau of Investigation (FBI) crime statistics serve as one source of estimation, the mail assessment process serves as a second source, and conventional statistical estimation techniques serve as yet a third. Of some limited assistance in this regard are national Uniform Crime Report (UCR) figures, reported annually by the FBI. These crime figures, unfortunately, are summary at best, and hence of rather limited utility. With these caveats in mind, a rough calculation of a 10-year figure for backlogged cases (murders and rapes) can be made using an average generated from the most recent three years reported by the FBI. This estimation approach leads to the conclusion that there are at least 49,000 unsolved murder cases in the U.S. (as of January 1, 2002). Because this method of backlog estimation does not assess truly old cases (older than 10 years), and because it does not include the immediately previous calendar years' figures, this figure is in all probability a low estimate. Applying the same cautious approach to the estimation of unsolved rapes leads to a figure of at least 470,000 unsolved cases. One significant shortcoming of UCR data as they relate to the purposes of this Report is that the FBI crime data summaries do not identify cases with biological evidence which could yield DNA findings. Using the data obtained through the mail assessment data collection process, it is possible (as was done for the Preliminary Report on this study) to extrapolate total numbers of backlogged cases as well. For purposes of validation, this was done by calculating an average figure for each type of case for each of the six strata of law enforcement agencies. That mean number was then multiplied by the total number of agencies of that size in the United States to obtain a national backlog subtotal for each stratum. Adding up these figures provides an estimated national total for each type of crime. This approach provides an estimated backlog of unsolved murder cases of more than 170,000 cases, more than 60,000 of which involve DNA evidence. The same estimation approach yields figures of more than 593,000 total unsolved rapes and more than 430,000 unsolved rape cases featuring forensic DNA evidence. The full range of calculations associated with this approach and the UCR estimations are set forth in the appendices to this Report.

However useful these figures might be for a rough estimation, both of these approaches are somewhat problematic. The UCR data are too summary in character, and they do not include DNA information. The raw data from the mail assessment study are skewed upwards by the presence of the very large agencies, and/or agencies with very strong evidence retention policies, and rely uncomfortably on data obtained from the "unspecified size" agency category – a category with low response rate and a high degree of variation in response. In order to compensate for these shortcomings in the data, other more complex statistical techniques must be employed which provide a higher level of confidence. Given the caution related to response rates discussed above, and the extremely skewed distributions of each of the measures being assessed in this section (unsolved rapes and homicides, and unsolved property crimes), which was driven by the large estimates from the larger law enforcement agencies, the following estimates were calculated in multiple ways to ensure that they are not the artifacts of a single method of statistical estimation. In particular, the following summary estimate figures were generated by a semi-parametric method that involved a *weighted decile* approach (excluding the cases at the 10th and 90th percentiles in the calculation of the mean and confidence interval estimates, and adding the excluded cases back into the end totals). This conventional statistical estimation approach was taken so that the estimates from the large law enforcement agencies would be reflected fully in the totals calculated, but would not disproportionately influence the calculation of the mean estimates. These results were then checked according to several standard statistical diagnostic procedures. These commonly used procedures in the management of estimation problems included performing log transformations on each variable of interest in order to correct for skewness (separate analyses for both log base 10 and "e" were conducted), and calculating separate estimates within each strata of agency size (under the assumption that pattern of skewness may vary according to the size of the agency, which it certainly did) with and without log transformations. In the end, none of the results from these several diagnostic statistical procedures produced backlog estimates that differed significantly (at $p<.05$) from those reported in this Report. The researchers, therefore, quite confident that the estimates arrived at here are not contingent upon any particular analytic strategy.[2]

A. Unsolved Rapes and Homicides

Table 3.1 contains the estimated total number of unsolved homicides and unsolved rapes extant in the U.S. at the time of the mail assessment data collection effort, along with estimates of the number of cases which likely feature possible forensic DNA evidence. Agencies were asked to count unsolved cases dating back to 1982 (twenty years). With regard to unsolved rape and unsolved homicide cases, there are currently an estimated 96,141 unsolved homicide cases and an estimated 304,178 unsolved rape cases reported by local law enforcement agencies in the U.S. in 2002-2003. Upon combining these two estimates, researchers arrive at an extrapolated total of 400,319 unsolved homicide and rape cases nationally. If the upper limits of the confidence intervals are used as an estimate (what will be referred to as "adjusted totals"), there may actually be as many as 432,179 unsolved homicides and rape cases nationally.

Local law enforcement agencies were also asked how many murder and rape cases contained possible biological evidence that had not been sent to a laboratory for testing. These findings, also displayed in Table 3.1, show that a substantial portion of the adjusted totals for rape (169,229) and homicide (51,774) cases have not been sent to a forensic laboratory for testing—indeed, using the adjusted totals, an extrapolated total of 221,003 cases may contain biological evidence that has not been sent to a forensic laboratory for DNA testing.

Table 3.1. Estimated national totals for unsolved homicides, rapes, and property offenses and estimates of cases with possible DNA evidence.[3]

Offense Type	Total	95% Confidence Interval
Unsolved Homicides	96,141	91,281 to 101,001
Unsolved Homicides with DNA	48,324	44,904 to 51,774
Unsolved Rapes	304,178	277,178 to 331,178
Unsolved Rapes with DNA	154,649	140,069 to 169,229
Total Property Crimes with DNA	253,931	243,491 to 264,371

Note: A similar table reports crime laboratory backlog estimates as well later in the text

B. Unsolved Property Offenses

The majority of law enforcement agencies report that forensic DNA evidence is *not* routinely collected from property crime scenes, and similarly a preponderant majority of local and state crime laboratories report that law enforcement does not perform "routine" collection of DNA from property crimes. The common assumption (made by nearly half of the law enforcement agencies) is that their local or state crime laboratory does *not* accept DNA evidence from property crimes for unnamed suspects. However, 75 percent of reporting local laboratories and 88 percent of state laboratories report that they *do* accept and process unnamed suspect property crime evidence. These mail assessment findings point to a shortcoming in the understanding by law enforcement of the policies of forensic laboratories that serve them. These findings also signal an inconsistency between local law enforcement's understanding of what forensic analysis is being done versus what the actual services of their crime laboratories are in practice. They could also signal an inconsistency between the reported versus actual practices of those forensic laboratories.

Despite this apparent "information gap" between local law enforcement agencies' perceptions and crime laboratory policies, the information collected in the law enforcement assessment process still allows an estimated total number of property crimes that may contain biological evidence across the nation. Accordingly, using the adjusted totals in Table 3.1, there is an extrapolated total of as many as 264,371 property offenses with possible biological evidence in the U.S.

Thus, upon adding the adjusted numbers of homicides, rapes, property crimes and "other" cases with possible DNA evidence from law enforcement agencies and state and local crime laboratories, there are currently as many as 542,723 unsolved homicide, rape, and property offense cases for possible DNA analysis known to law enforcement agencies and crime laboratories in the U.S.

C. Other Offenses

Other types of offenses for which DNA evidence could exist are not reflected in Table 3.1 because the assessment tool did not seek this information from local law enforcement agencies. Such offenses could include crimes such as assault, battery and kidnapping.

In designing the assessment tool, the researchers placed a considerable amount of emphasis on developing questions that would generate accurate responses without being overly burdensome on the responding agency. The initial emphasis of this question set was on counting the potential number of unsolved homicides and rapes with possible DNA evidence – those crimes typically considered the most heinous by society, and therefore the most important to solve. The researchers feel the general public come to expect DNA analysis for these types of cases.

The question regarding the number of unsolved property crimes was intended to provide a picture of where the United States could be headed in terms of future DNA analysis demands. While also asking for the number of "other" types of crimes with potential DNA evidence might have provided a broader picture of the number of backlogged DNA cases in the country, the researchers were concerned that requesting additional figures would only result in higher numbers of local agencies determining that they did not have the staff resources or automated systems required to complete the assessment.

Therefore, in reading the figures in the preceding sections A and B, it is important to bear in mind that these figures potentially exclude a large number of other types of crimes for which DNA evidence may be instrumental in solving. Because many crime laboratories do routinely track the types of cases for which DNA analysis is needed, a category for "other" case backlog was included in their assessment instrument. For comparison purposes, consider that of the over 57,300 backlogged DNA cases reported by state and local crime laboratories, at least 5,200 of these cases were classified as "other" – accounting for nearly 10 percent of all backlogged cases. (See Chapter IV, *Crime Laboratory Backlogs* for a further discussion of DNA backlogs at crime laboratories).

IV. Agency Capacity

This section addresses a number of issues concerning the capacity of the various agencies to collect and process forensic DNA evidence (see the appendix for the distributions of values for all variables in the law enforcement, local laboratory, and state laboratory assessments). In particular, this section is separated into the capacity issues facing law enforcement agencies versus local and state crime laboratories. The selected law enforcement issues to be considered include: (1) where law enforcement agencies typically send cases for DNA analysis; (2) biological evidence storage issues; (3) the reasons why DNA evidence for either unsolved homicides or rapes is not sent to a crime laboratory for testing; and, (4) cold case squad reviews. With regard to the local and state crime laboratories, the selected capacity issues highlighted in this section include: (1) those associated with the evidence typically compiled in backlogged cases; (2) the cases that are currently within the statute of limitations; (3) the expected backlog of cases estimated by the crime laboratories; (4) the average time for analysis and the output capacity of the laboratories; (5) the major barriers associated with processing DNA evidence, with particular attention to property offenses; (6) the potential need for mitochondrial DNA testing; and, (7) cost/funding issues.

A. Law Enforcement

Case Processing

With regard to general case processing, the findings set forth in Table 4.1 suggest that 80.1 percent of law enforcement agencies report that the primary location for sending DNA evidence for processing is state crime laboratories. Conversely, only 11.7 percent of law enforcement agencies reported that local and regional crime laboratories are the primary places to which they send forensic DNA evidence for testing. Another 4.2 percent reported that their evidence is sent elsewhere ("other"). However, in reviewing the description that these agencies included with their description of "other", it appears that this category in fact meets the definition of a "local" laboratory as used in this study; thus bringing the number of agencies using local laboratories up to 15.9 percent

Table 4.1. Primary locations where law enforcement agencies send DNA evidence for testing

Location to which DNA Evidence is Sent	Law Enforcement Agencies Responding (%)
State Agency Laboratory	80.1
FBI Laboratory	1.1
Private Laboratory/Commercial Laboratory	2.9
Local Agency Laboratory	11.7
Other (regional, medical examiner, county)	4.2

At first glance it may appear that state crime laboratories are performing the majority of casework DNA analysis. Even so, many of the larger U.S. cities and counties, where the majority of reported homicides and rapes take place, are served by local crime laboratories. Thus, although a greater number of law enforcement agencies report that they send their cases to state laboratories for DNA analysis, a relatively significant proportion of the overall DNA casework in the U.S. is in fact conducted in local crime laboratories. In point of fact, an estimated minimum of 80 million U.S. residents are being served by such local crime laboratories. With an estimated U.S. population of slightly more than 280 million according to the 2000 U.S Census Bureau data, local laboratory DNA testing accounts for nearly 30 percent of all DNA testing being done in the country. Moreover, of the 25 U.S. cities with the highest crime rate per capita (as reported in the 2001 UCR data), more than half (14) are being served by local crime laboratories. Additional analyses (see appendix) indicate that the larger jurisdictions also have greater needs for DNA testing. Specifically, in addition to having a larger caseload of rapes and homicides in general, the large law enforcement agencies reported a slightly higher estimate of the proportion of rape cases that are likely to contain DNA evidence, where 53 percent of large agencies estimated that between 75-100 percent of rape cases are likely to contain DNA evidence relative to 47 percent of all other law enforcement agencies. With regard to homicides, roughly 58 percent of both large and all other law enforcement agencies estimated that between 75-100 percent of all homicides are likely to contain DNA evidence. It should be noted that these estimates reflect the *expectations* of law enforcement, and are not necessarily indicative of the percentage of cases that test positive for DNA at the crime laboratory. These types of "local considerations" must be taken into full consideration in reviewing the findings reported here. Therefore, although it is undoubtedly true that the majority of forensic DNA analysis is performed by state laboratories, it is also the case that the local laboratories primarily serve major metropolitan populations that have high crime rates, and as a consequence may generate a higher level of demand for DNA analysis. Many of these large local jurisdictions may also benefit from from better evidence collection training programs, developed with the assistance of the local crime laboratory. Also of note, a relatively low number of law enforcement agencies utilize DNA analysis by either the FBI crime laboratory or private forensic laboratories. The FBI crime laboratory serves the agencies of the federal government, including the Bureau of Indian Affairs, and the District of Columbia almost exclusively. Though there is capacity at private laboratories for additional DNA analysis, many jurisdictions do not have the financial resources to pay the fees associated with such forensic testing.

Storage

Of those cases where biological crime scene evidence is not sent to a crime laboratory for testing, or evidence is returned to the local agency if current technology cannot produce results, a central concern for many law enforcement agencies is the availability of appropriate storage space for unanalyzed evidence. Pressures on evidence storage space can result in degradable biological evidence being maintained under improper conditions—or worse yet, being discarded or not collected at all for a lack of space to store it safely. Lack of appropriate storage space can lead to valuable DNA evidence becoming degraded and requiring a more expensive and potentially less exact DNA analysis process to be employed (see "Mitochondrial DNA Testing" section for further discussion). In addition to the need to retain evidence from unsolved crimes in the event that new advances in forensic technology (such as DNA testing) may identify a suspect in the future, law enforcement agencies are also facing increasing statutory requirements to preserve evidence pertinent to cases considered "solved." Cases where post-conviction DNA testing has resulted in extraordinary exoneration have led a number of state legislatures to impose requirements for the indefinite storage of evidence used in serious crime convictions. While such systematic storage activity is important to the enhancement of the criminal justice system's capacity to "do justice" for its citizens, such requirements for evidence storage frequently take the form of an unfunded mandate passed down to local jurisdictions from their respective state governments. It is also worth noting that over a fifth (22 percent) of law enforcement agencies reported that some of their unanalyzed evidence is stored at the crime laboratory rather than in agency evidence repositories. Among police agencies reporting that biological evidence is stored at the crime laboratory, nearly 40 percent were the largest jurisdictions. Again, considering that larger jurisdictions typically have higher crime rates and a high demand for forensic DNA analysis, this finding suggests that many crime laboratories may also be facing similar strains on evidence storage capacity. Moreover, many laboratories are also required to store evidence after analysis is completed, and therefore face many of the same unfunded mandates for evidence storage for "solved" cases as well as for "unsolved" cases. As a consequence many laboratories find they are responsible for not only storing their own cases – both unanalyzed backlog cases and analyzed evidence – but also those of the law enforcement jurisdictions they serve. In the area of lost forensic evidence, there have been widely publicized reports of large metropolitan law enforcement agencies discarding potential DNA evidence (e.g., rape kits) in an effort to create additional storage space for new evidence. Regardless of whether these reported actions were the result of honest mistakes or the consequence of faulty agency decision-making processes, the fact remains that this critical evidence is forever lost to future crime investigations. Table 4.2 summarizes these storage issues for local law enforcement agencies. As can be seen quite clearly in this table, most law enforcement agencies (79.0 percent) indicate that unanalyzed evidence is typically held in a centralized storage area. Six-in-ten (61.0 percent) of these agencies indicated that they currently have insufficient storage capacity for evidence retention needs relating to DNA evidence. It is also important to note that three-in-four (75.7 percent) of the large law enforcement agencies indicated that gaining additional space for the effective preservation of evidence was either of "critical"[4] or "highly critical"[5] importance (with 70.3 percent of all responding agencies responding similarly).

Table 4.2. Storage locations for unanalyzed evidence and long-term storage needs

Storage Issue for Local Law Enforcement Agencies	Law Enforcement Agencies Responding (%)
Where unanalyzed evidence is stored	
Centralized storage area	79.0
Decentralized storage areas/various district locations	3.1
Prosecutor's facility	2.0
Crime laboratory facility	22.2
Other	5.6
Does agency have sufficient space for long-term evidence storage?	
Yes	39.0
No	61.0
Is the need for more storage space "critical" or "highly critical"?	70.3

Failure to Send DNA for Testing in Rape and Homicide Cases

Part of what may be driving these backlog numbers and storage capacity issues at local law enforcement agencies are the specific reasons behind why forensic DNA evidence from unsolved homicides and unsolved rapes have not been sent to a crime laboratory for testing. Table 4.3 contains the percentages for common explanations provided to law enforcement agencies to choose from in the mail assessment instrument.

For those agencies indicating that rape or homicide evidence has not been sent to a crime laboratory for testing, Table 4.3 indicates that the primary reason is that a suspect has not yet been identified (31.4 percent of all responding agencies). Clearly, these "no suspect" cases are exactly the types of crime scene evidence that need to be submitted in order for the DNA database to be effective.

This finding is a strong indication that forensic DNA testing is not considered an investigatory tool by a significant portion of law enforcement agencies which have chosen not to send biological evidence to a crime laboratory for testing. Two other categories of response to this question are of a similar nature, and they warrant consideration as part of this discussion. The responses "A suspect has been identified but not yet charged," and "Analysis not requested by prosecutors" again show the bias towards using DNA analysis as a tool for the prosecution but not necessarily as an aid to identifying a suspect. When all three categories are combined, an estimated 50.8 percent of respondents indicated that forensic DNA was not considered a tool for law enforcement criminal investigations. Rather, DNA evidence is considered a tool for the prosecution – evidence to secure a conviction after traditional police investigations have already identified the suspected criminal.

This revelation is particularly important for the corresponding impact it has upon DNA databases – crime scenes in which there are no suspects are precisely the types of cases that need to be submitted in order for the DNA database to be effective. The purpose of the DNA database is to link known offenders to crimes with no known suspects, and to link unsolved crimes together, thereby providing detectives either with suspects or with new investigatory leads. The fact that law enforcement agencies are purposely not submitting these cases indicates that there is limited understanding as to the nature and purpose of DNA databases. In fact, the study found that in many instances law enforcement officials were unaware of the fact that a DNA database has been established. For illustration, consider the following comments:

One large law enforcement agency commented simply:

"National DNA Database Needed."

Three other law enforcement agencies recorded these comments:

"A database similar to automated fingerprinting should be the goal. Perhaps regional database established by the DOJ for the nation."

"This department would be interested in seeing a DNA database started. It could be accomplished by making the giving of samples mandatory after conviction of a crime."

"Need national database with rules for collecting samples, like with fingerprints."

It should be noted that these comments came from law enforcement agencies scattered throughout the U.S., and from agencies of varying sizes (NOT exclusively small agencies). This limited knowledge of the DNA database is troublesome, but it should not be construed as an accurate reflection of law enforcement's desire for such a tool. In fact, when asked if the law enforcement agency filling out the assessment would be interested in using forensic DNA databases more frequently if there was a reasonable expectation that an unnamed suspect could be quickly identified, an overwhelming 96.9 percent responded positively. Many of the agencies responding negatively indicated that they needed no access to the database since the state laboratory took care of database searches. However, a handful of agencies also explained that they believed DNA to be too expensive for their jurisdiction or they had too few crimes to justify DNA testing. Also reflective of law enforcement's interest in becoming more knowledgeable about forensic DNA evidence in crime fighting is the fact that two National Institute of Justice resources – *What Every Law Enforcement Officer Should Know About DNA Evidence – Beginning Level Module and Advanced Level Module* – are frequently requested by law enforcement professionals. In fact, numerous agencies responding to the assessment specifically requested additional information about DNA and expressed an interest in the availability of pertinent training on the use of DNA databases. (These agencies were all put in contact with the appropriate personnel at the National Institute of Justice for further assistance.) Another theme in agency responses regarding failure to submit biological evidence for testing relates to cost and resource (fiscal considerations). Individually, few agencies reported that evidence is not sent to crime laboratories because of a lack of funding for DNA analysis (9.4 percent), the inability of crime laboratories to produce timely results (10.4 percent), or because crime laboratories are not processing requests for DNA (3.8 percent). However, each of these reasons may be considered in the overall context of *fiscal limitations*. Timely results require the existence of adequate capacity on the part of crime laboratories to handle demand, and such capacity is limited by resources. Crime laboratories that may not be processing requests for DNA testing do so primarily as a fallback means of *caseload management*, which is limited by capacity, which is limited in turn by resources. So, taken together, an estimated 23.6 percent of agencies do not submit DNA cases for reasons relating to poor funding. This grouping represents the second most frequently indicated reason for not submitting evidence for DNA testing. In fact, the issue of *lengthy delays* in DNA analysis time was identified as a major concern by a significant number of respondents who chose to include comments with their assessment instrument responses. Police agencies throughout the country often face long delays in requested DNA analysis, which in turn limits the usefulness of DNA as an investigative tool for the police. Delays meanwhile are typically caused by crime laboratory resources that are inadequate to meet the demand for testing. The following comments regarding laboratory delays also reinforce the results discussed previously regarding the fact that law enforcement tends to view DNA as a tool for prosecutors and not for detectives:

> "[The] state laboratory has over a four-year wait for processing DNA from property crimes. Therefore we do not submit it unless the crime is of major significance."
>
> "DNA cases sent to laboratory with no suspect having been arrested are 1-2 year wait, even if a suspect is named and in [a] DNA database." "
>
> [The] State Police Laboratory system is inadequate for producing timely results – average waiting period is 1½ - 2 years."
>
> "DNA evidence is beginning to have a significant impact on our investigations. However, the process of DNA evidence is expensive and creates a financial burden for the local police and the state laboratories. If funding was not an issue, DNA would prove to be on [sic] of the most valuable tools in solving cases."

These comments represent a sampling of the over 100 responding agencies which felt strongly enough about this issue that they were compelled to add written comments on their assessment response. Clearly, the delay in processing time and associated fiscal considerations are issues that law enforcement agencies have identified as obstacles to their use of DNA evidence. There also appears to be a disconnect between local agencies who complain of one to two year delays on DNA testing (and one agency reporting four year), and laboratories who report average processing times of 23-30 weeks (see further discussion in the section on "Processing Time and Output Capacity"). These issues bring to bear a larger question relating to evidence collection. Specifically, if law enforcement officers do not see DNA as a primary part of their investigation, and those agencies which would like to use

DNA for investigations are limited in doing so due to evidence analysis turnaround times that are not constructive to ongoing crime investigations, then what effect do these factors have on the likelihood that investigators will identify, collect and submit DNA evidence? On the basis of discussions with law enforcement officials, that this situation of systematic disincentives occurs more often than would be preferred. Consider the following true story related to researchers in one of these background discussions. The owners of a car parked on a residential street heard a collision one night and ran outside to find their car had been hit by another vehicle. The local police department was called to the scene for an accident report. The owners of the damaged vehicle had noticed a section of the car where paint from the offending vehicle had been transferred during the collision, and asked the officers if they intended to take paint chip samples for forensic analysis. The officers agreed to collect a sample, but informed the owners that the sample probably would not be sent to the state laboratory for testing because it would be "too expensive." This was news to one of the owner's, who happened to be a state crime laboratory employee. Not only was he certain that local jurisdictions were not asked to pay for such testing, but the trace evidence unit also verified that they had the time and capacity to analyze these types of cases. After some follow-up with the investigating agency, the evidence sample was eventually forwarded to the laboratory for analysis.

While this example is not specific to DNA, it illustrates a line of reasoning which is worth contemplation: how much potentially valuable DNA evidence is simply not collected by law enforcement officials who have little hope that forensic analysis will be conducted in a timely manner? And when collected, how often is such evidence actually sent to the laboratory for testing? This scenario is quite likely for non-violent crimes such as property offenses where a large majority of law enforcement agencies report that their respective crime laboratories do not conduct such testing. In fact, some comments from law enforcement agencies on this issue seem to indicate that this may be a bigger problem than anticipated. For example, the comments from three responding agencies clearly suggest the scale of the problem in question:

> "I have just recently been trained in collection of DNA. Before my training, I am unaware of any cases where DNA was collected."

> "I am not familiar enough with DNA collecting to know how it effects [sic] my agency."

> "We provided all property detectives with DNA evidence training 2 months ago with the request to make testing routine. This is in progress. However, it is a cultural change that is difficult."

This type of observation makes accurate extrapolation extremely difficult, but by looking at the converse of this scenario, the potential value of a fully functional forensic DNA crime laboratory setting may be understood. Virginia's forensic DNA program is among the most mature in the nation and the state database has been averaging one cold hit per day for the last two years. Virginia's processing time for DNA evidence, while not ideal, is by far more efficient than the majority of other forensic crime laboratories in the country. Additionally, and perhaps most importantly, Virginia's crime laboratory does not limit (within reason) the type of case or the type of evidence that can be submitted. This means that the Virginia crime laboratory is just as willing to conduct DNA analysis in a murder case as it is for a breaking and entering case under investigation. These factors – short processing time, database successes, and liberal case submission policy – have resulted in a steady rate of growth every year in the number of cases submitted for biological testing. In fact the crime laboratory estimates that the amount of evidence submitted by law enforcement for DNA analysis grows by 30 percent every year. Does this mean that there were far *fewer* available DNA cases in previous years? Not likely, but rather the fact that crime investigators feel more encouraged to submit DNA evidence for analysis in Virginia likely accounts for that growth rate. This encouragement, coupled with the positive reinforcement of frequent DNA database matches, has resulted in a cadre of crime investigators across the state who tend to view the processing of crime scene DNA evidence as an effective means of reducing their caseload.

Table 4.3. Reasons why law enforcement agencies do not send DNA evidence from unsolved homicide and rape cases to a crime laboratory for testing

Explanation for Not Sending DNA Evidence from Unsolved Crimes to Crime Laboratories for Analysis	% of Law Enforcement Agencies Responding
A suspect has not yet been identified	31.4
A suspect has been identified but not yet charged	10.2
Guilty plea is expected	13.9
Uncertain how DNA analysis would be useful in case	6.1
Lack of funding for DNA analysis	9.4
Inability of laboratories to produce timely results	10.4
Laboratory is not processing requests for DNA testing	3.8
Uncertain where to send the case for DNA analysis	0.9
Analysis not requested by prosecutors	9.2
Other	9.7

Cold Case Review

The final backlog issue to explore is cold case review squads and policies. Cold case squads have been used in various jurisdictions throughout the country to reopen old cases for new investigatory leads. Many such cases have been found to contain DNA evidence which has been tested to solve crimes that are decades old. This type of review recently led to the identification of a suspect in the "Green River Killer" serial murders. The Green River Killer was thought to be responsible for 49 deaths over three years in the Seattle, Washington area. Biological evidence was collected from many of the murders, which began in 1982, and was kept in storage. After a review of the evidence in 2001, some pieces were selected and sent to the state crime laboratory for possible DNA analysis. The state crime laboratory was able to extract a DNA sample, and the analysis produced a match to a man who had always been considered a prime suspect by investigators. The suspect was initially charged with seven counts of murder, and eventually pleaded guilty to 48 counts of murder. The example of the Green River case is a valuable one because it demonstrates the utility of DNA to old investigations in which primary suspects are known but could not be linked directly to the crime.

Law enforcement agencies were asked if they have a "cold case squad" or other established policy for reviewing unsolved violent crimes for fresh investigatory leads, such as new DNA testing. It is important to note that many agencies, particularly the smaller ones, do not have the organizational resources to form actual "cold case" squads. For this reason, the assessment instrument question on this topic included language that allowed for "other policy for reviewing unsolved violent crimes." Of those agencies with a cold case squad (or a related periodic unsolved case review policy), the assessment also inquired as to the number of cases potentially eligible for review, how many cases have been reviewed recently, and how many cases have been sent for DNA testing.

Table 4.4 contains the results posed by these questions. As indicated, only slightly more than one-in-five (22.8 percent) law enforcement agencies report that they have a cold case squad or similar review policy, and possibly due to resource issues mentioned above the percentage for large agencies is somewhat higher at 38.6 percent. Among the group of agencies without a current cold case squad or related policy, 49.4 percent of the large agencies (and 37.9 percent of all agencies) report that they plan to review old, unsolved cases for new investigatory opportunities such as DNA testing. This leaves just under half (48.6 percent) of the agencies which neither have cold case review policies in place nor any plans for such a review. One large agency indicated that the task of responding to the DNA assessment inspired a discussion on cold cases in the jurisdiction that could potentially benefit from DNA testing. The agency had not previously considered reviewing cold cases for DNA, but was now planning a systematic agency review. Although it is encouraging to learn that this data collection effort has possibly spurred the review of solvable cases that may otherwise have remained in storage, it is also somewhat telling that the agency had not considered such a review beforehand.

Table 4.4. Cold case squad review

Assessment Item	Statistics	
Does agency have a "cold case squad"?	Yes = 22.8%	No = 77.2%
Of those jurisdictions that have a cold case squad		
	Median	*Mean*
Cases eligible for review	5.0	71.3
Cases reviewed	4.0	22.3
Reviewed cases sent for DNA testing	0.0[6]	6.3

Table 4.4 also shows a significant variation in volumes of cold cases that have been reviewed (or are considered eligible for review) by those agencies reporting the existence of cold case squads or periodic unsolved cases review policies. This variation is evidenced by the fact that the mean and median values are substantially different from one another—indicating significant positive skewness—in the distributions of these variables. In other words, there is a high degree of variation in the responses where many agencies report relatively small numbers and a few agencies report extremely large numbers on these items. Thus, a median number of 0.0 arose due to this severe "upward skewness." A median number of 0 indicates that a significant number of agencies with cold case review squads have not sent any of their cases to a crime laboratory for DNA testing; only a handful of agencies have been responsible for the majority of DNA testing coming out of these specialized units. This failure to submit DNA evidence could be due to a variety of factors, ranging from a determination of non-probative value, to a tendancy of law enforcement to rely more heavily on "traditional" investigative techniques -- particularly when confronted with long backlogs

at public crime laboratories and testing fees at private laboratories. While this assessment did not specifically ask cold case squads to quantify underlying reasons for why DNA evidence has not been submitted, clues to possible answers may be found in the previous section's general discussion on treatment of DNA evidence by law enforcement agencies ("Failure to Send DNA for Testing in Rape and Homicide Cases").

B. Local and State Crime Laboratories

Crime Laboratory Backlogs

State and local crime laboratories reported an estimated 57,349 backlogged cases awaiting DNA analysis, with 34,723 cases at state laboratories and 22,626 cases at the local and regional laboratories. It may be important to note that these backlogged cases appear to be only those crimes that have been identified by the crime laboratory as requiring DNA analysis. The assessment instructions defined a "backlogged case" as an unreported forensic case that has been in the possession of the crime laboratory for more than 30 days. However, after looking at data reported by one state crime laboratory it appears that law enforcement officials in most states have been counting only those cases for which it had already been determined that DNA analysis was needed. The state in question reported 14,695 rape cases, 12,023 homicide cases, 51,616 property crime cases, and 168,414 "other" cases in the "backlogged" crime cases category. While this state's crime laboratory will certainly not be performing DNA analysis on all 210,748 backlogged cases, it is a useful number in illustrating the great demand potentially facing crime laboratories in general, and in explaining the long turnaround times over which some police agencies express considerable concern. (This state crime laboratory also provided the number of backlogged cases that had been identified for DNA testing, which was used in calculating the national total.)

Table 4.5 displays the mail assessment-generated information regarding backlogged rape cases featuring rape kits and known DNA evidence. As indicated, both the local and state crime laboratories report that the majority of their backlogged rape cases (between 75-100 percent) contain rape kits only (additional analyses indicate that both local and state laboratories are also generally consistent in that the majority of these rape kits are likely to contain DNA evidence). Furthermore, a slightly larger percentage of local crime laboratories reported that over half of their backlogged rape cases feature rape kits as well as other forms of DNA evidence. Finally, both state and local laboratories note that backlogged rape cases with other DNA evidence exclusively are quite rare. These responses potentially point to a bigger issue of heavy reliance on rape kits for evidence. As the public acceptance and understanding of forensic DNA continues to grow, there is also a good chance that criminals may become increasingly savvy and begin leaving fewer obvious DNA clues behind at the scene of their crimes. Moreover, not all rape kits will necessarily yield a testable DNA sample. For these reasons, it is important that investigators do not begin to rely too heavily on the collection of a rape kit in sexual assaults for all of their physical evidence. Full processing of the crime scene may capture DNA evidence that may prove invaluable if the rape kit does not produce results.

One backlog issue *not* discussed in this report regards those cases that have previously been analyzed by crime laboratories, but which require additional analysis before they can be entered into the national DNA index system. These cases fall into one of two categories: cases analyzed using the RFLP method of testing, and cases for which only partial STR analysis was completed. For several years before the current method of DNA testing (STR analysis) was introduced and accepted by the scientific community, forensic DNA analysis was completed using a method called RFLP. Unfortunately, results from cases analyzed using RFLP are not transferrable into an STR result. This means that any testing that yielded RFLP profiles (either offender profiles, or unknown suspect profiles) must be reanalyzed before they can be compared to the database population of STR profiles. These particular cases are not typically counted in a laboratory's "backlog" of cases that need to be analyzed, since, indeed, these cases have already been analyzed. The number of RFLP cases requiring STR analysis for entry into the DNA index system is unknown.

The other type of possible uncounted backlogged DNA cases are those that have only been partially profiled. In order to be eligible for entry into the National DNA Index System, a DNA profile must be analyzed at 13 points, called *loci*. For a number of years many laboratories reduced their costs by analyzing fewer than 13 loci (usually 9 or 10 loci). While these results are typically adequate for evidentiary purposes, and are sufficient for entry into the Local or State level of DNA Index Systems, they are *not* permitted to be loaded to the national system for searching between states. Today there are only a handful of laboratories that are not using all 13 loci in their analysis of National DNA Index System eligible cases. However, the number of cases that were analyzed using partial profiles in the past has not been counted and could be quite sizeable in some jurisdictions. Moreover, since there are a number of laboratories that continue to use partial profiles, this number is likely increasing.

Table 4.5. Backlogged rape cases, rape kits, and DNA evidence from local and state crime laboratories

Backlog with biological evidence (%)	**Jurisdictions with Backlogged Cases with Rape Kits Only (%)**		**Jurisdictions with Backlogged Cases with Rape Kits and Other DNA Evidence (%)**		**Jurisdictions with Backlogged Cases with Other DNA Evidence Only (%)**	
	Local	**State**	**Local**	**State**	**Local**	**State**
0-10%	10.0	3.0	13.7	2.9	**56.9**	**64.7**
11-25%	30.0	18.2	13.7	14.7	31.4	26.5
25-50%	14.0	21.2	19.6	**41.2**	5.9	5.9
50-75%	12.0	24.2	**35.3**	20.6	3.9	2.9
75-100%	**34.0**	**33.3**	17.6	20.6	2.0	0.0

Statutes of Limitations and Anticipated Backlogs

Crime laboratories reported at least 1,637 backlogged rape cases that were expected to exceed the statute of limitations for prosecution by June 30, 2003. A significant number of these cases were reported to be held by the local laboratories. Furthermore, this number was generally expected to increase in the coming six-month period rather than decrease, thereby furthering the possibility that additional cases could have expiring statutes of limitation before the backlog is eliminated.

It should be noted that local jurisdictions were also asked to estimate the number of cases for which the statute of limitations may be a factor, but a very high number of agencies either did not respond to the question or indicated that an educated guess was not possible. This inability to track important information relating to cases points to a considerable deficiency in case management systems. Without such systems, the burden placed on law enforcement to review cases and respond to opportunities provided by advancements in forensic and other crime fighting technologies is overwhelming.

Table 4.6. Status of cases with regard to statutes of limitations (SOL) and anticipated backlogs

Laboratory Type	Cases within SOL	Cases to Exceed SOL by 6/30/03	Anticipated Backlog
Local Laboratories	Mean = 232.5	Mean = 49.1	Mean = 229.6
	Total = 7,440	Total = 1,522	Total = 10,789
State Laboratories	Mean = 372.1	Mean = 5.5	Mean = 377.6
	Total = 7069	Total = 115	Total = 20,371
Totals	14,509	1,637	31,160

Criminal justice professionals and policy makers also have been considering statute of limitations issues in conjunction with changes to forensic DNA policies. The issue is twofold. First, there are known instances where DNA backlogs – either in casework samples or offender samples – have resulted in DNA database matches that occurred after the statute of limitations for prosecution had lapsed for the likely guilty party. One state reported an estimated 150 such positive matches being made after the statutory period of exposure to prosecution had expired for repeat offenders in that state. Secondly, an abbreviated statute of limitations period negates the long-term effectiveness of the DNA database in that the crime investigators making use of the database will not be given a full opportunity to succeed in matching across crimes and/or persons. The DNA database is an effective tool to catch recidivists. In many instances, a known offender entered into the database will be identified at a later date when he or she commits a subsequent offense that leads to the collection of DNA forensic evidence. Even with a year-long backlog, DNA testing should still be completed in sufficient time for the prosecutors to bring forward legal charges. However, the reverse scenario is also equally important in making DNA matches. For example, a crime occurs, and at some later date when the offender commits a crime that requires a DNA sample for the database, a match is made retrospectively to the earlier unsolved crime(s). These "backwards" matches are those limited by short statute of limitations periods. Consider a state where the statute of limitations is six years where an unknown rapist victimizes a citizen in 2003 and eight years pass before the offender commits a crime that qualifies for the DNA database. In this situation, the 2003 rape can never be prosecuted. In such cases the crime victim may never receive closure, and the public safety is seriously compromised. To be certain, the statute of limitations represents a very important element of "quality control" in the criminal justice system. The limitation on prosecutorial exposure protects individuals from the natural tendency for most evidence to become increasingly less reliable over time. Eyewitness testimony becomes less certain; a person near the scene of a crime may have difficulties rebuilding the reason for his/her proximity over the passage of several years. The reliability of DNA testing, however, is quite different; it is largely undamaged by the passage of time. DNA forensic evidence has been used quite frequently to convict criminals decades after the commission of their crime. It should also be noted that while a fingerprint may be found at a crime scene for a variety of legitimate and/or illegitimate reasons, a semen sample has very few legitimate reasons for being part of the evidence found in a rape examination of an unknown suspect assault. Many states have responded to this statute of limitations problem by enacting new legislation intended to extend or remove the statute of limitations for specific violent crimes. One option that is quite popular among U.S. states is to remove the statute of limitations temporarily in sexual assault cases where DNA evidence is available. Once a match is made on the database, however, prosecutors have a set number of years to bring charges against the suspect in question. In this way, matches made on the DNA database can still be prosecuted, but prosecutors cannot indefinitely postpone a trial. Wisconsin, Delaware, and the federal government have enacted statutes that specifically permit "John Doe warrants" for specific crimes. However, Wisconsin subsequently completely removed the statute of limitations, negating the need for such warrants.

Processing Time and Output Capacity

State and local crime laboratories also differ substantially in terms of the average time for processing DNA evidence and the average annual output capacity. Laboratories were asked for the approximate length of time required for the analysis of a typical (non-priority) unnamed suspect case rape kit, assuming a vaginal swab with one perpetrator, one victim, and that the time runs from the date the rape kit is received by the laboratory until analytical results are reported. This question was worded very specifically to control for a number of factors that can affect processing times. For example, cases that have more than one perpetrator, multiple pieces of evidence, or where analysis must control for known consensual partners of the victim, can lead to longer analysis periods. Delays between the collection of evidence and actual submission of the evidence to the crime laboratory can also lengthen the overall turnaround time. Conversely, cases that become a priority, either for public safety reasons or because of publicity, can be sped through the system at a much quicker rate.

The findings reported in Table 4.7 show that state crime laboratories take an average of 23.9 weeks, and local laboratories average 30.0 weeks for DNA processing. In addition, state crime laboratories process an average of 1,284.5 samples per year as opposed to the local laboratories which average an output of 771.4 samples per year (with an extremely wide degree of variation between lows and highs). A potential explanation for this difference may lie in the fact that state crime laboratories tend to be slightly more process oriented because DNA evidence is generally submitted to the laboratory from remotely located agencies. In contrast, local laboratories are generally embedded in the law enforcement agencies they serve, and hence may have a more significant role in determining which evidence is of the most probative value.

A thorough understanding of the scope of capacity problems must also consider the wide range in existing capacity at crime laboratories. Consider the neighboring states of Virginia and North Carolina in this regard. Virginia has a population slightly smaller than North Carolina (by approximately 1 million, according to 2000 U.S. Census Bureau data), and Virginia's crime rate of 3,178 crimes per 100,000 is lower than that of North Carolina's at 4,938 (according to FBI UCR data). However, Virginia's leaders recognized the importance of DNA to public safety in the late 1980's and the state has steadily built its DNA program to rank among the finest in the country. To date, Virginia has approximately thirty-eight DNA analysts and processes approximately 8,172 DNA samples per year (with approximately 8 samples per case). In contrast, North Carolina has been slow to build its DNA program – its crime laboratories (a state forensic laboratory and a local laboratory serving Charlotte-Mecklenberg) employed a combined total of six DNA analysts (four at the state facility and two at the local laboratory) at the time of this Report. Moreover, as a matter of policy, North Carolina's state laboratory will not accept evidence for DNA analysis for any case in which there is no known suspect (with obvious exceptions for high profile serial cases) and has a processing time of three months. The local crime laboratory for Charlotte-Mecklenberg, which has a six-month processing time, accepts no suspect cases for violent crimes, but places limits on acceptance of property crime cases with no suspects. The two crime laboratories in North Carolina estimate their combined backlog of DNA cases at 720 (320 for Charlotte-Mecklenberg, 400 for the state). Virginia, in contrast, accepts nearly all cases (within reason), has a processing time of four months, and an estimated backlog of just over 2,000 cases.

Intuitively, it is reasonable to assume that higher output capacity should result in shorter processing times and smaller backlogs. However, when considering the Virginia-North Carolina comparison, the opposite was found to be the case. Virginia's capacity nearly doubles that of North Carolina, yet Virginia also has a larger backlog and generally a longer processing time. It seems unlikely that North Carolina simply has fewer crimes with biological evidence. In fact, given the higher crime rate in North Carolina, it is reasonable to assume just the opposite – that the state should have a larger number of crimes for DNA testing. This scenario begs the question of what is happening to biological criminal evidence in states such as North Carolina. There is good reason to believe that many of these cases are sitting in storage, either in crime laboratory evidence rooms or in local law enforcement evidence storage areas. It is also possible that biological evidence simply will not be collected for crimes if there is little real hope that it will be analyzed.

Another important comparison to make at this point involves the average DNA processing time considered acceptable in England. England's nationally established goal for the processing time of forensic DNA evidence is 24 days, and the Government has deemed as unacceptable the current processing time of 33 days for sex assault cases (See the attached report, *The Application of DNA Technology in England and Wales*). By comparison, in the U.S., the current average processing time for unnamed suspect rape kits is between 24 and 30 weeks (on the extremes, one local laboratory reported a 208 week backlog, and a state laboratory reported a 78 week backlog). Similar to England, many laboratories throughout the U.S. also have a stated goal of reaching a 30-day processing time. While this is a laudable goal, the problem is that most crime laboratories have no actual means of reaching this goal. Take for example the Oregon crime laboratory. In the late 1990's, crime laboratory administrators had announced a processing time goal of 30 days, although many on the DNA staff privately believed that target to be unreachable. However, due to a steady stream of funding and some changes to operational procedures, in 2000 the DNA section had reduced the DNA evidence processing time to sixty days or less. The next target of thirty days suddenly seemed to be an achievable goal. Unfortunately, at about the same time the DNA section was faced with a hiring freeze while demand for DNA testing continued to grow. Then, a budget crisis in 2002 saw the State Police budget decimated and the DNA staff was reduced by 65 percent (a staff of twelve DNA personnel were reduced to only four). By mid-2003, the DNA section was largely reconstituted, but the damage had been done. Oregon currently has a processing time of at least 10 weeks for a non-priority rape kit, and is still not operating at pre-2002 levels with regards to trained staff and output capacity. The goal of 30 days for processing of DNA evidence again seems far-fetched without a significant infusion of additional funding.

Table 4.7. Average analysis time and output capacity for state and local crime laboratories

Laboratory Type	Avg. Analysis Time (in Weeks)	Avg. Annual Output Capacity
Local Laboratories	30.0	771.4
State Laboratories	23.9	1,284.5

Note: Average analysis time is based on a non-priority, no suspect rape kit. Average annual capacity is measured in samples per year.

Barriers to Processing DNA Evidence of Property Crimes

State and local crime laboratories were also asked about the barriers associated with processing DNA evidence from property crimes (in particular, unnamed suspect property crimes). Table 4.8 displays the results of these items. The most frequently indicated barriers to the processing of evidence in such cases have to do with *personnel shortages* and the *backlog of cases* with higher priority. The more secondary concerns expressed by crime laboratories include reagents and equipment needs and the inadequacy of operational space.

Table 4.8. Reported barriers associated with processing DNA evidence from unnamed suspect property crimes for local and state crime laboratories

Barriers to Processing DNA Evidence	Local Laboratories (%)	State Laboratories (%)
Lack of Storage Space	5.2	9.3
More Personnel Needed	**34.5**	**30.2**
Backlogs/Other Priority Cases	**39.7**	**30.2**
Reagents and Equipment Needed	12.1	18.6
Lack of Operational Space	10.3	16.3
Prosecution Must Request	8.6	4.7
Investigator Must Request	17.2	4.7
Other	6.9	4.7

On a related note, an item was included in the local laboratory mail assessment instrument concerning the various obstacles facing local crime laboratories in getting DNA evidence from either unsolved rapes or unsolved homicides in queue at the laboratory. As indicated, and consistent with the previous set of analyses, the findings reported in Table 4.9 indicate that funding and backlog considerations both play an important role in getting DNA evidence from unsolved homicide and rape cases into the queue. This question was not posed to state laboratories because it essentially asks the respondent to opine on why detectives in their jurisdictions have not submitted cases. While local laboratories could reasonably be expected to have good insight on this issue given their closer proximity to the investigative unit, state laboratories, which sometimes serve hundreds of jurisdictions, cannot be expected to have the same detailed understanding.

Even so, several important differences do emerge here. In particular, local laboratories noted the importance of at least three additional reasons why DNA evidence from these types of cases may not be processed: a suspect has not yet been identified (noted as important by 37.0 percent of local laboratory respondents), a guilty plea is anticipated (30.4 percent), or the DNA analysis may not be requested by the prosecution (34.8 percent). Other important factors included the situation in which the subject has yet to be charged (26.1 percent) and cases wherein the agency may be uncertain as to how the DNA analysis my help close the case (28.3 percent).

In short, while both local and state crime laboratories indicate that staff personnel and backlog issues are the primary barriers to processing DNA evidence from property crimes, the results from the local crime laboratory assessment indicate a much more complex picture with regard to the processing of DNA evidence from unsolved homicide and unsolved rape cases.

Table 4.9. Reported barriers associated with processing DNA evidence from unsolved homicides and/or unsolved rapes for local crime laboratories

Barriers to the Processing of DNA Evidence	Local Crime Laboratories (%)
A suspect has not yet been identified	**37.0**
Suspect identified but not yet charged	26.1
Guilty plea is anticipated	**30.4**
Agency uncertain how DNA may help case	28.3
Lack of funding for DNA analysis	**30.4**
Backlog at laboratory prevents timely results	**45.7**
Laboratory is not processing requests for DNA testing	2.2
Agencies uncertain as to where to send case for analysis	15.2
Analysis not requested by prosecution	**34.8**
Other	30.4

Mitochondrial DNA Testing

Another DNA testing option that warrants some discussion in this study is the analysis of mitochondrial DNA (or mtDNA). Testing of nuclear DNA is by far the most common analysis conducted in the United States and in other countries. This testing results in the measurement of the *short tandem repeats* of nuclear cells in DNA, and is therefore commonly referred to as STR testing. However, only two copies of nuclear DNA are present in human cells (once copy from the biological mother and one copy from the biological father), which means that a deterioration of the cell sample, or a sample that has only a few cells, may not be testable through STR analysis. On the other hand, mitochondrian, which contain mtDNA, are present in hundreds to thousands of copies per cell, and therefore not only withstand degradation better but can also provide more testable molecules per sample. This type of testing is particularly useful for evidence such as bone fragments and hair samples where nuclear DNA may not be present. However, mtDNA testing is rather limited in criminal forensic identification applications. MtDNA is passed down through maternal lines, with all descendants in a given maternal line sharing the same mtDNA sequence. So, while mtDNA may conclusively prove that a particular person is related through maternal lineage to a specified woman, it does not serve the purpose of uniquely identifying the individual in question. Indeed, persons who would appear to be unrelated may in fact share a common maternal relative at some point in their lineage, and this would lead to the same mtDNA results. As a result, mtDNA testing can be used in criminal cases to positively include or exclude a person as a possible suspect, but does not provide the discriminatory power that the forensic community has come to expect from nuclear DNA analysis. MtDNA testing is also more labor intensive, and therefore considerably more expensive than nuclear DNA testing. Both state and local laboratories were asked about the degree to which their unsolved cases may benefit from mitochondrial DNA testing. Specifically, the laboratories were asked to estimate: (1) the total number of forensic cases (for the calendar year 2002) analyzed in the laboratory that failed to yield testable amounts of DNA for STR analysis, but could potentially benefit from mitochondrial DNA testing; and, (2) the number of hair analysis cases received by the laboratory that would benefit from additional mitochondrial testing.

Table 4.10 contains the results of these items. Both local and state laboratories reported that, although not as substantial as that for nuclear (STR) DNA analysis, a number of cases could potentially benefit from mtDNA testing. To be sure, local laboratories note that a total of 956 cases could benefit from such testing, and state laboratories indicated an additional 2,043 cases.

This question was not posed to local law enforcement agencies given that a need for mtDNA testing is primarily a scientific determination for which general law enforcement personnel do not have the appropriate expertise to ascertain. However, it is probable that, of the estimated 542,743 backlogged cases with biological evidence held by local law enforcement agencies and crime laboratories, some number of these cases may require mtDNA testing.

This may be especially true for those jurisdictions (70.3 percent) that reported that the need for additional evidence storage space was either “critical” or “highly critical.” Many of the evidence storage rooms across the country do not necessarily maintain the climate control conditions that are ideal to DNA evidence preservation. Although DNA can typically withstand fluctuating temperatures and endure over very long periods of time, it is not indestructible. Moreover, many of the evidence policies and protocols at local law enforcement agencies may not be conducive to long-term storage of biological materials. Although this study turned up no such admissions, stories of biological evidence being “stored” in squad car trunks or under stairwells at the stationhouse are commonplace in the forensic science community.

In addition to the evidence contamination and chain of custody problems that the inappropriate storage of any crime scene evidence could present, haphazard storage is also far from an ideal manner of storage for the preservation of biological evidence. In cases where DNA evidence has deteriorated to a point where the more common STR testing cannot be completed, mtDNA testing may be appropriate. Currently, there are only a few crime laboratories around the country with the ability to conduct mtDNA testing. With demand being present but not overwhelming, the question has been raised as to whether it may prove more cost-effective to maintain regional mtDNA testing laboratories rather than attempting to establish this capacity at each state and local forensic laboratory.

Another factor possibly affecting demand for mtDNA testing is that fewer than half of all states have obtained court decisions permitting mtDNA test results as evidence at trial in criminal cases. It is possible that the need for mtDNA testing could expand as more states rule on its admissibility as evidence. It is also worth noting that mtDNA testing results are not comparable to nuclear DNA testing results, and therefore cannot be loaded into criminal DNA database indexes (see CODIS discussion in section V). However, an index for mtDNA analysis has been included as part of the CODIS *Missing and Unidentified Persons Database.*

MtDNA testing is being used by a growing number of state laboratories which intend to participate in this database program. According to statistics maintained by the FBI's National Crime Information Center (NCIC), there are nearly 5,000 reported unidentified persons in the United States at this time.

Table 4.10. Forensic and hair analysis cases that may benefit from mitochondrial DNA testing

Case Type	Local Laboratories Total (avg.)	State Laboratories Total (avg.)
Forensic Cases	336	897
	(8.6)	(28.9)
Hair Analysis Cases	620	1,146
	(17.2)	(47.8)
Total	956	2,043

Cost/Funding Issues

Many of the major obstacles associated with DNA analysis concern the costs/funding issues involved. Accordingly, the local and state crime laboratories were assessed on a number of these issues. As a first step in this process, local and state crime laboratory administrators were asked to indicate from what sources the bulk of their funding comes. Table 4.11 shows that the majority of funding for the local crime laboratories derives from local sources. Accordingly, state crime laboratories receive most of their funding from state sources. Conversely, most state laboratories (91.6 percent) receive little to no funding from local sources, and 88.9 percent of local laboratories report a similarly low level of assistance from the state.

What this table also reveals is that federal funding is not a significant portion of the overall DNA budgets of state and local crime laboratories. Indeed, only 20.5 percent of state laboratories receive at least half of their funding from federal sources—a figure that drops to a mere 4.5 percent for local laboratories. Moreover, nearly half of all local laboratories reported that 10 percent or less of their DNA budget was attributable to federal sources. On the other hand, only 23 percent of state laboratories reported this lowest level of funding (see appendix). When considering that many of the local laboratories handle extremely high volumes of forensic DNA cases, this difference in reliance on federal money is startling.

However, there may be two plausible explanations for this difference. First, local crime laboratories are not permitted to apply directly for federal funding grants for DNA analysis. Instead, local laboratories must apply as a consortium through the state laboratory. Although this application process works well for a number of state and local laboratories, some local laboratories privately complain that they do not get a fair amount of this grant money. This situation also potentially leaves local laboratories at the mercy of a state's level of interest in applying for federal funding. Additionally, the process of coordinating a consortium application – particularly in those states where local laboratories are numerous – can be difficult.

A second reason why these data show a higher degree of reliance at the state level on federal funding is because the question did not allow for a distinction between funding received for casework versus funding received for offender samples. Offender DNA samples are the sole responsibility of the state, and therefore local crime laboratories are not eligible to apply for federal grants for offender DNA analysis.

Table 4.11. Sources of funding for state and local crime laboratory budgets for DNA analysis

Funding Source	Less than 50% of Funding	50% or Greater of Funding
Local Crime Laboratories		
Local	19.6	**80.4**
State	**88.9**	11.1
Federal	95.5	4.5
State Crime Laboratories		
Local	**91.6**	8.4
State	27.8	**72.2**
Federal	79.5	20.5

Local and state crime laboratories were also asked to estimate the average cost of processing an unnamed suspect rape kit (assuming a vaginal swab with one perpetrator and one victim). Table 4.12 indicates that both state and local laboratories arrived at the same approximate cost of $1,100. In arriving at this estimate, the majority of local and state laboratories included the costs of reagents and salaries, but very few included costs associated with overhead and equipment. It is important to remember that these estimated costs are for what is considered a very simple rape kit case, as defined above. There are a variety of other factors that can significantly increase costs associated with DNA analysis, including the size, quantity and condition of the evidence, the number of perpetrators involved, and contaminants. To repeat, the $1,100 per case estimate is only for the most rudimentary of rape cases, and it does *not* include many overhead considerations. As forensic cases become more complex, the cost of analysis will quickly rise.

Table 4.12. Average cost of rape kit analysis and frequency that factors associated with costs were included in the estimate

	Local Laboratories	State Laboratories
Average cost of rape kit analysis	$1,153.95	$1,041.27
Factors associated with costs		
Reagents	**75.9%**	**67.4%**
Equipment	34.5%	27.9%
Salaries	**65.5%**	**48.8%**
Overhead	39.7%	11.6%
Other	15.5%	9.3%

Table 4.13 presents the responses from laboratories regarding how they would choose to spend supplemental funding for their DNA programs. Essentially, the question asks laboratories where there biggest needs lie. The sum totals for all laboratory responses indicates that reagents and analytical equipment were the areas most frequently identified by

laboratories for such funding. However, this table shows only how often a particular response was chosen, and no limit was placed on the number of response chosen.

Table 4.13. Projected use of supplemental funding for DNA analysis for local and state crime laboratories (frequency of selection)

Funding Priority	Local Laboratories (%)	State Laboratories (%)
Salaries	63.8	59.5
Overtime	46.6	48.8
Training	58.6	62.8
Equipment	60.3	67.4
Robotics	31.0	58.1
Reagents	**67.2**	**76.7**
Construction/Lease	29.3	48.8
Offender Collection	10.3	41.9
Suspect Case Backlog	51.7	41.9
No Suspect Case Backlog	55.2	51.2
Outsourcing	29.3	34.9
Other	6.9	27.9

Table 4.14 sets forth study results in this area in the form of a priority listing of spending priorities for local crime laboratories and state crime laboratories. Of the responses listed in Table 4.13, laboratories were asked to rank the top three most significant priorities, in order of importance. A review of these data clearly shows that salaries were, by far, considered the single most significant need. Crime laboratories were also subsequently asked if by "salaries" did they mean additional funding to augment current analyst salaries or funding to pay for hiring new personnel? Although a handful of laboratories indicated that current staff needed augmented salaries, the majority of laboratories indicated that the need was for new hires. This issue of salaries is significant because federal grants for DNA analysis may not be used in this manner. Instead, DNA laboratories are solely dependent on state and local funding for salary needs. Two other personnel issues – training and overtime – also ranked among the top needs reported.

Additionally, the fact that local laboratories ranked funding for no suspect casework as a mid-level priority, but state laboratories ranked it last is a point for consideration. Current federal grants for DNA analysis fall into two categories. One grant can be used for DNA analysis of backlogged offender samples, and the other grant is for DNA analysis of backlogged cases with no suspect. As discussed previously, local laboratories privately complain that they do not receive a fair pass-through of the federal funding that is awarded to the state. This complaint would seem to be reinforced by the high priority that local laboratories place on the need for additional money for no suspect casework. This significantly higher need could also be reflective of the fact that many local laboratories serve large metropolitan jurisdictions with high crime rates, as discussed previously in this Report.

Finally, "construction/lease" was selected as a priority by a small number of laboratories, but for those laboratories that indicated this need, it was typically identified as the most significant priority. Of the twenty-five laboratories rating construction/lease as a priority, 14 rated it as the top priority, and eight rated it as the middle priority. Therefore, funding for construction/lease, though not a priority for the majority of laboratories, becomes a significant concern once the need develops.

Table 4.14. Rank ordering of spending priorities for local and state crime laboratories

Local Crime Laboratories		State Crime Laboratories	
1.	Salaries	1.	Salaries
2.	Reagents	2.	Equipment
3.	Equipment	3.	Construction/Lease
4.	Training	4.	Reagents
5.	Construction/Lease	5.	Outsourcing
6.	Overtime	6.	Training
7.	No Suspect Case Backlog	7.	Robotics
8.	Suspect Case Backlog	8.	Overtime
9.	Robotics	9.	Offender Collection
10.	Other[8]		Other[7]*
11.	Outsourcing	10.	Suspect Case Backlog
12.	Offender Collection		No Suspect Case Backlog*

* Ranking of "Offender Collection" and "Other" categories resulted in a statistical tie.

** Ranking of "Suspect Case Backlog" and "No Suspect Case Backlog" categories resulted in a statistical tie.

V. CODIS ANALYSIS

In 1982, California became the first state to begin requiring blood samples from certain sex offenders. Although DNA was not specifically mentioned in statute, and indeed the basis for modern forensic DNA analysis was not first introduced until 1985, California's identification of the utility of collecting blood samples from a specified group of known offenders was ground-breaking at the time. In 1988, Colorado became the first state to specify through statute the requirement for DNA samples from certain offenders, and in 1990, Virginia became the first state to enact a law requiring DNA from all convicted felons. In the following year (1991), the FBI established guidelines for states on sex offender DNA database laws and began developing the concept of a computer software program that would operate similar to the national criminal fingerprint database (IAFIS). In 1994, this DNA database program was officially created in statute by Congress through the *DNA Identification Act (P.L. 103-322)* and was formally named the Combined DNA Index System, or CODIS.

Today, every State has a DNA database statute that allows collection of DNA from specified offenders. All 50 States require DNA from sex offenders and murderers, and 46 States require DNA from all violent felony convictions (including assault and battery and robbery). Over the past several years, a growing number of states have been expanding their databases to include non-violent felony convictions; 45 States require DNA from burglary convictions, 36 States require DNA from certain drug convictions, and 31 States require DNA from all felony convictions. (These figures are current through July 2003). (See appendix for chart of state statutes.)

An easily understandable description of CODIS was included in a July 2002 Special Report from the National Institute of Justice (U.S. Department of Justice) titled, "Using DNA to Solve Cold Cases" (NCJ 194197). The Special Report's description is as follows:

> CODIS is a computer software program that operates local, State, and national databases of DNA profiles from convicted offenders, unsolved crime scene evidence, and missing persons. Every State in the Nation has a DNA database that allows for the collection of DNA profiles from offenders convicted of particular crimes. CODIS software enables State, local, and national law enforcement crime laboratories to compare DNA profiles electronically, thereby linking serial crimes to each other and identifying suspects by matching DNA profiles from crime scenes with profiles from convicted offenders. The success of CODIS is demonstrated by the thousands of matches that have linked serial cases to each other and cases that have been solved by matching crime scene evidence to known convicted offenders…
>
> …CODIS uses two indexes to general investigative leads in crimes for which biological evidence is recovered from a crime scene. The convicted offender index contains DNA profiles of individuals convicted of certain crimes ranging from certain misdemeanors to sexual assault and murder. Each State has different "qualifying offenses" for which persons convicted of them must submit a biological sample for inclusion in the database. The forensic index contains DNA profiles obtained from crime scene evidence, such as semen, saliva, or blood. CODIS uses computer software to automatically search across these indexes for a potential match.
>
> A match made between profiles in the forensic index can link crime scenes to each other, possibly identifying serial offenders. Based on these "forensic hits," police in multiple jurisdictions or States can coordinate their respective investigations and share leads they have developed independent of one another. Matches made between the forensic and convicted offender indexes can provide investigators with the identity of a suspect(s). It is important to note that if an "offender hit" is obtained, that information typically is used as probable cause to obtain a new DNA sample from that suspect so that the match can be confirmed by the crime laboratory before an arrest is made.
>
> LDIS, SDIS, and NDIS
>
> CODIS is implemented as a distributed database with three hierarchical levels (or tiers)—local, State, and national. All three levels contain forensic and convicted offender indexes and a population file (used to generate statistics). The hierarchical design provides State and local laboratories with the flexibility to configure CODIS to meet their specific legislative and technical needs.
>
> A description of the three CODIS tiers follows
>
> Local. Typically, the Local DNA Index System (LDIS) installed at crime laboratories is operated by police departments or sheriffs' offices. DNA profiles originated at the local level can be transmitted to the State and national levels.
> State. Each State has a designated laboratory that operates the State DNA Index System (SDIS). SDIS allows local laboratories within that State to compare DNA profiles. SDIS also is the communication path between the local and national tiers. SDIS is typically operated by the agency responsible for implementing and monitoring compliance with the State's convicted offender statute.

National. The National DNA Index System (NDIS) is the highest level of the CODIS hierarchy and enables qualified State laboratories that are actively participating in CODIS to compare DNA profiles. NDIS is maintained by the FBI under the authority of the DNA Identification Act of 1994.

There are three states (Louisiana, Texas, and Virginia) which, in addition to requiring DNA from all convicted felons, also require DNA from certain offenders prior to conviction (upon arrest or indictment). However, the current national DNA database law only permits those samples that are taken from convicted offenders to be uploaded to NDIS. The wording of this law also does not permit samples from juveniles to be uploaded to NDIS since most juveniles are adjudicated delinquent rather than convicted of crimes. However, individual states may maintain these samples at the SDIS tier, as state laws permit.

Offender DNA Profiles

According to the FBI CODIS program office, there were 1,321,854 offender DNA profiles in NDIS as of April 2003. Additionally, 41 State CODIS laboratories reported 463,209 offender samples that were expected to be part of the laboratory backlog by June 30, 2003. As a comparison, the English DNA database contains over two million DNA profiles. Given that the United Kingdom's population is approximately 52 million, the two million offender samples on file represent a significantly larger percentage of the entire population than what is represented in CODIS (see the attached report, *The Application of Forensic DNA Technology in England and Wales*). The U.S. DNA database system would need to reach almost ten million profiles to achieve a similar percentage of the total population covered. The difference between these proportions go a long way towards explaining the greater success of England's forensic DNA program compared to that of the United States.

The mail assessment instrument asked those state laboratories with statutes that did not yet require DNA from all convicted felons to provide an estimate of the additional samples that the enactment of such a law would add in the first year, along with the estimated number of annual samples expected in future years. Those laboratories estimated that an expanded DNA database statute would add a combined total of 2,281,000 offender profiles in the first year, with an annual rate of 504,484 additional profiles in future years. Anticipated offender profiles for the first year are more than in future years because laboratories were asked to assume that the expanded requirement would be made retroactive to include offenders who were still incarcerated. A potential pool of backlogged offender samples that these figures do not capture are the uncollected offender sample in states where a requirement for an all felons DNA database has been enacted in statute, but not yet implemented (usually as a result of funding problems).

In the majority of states, offender DNA samples are taken at some point prior to release (72 percent) rather than at the point of sentencing or intake (52 percent). These numbers do not total 100 percent due to the fact that many laboratories responded that samples are collected at both points, presumably depending on the particular circumstances of each offender's conviction. For the purpose of solving crimes, it is most desirable to capture DNA samples from the specified offenders at the earliest point possible. Collecting DNA from offenders shortly after sentencing not only allows sufficient time for the sample to make its way through the backlog, but also, if a DNA database match is made to a previously unsolved crime, investigators and prosecutors will have ample opportunity to determine whether additional charges should be pursued while the offender is still in custody.

Another factor determining the number of offender profiles on the DNA database and related backlogs is whether the state requires DNA from specified offenders who are not sentenced to state prison terms. There are a large number of felony convictions in which the offender is either sentenced to a county jail or to community probation. In 2002, Washington State expanded its offender DNA database to include all felony convictions. The State estimated that limiting the database to only those felony offenders sentenced to state prison would mean an additional 5,600 DNA profiles annually. However, including those felony offenders sentenced to jail would mean an additional 15,000 offenders annually, and felons sentenced to serving community probation would add 840 offenders per year. In addition to the large number of felony convictions that these sentences represent, these are also offenders who are likely to have shorter sentences and therefore earlier releases back into the community.

Moreover, the size of the DNA database in the U.S. is further limited by whether the state elects to require DNA samples from persons who had been convicted of qualifying crimes prior to the time of the database expansion statute and are still serving sentences. Many states choose to omit these offenders, primarily due to the additional analysis and logistical problems associated with collections. Again using Washington State as an example, including those offenders who were incarcerated at the time of enactment would have added 6,100 state prison inmates and 1,800 county jail inmates. Making the statute retroactive to include those persons currently on probation and parole would mean adding an additional 10,300 DNA profiles. While this group of offenders included retroactively represent a significant cost increase, it is also worth pointing out that retroactive provisions represent a one-time cost, with no recurring collection issues. And as with the jail and community probation sentences, the groups of felons already serving time for qualifying offenses are the ones most likely to be released into the community soonest.

The type of biological sample required from offenders is another factor affecting both collection and analysis costs. Over half of the state laboratories (52.4 percent) indicated that a blood sample is collected from offenders, with 28.6 percent of states collecting buccal (cheek) swabs. Nearly one-in-five (19 percent) states are taking both types of samples, as conditions warrant. The move towards taking buccal swabs instead of blood draws represents a recent switch. Buccal swabs are less problematic, particularly for those local jurisdictions that are responsible for taking DNA samples from jailed offenders and offenders on probation and parole. Blood collections require a trained phlebotomist and are therefore considerably more expensive for local agencies. Buccal swabs, in contrast, can be accomplished easily with a minimal amount of training. Additionally, many people consider a buccal swab to be less invasive than blood draws. Fortunately, at the same time that the demand for buccal swabs was increasing, the kits for buccal swab collection were becoming increasingly reliable. As evidenced by the crime laboratory assessment responses, many states now use buccal swabs exclusively for offender DNA testing and have independently indicated that they receive adequate samples for analysis. However, for crime laboratories making the switch from the analysis of offender blood samples to offender buccal swabs, it is not an overnight change and requires some planning and changes to laboratory operations.

Characteristics of CODIS Hits

Over the past few years as DNA databases have become increasingly successful, the need for information on the types matches made (or "hits") has become apparent. Virginia's CODIS office has a strong tracking program for identifying the types of crimes solved and the types of offenders linked to such crimes. As other states have considered following the Virginia model of an all felons DNA database, the Virginia information has been a significant tool in driving the debate. However, Virginia's data have brought to light the lack of any comprehensive CODIS hit data on a national scale. As part of the state and local laboratory assessment form, respondents were asked to supply this information. The figures contained in this Report cover 38 states that reported DNA database hits, plus 70 local laboratory hits that were determined to be cases that had not been reported to the state. The local crime laboratory hits reported are matches made at the LDIS tier, but should not be viewed to represent the only hits made at the LDIS tier since many local jurisdictions regularly report such hits to their state CODIS office.

In reporting forensic hits and offender hits, crime laboratories were requested to follow the "CODIS Hit Counting Guidelines" as prepared by the FBI. However, it is possible that there are inconsistencies among states in the manner in which hits were reported. Another issue to bear in mind when reviewing Table 5.1 is that not every "hit" results in an "investigation aided." For example, a DNA profile from an unknown suspect rape case could hit upon the victim's boyfriend, assuming that the boyfriend has a prior offense which resulted in his inclusion on the database. If the victim is certain that her boyfriend was not the rapist, then the "hit" is not valuable to the investigation. Most often consensual partners are controlled for in DNA analysis cases, but such "hits" are not unheard of.

Table 5.1 displays the characteristics of the SDIS hits (hits made within a state) and NDIS hits (hits made between states). As indicated, most of the hits are from state crime laboratories. Furthermore, most (approximately three-in-four) are SDIS offender hits. With respect to the qualifying offense distribution, offenders were more likely to be entered into the CODIS database for a non-violent qualifying offense as a violent offense.[9] With regard to types of crimes linked to offenders, however, violent crimes predominate; approximately six-in-ten of the crimes solved with DNA hits were violent crimes in the SDIS subset of cases. For the NDIS hits, violent crimes predominate on both the qualifying offense and crimes cleared sides of the equation. A majority of the inter-state hits entailed offenders who had violent qualifying offenses, and nearly three-in-four crimes linked either to offenders or to other cases through DNA evidence were violent crimes.

As is clear from the findings set forth in Table 5.1, the majority of types of crime solved through DNA database hits in the United States have been sexual assaults and other violent crimes. Considering that many crime laboratories will not process non-violent cases (such as property crime cases), or will only do so under a narrow set of circumstances, it is not surprising that the majority of unsolved crimes matched to offenders through the DNA database have been violent crimes. However, a comparison to hits on England's database, which has had an aggressive policy of encouraging submissions from property crimes, shows over 31,000 residential burglaries and over 29,000 commercial burglaries have been matched through hits on the database. In fact, only 14 percent of all DNA cases submitted to England's crime laboratory agency in 2001-2002 were violent crimes. With the FBI reporting that the estimated dollar loss attributed to property crime (excluding arson) in the U.S. was $16.6 billion in 2001, it is reasonable to assume that the untapped potential for using CODIS to solve non-violent crimes is immense. (See attached report, *The Application of Forensic DNA Technology in England and Wales*, for further details.)

The importance of considering non-violent qualifying offenses is also seen in Table 5.1. These figures indicate that in the United States only between 16.8 percent and 25.6 percent of the qualifying offenses for offenders linked to crimes are specified as violent offenses. It is quite possible, however, that a large number of cases comprising the "unknown qualifying offense" category—which contains the majority of responses—are violent offenses. Such a high proportion of violent offenses would be expected since most state DNA databases began as sex offender databases, and slowly expanded to include other violent crimes. For a majority of states, it has only been within the last three years that the database has grown to include nonviolent felonies. Consequently, for the non-violent offenders on the database a majority of the hits recorded at this time are for crimes that were previously committed. It will likely take several years before these offenders matriculate through the penal system and new offenses are committed to which they can be linked. This delay in hit levels as the database grows was experienced by Virginia. Although Virginia has had an all felons DNA database since 1990, it has only been since 2001 that the state has been reporting approximately one hit per day.

In addition to having all convicted felons on the database, another reason that Virginia's program has been so successful is due to its policy of processing a wide array of DNA cases. DNA databases will be limited in success if either the crime file index or offender file index is limited. The FBI reports a total of 54,895 forensic case profiles on the database as of April 2003. This number pales in comparison to the more than 200,000 similar profiles included on England's database – again contributing to the relatively higher level of success of their database compared to that of the United States.

Table 5.1. Descriptive statistics for CODIS hit characteristics

Characteristics of CODIS Hits	SDIS Hits % In State Matches (n = 4,092)	NDIS Hits % Between State Matches (n = 289)
Type of Crime Laboratory*		
Local	8.5	8.5
State	91.5	91.5
Type of Hit*		
Offender	72.3	57.7
Forensic	27.7	42.3
Offense Characteristics		
Non-Violent Qualifying Offense	23.9	15.9
Violent Qualifying Offense	16.8	25.6
Qualifying Offense Unknown	59.3	58.5
Non-Violent Crime Solved	16.4	12.1
Violent Crime Solved	39.2	46.8
Type of Crime Solved Unknown	44.4	41.1

* Note: these estimates are based on the 2,706 SDIS cases for which states provided case-level information.

In order to portray these findings in a more concrete and detailed format, Tables 5.2 and 5.3 set forth in raw numbers the case combinations between qualifying offenses and the unsolved crimes linked for all SDIS and NDIS cases where such information was available.

Many of the responding laboratories were able to supply both the matched offender's qualifying offense (i.e., the reason the offender was included on the database), and the type of crime linked to the offender. However, a crime laboratory's ability to provide this information depends upon several factors. First, many crime laboratories do not have ready access to offender criminal history information, and therefore may not be able to identify the qualifying offense. Also, several laboratories have not instituted programs that allow them to track database hits. Although such tracking may seem like a simple thing, it requires additional resources from laboratories that are already facing extreme resource shortages. For this reason, there are a considerable number of offenders in the "unknown" category of Table 5.2 and 5.3. Additionally, a few agencies were able to provide the total number of hits recorded, but could supply neither the offenders' qualifying offense nor the type of crime solved. By default, these hits are recorded in the "unknown" category as well.

Table 5.2. SDIS hit distribution by qualifying offense and type of crime solved

SDIS TIER OFFENDER HITS (Within State Matches)								
Qualifying	**Forensic Case Type**							
Offense	Murder	Sex Offenses	Assault	Robbery	Burglary	Misc.	Unknown	Total
Murder	24	18	0	3	2	3	4	54
Sex Offenses	30	220	2	5	11	6	53	327
Assault	18	61	6	3	9	11	2	110
Robbery	27	75	4	25	53	12	2	198
Burglary	18	99	4	31	168	16	79	415
Property Offenses*	18	21	3	22	43	15	0	122
Drug Offenses	43	94	2	16	47	26	0	228
Supervision Violation	0	4	0	0	3	0	1	8
Misc.	21	87	4	16	55	18	2	203
Unknown	61	485	3	33	137	36	1672	2427
Total	260	1164	28	154	528	143	1815	N=4092

* Note: property offenses include theft, forgery, and breaking and entering. Miscellaneous offenses include: violation of oath as a public official; obstruction as a law officer (7); criminal attempt (3); entering vehicle; driving habitual violator (2); possession of firearm during felony; miscellaneous judicial proceeding; impersonating an officer; cruelty to children; criminal mischief; public lewdness.

The findings set forth in Table 5.2 indicate the presence of many repeat offenders – that is, criminals who tend to specialize in one type of crime and re-offend frequently. For example, the most frequent qualifying offense for burglars was burglary, and for rape and sex offenses was rape and sex offenses. It is also clear, moreover, that property offenses were qualifying offenses for many violent crimes – more than 100 among the cases displayed here. A somewhat different pattern is evident for drug offenses as qualifying crimes. Such offenses are matched to a wide range of types of crimes solved through DNA evidence. These data begin to show that the nonviolent felons, in fact, commit a wider array of crimes than the violent felons. In fact, Virginia estimates that limiting its DNA database to violent offenders would have resulted in missing 82 percent of its hits to offenders.

It also bears pointing out that the "unknown" category for qualifying offenses is quite large. Also, the qualifying offense as reported by states is merely a record of the crime that resulted in the offender's inclusion on the database. As illustrated in the New York data discussed later in this Report, many of these offenders have extensive criminal histories – and many carry convictions for other "lower-level" felonies that were not crimes included on the database at the time of the conviction[10]. Therefore, the relatively larger number of violent offenders matched to crimes on the database is possibly inflated both because most databases began as violent offender only databases, and also because the qualifying database offense is not necessarily the only conviction attributable to the offender.

The likelihood of this scenario is illustrated in the New York study that found that for more than half of the offenders studied, the qualifying offense that resulted in the inclusion of the offenders profile on the database was committed an average of four and a half years after the first criminal conviction[11]. Moreover, these data are supported in some of the hit data submitted by states. Several states were able to include criminal histories for their offender hits. These criminal histories were, more frequently than not, extremely lengthy with multiple arrests and convictions. A hit in one state linking an unsolved sexual assault to a felon whose qualifying offense was robbery, shows a criminal history that covers two states as well as some federal felonies. The record includes charges on: two rapes, a kidnapping, four robberies, three assaults, two burglaries, three thefts, two counterfeiting crimes, driving while intoxicated, resisting an officer, trespassing, defrauding an innkeeper, and three parole/probation violations. These twenty-one charges (excluding the parole/probation violations) resulted in nine convictions – only the last of which required a DNA sample for the database.

Table 5.2 also reports data which may be of interest for further criminological research. Of the 228 drug offenders linked through the database to another unsolved crime, almost 70 percent of these unsolved crimes were violent offenses. Overall, drug offenders accounted for more than 21 percent of the hits made to unsolved murders and 14 percent of hits made to unsolved sexual assaults. When looking more closely at the sexual assault crimes solved through the DNA database, approximately one-third of these crimes were linked to sex offenders. More surprisingly, nearly 18 percent of the unsolved sex assaults were linked to burglary or property crime offenders; this figure combined with the 14 percent attributed to drug offenders may reveal patterns of criminal activity for study and use in police investigation practices. (For the purposes of these calculations, the "unknown" number of forensic cases was subtracted from the denominator.)

The findings set forth in Table 5.3 address the same question of type of qualifying offense matched to crimes for NDIS hits. This table includes NDIS tier offender hit information for 31 states. Significant efforts were made to ensure that hit counting was not duplicated, but it is possible that some of the hits were counted twice, particularly for those states that were unable to give a breakdown of qualifying offense of type of forensic case matched. A significant number of database hits were made between neighboring states, with Illinois reporting fourteen hits with Wisconsin, and six hits with Missouri. However, hits were also reported between states with little geographical proximity – such as Alaska and Arkansas, Washington and Florida, and Maine and Texas. In addition, there were five hits reported to the District of Columbia, one hit involving the military, and one international hit with Canada. (See appendix).

Moreover, at least 73 forensic case matches have been made between 27 states, the District of Columbia and the FBI. These cases included 56 sex offenses and 21 homicides and 15 burglaries. The total number of forensic hits is substantially lower than the number of crimes involved because one forensic hit will necessarily link at least two crimes together. Therefore, although only 73 forensic hits were made, 166 unsolved crimes were involved.

Table 5.3. NDIS hit distribution by qualifying offense and type of crime solved

NDIS TIER OFFENDER HITS (Between State Matches)								
Qualifying	**Forensic Case Type**							
Offense	Murder	Sex Offenses	Assault/ Battery	Robbery	Burglary/ BandE	Misc.*	Unknown	Total
Murder	0	4	0	0	1	0	0	5
Sex Offenses	8	27	0	0	3	0	8	46
Kidnapping / Restraint	1	3	0	0	0	0	0	4
Assault	2	8	1	0	0	0	1	12
Robbery	1	1	0	1	3	0	1	7
Burglary	4	2	0	1	8	2	1	18
Theft and Receiving	4	4	1	0	1	0	0	10
Misc.	1	10	0	0	4	1	2	18
Unknown	7	38	3	2	11	1	107	169
Total	28	97	5	4	31	4	120	**289**

*Miscellaneous forensic crimes include vehicle theft, criminal trespass, DUI/vehicle accident. Miscellaneous Qualifying Offenses include theft, drug charges, forgery, tampering with evidence, weapons violations, passing bad checks, and juvenile adjudications.

It is clear from the findings set forth in Table 5.3 that most cases entailing complete data for qualifying offenses and crimes solved among the NDIS hits relate to rapes and sex offenses. The vast majority of rape and sex offense crimes cleared entailed rape and sex crime qualifying offenses. However, again there is a large number of "unknown" offenders and forensic cases, which could potentially cause the distribution. This finding, coupled with the same strong pattern of repeat offending witnessed in Table 5.2, highlights the importance of collecting and processing rape kits and other biological evidence that might render DNA evidence for DNA databases. The following section will add further to our understanding how DNA evidence, if collected and processed with proper dispatch, could in fact prevent re-offending and spare many citizens from avoidable crime victimization.

VI. FORENSIC DNA AND CRIME PREVENTION

Solving a crime -- and solving it quickly -- has a direct effect on preventing additional crimes by the same perpetrator. An offender who is not apprehended in a timely manner remains free to commit more crimes. The most recent federal studies on recidivism tracked 272,111 released prisoners from 15 states[12]. The study found that 29.9 percent of the released prisoners were rearrested for a new offense within six months of release; and after three years this percentage grew to 67.5 percent. The arrests in question were almost exclusively either for new felonies or serious misdemeanors. The same study found that the offenders accounted for 4.1 million arrest charges prior to their most recent incarceration, and were responsible for another 744,000 arrest charges within three years of release.

It is precisely such repeat offenders that DNA databases are established to identify to enable timely intervention and the prevention of new crimes by habitual offenders. A match on the DNA database necessarily means that the same offender has committed at least one other criminal offense. Therefore, DNA databases serve the purpose not only of bringing criminals to justice and achieving closure for the victims of crime, but they also offer the prospect of preventing the same perpetrator from victimizing additional citizens. Given the relatively high rates of recidivism in the U.S., the potential for DNA databases to help solve and prevent crime is substantial. DNA analysis cannot stop the first crime from occurring, but it can provide investigators with the tools they need to identity a suspect and remove the threat to public safety before the same perpetrator can re-offend.

However, the effectiveness of DNA databases is restricted by a number of factors. First, to have an effective DNA database, biological evidence must be routinely collected from crime scenes, and that evidence must be sent to crime laboratories for forensic analysis. This set of activities on the part of law enforcement personnel assumes that crime scene investigators have the proper training to identify and collect the DNA specimens, and that the samples are submitted to the crime laboratory in a timely manner.

Secondly, crime laboratories must have a reasonable processing time for DNA analysis of crime scene samples, along with a policy to accept and process most reasonable requests for DNA testing – including crimes with no suspects and property crimes. In England, the current processing time of 33 days has been deemed unacceptable by the Government, which has set a processing time goal of 24 days. As discussed previously in this study, the average turn-around time in the U.S. is approximately 30 weeks, or for purposes of comparison to England's numbers, 210 days.

Additionally, the crime laboratory must accept requests for DNA testing for a variety of crimes. As discussed previously, states with progressive DNA polices have had great success in solving an increasing number of crimes through their DNA database. Limiting the numbers and types of acceptable cases for DNA testing will necessarily limit the number and types of crimes that can be solved through the use of forensic DNA. Lastly, the DNA database must have a strong pool of offenders for comparison. As described in Section V, the DNA database is a two-index system – a crime scene sample index, and an offender index. The effectiveness of either index is necessarily restricted by any limitations on the other index. As previously discussed, those states with statutes requiring DNA from all convicted felons have shown a high success rate in matches on their DNA database. A 2002 Research Note by the New York Division of Criminal Justice Services further supports this argument[13]. The study reviewed the first 102 DNA database matches occurring after a 1999 expansion of the database to include considerably more convicted felons. For 55 of the 102 offenders on the database who were matched to unsolved crimes, the review found that the first conviction was not for an offense that would be included on the DNA database under the current statute. Instead, the conviction that resulted in the offender's inclusion on the database occurred about 4½ years after the first criminal conviction – during which time these particular offenders accumulated an average of 10.2 felony and 5.6 misdemeanor arrests. These types of numbers on repeated offending by known felony offenders are supported by the recidivism study discussed previously. These observations on repeat offenders highlight a clear public safety need – that of identifying these repeat offenders as quickly as possible and monitoring their activities carefully. Quantifying the number of crimes that could be prevented through a more systematic use of forensic DNA testing presents a difficult problem. As in all matters of documenting the "prevention" of crime, it is difficult to count crimes that did not happen. As a way to deal with this fundamental problem, the following case studies were developed to provide examples of crimes that potentially could have been prevented had a strong forensic DNA program been in existence to call upon. The research on these cases specifically focused on those states that did not require DNA from all convicted felons at the time that the research for this Report began. Such states were chosen for the greater likelihood of uncovering preventable crimes due to a limited offender database. Moreover, many of these states have not expanded their offender databases largely due to resource problems which also affect criminal evidence analysis. The case studies were developed through the assistance of investigators and prosecutors around the country, and reflect the following assumptions:

- State statutes requiring DNA from all convicted felons were feasible by 1990. This assumption is based on the fact that Virginia enacted such a law in 1990.
- In addition to all felony offenses, state databases could include misdemeanor convictions that arose out of felony charges. Several states currently have such requirements due to the number of felony offenders who plea to misdemeanor crimes.
- A 30-day turn-around time is both desirable and possible, given sufficient resources. In fact, laboratories will often expedite testing and can finish analysis in a week or less if the crime(s) warrant priority treatment.

When reviewing the cases presented below, the reader should bear in mind the following points:

- Backlogs at crime laboratories are primarily the result of growing demand and limited resources. "Preventable crimes" that may in part be due to backlogs at crime laboratories, should be considered as a byproduct of resource limitations. In fact, crime laboratory analysts often work overtime and weekends to complete analysis on high profile cases.
- Law enforcement and prosecutors should not be expected to be able to identify offenders of unsolved crimes when they have not been given access to the necessary tools, such as DNA. These case studies should not be read to point blame at criminal justice professionals who did not immediately detect the offender's involvement in

additional crimes. Indeed, many of these cases would still be unsolved if not for other extraordinary detective work.

- States with multiple case studies should not be considered to have a particular deficit in DNA testing. For several of the case studies, it was the fact that DNA testing is being conducted that allows law enforcement to determine that serial offenders were at work.

Alaska

Four Preventable Rapes

Between January of 2000 and January of 2001, an unidentified perpetrator raped five women in the area of Anchorage. All five rapes were all linked to the same unknown offender through DNA analysis.

Police identified a suspect after the January 2001 rape, and that individual has since been convicted of all five attacks.

> The suspect in question had a long criminal history of felony charges which resulted in misdemeanor convictions. Felony charges levied against him included burglary with sexual intent, and his misdemeanor convictions ranged from criminal trespass to forgery. If this individual had been required to supply a DNA sample from a 1995 felony burglary charge that was reduced to a criminal trespass conviction, he could have been identified after the first rape in January 2000, *thereby preventing the following four rapes.*

One Preventable Rape

In 2000 in Anchorage, a woman was raped by a stranger and a DNA sample from the crime was entered into the state DNA database. No DNA hit was made, and the crime remained unsolved.

In 2001, another woman was raped in the remote village of Kotzebue on the Seward Peninsula – an area primarily accessible only by airplane. In this case, authorities identified the suspected perpetrator and he was convicted of sexual assault. Upon his conviction, a DNA sample was collected for the DNA database, and was matched in June of 2002 to the 2000 Anchorage rape.

> A review of the offender's criminal history shows at least nine prior convictions for a variety of crimes ranging from criminal trespass to felony burglary. Several of the convictions also carried sexual assault charges which were dismissed. In 2000, Alaska expanded the DNA database to include burglars, but did not make the provision retroactive to include prior convictions for those still serving probation or on parole. If the state had required DNA from this group of offenders, the DNA database would have matched the offender to the 2000 rape, *thereby preventing the rape in 2001.*

One Preventable Property Crime

In 1993, a murder was committed in Kodiak, but with no suspect the case remained unsolved. In recent years, the case was reopened and a cigarette butt collected from the crime scene was tested for DNA. A DNA profile was extracted, and it matched up with a felon on the database for a 1996 felony armed robbery.

However, before this murder identification was made, the offender remained criminally active in the community and was arrested and convicted of another theft in 2002.

With proactive policies to review cold cases for possible DNA evidence, the offender's DNA sample could have been matched to the 1993 murder prior to the 2002 theft – *thereby preventing at least one property crime.*

Arkansas

Four Preventable Rapes

Between 1995 and 1997, seven rapes were committed against women and young girls across four counties in Arkansas. In at least four of the cases, the victims were assaulted after being stopped by a man posing as a police officer, whom newspapers subsequently dubbed the "Blue Light Rapist."

In 1997, a suspect was identified as the suspected rapist through the assistance of one of his acquaintances who was working with law enforcement. Subsequent DNA testing linked him to several of the rapes, with other evidence and victim descriptions tying in the remaining cases.

The suspect had been convicted in 1996 on charges of theft by receiving a stolen rifle. Had the state required a DNA sample for this felony conviction, *up to five of the subsequent rapes could have been prevented.*

California

Six Preventable Rapes

In the Alameda County area, a series of 12 sexual assaults occurred in 1997 over a two-month period, all of which were attributed to the same unidentified suspect. The offender wore a ski mask in all the attacks, often robbed his victims, and in many instances attacked two women on the same day. This rapist struck quickly and frequently – his first five detected attacks occurred over a period of 10 days. Due to the extremely violent nature of the offenses and other similarities linking the attacks, it is reasonable to expect that DNA analysis would be expedited in these cases, as is often done when a serial offender is at large in a community.

A latent fingerprint found at the scene of the 12th attack was linked to a former high school track and field coach who had an extensive criminal record. This individual was formally charged and convicted in 6 of the cases, and is currently serving a 59-year to life imprisonment sentence.

The perpetrator's criminal record included 21 prior arrests, most of which were felony charges ranging from murder to interfering with a police officer. Although most of the offenses occurred prior to the introduction of DNA databases, the man's last brush with justice was a 1993 parole violation for a 1989 felony burglary conviction; the offender was discovered to be in possession of weapons and spent another 16 months in prison.

> DNA evidence from the first rape in 1997 could have been matched to the offender by the time of the sixth attack (occurring 11 days after the first attack) if the state had required DNA from all convicted felons – *thereby preventing six rapes.*

Three Preventable Rapes

In 1998, a woman was raped in Ventura County. A DNA profile from the criminal evidence was uploaded to the DNA database, but no match was made. Two additional rapes that occurred four months apart in 2002 were subsequently matched to the 1998 case, and new testing of a 1993 case was also eventually linked to the same unknown offender.

The offender became a suspect in these crimes after being identified in another case. He provided a DNA sample that linked him to the four rapes. He is currently awaiting trial.

> The suspected rapist had a prior conviction of felony drug possession in 1990. If the state statute had required DNA from all convicted felons, including felony drug possession, and if the 1993 rape case had been submitted for DNA testing in a timely manner, *at least three rapes could have been prevented.*

One Preventable Assault

On an April evening 1997, an intruder entered a residence in the Berkeley area and sexually assaulted a woman in her bed while threatening her with a knife. Before burglarizing the house and fleeing the scene, the intruder bound the victim with duct tape and stockings and viciously beat her.

In a second incident in 1997, an intruder entered a residence in Berkeley and began to burglarize the house. A male resident awoke and a struggle ensued during which the resident was stabbed in the face and back. In a sweep of the neighborhood, police stopped a suspect who was eventually determined to be responsible for both attacks.

> The offender had a prior record that included charges on 13 felonies. However, only six of these charges resulted in convictions and all six convictions were reduced to misdemeanors. Had California required DNA from criminals whose misdemeanor conviction arises from the same set of circumstances as a felony charge, *at least one potentially deadly assault could have been prevented.*

Hawaii

Two Preventable Sexual Assaults, Two Preventable Assaults

Over a period of two months in 1994, two women were sexually assaulted at knifepoint in parking garages in Honolulu. These two crimes occurred two weeks apart, so it is reasonable to assume that the case could have been prioritized and expedited DNA testing could have been conducted. More than a month later, a third attack was attempted, but the offender broke off the attack when a man nearby heard the victim's screams. The offender then chased after the man, but both the male and female were able to evade further contact with the offender.

Relying on latent fingerprints and victim identifications, police eventually arrested a suspect. During the course of the investigation that suspect was also linked to two unsolved home invasion sexual assaults. He pled guilty to 21 counts pursuant to a plea agreement, and ultimately was sentenced to 40 years in prison.

> The criminal in question was a registered sex offender in Hawaii, but his sentence terms were completed prior to the establishment of a DNA database in Hawaii in 1992. As it turns out, the 1994 attacks coincided with dates when he was required to check in with his parole officer in the downtown area. Had Hawaii extended its DNA database to include all registered sex offenders, he could have been identified prior to the third attack. Moreover, this individual's criminal record contains a kidnapping conviction for which he was paroled in 1994. If the state had required a DNA sample from persons incarcerated for kidnapping at the time of the DNA database establishment, *at least two sexual assaults and two related attempted attacks could have been prevented.* Hawaii is the only state that still does not require DNA from kidnapping convictions.

Idaho

One Preventable Death

In September of 2002, a woman was kidnapped, raped and murdered. DNA collected from the crime scene was entered into CODIS, but no offender was identified. In March of 2003 another woman was raped and murdered, and the DNA database linked that crime to the 2002 unsolved murder case. The man who was a suspect in the 2003 murder case was arrested and confessed to the crime. Further DNA testing reconfirmed that the man had in fact committed both murders.

> The murder suspect had been convicted on felony burglary charges in 1991. If the state had required DNA for this conviction, *one death could have been prevented.*

Indiana

One Preventable Death, Several Preventable Property Crimes

In May of 2000, an elderly woman was brutally raped while on her way to vote in an election. Ten days later a suspect, who had not been identified as the woman's rapist, was charged and subsequently convicted of felonious receiving of stolen property and trespass. Upon his release, he was remanded to another jurisdiction where he was wanted on felony theft charges. The suspect was released from this county correctional facility in May of 2001, and the next day an elderly woman was found raped and murdered. Tracking dogs lead police to an area where the suspect's mother lived, and within a few days the suspect was arrested for the murder. Subsequent DNA testing linked both the 2001 murder and the 2000 rape to the suspect in question.

> In 1998, the perpetrator of these crimes was convicted on felony charges of receiving stolen property, and he was again convicted on a similar charge while still under confinement in prison. From 1999 through 2000, he was charged or arrested on four separate occasions for felony theft by receiving, one of which resulted in a misdemeanor conviction and the last one brought the felony conviction in May of 2001. If the offender in question had been required to give a DNA sample upon the 1998 felony conviction, the

2000 rape could have been solved, *and the rape and murder of an elderly woman, and several property crimes could have been prevented.*

Two Preventable Sexual Assaults

In October of 2001, a woman was raped by an unknown assailant who broke into her home; a rape kit was collected for analysis in this case. In July of 2002, another woman was raped and burglarized, and another rape kit was collected for forensic analysis. Then once more in August of 2002 a third woman was burglarized and sexually battered. All three violent assaults took place in the Indianapolis area.

Use of the Indiana state DNA database eventually led to the matching of the rape that occurred in October of 2001 to the rape of July 2002. In addition, a match was also made to a DNA sample obtained from a suspect. Upon questioning by detectives, the suspect in question incriminated himself in a third sexual assault which had taken place in August of 2002.

> The perpetrator in this set of cases received a 20-year sentence for his second rape conviction in December 1986, and was released from prison on parole in October 1995. However, the Indiana DNA database did not become effective until July 1996, and upon going into effect it did not require DNA samples from qualifying offenders who were still serving community sentences of probation or parole. Had the Indiana statute on DNA evidence collection included a provision to collect DNA from persons still serving community sentences, *at least two sexual assaults could have been prevented.*

Kentucky

Seven Preventable Rapes

In October 1998 a female attendant at a gas station was raped. In this case, DNA was collected but was not tested. Approximately ten days later, another female gas station attendant was raped, and over the next three years an additional seven rapes were committed by the same repeat offender.

Investigators identified a suspect in the last rape in August of 2002 after he used the victim's ATM card. In 2003, DNA testing finally linked the man to the first two rapes in 1998, and other evidence linked the remaining cases to one another.

> The suspect was a known sex offender in Kentucky who had committed twelve documented rapes as a juvenile. His first rape committed as an adult occurred within a month of his release from juvenile detention facilities. Unfortunately, the State of Kentucky did not require DNA from juvenile offenders adjudicated delinquent of sex crimes at the time of the suspect's juvenile sentences. If the state had required DNA from juveniles adjudicated delinquent of felonies, *at least seven rapes could have been prevented.* Moreover, in 2002, the requirement was not made retroactive to encompass persons on probation or parole. Had it not been for good police work, this rapist could still be a threat to public safety today. when amending the state's DNA evidence law governing the DNA database to include juveniles

Five Preventable Rapes

From June of 1997 through October of 2000 six rapes and several attempted rapes took place in the Louisville area. In addition to DNA evidence that linked these rapes to one another, the rapist frequently used a flashlight to blind his victims -- thus earning the nickname of the "Flashlight Rapist."

In November of 2000 a suspect was arrested and subsequently convicted on numerous burglary charges in Louisville. A sex crime detective began to suspect the man as the Flashlight Rapist and obtained a warrant for a DNA sample. The DNA analysis positively identified the man as the Flashlight Rapist, and he later pleaded guilty to the crimes.

> The flashlight rapist had been previously convicted on felonious burglary charges in 1991 in Florida, which did not yet require DNA from all convicted felons. Had DNA been required, *at least 5 rapes could have been prevented.* Moreover, although Kentucky altered its law to require DNA for burglary convictions in 2002, the provision was not made retroactive to include probationers or parolees and the implementation date of the law was delayed. Thus the 2000 burglary conviction in Kentucky may also have "slipped through the cracks" and allowed the crimes to remain unsolved if not for good detective work.

Louisiana

Four Preventable Deaths

Between September of 2001 and March of 2003 five women were raped and murdered in the Baton Rouge area. All five crimes were linked to the same unidentified perpetrator through DNA testing. In May of 2003, a volunteered DNA sample collected from a mass sampling of potential suspects resulted in the identification of a suspect. Subsequent to this match, at least one additional murder has been tied through DNA to the suspect, and over 20 additional cases are being reviewed for possible connections to the suspect in question.

> The suspect had a 1993 conviction on felony burglary charges arising from an attack on a 74 year-old man. If his DNA sample had been collected and entered into the database, *at least four deaths could have been prevented.* The suspect also had prior convictions for beating up his girlfriend in a bar and trying to run over a Sheriff's deputy at a roadblock.

One Preventable Rape and Burglary

In 1997 and unknown suspect committed attempted aggravated rape on a child in her home. A DNA sample was collected as evidence, but was not matched to an offender.

In December 1998, a woman was raped and her home burglarized by an unknown assailant. A suspect who was in close proximity to the crime scene and matching the victim's description was arrested. Subsequent DNA testing linked him to both the 1997 and 1998 crimes. The same perpetrator is suspected in the commission of two other similar crimes for which no DNA evidence was available. He has been sentenced to 50 years of imprisonment.

> The offender's criminal history included a 1990 conviction on unauthorized entry of a place of business, and a 1996 felony theft conviction. If a DNA sample had been required for either of these crimes, the database could have matched the offender to the 1997, *thereby preventing the 1998 rape and burglary.*

Massachusetts

Three Preventable Rape/Murders

In late 1997, a woman was found raped and murdered in her home in Springfield. In early 1998, another three women were found raped and murdered – one in her home, two others in alley ways. All four murders were linked through DNA, and due to the unique positioning of the bodies which became the offender's "signature."

Following the fourth murder, a voluntary DNA sample was collected from a person who had become a suspect in the case. Within a few weeks, that suspect was tied through a DNA match to the crimes.

> The suspect's criminal record included two prior felony convictions in 1996 – one for larceny and the other for breaking and entering, for which he was sentenced to community supervision. If Massachusetts had required a DNA sample for either of the 1996 non-violent felony convictions, a DNA match could have been obtained after the first rape/murder, *thereby preventing the subsequent three rape/murders.*

Missouri

Ten Preventable Rapes

Between 1988 and 1997, an unidentified masked man was beating up and raping women in areas of Missouri and across the Mississippi River in Illinois. Because many of the 29 or more attacks happened in south St. Louis, the media dubbed the attacker the "South Side Rapist." DNA linked at least 13 of the cases together, but the police were unable to identify a perpetrator.

In October of 1998 St. Louis City Police were called when a man was seen breaking into a house. A van registered to a person known to the police was reported leaving the scene of the break-in. This person's appearance matched a physical description of the South Side Rapist and police asked for a DNA sample. The suspect voluntarily agreed to have his mouth swabbed. Several weeks later the DNA results were returned and positively identified the suspect as the South Side Rapist, who by this time had disappeared. He was arrested several months later in Albuquerque, New Mexico after a worried mother found his hotel number in her daughter's belongings. The suspect ultimately confessed to raping at least 100 women since his late teens.

> Sometime in 1991 the suspect was convicted of felony burglary for which he served a sentence in the state prison. Prosecutors indicate that there were a minimum of ten rapes occurring after this conviction that are attributable to the suspect. If the state had required a DNA sample from this perpetrator after the burglary conviction, the suspect could have been linked to serial rapes occurring prior to his conviction, *thereby preventing at least 10 additional rapes.*

Eleven Preventable Rapes and Murders

From April of 2001 through May of 2002, police began finding the bodies of women who had been raped and murdered in the St. Louis/western Illinois area. Investigators recovered semen from the victim's bodies that was sent for crime laboratory analysis. The DNA profiles from the semen recovered from the victims all matched.

A person known to the police became a suspect in the crimes after he wrote an anonymous letter to a local newspaper. An internet-generated map enclosed with the letter led to some computer forensics that eventually identified the specific computer that downloaded the map. The suspect was ultimately arrested in June of 2002 when police found videotapes of himself killing and torturing his victims. On the videotape, the suspect states that he had just committed "murder number seventeen". Police have conclusively linked 12 victims to this offender thus far, and believe the number could be as high as 20. This individual committed suicide shortly after his arrest.

In March of 1988, this offender committed a series of five robberies and was sentenced to fifteen years for robbery and armed criminal action. In June 1994, he was paroled after serving five years and three months of his sentence. Unfortunately, Missouri does not require DNA from convicted robbers, and this offender was released without submitting a DNA sample for the state database. With a DNA sample in the database, this offender could have been identified as the killer of the first victim *long before a minimum of eleven additional women lost their lives.*

Nebraska

Two Preventable Sexual Assaults

In 1995, an unknown perpetrator raped a woman in Ohio. DNA was collected during the investigation, but was not submitted for testing.

In 1999, a woman was sexually assaulted by an unknown assailant at a hotel in Nebraska. DNA evidence was collected from this crime scene. Later the same day in Colorado, a woman was sexually assaulted by a man who had answered an advertisement in the newspaper for furniture that she was selling. DNA was collected from this crime scene as well.

Using an electronic bulletin board that serves a nine-state area in the Midwest, a Nebraska police detective posted a digitized photo of the suspect in the Nebraska hotel attack. Within 30 days police in Iowa identified the person in the photo as a known offender resident in their area. The man in question was arrested and subsequent DNA testing linked him to both 1999 attacks.

Subsequently, an Ohio police detective noticed similarities to the 1995 attack, and the DNA from that crime was submitted for testing and was found to match that of the offender.

The offender's extensive criminal history dates back to a 1979 felony burglary conviction, and included two separate burglary convictions in Iowa in 1989 (for which he was sentenced to a maximum of 25 years) plus a 1993 misdemeanor indecent exposure conviction and several acquittals on sexual assault. If Iowa had required DNA prior to releasing the offender for the 1989 felony burglary charge, and if the DNA evidence in the Ohio case had been submitted and analyzed in a more timely manner, *at least two sexual assaults in Nebraska could have been prevented.*

This case is an excellent example of the importance of each state's DNA program to solving and preventing crimes in other states. It is also worth noting that Iowa expanded its offender DNA database to include all convicted felons in 2002, but Nebraska still does not require DNA from felony burglary charges.

Three Preventable Rapes

In July of 2000, a woman was raped in her home after answering a knock at her door, but no DNA was collected. Between September of 2001 and September of 2002, four more rapes were committed by a perpetrator using the same modus operandi – but in these cases DNA was collected and linked to the same unidentified perpetrator.

Acting on a tip, police tracked down a suspect in November of 2002 and the man was subsequently convicted on all four rape cases for which DNA was collected. He is eligible for parole in 140 years.

> The rapist in question had several convictions for misdemeanor thefts from 1996 through 1998. Moreover, he was convicted as a juvenile on felony theft charges in 1996. If a DNA sample had been required for the felony theft adjudication, *at least three rapes could have been prevented.*

New Jersey

Three Preventable Rapes

In mid-May 1998, a woman was raped at a public library in Essex County. One month later, a second woman was raped in a library. DNA samples were taken from both cases and loaded into the DNA database, where it was discovered that the two rapes were linked. Importantly, in matching these cases to each other, DNA also excluded two men being held by police as possible suspects.

In late June of 1998, a child was abducted and raped. A DNA sample was collected and sent to a private laboratory for testing, and the victim provided a description of the attacker to police.

The police eventually identified a suspect, and DNA testing subsequently tied him to the child attack. After the sample was loaded into the state database, it was discovered that the same offender was the library rapist. Additionally, the same DNA profile was eventually matched to an October 1999 rape in New York City.

> The offender had a prior felony arrest on a weapons possession charge. The charge was later reduced to a misdemeanor crime to which the offender pled guilty. If a DNA sample had been required of felony charges that result in misdemeanor convictions, the perpetrator could have been identified after the first rape, *thereby preventing the following three rapes.*

Seven Preventable Robberies, Five Preventable Rapes

In October of 2002, the first in a series of ten robberies began. The incidents included seven aggravated sexual assaults, spanned four months and included victims in at least nine different New Jersey cities.

A person known to the police became a strong suspect in the first offense, and a DNA sample was collected from him four days later. A DNA match was finally made in January of

2003 to the third offense, but only after a unit commander requested expedited testing of the evidence.

> The offender in question was convicted in the 1980's on federal felony robberies charges, and was released from a federal prison in 1999. Unfortunately, the federal government did not begin requiring DNA from felony robbery convictions until 2000. Moreover, law enforcement had custody of all the DNA information that they needed to arrest this offender within only a few weeks of the first offense. The omission of his DNA from the federal DNA database, along with the backlog delay in processing DNA evidence, allowed the offender to remain on the streets. With stronger federal statutes and shorter DNA testing delays, the perpetrator could have been identified after the third attack, *thereby preventing the subsequent seven robberies and five rapes.*

Four Preventable Rapes

Between April of 2002 and May of 2003, five women were raped in the Trenton area. DNA testing linked all five offenses to the same unknown perpetrator. After police released a composite sketch of the suspect in 2003, nearly 75 tips were called in identifying the same person. In June 2003, U.S. Marshals eventually arrested the suspect in Pennsylvania on a parole violation warrant that was issued in July of 2002. Trenton Police obtained a DNA sample from the suspect through a court order, and thanks to expedited testing at the state laboratory the man was linked to the crimes within a few days. The charges on 16 counts involving five victims are pending as the suspect awaits extradition to New Jersey from Pennsylvania.

> The suspect's criminal record included two felony convictions for theft and forgery related offenses in New Jersey, and nine felony convictions for theft, forgery, and receiving stolen property in Pennsylvania. If the suspect had been required to give a DNA sample for any of these crimes *in either state*, he could have been identified after the first assault, *thereby preventing the subsequent four rapes.*

New York

Thirteen Preventable Rapes

In August of 1993 a young woman was raped in the Bronx in what was to be the first of up to 51 rapes attributed to the same offender over a five-year period. The perpetrator was dubbed the "Bronx Rapist" by the media.

A person known to the police became a suspect when he was identified in a transaction involving a victim's jewelry at a pawnshop. He was arrested and subsequent DNA testing linked him to several of the rapes. He has been convicted on fourteen counts of rape in the Bronx, six counts of sexual abuse, nineteen counts of robbery, and two counts of criminal possession of a weapon. He has been sentenced to two life sentences.

> This offender had a prior conviction in 1989 for felony robbery and assault, for which he received a seven-year sentence. If the State of New York had begun requiring DNA from all convicted felons in 1990 this offender would have been on the DNA database prior to the first rape in 1993, and *at least thirteen rapes could have been prevented.* Moreover, when New York's database was established in 1994, an inclusion of all convicted felons

and retroactive application to persons previously convicted but still under supervision would have captured this offender's DNA sample much earlier in the investigation.

Two Preventable Sexual Assaults, One Preventable Death

From 1991 to 1999, three young women were murdered in New York City and four others were raped. The youngest victim was 13, and several of the crimes were noted for their brutality. During the course of the investigation, police identified a man who had just been released from jail for a sex crime in the same area in which a victim had been raped. He had been seen in the neighborhood just before and after the rape, and was picked out of a lineup. The man was jailed for four months, but DNA testing subsequently eliminated the man as a suspect.

Another person known to the police became a suspect in these crimes in 1999 and was placed under surveillance by police. He was eventually arrested on petty theft charges and DNA testing later linked him to evidence from the crimes. This person had been released from custody pending the DNA testing, and was arrested again in Miami after the DNA match was made. He was found with a young woman who may have been his next victim. This offender was found guilty on twenty-two counts, and sentenced to 400 years in prison.

> This offender had been convicted of felony robbery in 1992 at a time when New York did not collect DNA samples from criminals convicted of felony robbery. Moreover, if a 1996 expansion of the database to include robbery convictions had been applied retroactively, he could have been required to provide a DNA sample at this point. The sample would have been linked to one of the previous crimes, *thereby preventing at least two sexual assaults against juveniles and one death.* It is also worth noting that a sooner DNA match would have prevented an innocent man from spending four months in prison.

Seven Preventable Rapes and Robberies

In 2001 it was revealed that New York City had between 14,000 and 16,000 unanalyzed rape kits that were sitting in a storage rooms. Through a focused backlog reduction program, the City has been analyzing the rape kits and loading them into the state DNA database system.

In 2002, two unsolved rapes that were part of the backlog reduction project were connected to the same offender. The offender's criminal history included five prior arrests which resulted in two separate felony convictions – in 1991 for robbery and sexual abuse, and in 1997 for armed robbery. Although New York was not collecting DNA from robbery convictions in 1997, a 2000 law expanded the database to include robbery and included offenders who were still incarcerated for previous convictions. Upon release in 2001, the offender in question was required to give a DNA sample for the database.

> This offender was arrested in December 2001 for a series of rapes and robberies (seven separate incidents). If the 1996 rape kits had been tested sooner, this person would have been linked to these assaults in 2001 prior to his release, *thereby preventing the subsequent 7 attacks occurring after his release.*

North Carolina

Two Preventable Rapes

A series of three undetected rapes occurred in the Charlotte-Mecklenberg County area – one in February of 2000, and two more in May of 2002.

Police identified a suspect after the first attack in May, and positively identified the perpetrator through fingerprints found at the scene. Subsequent DNA testing also linked all three rapes to the suspect.

> The offender was convicted in December of 2000 on felony breaking and entering and larceny charges. However, the North Carolina DNA database statute did not include either felony crime as a qualifying offense for the DNA database. If the suspect had been required to give a DNA sample for his December 2000 conviction, he could have been connected to the February 2000 rape, *thereby possibly preventing two rapes in May of 2002.*

North Dakota

One Preventable Rape

In June 2000, a woman in Fargo was sexually assaulted in her home by an unknown intruder. DNA evidence was collected from the crime scene, but was not matched to an offender. Police had identified a man as a possible suspect, but did not have sufficient cause to obtain a warrant for a DNA sample.

In August 2002, a teenager was sexually assaulted by an intruder in an apartment where she was babysitting. Several days later, police were finally able to obtain a warrant for a DNA sample from the suspect, and he was linked to both rapes.

> The offender was convicted in Minnesota for felony possession of stolen property and burglary in September 1996, and for felony burglary in June 1997. At the time Minnesota did not require DNA from convicted burglars. North Dakota still does not require DNA from convicted burglars. If a DNA sample had been collected from the offender for either the 1996 or 1997 felony conviction, the June 2000 sexual assault could have been solved and the perpetrator apprehended, *thereby preventing one rape.* The offender also had a 1996 domestic assault misdemeanor conviction, which is also a DNA database crime in some states.

Ohio

One Preventable Rape

In early April of 2002 a man who was hired for yard work at a Columbus residence returned in the evening and burglarized the home where he had worked. In gaining entry, the burglar left blood that was collected and analyzed for DNA. The man had given the owner of the home a fictitious name and false credentials. However, through diligent detective work investigators assigned to the case identified a possible suspect and requested a DNA sample from him. The suspect complied with the request and the police returned to arrest the suspect in question after DNA forensic analysis matched the suspect's DNA and the DNA collected at the scene of the crime. Unfortunately, the suspect had disappeared in the interim.

In mid May of 2002, the offender in question raped a young girl who was able identify him. Investigators arrested him and found that his fingerprints matched felony prints on file noting that he was wanted in the April burglary. DNA testing subsequently confirmed that the suspect in question raped the young girl, and that he was the missing suspect in the home burglary.

> The perpetrator in this case had a prior conviction in 1996 on felony drug trafficking and drug conspiracy charges. If the state of Ohio had required DNA from convicted felony drug offenders, police could have arrested this man after the burglary offense rather than asking him for a DNA sample which prompted his disappearance. This offender would have been incarcerated for the burglary rather than being allowed to go into hiding, *and the rape of a young girl could have been prevented.*

Two Preventable Rapes

Between 1993 and 1994, three rapes were committed by the same unknown perpetrator in the Hamilton County area. After the third rape, the victim was able to notify police officers promptly and they were able to apprehend a suspect in short order. DNA testing linked the suspect in question to all three rapes.

> The perpetrator had a 1993 felony conviction for carrying a concealed weapon and served a sentence in state prison. He also had a 1984 conviction in California on felony sexual battery. If Ohio had required DNA from the 1993 concealed weapon conviction, the 1993 rape could have been solved, *thereby preventing two subsequent rapes.*

One Preventable Rape, One Preventable Property Crime

In 1999, two rapes occurred several months apart in nearby counties. Both rapes were linked through DNA, and the database was used to identify a suspect in 2001.

> The perpetrator's criminal history includes a 1994 burglary for which he was required to give a DNA sample for the database. The DNA sample was collected in 1997, and he was released from prison in 1999 on "shock probation" -- three months prior to the first rape. Unfortunately, the offender biological sample was in a backlog and remained unanalyzed until 2001 when the "cold hit" was made to both rapes. If not for the backlog, the man would have been identified and arrested as a suspect in the first rape, *thereby preventing the subsequent rape.* The offender in question was also convicted in late 1999 of a home burglary and theft of prescription drugs – *another crime he would not have been free to commit if the DNA match had been made sooner.*

Pennsylvania

Two Preventable Rapes

In 1994, an elderly woman was raped in her home by a stranger. This case was followed in 1998 by two similar attacks on elderly women – one of whom lived independently before the attack but was particularly traumatized and moved to a nursing home thereafter. She died before the case was solved. DNA linked all three cases to one unidentified offender.

A person known to police became a suspect in the case when detectives realized the modus operandi was similar to a local known repeat offender who targeted elderly victims. The offender's parole officer supplied detectives with an envelope that had been sent by the suspected person, and DNA from the saliva was determined to be consistent with that of the attacker.

Detectives subsequently procured a search warrant for a blood sample, and that lead to a match between the three crimes and this specific offender.

> The offender's criminal record included two separate felony convictions for a series of home invasion burglary crimes committed against elderly victims. His first sentence began in 1987, and he was released on parole in 1992. The second sentence began in 1995. If Pennsylvania had required DNA from felony burglaries in either 1992 or 1995, this repeat offender could have been linked to the 1994 rape, *thereby preventing two rapes in 1998.*

Five Preventable Rapes

In 2002, an unknown assailant in the Pittsburgh-area raped or attempted to rape six women and assaulted two other women. The youngest victim among these women was 14. In each case, the suspect approached the victim from behind, attempted to make conversation, and either made threats with a gun or displayed a firearm.

The suspect was eventually apprehended when his last victim shot him. The woman, who worked as a security guard, was approached by the offender in question in a park and she narrowly escaped him after he threatened her life. After reporting the incident to police, she continued her walk and was again approached by the same man. This time, instead of running away she shot the assailant twice in the stomach and then notified police. The offender in question has been linked to several of the crimes noted through DNA testing, and he is currently awaiting trial on multiple charges.

> The offender's felony record included convictions in 1997 and 2002 for felony receiving of stolen property, and a 2001 conviction for felony theft. This offender's most recent release from incarceration occurred just weeks before the first rape. If the state had required DNA from all convicted felons at any point since 1997, the offender's DNA profile would have been on record and potentially could have identified him after the first rape, *thereby preventing the subsequent 5 rapes.* Pennsylvania still does not collect DNA from these felons.

Rhode Island

One Preventable Sexual Assault

In Providence in 2000 an assailant kidnapped at gunpoint a male college student who was attempting to enter his apartment. The offender forced the student withdraw funds from two banks, then returned to the student's apartment and burglarized it.

In a second incident, a female and a male college student were both kidnapped and the two victims were robbed at gunpoint. The male student was forced to withdraw money from a bank, and both students were sexually assaulted. DNA was collected from this crime scene.

In a third incident, a female college student was kidnapped at gunpoint while she was entering her apartment. She was robbed of her money and her apartment was burglarized. The woman was then forced to drive to a bank in an attempt to have her withdraw additional money from the ATM. The offender then drove the female student to a secluded area and sexually assaulted her.

The offender in this case was ultimately identified through a photograph taken by an ATM Bank surveillance machine during commission of the second crime. The offender was arrested by police one day after the third crime, and he eventually received a 70-year sentence for his violent gun-involved crimes.

> The offender was charged of felony possession of a stolen vehicle in 1999, which is not a crime included in the Rhode Island DNA database. With a DNA sample from this conviction, the crime laboratory could have linked the second incident to the offender, *thereby possibly preventing the third crime involving a sexual assault.*

South Carolina

Unknown Preventable Crimes

In August of 2000 a teenager in Aiken was raped and murdered in her home. There was no suspect in the case, but DNA evidence from the crime was sent to the laboratory for testing and a profile was sent to the national database. Meanwhile, police actively pursued the investigation, conducting between 300 and 400 interviews and collecting 94 DNA samples for comparison.

In August of 2002 an offender's DNA sample was submitted to the Georgia DNA database after he was returned to state prison for violating his parole on a felony theft by taking conviction. When the sample was compared against the national database, it was matched to the South Carolina murder. The person in question had worked for a package delivery service in 2000. During one of his deliveries, the offender met the teenager and later he returned to kill her.

> The offense which resulted in this offender's inclusion in Georgia's DNA database, and which eventually lead to the closure of the teenager's murder, is a crime that is excluded from the South Carolina database. Had the offender committed his prior crimes in South Carolina instead of Georgia, he would likely still be undetected and living unsuspected in the community. In addition to the theft by taking conviction, the repeat offender in question also had convictions for numerous other crimes. Among those crimes are escape, possession of a firearm by a convicted felon, theft of a motor vehicle, and entering a vehicle – none of which are qualifying offenses for the DNA database in the State of South Carolina.

Three Preventable Rapes

In September 1995, a woman was raped by a stranger and a rape kit was collected at the scene of the crime and submitted to the crime laboratory. The DNA profile was loaded into the state database system, but no match was made. In July, September and November of 1996 three more women were raped, but no rape kits were collected from these crime scenes. However, all three women identified the same suspect as their attacker through mug shot photographs. Investigators interviewed a suspect at his home and made an arrest in early 1998. A DNA sample was collected from the suspect and was matched to the DNA profile from the first rape. The offender was tried and convicted for rape and burglary, and he was sentenced to life over 30 years in prison.

> The offender was convicted in 1980 on two separate rape and burglary charges. He completed his sentence in June of 1995. Unfortunately, while the South Carolina database statute was enacted in 1994, it did not contain an emergency clause and therefore it did not come into effect until July of 1995 – one month too late to capture this offender's DNA sample. If the South Carolina statute had become effective immediately upon enactment, this offender could have been identified after the first rape, *thereby preventing the following three rapes*.

Conclusion

The case studies reported here serve their purpose well – namely, they illustrate quite clearly the concrete benefits to crime prevention of DNA databases. Many violent and property crimes committed by repeat offenders could have been prevented in these cases. Of course, the few cases set forth here only represent the tip of the iceberg; many more exemplary cases could be listed for each of these states. The following section moves on to the cost factors associated with gearing up to use DNA databases for proactive crime prevention and the clearance of unsolved cases.

VII. Cost and Benefit Questions

A full cost-benefit analysis of forensic DNA testing and DNA databases is problematic since many of the potential benefits do not lend themselves to direct quantification. This Report did not attempt to develop this type of analysis, but presents the following discussion as a listing of relevant matters for consideration and possible further study.

The costs of DNA testing at crime laboratories are generally known, and have been discussed to some extent in other sections of this Report. In addition to the costs of equipment and reagents needed to complete DNA testing, an ever-increasing demand for DNA testing means a corresponding increase in the need for more capacity. Increased capacity, in turn, means more personnel, more equipment, and occasionally more space. Personnel costs, as demonstrated elsewhere in this Report, pose a considerable hurdle to DNA testing at many crime laboratories. The fact that these costs are relatively easy to calculate, and nonetheless have not been addressed adequately in some jurisdictions, raises an interesting question of funding priorities geared properly to community needs.

Beyond the quantifiable crime laboratory costs, there are also costs associated with the proper training of criminal justice professionals. Law enforcement training is needed to ensure the identification and collection of appropriate DNA evidence, as well timely collection of evidence from offenders. In order to ensure that DNA analysts are receiving quality DNA samples, there is also a need to ensure that medical professionals, particularly those responsible for rape kit collection, are adequately trained in evidence gathering and storage. Another group sometimes overlooked in this equation are the victim service providers who could prove instrumental in integrating the victim into the evidence gathering process and ensuring his/her informed participation so that DNA analysis is not performed needlessly.

Of course, once a DNA match has been made and a suspect arrested, criminal investigators, prosecutors and defense lawyers must devote their limited resources to determining whether to bring the case to trial. The training of prosecutors, criminal defense lawyers, and judges poses problems for legal professionals who must now be versed in the scientific issues of DNA analysis and related population probability statistics. Beyond training is the cost of simply having additional cases to be investigated, prosecuted and defended in an already over-burdened criminal justice system. Newspaper accounts quite frequently report on offenders who, when faced with DNA evidence, become inclined to accept plea bargains or provide admissions of guilt. Although this is certainly true for some cases, this study did not undertake to determine if the additional justice system caseload resulting from cases due to DNA matches is offset by increasing plea bargains. Moreover, some attorneys have argued that prosecutors actually may be less inclined to allow plea bargains once they have the advantage of DNA evidence, thus resulting in a heavier caseload.

Some of the most obvious benefits to forensic DNA testing are the potential to bring criminals to justice and closure to victims and their families. These, again, are largely immeasurable benefits. The "preventable crimes" case studies presented in this Report begin to paint a picture of potential added benefits to public safety from investment in DNA programs, but they do not provide a calculable measurement. There are certainly benefits to victims in DNA cases that bring an offender to justice, and individual stories can again give a glimpse into this world, but these cannot be computed in a manner that can be compared easily against costs. The question has also been raised as to whether DNA testing and DNA matches have an indirect effect in encouraging victims of violent crimes to come forward. Again, anecdotally there are victims who will say this is the case, but further study of this question might be useful in providing reliable cost efficiency data.

Moreover, every match of an offender to a crime on the DNA database represents a case that an investigator may soon consider "cleared." Clearing these cases in turn allows the investigator to turn his or her attention to other unsolved crimes. To understand cost efficiencies to investigations, data including man-hours involved in a "typical" investigation in cases without DNA, would need to be compared to "typical" case with DNA – and/or cases in which DNA matches have named potential suspects. Without this type of data, it is difficult to have a full understanding of potential cost efficiencies.

And last, but by no means least, benefits are also derived from ensuring that the appropriate person faces justice for a crime. Post conviction DNA testing in the United States has been instrumental in the release of over 100 persons who have been wrongly convicted. Increasingly, DNA testing is now being used to exonerate persons prior to conviction. Indeed, crime laboratories estimate that in cases requesting a match of DNA evidence from an unsolved crime to a DNA sample from a known potential suspect, the analysis exonerates the suspect identified by investigators in approximately a third of the cases. Such exonerations not only have a significant benefit to the misidentified suspect, but also allow law enforcement to refocus their efforts and avoid wasting time investigating the wrong person. In addition to the direct benefit supplied to both the accused and investigators, DNA exonerations provide the general public with a greater level of confidence in the criminal justice system.

VIII. Conclusions and Policy Implications

In the relatively brief amount of time that forensic DNA has been available to the criminal justice system, its impact has already proven remarkable – from the conviction of rapists and murderers to the exoneration of wrongly convicted inmates on death row. However, the proven effectiveness of forensic DNA has resulted in a tremendous demand for additional testing which has not been met by a corresponding increase in available supply. The purpose of this study was to provide a basis for extrapolating the potential number of DNA cases sitting in law enforcement evidence rooms and storage areas throughout the country. In developing these figures, crime laboratories were also asked to supply data regarding their backlogged cases in order to arrive at a more precise national sum. It was also important in this study to have a discussion as to the reasons for the unanalyzed DNA cases found both at the law enforcement agencies and the crime laboratories. This discussion included capacity issues facing both law enforcement and crime laboratories as well as a discussion of how forensic DNA is viewed by law enforcement. Finally, the study also assembled an overview of DNA database matches in the United States along with a discussion on the potential of DNA to not just solve crimes, but also to prevent crimes. The following summarizes the major conclusions drawn from the Report.

1. The Backlog of Unsolved Rapes and Homicides in the U.S. is Massive

When unsolved property offenses with possible biological evidence are added into the equation, there are an estimated 700,000 of these unsolved cases nationally. Furthermore, of the 400,000+ unsolved rapes and homicides nationally law enforcement agencies reported that roughly half of such cases are likely to contain biological evidence for DNA testing. Thus, when including the extant unsolved property offenses with biological evidence, there may be a national total of 553,821 unsolved rapes, homicides, and property offenses that may be amenable to DNA testing.

2. The Majority of Law Enforcement Agencies Have Insufficient Evidence Storage Capacity

This issue is critical since, as demonstrated in Section III, pressures on storage space can result in biological evidence being maintained under improper conditions or, even worse, discarded or not collected at all. This issue is also significant given the finding that the overwhelming majority of law enforcement agencies (over 70 percent) reported their storage capacity limitations to be either “critical” or “highly critical.”

3. A Significant Proportion of Law Enforcement Agencies Continue to Misunderstand the Potential Benefits of DNA Testing

As reported by nearly one-fourth of all law enforcement agencies, one of the primary reasons for not sending DNA evidence to a crime laboratory is due to the lack of a suspect. To be sure, this is exactly the kind of situation where an offender DNA database would be most useful.

As a particularly notable example of this lack of understanding of the potential utility of DNA testing, during a telephone conversation with researchers the sex assault unit commander of the largest local law enforcement agency in a particular state reported that it had *never* submitted a DNA sample for testing.

4. Both State and Local Crime Laboratories are Overworked, Understaffed, and Insufficiently Funded

These agencies simply do not have the capacity to handle their current caseloads—let alone their anticipated backlogs for the near future—in a timely manner. This problem would appear to be broadly present across the country.

5. The Role of the Federal Government in Funding Forensic DNA Analysis has been, Up to this Point, Important but Rather Minimal

Indeed, the majority of funding for local crime laboratories is derived from local sources, and the majority of funding for state crime laboratories comes from state sources. Only one-in-five state crime laboratories, and fewer than one-in-twenty local crime laboratories, report that the majority of their funding comes from federal sources. Clearly, not only is there a greater potential role for the federal government to play in assisting with the current backlog problem, but there is also a certain need for state and local governments to re-evaluate their degree of investment in their forensic crime laboratories given that demand for services has far outstripped availability of analysis over the past several years.

6. Forensic DNA Databases are Important Tools in Solving a Variety of Crimes, Committed by a Variety of Criminals

The DNA database system has been used by an increasing number of law enforcement agencies throughout the nation to identify recidivist criminals and to provide investigatory leads to detectives, particularly in cases involving serial crimes. While the DNA database, to date, has been limited largely to violent offenders and violent unsolved crimes, this trend is changing. As demonstrated by states such as Virginia, the potential for DNA to play a vital role in solving nonviolent crimes is considerable.

7. There are Numerous Crimes that are Potentially Preventable Through Better, More Efficient Use of Forensic DNA Analysis

Although it is extremely difficult to document the number of preventable crimes associated with the timely availability of DNA evidence, a look at specific case studies from a variety of states clearly demonstrates the potential for DNA to prevent repeat offender criminals from victimizing multiple citizens.

8. The Cost, and the Offsetting Benefits Associated with DNA Testing Present Several Questions Relating to Return on Investment which Merit Further Study

Many of the costs associated with DNA testing are discussed in this study, but a more comprehensive study of the costs of DNA forensic evidence collection and processing is needed to provide policy makers with additional valuable information required to make informed decisions during budgetary discussions. The benefits of DNA analysis to investigators, prosecutors, victims and the falsely accused are an important part of the cost/benefit puzzle that budget writers must take into consideration in allocating resources to the national DNA collection and analysis system.

ACKNOWLEDGEMENTS

This report could not have been completed without the participation and support of a great number of criminal justice professionals spread throughout the country. We wish to thank the nation's public forensic DNA laboratories whose response rate of 100 percent has guaranteed confidence in many of the results documented in this Report. The willingness of the heavily burdened state and local forensic laboratories to devote their limited resources to the detailed assessment tool sent for their completion is a testament not only to their professional dedication, but also to their recognition of the great need for national policy attention in this arena from all levels of government – local, state and federal.

We are also particularly grateful to those professionals in the law enforcement and forensic communities who participated in the pre-administration review of the draft assessment tool developed for this study. Given the considerable diversity in law enforcement agencies throughout the country, and the substantial variation in level of understanding and rate of utilization of forensic DNA, a thorough review of issues relating to the interpretation of and possible responses to the assessment tool was a primary concern of the researchers. Our topnotch review team was extremely instrumental in examining the draft assessment tools for weaknesses and omissions, and in providing a high level of confidence in the responses the assessment instrument ultimately generated.

In addition to the criminal justice professionals specified above, we also wish to express our gratitude to each local level law enforcement official who took the considerable time required to fill out the detailed assessment form. This group of public servants includes Police Chiefs and Sheriffs across the nation, as well as many tribal law enforcement executives.

Similar thanks are owed to those many local prosecutors and crime investigators who assisted with the case studies and other research on DNA forensics.

And lastly, a very special thank you is owed as well to the officials at the *National Institute of Justice* who recognized at an early stage the importance of forensic DNA to the protection of public safety. This study is a reflection of their commitment to seeking to quantify the problems related to DNA analysis backlogs and to provide law enforcement and crime laboratories with workable solutions to those problems.

AUTHORS' NOTE

In order to ensure accurate and honest responses, law enforcement agencies and crime laboratories were assured anonymity in the final published document. For this reason, some data are intentionally broad or not attributed to a specific source. In those instances where a law enforcement agency or crime laboratory is named, permission was obtained to both identify the agency and utilize specific data.

REFERENCES

[1] Where a state forensic DNA laboratory does not exist, the local crime laboratory appointed as the FBI CODIS point of contact is treated as the state laboratory in this study. This is the case for Nevada (Washoe County Sheriff's Office laboratory), and Hawaii (Honolulu Police Department Crime Laboratory). The local laboratory in Albuquerque, New Mexico serves as the CODIS point of contact instead of the DNA state laboratory. As such, Albuquerque assisted in completing two assessment forms – one on behalf of the local laboratory, and the other calculating state laboratory figures.

[2] Since we are dealing with extrapolating to the total population of law enforcement agencies (18,000) with our sample (over 1,500), researchers have taken the most methodologically rigorous (and therefore conservative) approach possible so that they could avoid any potential charge that these estimates are inflated. Accordingly, there is a possibility that the true numbers of unsolved homicides and rapes are actually higher than what is reported here.

[3] The assessment form specified that law enforcement agencies should only count those cases that "were still in your control (i.e., had not been sent to a laboratory for testing)." Similarly, crime laboratories were asked for the number of cases "backlogged at your laboratory." For this reason, double counting of cases by law enforcement agencies and crime laboratories was not an issue.

[4] "Critical" was defined as "available storage is quickly disappearing."

[5] "Highly Critical" was defined as "no additional storage space available."

[6] A "median" figure of 0.0 results from a severely skewed distribution featuring many zero values.

[7] "Other," as defined by state laboratories, included expert software for CODIS review, IT support/informatics, in house offender analysis, software for case management, equipment and reagents used to address suspect/no suspect backlogs, and personnel (3).

[8] "Other," as defined by local laboratories included personnel (2) and validation projects.

[9] The non-violent offenses include property offenses (theft, forgery, breaking and entering, burglary), drug offenses, and supervision violations. The violent offenses include murder/homicide, rape and sex offenses, assaults, and robbery.

[10] Gilmer, James A., van Alstyne, David J., *The First 100 Hits — Forensic-Offender Matches on the New York State DNA Data Bank,* Research Note, New York State Division of Criminal Justice Services, Bureau of Research and Evaluation: 1.

[11] Ibid., 1.

[12] Langan, Patrick A., Levin, David D., *Recidivism of Prisoners Released in 1994*, Special Report, Washington, DC: U.S. Department of Justice, Bureau of Justice Statistics, January 2002, NCJ 191191: 1.

[13] Ibid., Gilmer, *The First 100 Hits*, 1.

In: Forensics in Law Enforcement
Editor: M. V. Shoester, pp. 65-122
ISBN 1-60021-164-X

Chapter 2

INCREASING THE PREDICTABILITY AND SUCCESS RATE OF SKELETAL EVIDENCE TYPING: USING PHYSICAL CHARACTERISTICS OF BONE AS A METRIC FOR DNA QUALITY AND QUANTITY*

David Foran

ABSTRACT

Owing to their longevity, skeletal remains can supply important forensic information long after death occurs. Further, when simpler tests are not available, bone DNA can be invaluable in skeletal identification. Unfortunately, while bones are the longest lasting tissues postmortem, they degrade over time, as does the DNA within. This relationship between bone weathering and DNA degradation is poorly understood, and an analyst can only make an educated guess as to which bones might harbor useful DNA, and how degraded that DNA might be. If the appearance of bone could be related to the quantity and quality of the DNA within before testing commences, substantial time and effort would be saved, and laboratory productivity would increase.

Previous studies on DNA from aged bone have used samples of va rying age and type, obtained from different environments. To avoid these confounders, a large set of discovered skeletons from a mid-1800's cemetery near Pittsburgh were tested. Long bone, flat bone, rib and tooth were collected from remains at varying stages of degradation. Quantitative PCR was used to measure the amount of mitochondrial DNA remaining, while DNA quality was assayed by amplifying progressively larger segments of DNA. Results indicate that there is little relationship between skeletal/bone weathering and DNA quantity or quality. In contrast, bone type played a significant role in obtaining DNA results. Long bones contained more DNA and were more likely to produce usable results than ribs, which were more likely to produce usable results than flat bones. The amount of DNA recovered did not play a significant role in the ability to amplify DNA, though there was a trend in that direction. Neither sex nor age of the individual were related to DNA typing success.

---

* Excerpted from http://www.ncjrs.gov/pdffiles1/nij/grants/212869.pdf.

Several ancillary projects were undertaken related to this research. Soil samples assayed indicate pH influences bone preservation, while several other factors do not. PCR inhibition was found to greatly affect quantitative PCR results, remedied to some extent by the addition of BSA. Amplification using primers moved in towards the target sequence (Mini-STRs) made little difference on the ability to amplify nuclear DNA, while the use of nested PCR did. Whole genome amplification, while promising for high molecular weight DNA, was of little use on aged skeletal material.
Overall, the research indicates that while the outward appearance of bone is generally not related to successful DNA typing, the bone type chosen for analysis needs to be considered.

Executive Summary

Background

Skeletal material, including bones and teeth, are the biological samples most likely to require analysis by the forensic scientist well after an individual's death. Although bone persists in general, it does degrade over time, in part due to the dissolution of the minerals, most importantly hydroxyapatite. Likewise, the organic molecules in bone, including DNA, break down over time. This breakdown can result from direct strand breakage, chemical modification, or enzymatic actions of microorganisms. It is not known however, how the breakdown of bone and DNA correlate.

For the forensic scientist a knowledge of the relationship between bone and DNA degradation would be advantageous. If an analyst could look at a skeleton or bone and, based on its appearance or level of weathering, make a reasonable prediction regarding the likelihood of successfully obtaining DNA, valuable time and resources could be saved. When a certain level of bone degradation was reached the analyst would know not to expend the effort on DNA analysis. Likewise, if the level of bone weathering related to DNA degradation levels, the analyst could more accurately predict what size fragment of DNA could successfully be analyzed. On the other hand, if no such relationship exists, this too is important, as the analyst will know that just because skeletal material appears to be poorly preserved, it does not preclude successful DNA analysis.

While there have been numerous studies on DNA and bone, most have worked with mixed skeletal samples. Some varied greatly in age, some in the environment where they existed prior to analysis, some in bone type analyzed, and some in all of these variables. Comparing results from a 20 year old bone with one 150 years old makes little sense. Similarly, trying to draw conclusions on DNA degradation from a bone found in a woods to one found in a swamp or one found in a desert is nearly impossible. Likewise, it is not known to what extent DNA results from one bone type, for instance a long bone like a femur, can be extrapolated to a flat bone such as the pelvis.

The goal of this study was to use a more uniform set of skeletal remains to analyze the relationship between bone weathering and DNA degradation. For this, a set of burials from a cemetery used over a relatively short period of time was tested (details below). Weathering was graded at both the overall skeletal level as well as for individual bones. Similar bone types (generally femur, rib, pelvis, and tooth) were collected from skeletons over a range of weathering states. DNA quantity was assessed using quantitative (real time) polymerase chain reaction (PCR), while DNA quality was estimated by attempting to amplify progressively larger pieces of DNA. The focus of the research was on mitochondrial DNA (mtDNA) as its analysis is more likely to be successful in aged skeletal remains than is nuclear DNA, although nuclear loci were examined as well. Soil was analyzed to help determine what role it plays in degradation. Age and sex of individuals was considered. Finally, a series of experiments designed to better isolate and analyze DNA from samples with limited DNA quantity or quality was performed.

Skeletal Samples

The primary skeletal material used in this study originated from the Voegtly Cemetery, associated with the First Evangelical Church of Allegheny (The Voegtly Church), near Pittsburgh. The cemetery was used between 1833 and 1861, thus all the remains are about 150 years old. The plot was small, and church members were buried in a uniform fashion, therefore environmental conditions should be similar for all burials except perhaps at the extremely localized level. When the church and long-forgotten graveyard were declared to be in a highway right-of-way, the church was largely disbanded. When highway construction commenced the cemetery was discovered. Because there were no records on these individuals, all skeletons were donated to the Smithsonian Institution. There, anthropologist Doug Ubelaker and co-workers estimated age and sex of each individual, and gave each skeleton an overall weathering score, based on a 0 – 5 scale, with 0 being bone showing no weathering. Sections of long bone (primarily femur), flat bone (generally pelvis), rib, and a tooth were collected from up to 20 individuals at each weathering stage (when available) for DNA analysis.

A second, separately funded study in our laboratory, involves analysis of skeletal material from a large burial mound near Kamenica, Albania. This material ranges from 2500 – 3000 years old. Sections of long bone, teeth, and the hardest bone in the human body—the petrous portion of the temporal bone—were collected.

Methods

Bones were cleaned and either drilled or ground to obtain bone powder. Bone powder was weighed and DNA isolated using a standard organic extraction method. MtDNA primers and an internal oligonucleotide probe were generated for the quantitative TaqMan assay. MtDNA was quantified on an ABI 7700. The effect of PCR inhibition on quantitation was tested by adding known amounts of target DNA to DNA samples that had shown inhibition in previous experiments, and observing how the known DNA quantity was altered. The same experiment was conducted with the addition of substances thought to reduce PCR inhibition, a commercial PCR enhancer, as well as bovine serum albumin (BSA). MtDNA quality was assayed by attempting to amplify a 220 base pair (bp) fragment of mtDNA. If this was successful, progressively longer amplifications were attempted. If it failed, a 107 bp amplification was attempted. If this failed the sample was considered negative.

Both quantity and quality data were compared to skeletal weathering stage and bone type using single factor Analysis of Variance (ANOVA). During the study it was found that individual bones often differed in their level of weathering in comparison to the skeletal grade, thus each bone was restaged on a 4 point scale, allowing a second comparison of DNA quantity and quality to individual bone weathering using ANOVA. Quality and quantity results were compared to one another using a t-test.

Although direct comparison was difficult given the very different nature of the Albania bone samples, these samples were prepared and mtDNA amplified similarly to the Voegtly bones. Comparisons of amplification success of the different bone types were made.

A number of techniques were tested for enhancing PCR results from low copy or degraded DNA. Mini-STR sets, in which the PCR primers are moved closer to the DNA region of interest thus producing a shorter amplicon (more likely to be successfully recovered from degraded DNA) were obtained for 6 nuclear loci from scientists at the National Institute of Standards and Technology (NIST). Mini-STR primers for the sexing locus amelogenin were produced in-house. Both sets of primers were tested on a subset of the Voegtly bones that amplified using mtDNA primers. Nested PCR, in which two rounds of amplification are conducted, uses an external set of primers for the first round of amplification, followed by a second round using primers internal to (nested within) the first set. This allows for an increased number of PCR cycles (advantageous when very little DNA is present) without causing non-target DNA to amplify—which often happens when DNA is over-amplified using a single set of primers. Nested PCR was conducted on mtDNA when necessary, on the amelogenin locus, and on a set of STR loci using a commercially available PCR kit (Identifiler™) followed by the NIST Mini-STR set.

Whole genome amplification (WGA) are methods for amplifying all the DNA in a sample prior to DNA testing. Two methods of WGA, Improved Primer Extension Preamplification (I-PEP) and Multiple Displacement Amplification (MDA), were tested on a subset of the Voegtly bones that amplified using mtDNA primers. Following WGA, mtDNA amplification was attempted.

Soil samples from a number of Voegtly remains were tested for levels of a variety of organic and inorganic compounds, to determine if any had an effect of bone decomposition. The pH of the soil was also analyzed.

Findings

MtDNA quantities showed a statistically significant difference when skeletal weathering was taken into account, although this outcome was not as expected. When all individuals were considered, the most weathered skeletons tended to produce the highest levels of mtDNA ($p=0.036$) (but see individual bones below). It is surmised that this might result from the relative ease of retrieving DNA from the more friable material, although it is also possible that factors or conditions that help preserve skeletons (those with the least weathering) are disadvantageous for DNA. In this regard, the only soil factor that showed a correlation with overall skeletal weathering was pH; more degraded skeletons tended to have lower soil pH ($R2=0.21$). It seems possible that while the lower pH tended to lead to skeletal breakdown, it was likely not low enough to damage DNA. On the other hand, the more neutral pH found with the less-weathered bones may have created conditions detrimental to DNA, perhaps by encouraging microbial activity.

DNA quality was not significantly correlated with skeletal weathering, although the most degraded stage generated the highest percentage of positive results. When the quantitative and qualitative results were broken down by bone type for each skeletal weathering stage (e.g., stage 5 femora) there was no significant differences in stages, however this practice reduced sample sizes considerably. When quantitative and qualitative results were compared against each other, there was no statistical relationship between the number of DNA copies in a sample and the maximum amplicon size produced.

The restaging of each individual bone (as opposed to overall skeletal staging, above) did not result in a significant effect of bone weathering on DNA quantity or quality, contrary to the quantitative skeletal results. On the other hand, when bone type was taken into consideration it was readily apparent that certain bones produced more amplifiable DNA than others. While this was not significant in DNA quantity, bone type and the likelihood of successful PCR amplification was very significant ($p=0.006$). Femora had the highest amplification success (79%) as well as the most DNA. Ribs were next in PCR success (64%) while pelves were lowest (36%). Ribs and pelves produced similar amounts of DNA. Similar percentages were obtained for the Albanian samples, with both femora and petrous portions amplifying greater than 80% of the time.

No effect of age was observed on DNA quantity or quality, while sex did appear to have an influence, although the actual sex of many of the remains was tentative based on anthropological sex estimation of poorly persevered specimens.

PCR inhibition was measured by adding target DNA to samples that had previously shown inhibition. Target copies ranged from 600 – 6,000,000 in 10-fold dilutions. The same experiments were conducted with the addition of a commercial PCR enhancer or BSA. The untreated samples showed substantial inhibition, with estimated quantities of the target DNA reduced by 79 – 96%. Samples with the enhancer added also had high levels inhibition (41 – 99%) and were not significantly different from those without. In contrast, samples with BSA added had significantly lower levels of inhibition at all levels except at 6,000 and 60 target copies.

The enhanced techniques for use on low copy or degraded samples met with mixed success. The NIST Mini-STRs for nuclear loci did not amplify any of the Voegtly samples, nor did the amelogenin primer set produced in-house. On the other hand, nested PCR using the amelogenin primers allowed the nuclear DNA to be amplified in 12 of 65 Voegtly samples and 4 of 17 Albanian samples. Similarly, DNA from Voegtly teeth could not be reliably amplified until nested PCR was initiated.

WGA, while successful on high quality DNA, was not useful on the more degraded DNA of the Voegtly samples. Because WGA reduces DNA size it is assumed that the vast majority of DNA produced is too small to be amplified.

Conclusions

From the experiments and results presented here it seems clear that skeletal weathering/appearance cannot be used as a reliable metric of mtDNA quantity or quality, and indeed the only statistically significant result obtained was that more weathered burials resulted in higher DNA yields (other factors being equal). Likewise, the weathering stage of an individual bone is not a useful measurement of DNA quantity or quality. On the other hand, bone type plays a substantial role in DNA results, particularly the ability to successfully produce an amplicon. This should be taken into account when selecting skeletal material for processing. Likewise nested PCR can be a powerful tool when amplifying very small amounts of DNA. Owing to its extreme sensitivity precautions need to be made, particularly running reagent blanks and negative controls to test for contamination, however with these in place DNA results can be obtained from material that would otherwise generate a negative result.

INTRODUCTION AND HISTORY

An important goal of any forensic investigation involving unidentified human remains is positive identification. Forensic specialists including anthropologists and odontologists may evaluate the remains, estimating the individual's sex, stature, age at death, and ancestry. Any identifiable characteristics such as fingerprints, if flesh is still intact, unique skeletal features, and dental arrangement are also noted. However, when antemortem reference records are not available for comparison or remains are fragmented or otherwise in a state in which definitive conclusions cannot be made as to the person's identity, DNA analysis may be required. Indeed, identification through analysis of DNA from human skeletal remains has been used in numerous cases, beginning in 1989 (Pääbo *et al.*, 1989). Advancements in techniques and applications occurred in the 1990's (Boles *et al.*, 1995; Hagelberg *et al.*, 1991; Primorac *et al.*, 1996; reviewed in O'Rourke *et al.*, 2000), and in 1991 the Armed Forces DNA Identification Laboratory was established for the identification of the remains of U.S. military personnel (Holland and Parsons, 1999). A decade later a high-throughput method was developed for the analysis of the thousands of bones connected with the attacks on the World Trade Center (Holland *et al.*, 2003).

Bones encountered by the forensic biologist often vary in their degree of degradation, and if more than one bone is available, the scientist may sensibly choose which bone to analyze based on its appearance; a bone in good condition would logically contain 'better' DNA than a more weathered sample. However, the lack of any proven association between the degradation level of a bone sample and the quality or quantity of its DNA means that it is currently difficult or impossible to reliably predict DNA typing success for aged bones. Further, because of the high levels of variability among aged skeletal samples that have been studied to date (including bone type, age, the environment where it was found, etc.), DNA preparation and typing techniques that have been shown to work well on one sample may not be useful for another. If criteria were available for relating the appearance of aged bone to the DNA within, the efficiency, affordability, and reliability of analysis could be greatly enhanced. Given the type of skeletal material (long bone, flat bone, tooth, etc.) and its level of weathering, valuable predictions could be made about the probable amount of obtainable DNA and its level of degradation, thus leading the scientist to the best genetic loci and polymerase chain reaction (PCR) primers for analysis.

Genetic Analysis of Aged Skeletal Material

Although bone (and relatedly, dental remains) can persist for exceedingly long periods of time, this does not mean that bone, at either the gross or molecular levels, does not change with time (the so-called taphonomic process). Like any tissue, bone breaks down postmortem, and given enough weathering becomes so fragmented that it may be unidentifiable. Likewise, the organic molecules within a bone sample used for individual identification, including DNA, mutate and degrade as time passes. It is not known however, how these two species of degradation inter-relate. Bone, for instance, is often damaged mechanically, hastening its breakdown, but this may or may not have a large influence at the molecular level.

In describing bone diagenesis, Hedges (2002) summarized the histological and biochemical changes that occur as a bone degrades. The primary medium in which skeletal remains are located is soil. Analyzing the effects of soil conditions, soils of neutral pH often have calcium and phosphate concentrations similar to those found in hydroxyapatite (Ca10(PO4)6(OH)2; the major bone mineral), which likely leads to a slower bone dissolution rate. In contrast, soils of low pH generally have lower calcium and phosphate concentrations and dissolution occurs faster, as the protons from the soils replaced the calcium ions in the hydroxyapatite of the bone. DNA is also negatively impacted by acidic conditions, although other variables, such as warm temperature and high moisture, accelerate DNA degradation as well, and may be as or more important than soil pH (Parsons and Weedn, 1996; Smith *et al.*, 2003). DNA from bone can also be broken down enzymatically or chemically with nicks, chemical cross-bridges, or extraneous molecular attachments occurring (e.g., Rogan and Salvo, 1990; Tuross, 1994; reviewed in O'Rourke *et al.*, 2000). Microorganisms also affect the stability of bone DNA, producing nucleases that directly attack it (Rogan and Salvo, 1990). Finally, as long as soft tissue persists, additional enzymatic attack can occur from autolytic enzymes.

Multiple authors (e.g., Gilbert *et al.*, 2003; Gotherstrom *et al.*, 2002; Kalmar *et al.*, 2000; Pääbo *et al.*, 1989), have noted that mitochondrial DNA (mtDNA) analysis is the primary mode of DNA typing of aged skeletal remains. Mitochondria are cytoplasmic organelles containing a small, maternally-inherited, circular piece of DNA distinct from the linear chromosomes of the nucleus. Thousands of mitochondria can exist in a single cell, and as such there are thousands of copies of mtDNA as well. This is far different then the two copies (maternal and paternal) of a DNA locus that are examined in most forensic analyses. Human mtDNA was first sequenced in its entirety in 1981 (Anderson *et al.*, 1981) and is approximately 16569 bp in length. The majority of genes in mtDNA encode proteins essential to mitochondrial function, thus these areas are highly conserved among individuals, and are generally not useful for identification. However, an approximately 1125 bp stretch of non-coding DNA known as the control region contains two segments that mutate frequently and therefore vary among unrelated individuals. The sequence variation of these two areas, known as hypervariable region I and II (HVI and HVII), are generally the focus of forensic analysis (reviewed by Holland and Parsons, 1999). Typically, this involves amplification of both hypervariable regions using PCR followed by a sequencing procedure to determine the exact DNA sequence, which is then compared to the Anderson reference sequence. The nucleotide differences between the sample and the reference sequence constitute the mtDNA profile for that sample, which can then be compared back to a known sample or a maternal relative for identification.

Project Goal

The objective of this project was to determine if the visual appearance of skeletal remains can be used as a reliable metric of the DNA (particularly mtDNA) found within, or: is there a relationship between the level of bone weathering and the quantity and/or quality of DNA that may be used for analysis? While many scientists have obtained DNA from bone, no study to date has systematically looked at bone appearance and related it to successful DNA typing. The utility of this to the forensic scientists is plain: can we examine a skeletal specimen and make a reliable estimate about how much DNA it might contain, and how large a fragment of DNA exists for analysis?

To accomplish this goal it was necessary to eliminate confounding factors that exist in most research on DNA and skeletal remains. Foremost among these is nonuniform samples. In a systematic study it is not useful to begin with samples of different ages, that come from different peoples, have been 'stored' under different environmental conditions, and otherwise do not resemble one-another, and then try to directly compare results from sample 1 to sample 2. Therefore, a set of skeletal remains was sought that eliminated most confounders, and instead differed only by their appearance (or weathering level) to the greatest extent possible. From these we could start to address the relationship between bone appearance and DNA quality and quantity in an objective and systematic way. These results could then begin to be compared to other skeletal samples to see how generalized the findings were. Bone type (long bone, flat bone, teeth, etc.) was considered, as it is possible that different bones generate different results. Other factors that might affect bone diagenesis, most notably soil conditions, were tested as well. Finally, methods for enhancing the acquisition of DNA data from aged skeletal remains were examined.

The Samples: The Smithsonian Institution and the Voegtly Cemetery

The two key features of this study were having 'uniform' samples for the controlled, correlative portions of the work, and having large sample sizes for statistical analysis. Skeletal material for this study came through collaboration with Dr. Doug Ubelaker of The Smithsonian Institution. These samples originated from a single burial site that was utilized for a short period of time about 150 years ago, known as the Voegtly Cemetery.

The Voegtly Cemetery was associated with The First Evangelical Church of Allegheny (The Voegtly Church), located in 'Old Allegheny Town', across the Allegheny River from Pittsburgh; its history is documented in Ubelaker and Jones (2003). The founders were Swiss-German immigrants (the Voegtly family immigrated to the area in 1822) who started Voegtly Church in 1833. The cemetery, adjacent to the church, was utilized from that point until 1861, when a new cemetery site was purchased. The Church was expanded and modified over the next century, and the historic cemetery, without permanent markers or other identifying materials, was built over.

In 1959 it was announced that the Church was located in the right-of-way for a new highway, and thereafter membership declined. In 1972 the last Voegtly associated with the church died, the parsonage was destroyed, and in 1984 the Pennsylvania Department of Transportation acquired the entire property. The Church was officially disbanded in 1985; its original cemetery was discovered two years later when highway construction unearthed the first human bones. Church records from the time, written in a rare German dialect, had deteriorated and were of little use in immediately determining which or how many persons were buried at the site. Official city records of burials were not initiated until 1882, and remaining parishioners had no knowledge of the cemetery's existence as it had been largely assumed that all bodies had been moved to different sites in the 1860s.

The Layout and Excavation of the Cemetery

The ¾ acre Voegtly Cemetery was excavated over a relatively short period (June – September of 1987). As no gravestones or other markers were present the site was treated as an archeological dig (Figure 1, photo and burial map). Excavations consisted of mechanical removal of topsoil followed by shoveling and hand-excavation to expose, map, and record each grave. Coffins were all similar—wooden, six sided, and wedge shaped—with the major differences being in the degree of ornamentation. Following primary bone and artifact collection, soil was sifted through 0.25-inch hardware cloth to collect remaining artifacts and small bone fragments. All skeletal material was wrapped in aluminum foil, placed in plastic bags, and labeled.

Since 1987 the German church records have been interpreted and analyzed; these indicate approximately 823 individuals were buried, however remains from only 724 were located. Over the years church pastors kept different records; in some cases very little information about the deceased was given. This was most true of children, some labeled as "not seen", indicating miscarriage or stillbirth. For the 799 persons to which church records assigned age, 39% were less than 1 year old, 24% were between 1 and 5 years, and 8 % were between 5 and 20. The mean age at death was 14.6 years, a datum influenced by the high level of infant mortality. For known sexes (47% female) 99 females and 131 males were age 20 or over, while 266 females and 278 males were younger.

Figure 1. The excavation and layout of graves at the Voegtly Cemetery site

Causes of death were varied and often unrecorded, but beyond stillbirths (the most common), illnesses such as cholera, typhoid, scarlet fever and consumption (tuberculosis) were seen, and often ran through families. Other illnesses are more poorly described, with only brief notations such as "Long Illness" or "Feverish Illness". The highest percentages of deaths occurred in July and August (13.4 % and 11.9 % respectively) generally affecting children. Seventy percent of individuals were buried 1 day after death, 23% after 2 days, and 5% on the same day.

The Skeletal Remains

All skeletal remains were transported to The Smithsonian Institution in Washington DC for physical analysis. While preliminary cataloging began several years ago, an intensive effort to finalize the visual analyses began in 2000 and is now complete. Bones were unpacked, cleaned, soil samples collected, and a variety of data recorded. The nature of the cleaning depended on the state of the bone (detailed below), with those in excellent condition washed under water while more fragile specimens were gently dry-brushed to remove dirt. Data were collected according to the Standards for Data Collection from Human Skeleton Remains (Buikstra and Ubelaker, 1994). Sex, age and stature were estimated when possible using all available material. Sex of children was not determined, and higher emphasis was placed on the pelvis, when available, for adults. Ages were placed into general ranges, these being typically more refined in children due primarily to dental development. Stature was estimated using the femur. Results relevant to this proposal are given below, while complete data can be found in Ubelaker and Jones (2003).

The overall condition (degree of weathering) of each skeleton was carefully assessed and logged. The classification scheme was taken from Behrensmeyer (1978) and is detailed in Buikstra and Ubelaker (1994). Briefly, a 0 to 5 scale is generated:

Stage 0—A bone sample whose surface shows no sign of cracking or flaking due to weathering;
Stage 1—Bone shows some cracking, usually longitudinally in long bones;
Stage 2—Cracks and some flaking of bone;
Stage 3—Bone surface has rough patches of weathered compact bone down to 1.5 mm, with extensive flaking although bone fibers are still attached to each other;
Stage 4—Bone surface is course, splinters may exist and fall out, and weathering reaches the interior portions (Figure 2);
Stage 5—Bone is easily broken and is disintegrating. Original shape may be hard to determine.

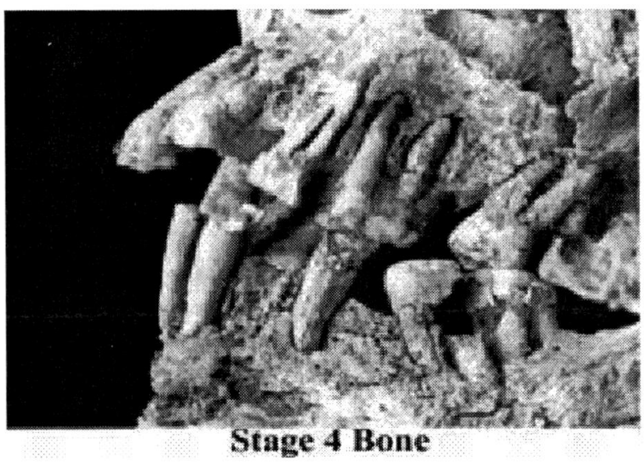

Figure 2. Example of skeletal weathering stage 4

Individual records for each of the burials are available in Ubelaker and Jones (2003) . These records encompass several hundred pages and hence cannot be reproduced here, but in brief they include as much information as available on: Each bone detected; Skeletal weathering score; Teeth present; The deceased's age range and sex if possible; Cultural information (coffin and other artifacts found); Other observations (e.g. discoloration of bone, dental decay, evidence of disease, etc.).

The vast majority of bones in the Voegtly sample are in weathering stages 2 – 5, with a smaller number classified as stage 1. It is not surprising for samples that have been buried for 150 years that virtually no bones were found at stage 0 (showing no weathering). This is not of particular concern for this study as bones at this stage are basically 'fresh' and as suc h are not usually challenging for identification or genetic studies. In general, confirmed male samples were in slightly better condition than females in the same age class, and younger adults were in better condition than the very old, presumably resulting from osteoporosis. Also, when compared to the church records, a large number of infant burials were not located. Because of the high number of stillbirths and similar deaths described in the records, it seems likely this deficit results from a lack of calcified bone in the very young.

Figure 3. Example of (double) burials at the Tumulus at Kamenica, Albania

While the burials at Kamenica appear to be in excellent condition (Figure 3), upon their recovery it was discovered that they were extremely friable, therefore only small fragments were recoverable. Because of this, the hardest bones available, the femur, teeth, and the petrous portion of the temporal bone, were collected for DNA sampling.

Comparison to other Skeletal Samples: The Albania Project

In addition to the skeletal remains from the Voegtly Cemetery, extensive research has now been conducted on a set of skeletal remains from a tumulus (burial mound) in Kamenica, Albania, in collaboration with Dr. Todd Fenton. The site at Kamenica is a Late Bronze Age,

Early Iron Age tumulus located in eastern Albania just outside the village of Kamenica in the southeastern corner of the fertile Korca basin. The Tumulus at Kamenica was utilized as a cemetery over many centuries, ranging from approximately the 12th to 6th century BC, introducing the variable of age to these analyses. The site was first identified in the early 1990s. Excavations began at the tumulus in 2000 as a rescue effort to preserve the burials after the site was badly damaged by looters from 1997 to 1999. There were three seasons of excavation from 2000 – 2002, which unearthed approximately 400 human skeletons.

Experimental Studies

Determining MtDNA Quality

The degree to which DNA is degraded in a sample dictates the size of DNA fragments that can be amplified, and thus the level of genetic information that can be retrieved. If a sample is too far degraded the remaining small fragments of DNA are of no use for identification. In contrast, a sample retaining high molecular weight DNA, regardless of age, can yield a wealth of data.

DNA fragment length isolated from ancient DNA is typically small (O'Rourke *et al.*, 2000). To more exactly pinpoint useful size ranges for analysis, PCR can be used to determine the largest size class of DNA existing in each sample by targeting a series of amplification products. Progressively larger segments of DNA can be amplified until a negative result is obtained, this cutoff size can indicate how degraded a sample is. Amplicon sizes can then be compared within a weathering stage to see what generalities can be observed, within a stage and among stages, to discern any statistically meaningful differences in degradation levels.

It is important of course to distinguish between samples that do not amplify because there is no target DNA of a given size, and samples that do not amplify owing to the presence of PCR inhibitors. One way to test this is to add a small amount of high quality DNA to the PCR reaction containing a non-amplifying sample (or 'spike' it). If a positive PCR result is obtained, it indicates that the sample is clean enough for PCR to occur, and that there is not adequate product in the sample. On the other hand, if the control DNA does not amplify it indicates that inhibitors are present and that the sample requires additional purification.

Determining mtDNA Quantity

DNA quantity can also be assessed from bone samples and compared among weathering stages and bone type. In aged skeletal remains it is likely that not enough DNA exists for more traditional forensic methods of quantitation (such as Quantiblot), therefore a DNA amplification method is requisite. Quantitative PCR (QPCR, also called real time PCR) works by detecting increases in amplified DNA product (the amplicon) during the amplification process. In standard PCR, the amount of DNA produced bears little relationship to the starting amount of DNA, as a plateau exists when one or more reagents become limiting and amplification ceases. QPCR takes advantage of the fact that at lower concentrations of DNA, the rate of amplification proceeds in an exponential manner. During the exponential growth phase of amplification, samples pass a preset threshold of amplification rate. This value is taken as a sample's critical threshold (Ct) value, which is directly related to its starting DNA concentration. In order to assess the relationship between Ct and starting concentration, DNA standards—samples of known concentration—are amplified at the same time as unknown samples. A standard curve is then derived from a dilution series of these standards by plotting the concentration of the standards versus their Ct values.

Detection of the amount of amplicon in a reaction can be done in one of two ways. Double stranded DNA in the reaction can be detected with a dye, such as Syber Green, which intercalates between the strands of DNA, causing the dye to fluoresce when excited by a laser. This fluorescence will increase in a linear relationship to the concentration of double stranded DNA in a sample. The second method of detection is a probe that can hybridize to a specific sequence in the amplicon. Depending on the nature of the probe, it may fluoresce only when hybridized to the amplicon or after degradation of the probe. In the research detailed below a TaqMan probe was used for detection, which is a short length of DNA, typically between 18–27 bp, with a fluorescent molecule at the 5' end (a "reporter") and a "quencher" molecule at the 3' end. The reporter is excited throughout the amplification process. However, when the probe is intact, the reporter is in close proximity to the quencher, which absorbs any emissions from the reporter. When the amplicon is present, the probe hybridizes to it and is digested by the 5' exonuclease activity of the polymerase, freeing both the reporter and quencher. This allows the fluorescence of the reporter to be detected by the QPCR instrument. Since the target level of fluorescence increases in a linear relationship to the concentration of the target amplicon, the starting concentration of DNA can be calculated using a standard curve.

Enhanced Techniques

When dealing with degraded skeletal samples, DNA cannot always be amplified using standard PCR. Bone diagenesis may leave little DNA to be extracted, and any DNA can be highly fragmented. One solution is to increase the chance of amplifying degraded DNA targets by moving primer sites closer to the DNA region of interest. This method can be useful on both nuclear and mtDNA. A second tactic is to increase DNA yields by increasing the number of PCR cycles attempted. A problem with this approach is that excessive PCR cycles often result in amplification of undesired, non-target DNA, that can jeopardize subsequent analyses. In addition, methods exist for pre-amplifying all the DNA that exists in a sample. One final solution may be to modify DNA isolation procedures to increase DNA yields; for instance, most bone DNA preparation protocols leave visible bone behind, which may harbor useful DNA. These methods have the potential to generate large amounts of DNA and allow for multiple rounds of testing.

Mini-STRs Sets for DNA Analysis

Moving primers closer to the DNA region of interest can be advantageous when analyzing degraded DNA. For instance, most commercial STR kits amplify DNA segments from 100 to 450 bp. However, if a DNA sample is degraded, its length can be reduced to a size range smaller than this (Zelman and Moran, 1996), resulting in allelic or locus dropout and an incomplete genetic profile (Whitaker *et al.,* 1995). By moving primers as close as possible to the ends of the repeat region, successful amplification of smaller fragments of DNA may occur (Chung *et al.,* 2004). Butler *et al.* (2003) developed primers for amplifying CODIS STRs and additional markers. Likewise, multiple primers exist for the mtDNA control region, which can be used in various combinations to better amplify degraded material.

Nested PCR

It has been shown that DNA existing at very low copy number can be successfully amplified using nested PCR (Strom and Rechitsky, 1998), a technique in which two successive rounds of PCR are used to amplify small amounts of DNA. In the first round, DNA is amplified under standard conditions. In the second round, the reaction is supplemented with product from the first round reaction, providing it with an enriched template. This subsequent round utilizes primers that sit internal to the first round primers, meaning that only fragments amplified in the first round that contain the second round primer sites are amplified. This allows for a greater number of PCR cycles while eliminating non-specific amplification products, and serves as a powerful technique for amplifying very small copy number samples with relatively high fidelity. A related technique is semi-nested PCR, in which the second round of PCR uses one of the primers from the first round and a second primer internal to the first set.

Whole Genome Amplification

Another potential method for dealing with limited starting DNA is to increase the overall amount of DNA prior to beginning standard laboratory procedures. Whole genome amplification (WGA) is a procedure used to duplicate DNA, but unlike PCR, which generally amplifies small sections of the genome, WGA is capable of replicating the genome in its entirety. WGA methods utilize random primers (oligonucleotides) to amplify large portions of the genome. Two WGA methods, I-PEP (Improved Primer Extension Preamplification) and MDA (Multiple Displacement Amplification) are widely used in clinical research for this purpose.

I - PEP is completed under conditions similar to that of typical PCR, except that random 15-mer oligonucleotides are utilized. I-PEP WGA reactions are, in theory, capable of replicating the genome in an unbiased manner as the random 15-mer oligonucleotides can locate a complimentary sequence anywhere in the sample DNA. IPEP WGA has been shown to result in a 30 fold increase in product yield (Dietmaier *et al.*, 1999).

MDA was first described by Dean *et al.* (2002) and utilizes the DNA polymerase Phi 29. This polymerase is very processive and also displaces double stranded DNA in front of it. This results in longer product length and more access to the template and non-template strands so random primers can anneal. In MDA, random hexamer primers are used to amplify the genome. Hosono *et al.* (2004) determined that up to a 10,000 fold increase in DNA yield can be achieved with MDA.

Methods Collection of Samples

A subset of 89 bones from the total set obtained from The Smithsonian Institution was ana lyzed in this study. Upon recovery of the skeletal remains, the bones were described in terms of sex, estimated age, and one of the six skeletal weathering stages (Stages 0 – 5). As detailed above and by Ubelaker and Jones (2003), the weathering stages originally assigned to the samples by the anthropologists at The Smithsonian considered the condition of the skeleton as a whole. In order to allow ratings on individual bones, a new staging system was developed at MSU and assigned to each bone based on visua l inspection for the DNA study. This individual bone staging system was separated into four categories:

Stage 1: Bone surface shows minimal flaking. The bone piece is still whole, with no large pieces broken off.
Stage 2: Bone surface shows some flaking, pieces of bone are coming off in sheets. Small pieces of bone are breaking away from the cut piece.
Stage 3: The bone is fragmented into several pieces. At least one large piece is still present.
Stage 4: The bone is extensively fragmented. No large pieces are present.

Various bone types were collected for this study. When possible, femur sections represented long bone while pelves represented flat bones, and ribs an intermediate. If femora were not available, another long bone was sampled. If pelves were not found among the skeletal remains, crania were chosen. In addition, teeth were also collected from the burials. A total of 2 crania, 28 femora, 1 fibula, 25 pelves, and 33 ribs were tested, coming from a total of 36 individuals. In addition, 31 teeth were examined.

The bones samples presented here spanned five of the six weathering stages assigned by Ubelaker and Jones (2003): 6 from stage 1, 23 from stage 2, 22 from stage 3, 18 from stage 4, and 20 from stage 5. The three samples from the single individual classified as stage 0 were not tested due to the insufficient sample size and nonexistence of comparison samples. Of these, 11 were female, 17 were male, 1 was labeled as "possibly male", and 7 were undetermined. This possible male had large mastoid processes and supraorbital ridges, but female sex could not be ruled out.

For the Albania bone samples, specific burials were chosen for testing based on the information mtDNA analysis could contribute to the Kamenica project. Long bones, such as femur, and teeth were collected whenever possible. In addition, the petrous portion of the temporal bone was taken if available, as it is one of the hardest bones in the body. Integrity of the bone samples was rated using a 0 through 5 system (below) based on their completeness. Teeth were rated in a similar fashion, but with some descriptive adjustment made within the scale to represent their unique endurance. Unfortunately, because the skeletons had already been removed to a new location, and because the bones were largely broken, the anthropologists on site were forced to use rating criteria modified from those used on the Voegtly material. Rating systems were as follows: Bones (excluding teeth)

0 – bone is complete; surface of bone has a sheen
1 – proximal/distal ends beginning to break; sheen may be present
2 – 3/4 to 2/3 bone present
3 – 1/2 to 1/4 bone present
4 – small pieces (1 – 4 inches) of identifiable bone
5 – tiny (less than ½ inches), unidentifiable pieces of bone

Teeth

0 – no erosion visible
1 – little erosion
2 – moderate erosion
3 – great erosion, but crown still attached to root
4 – crown and root attached, but one or both is/are broken
5 – only crown or root present

Sample Preparation and DNA Extraction

Approximately 1 cm3 of bone was cut from the source section using a Dremel MultiPro tool and was collected in a tube. For tooth samples, the tooth was cut in half exposing both the crown and the root. Samples were then immersed in filter-sterilized wash buffer (1% SDS, 25 mM EDTA) and 0.1 mg/ml proteinase K, and incubated for one hour at room temperature. Following the incubation, the wash buffer was poured off and each sample was washed with 1ml of sterile dH2O six consecutive times. Samples were allowed to air dry. Bone powder from the dried bone samples was collected in one of two ways. Bone was either ground to powder using an IKA A11 Basic Grinder or drilled using a the Dremel tool or a 12 inch Craftsman drill press, both fitted with 1/16th inch drill bits. Teeth were drilled in all cases. The resultant powder was collected in a microfuge tube and weighed. Between samples the grinder was rinsed with digestion buffer (see below), which was carried through the entire analysis as a reagent blank.

Four hundred microliters of digestion buffer (20 mM Tris, 100 mM EDTA, 0.1% SDS) and 0.4 mg/ml proteinase K was added to each ground bone sample and incubated overnight at 56°C. A standard phenol/chloroform organic extraction was performed on each of the samples. DNAs were precipitated using 3M sodium acetate and 95% ethanol, vacuum dried, and resuspended in TE buffer (10 mM Tris, 1 mM EDTA) based on the original mass of the bone powder. For the Albania bone samples, the final aqueous layer was processed using a Microcon-30 column and retentate volume adjusted based on the original mass of the bone powder.

Several precautions were taken to prevent contamination during the experiments. Grinders and drills used to generate bone powder were washed with 70% EtOH and 10% bleach, and were UV irradiated between each sample prep. Pre-amplification and post-amplification steps were carried out in separate rooms. Finally, negative controls and reagent blanks were included in all experiments.

Optimizing DNA Amplification

Multiple steps were taken during DNA amplification procedures to decrease the effects of PCR inhibitors found in the amplification reaction. If amplification was inhibited using undiluted DNA extract, a 1:20 dilution of the DNA was used. In addition, 5X HotM Enhancer (Eppendorf) and/or bovine serum albumin (BSA) was added to the amplification reaction to decrease inhibition. A hot-start Taq polymerase (HotMaster, Eppendorf) and accompanying

10X buffer were also used. Finally, the use of the Microcon columns was incorporated as part of Voegtly DNA preparations when a sample caused PCR inhibition. This allowed removal of both small pieces of DNA that could potentially act as random primers, and small water soluble inhibitors not removed during organic extraction.

Table 1. Mitochondrial and nuclear primers used for DNA amplification. Also included is the TaqMan® probe used in QPCR experiments

Name	Sequence	Region
Mitochondrial Primers		
F82	5 'ATAGCATTGCGAGACGCTGG3'	HVII of mtDNA
F155	5'TATTTATCGCACCTACGTTC3'	HVII of mtDNA
R285	5'GTTATGATGTCTGTGTGGAA3'	HVII of mtDNA
R484	5 'TGAGATTAGTAGTATGGGAG3	HVII of mtDNA
F15989	5'CCCAAAGCTAAGATTCTAAT3'	HVI of mtDNA
F16144	5'TGACCACCTGTAGTACATAA3'	HVI of mtDNA
F16190	5'CCCCATGCTTACAAGCAAGT3'	HVI of mtDNA
R16251	5'GGAGTTGCAGTTGATGT3'	HVI of mtDNA
F16400	5'ACCATCCTCCGTGAAATCAA3'	HVI of mtDNA
R16410	5 'GAGGATGGTGGTCAAGGGAC3'	HVI of mtDNA
D- loop	5'ACCCTGAAGTAGGAACCAGA3'	D-loop of mtDNA
Nuclear Primers		
BF	5'CCCTGGGCTCTGTAAAGAATAGTG3'	Amelogenin Gene
BR	5'ATCAGAGCTTAAACTGGGAAGCTG3'	Amelogenin Gene
LF	5'AAGAATAGTGTGTGGATTCTTTATCCCA3'	Amelogenin Gene
LR	5 'GGAACTGTAAAATCGGGACCACTTGAG3'	Amelogenin Gene
Forward Amel	5'CTCCCCTCCTCCCTGTAAAA3'	Amelogenin Gene
Reverse Amel 496bp	5'AGCAGAGGCAAGCAAGAGAC3'	Amelogenin Gene
Reverse Amel 200bp	5'TAAACTGGGAAGCTGGTGGT3'	Amelogenin Gene
Probes		
TaqMan® probe	5'CCTCGCTCCGGGCCCATAAC3'	D-loop of mtDNA

DNA Quality: PCR Amplification and Sequencing

Voegtly and Albania Bone Samples

DNA quality (maximum obtainable amplicon size) from the Voegtly bone samples was assayed using several different mtDNA primers in hypervariable region I (HVI). Primer sequences used for amplification can be found in Table 1. Initially, PCR was performed using F16190 and R16410. If the sample did not produce the 220 bp amplicon, F16144 and R16251 were used to produce a 107 bp amplicon. When amplification of the 220 bp amplicon was successful, amplification of progressively larger amplicons (329 bp followed by 402 bp) was attempted. The amplification reaction consisted of denaturation at 94°C for 2 min, followed by 35 – 40 cycles of denaturation at 94°C for 30 s, annealing at 56°C for 45 s, and extension at 72°C for 45 s. The last cycle was followed by an additional extension step at 72°C for 5 min. PCR reactions were in 20 µl volumes, containing 1U of enzyme, 1X buffer, 0.2 mM each of dNTP, and 2 µmol each of mtDNA-specific primers. Fragment size and amplification quality were visualized by running 5 µl of the PCR product on a 2% agarose gel followed by staining with ethidium bromide. If only a light PCR product was seen, an additional amplification reaction was performed to increase the amount of product to be used in sequencing reactions. In these reactions, 1 µl of the original PCR product was used as a template and the number of cycles was reduced to 20.

Voegtly Tooth Samples

Samples were amplified using a semi-nested PCR technique because single PCR did not provide enough DNA for sequencing. A portion of the HVI was amplified. For the first round of PCR, primers F16144/R16410 were used. The primer set F16190/R16410 was used for the second round of PCR, resulting in a 220 bp amplicon.

MtDNA Sequence Determination

When amplification was successful, the remaining 15 µl of PCR product was purified using a Microcon-30 column with 300 µl of TE. The samples were washed two additional times with TE before retentate was brought back to 15 µl with TE. Up to 5 µl of template DNA was sequenced using a BeckSeq kit (Beckman-Coulter). Per the manufacturer's recommendations, 50–100 femtograms of DNA were used for sequencing reactions; estimations of concentration were made from the yield gel of the original amplification. The primers used for sequencing were the same as those used for amplification, and as a modification to the protocol provided with the kit, the total reaction volume was reduced to 10 µl. The sequencing reaction was followed as outlined in the kit manual. Following sequencing, 4 µl of stop solution (1.5M NaAc, 50 mM EDTA, 2.5 mg/ml glycogen) and 30 µl of cold 95% EtOH were added to each reaction, which was then centrifuged at 14000rpm for 15 min. The supernatant was removed and the sample was washed twice with 200 µl of cold 70% EtOH with a 2 min, 14000rpm spin between washes. After the final wash, the supernatant was removed and the sample was vacuum-dried for approximately 10 min, then resuspended in 40 µl Sample Loading Solution (SLS, Beckman-Coulter). Samples were sequenced on a CEQ 8000 Genetic Sequence Analyzer (Beckman-Coulter), using the LFR-1-60 program (capillary temperature 50°C, denature 120 s at 90°C, inject 15 s at 2.0kV, and separate 60 min at 4.2kV). Resulting sequences were aligned using BioEdit Sequence Alignment Editor (Hall, 2004) and compared to the Anderson *et al.* (1981) reference sequence.

MtDNA sequences for scientists conducting the DNA work were determined in all cases, to ensure DNA sequences were not derived from laboratory personnel. To be considered a 'positive' result, the same mtDNA sequence had to either be obtained from more than one bone from a skeleton, or obtained from two independent DNA preparations of a bone. Further, reagent blanks had to be negative throughout.

DNA Quantity: Quantitative PCR

A subset of 60 bones that had previously produced mtDNA PCR products was used for quantitative analyses. Also included were samples that did not produce amplicons yet did not show PCR inhibition, in order to address DNA levels that resulted in unsuccessful amplification. Samples that had PCR inhibition were not chosen for this portion of the DNA quantity experiment. The two mtDNA primers used in the QPCR reactions, F16400 and D-loop, amplified a 118 bp region in HVI. A TaqMan® probe was then designed to sit between the forward and reverse primer sites (Table 1). Primer/probe concentrations were optimized. The parameters recommended for quantitative TaqMan® assays (as described in the TaqMan® Universal PCR Master Mix protocol, 2002) were utilized, except that the reaction volume was decreased to 10 µl. Further, based on the work of Andreasson *et al.* (2003), cycle number was increased from forty to fifty. Based on optimization experiments, bone DNAs were diluted 50-fold for amplification, and BSA was added. Standards (known amounts of the same region of human mtDNA) were designed as ten-fold dilutions, from 6x107 copies/µl down to 6 copies/µl. The samples were processed in triplicate on an ABI 7700. Results were analyzed using the standard curve method.

Effects of PCR Inhibition

A set of 11 Voegtly bone samples that showed extens ive/complete PCR inhibition were tested to determine what effect it had on DNA quantity estimates, and how addition of substances used to reduce PCR inhibition altered results. One microliter of DNA extract was spiked with 1µl of the mtDNA standards (in ten-fold dilutions from 6,000,000 – 60 copies/µl) and analyzed by QPCR. The 11 spiked samples were also tested in the presence of a commercial product designed to augment PCR (TaqMan® 5x PCR Enhancer (Eppendorf)) and BSA.

Enhanced Techniques

Mini-STR Experiments

Mini-STR primers were supplied by Michael Coble and John Butler of NIST. These included 6 individual primer pairs, and one mini A1 primer set that contained a combination of all primers. Table 2 lists the primers included in the set, and additional information on each. The DNAs analyzed were selected based on results from the amelogenin nested PCR amplification results and in some cases, on previous ability to obtain mtDNA sequence.

Table 2. Mini-STRs utilized in this study. Information from But ler *et al.* 2003

STR Locus (Dye Label)	Allele Range	Allele Spread	Product Size (STR Kit)	Mini- STR Size	Size Reduction
FGA (6-FAM)	12.2 – 51.2	156 bp	196 – 352 bp	125 – 281 bp	71 bp
TH01 (6-FAM)	3 – 14	44 bp	160 – 204 bp	51 – 98 bp	105 bp
D16S539 (NED)	5 – 15	40 bp	233 – 273 bp	81 – 121 bp	152 bp
D18S51 (VIC)	7 – 27	80 bp	264 – 344 bp	113 – 193 bp	151 bp
D2S1338 (PET)	15 – 28	52 bp	288 – 340 bp	90 – 142 bp	198 bp
Amelogenin (6-FAM)	X, Y		106 – 114 bp		

Amplification parameters were based on the authors' recommendations, although increased cycle number was also attempted. In addition, the Mini-STRs were tested using a nested technique. DNAs were first amplified for 30 cycles using an Identifiler™ kit and the manufacturer's protocol at 30 cycles in a 10 µl sample volume. One microliter of the resultant product was transferred to a reaction mix containing the Mini-STR set and PCR components listed above, and amplified for an additional 30 cycles. Half the reaction was electrophoresed on a 2% agarose gel, and examined for PCR product. Amplification products visible on the gel were electrophoresed on an ABIPRISM® 310 Genetic Analyzer.

Nested PCR of Nuclear Loci

Nested amelogenin primer sets (Sullivan *et al.*, 1993) were created based on the amelogenin sequence from Genbank (Figure 4). The external primer pair amplified a 112 bp region in males and a 106 bp region in females. The internal primers, one of which was labeled for capillary electrophoreses, produced 68 bp and 62 bp amplicons.

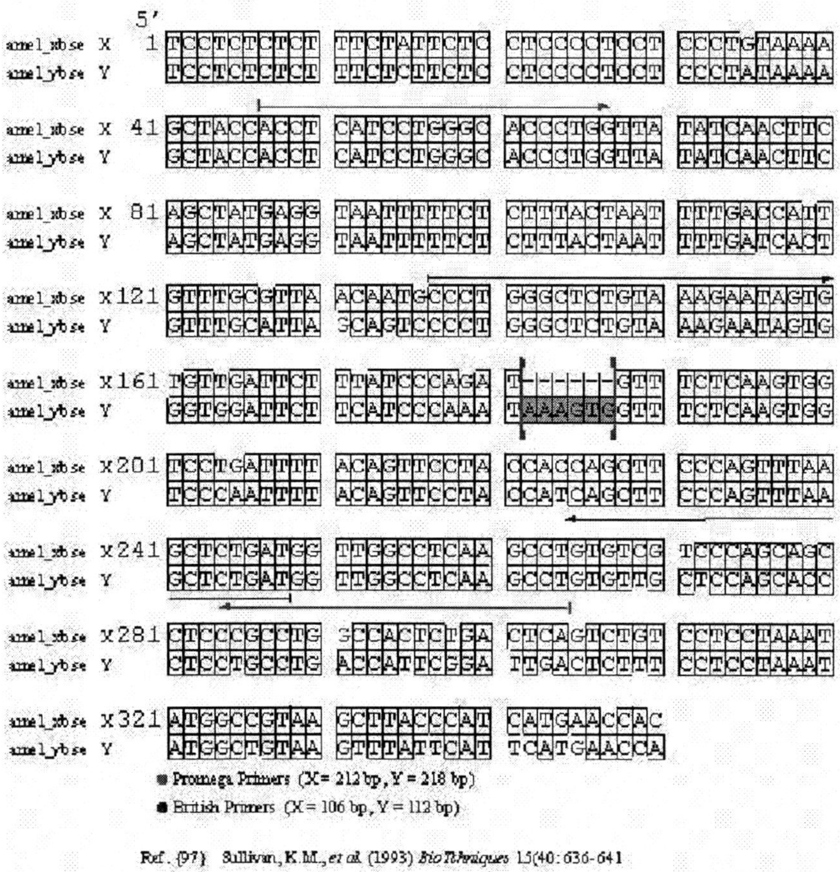

The amelogenin sequence from Genbank for both the X and Y chromosomes. The British Primer set, labeled in blue, was chosen as the external primers for nested PCR. Primers for the second round of amplification were chosen internal to the British primer set (see Table 1). Figure taken from www.cstl.nist.gov/ div831/strbase/jpg_amel.htm.

Figure 4. Amelogenin gene sequence and primer positions

Voegtly DNAs shown to have amplified using mitochondrial primers were tested. A 1:10 dilution of the DNA was used in the first round of PCR in a 10 μl volume. Cycling parameters were as above, for 30 cycles. One microliter of product was transferred to a second tube containing the PCR mix and the internal primers in a 20 μl volume. This too was amplified for 30 cycles. Five microliters of the reaction was electrophoresed on a 3% agarose gel and examined for the presence of bands. Samples that had an amplification product were analyzed on a Beckman-Coulter CEQ™ 8000 Genetic Analysis System

Whole Genome Amplification

Five Voegtly femur samples (burials 27F, 114F, 249F, 448F, and 704F) were tested using WGA. A 1:20 dilution of the DNAs was amplified using two techniques, IPEP (Dietmaier *et al.*, 1999) and MDA (Dean *et al.*, 2002). I-PEP was performed using Expand High Fidelity PCR system (Roche Applied Sciences) and MDA was performed using a GenomiPhi DNA amplification kit (Amersham Biosciences). The whole genome amplified products were purified using a Microcon-100 column and amplified using mitochondrial DNA primers F16190/R16410, a 220 bp region of HVI. In addition, F155/R484 were used to amplify a 329 bp region of HVII. PCR products were visualized by running 5 μl of the PCR product on a 2% agarose gel. Purified mtDNA amplified DNA was sequenced on a Beckman-Coulter CEQ™ 8000 Genetic Analysis System as detailed above, and sequences compared to those previously obtained.

Soil Analyses

Samples were collected from all Voegtly burials in which soil could either be brushed off skeletal remains or collected from the box where the skeletal remains had been stored. Control soils samples were collected from the Voegtly Cemetery site in early 2004. Descriptions of the soils were generated using particle size analysis. Soils were tested for relevant inorganic compounds, including phosphorous, magnesium, potassium, calcium, beryllium, cobalt, indium, cerium, cerium oxide, bismuth, uranium, berkelium, arsenic, zinc, uranium oxide, lanthanum, and barium, as well as total organic carbon, based on X-ray fluorescence. Calcium, magnesium and potassium levels were determined using ammonium acetate extraction followed by atomic absorption. Extractable phosphorous was isolated using acidic Bray extraction and analyzed by atomic absorption. Additional elemental analysis was conducted using inductively coupled plasma in line with mass spectrometry (ICP-MS). Finally, the pH level of each soil sample was determined using a pH meter with a standard two point calibration.

Statistical Analyses

Statistical analyses were performed in Microsoft Excel. Single factor Analysis of Variance (ANOVA) was used to examine the effect of weathering stage, sex, age, and bone type on the DNA quantity and quality results from the Voegtly bone samples. ANOVA was also used to examine the effect of skeletal weathering on amplification success of multiple bones from a single individual, as well as the effect of skeletal weathering, bone weathering, and bone type on amplicon size. DNA quantities for sex and age statistics were averaged when multiple bones originated from a single individual. Amplification success vs. DNA quantity was examined using a t-test with equal variance assumed. The effect of PCR inhibition during QPCR on spiked samples with and without anti-inhibitory addition (BSA or commercial enhancer) was examined using a two-tailed paired t-test. In all cases results were considered significant at $p<0.05$.

Results the Voegtly Samples

The Voegtly bone samples tested, bone type, mtDNA QPCR yields, maximum mtDNA amplicon size obtained, and PCR inhibition are detailed in Table 3.

The Voegtly mtDNA quantity and quality results are displayed below. Headings denote burial number, bone type, mtDNA quantity (copies/μl), and the maximum obtainable mtDNA amplicon size. Samples that were not tested for mtDNA quantity are left blank in the mtDNA quantity box. Those samples in which an amplicon was not produced and there was no primer activity are labeled as "inhibited". Samples which did not produce an amplicon but showed primer activity were considered negative and all boxes were left blank. * indicates samples that were processed with a Microcon-YM 100 column.

MtDNA Quantity

Skeletal Weathering Stage

The mtDNA quantity calculated for each sample was categorized by the complete skeletal weathering stage of the Voegtly samples, where a degradation level was assigned to each skeleton. Table 4 gives the average mtDNA quantity values obtained for each skeletal weathering stage. There was a notable trend (Figure 5) between mtDNA quantity and the skeletal weathering stage, with more weathered skeletons producing more mtDNA, and differences among stages were statistically significant ($p=0.036$).

Skeletal Weathering Stage Categorized by Bone Type

The mtDNA quantity was further broken down by bone type (ribs, femora, and pelves) in each skeletal weathering stage (Tables 5, 6, and 7, Figure 6). For all samples, the greatest average DNA quantity was found in stage four or five, and the lowest quantity was found in either stage one or two. The average mtDNA quantity found in ribs increased from stage one to stage two, then decreased in stage three. The quantity then increased from stage three to stage five. The quantity of mtDNA in femora stayed approximately the same between stages one and two, then increased sharply from stage two to three. The quantity increased between stages three and four, then decreased in stage five. The average mtDNA quantity in pelves decreased between stage one and two, then increased in stages two through five.

Table 3. Overall DNA quantity and quality results from Voegtly samples

Burial Number	Bone Type	MtDNA quantity (copies/µl)	107 bp	220 bp	329 bp	Inhibited
27	Femur	76.2		X		
27	Rib	508		X		
30	Femur	64.2		X		
34	Femur	304.3	X*			
34	Pelvis	61.9				
34	Rib	162.2		X		
47	Femur					
47	Pelvis	141.8		X		
47	Rib	122.2		X*		
47	Rib					
111	Femur	67.8	X			
111	Rib	146.5	X			
111	Pelvis		X			
114	Femur	122.9		X		
124	Femur	277.1	X			
124	Pelvis	138.6	X			
124	Rib	117.9		X*		
126	Femur	63.7				
126	Pelvis	14.9				
126	Rib	78.6				
132	Femur	49.2	X			
132	Pelvis	24.2		X*		
132	Rib	66.21	X			
164	Femur	38.9			X	
164	Pelvis	134				
164	Rib	110.9			X	
167	Femur	10.3		X		
167	Pelvis	22.4				
167	Rib	175.4				
192	Femur	101.2		X		
192	Pelvis	53.4		X		
192	Rib	9.5				
203	Cranium				X	
203	Fibula	64.9		X		
203	Rib					
256	Femur					
256	Pelvis					
256	Rib					
260	Femur	31.8	X			
260	Rib	78.8	X			
322	Femur	24	X			
322	Pelvis	69		X		
322	Rib	13.9	X			

Table 3. Overall DNA quantity and quality results from Voegtly samples(Continued)

Burial Number	Bone Type	MtDNA quantity (copies/µl)	107 bp	220 bp	329 bp	Inhibited
328	Femur	34.3	X			
328	Pelvis					X*
328	Rib	71.4		X*		
331	Femur	161	X			
331	Rib	100.2	X			
345	Femur					
345	Pelvis					X*
345	Rib	27			X	
345	Rib				X	
348	Femur	74.7				
348	Pelvis	57.1				
348	Rib	92.7	X			
349	Femur			X		
355	Femur					
355	Rib					
381	Femur	107.1	X			
381	Pelvis	157.4				
381	Rib	11.2	X			
389	Pelvis					
389	Rib					
402	Pelvis					X*
409B	Femur	195.6	X			
409B	Pelvis					
409B	Rib	57.5		X*		
447	Femur			X		
447	Rib			X		
448	Femur	52.1		X		
448	Rib	7.2		X		
489	Pelvis	45.8				
489	Rib					X
529A	Femur	251.4		X		
529A	Pelvis					
529A	Rib	0.6		X		
539	Pelvis					
539	Rib					X*
540	Pelvis	76.9		X		
540	Rib					
545	Femur	55.7	X			
545	Pelvis	56.3				
545	Rib	42		X*		
546	Pelvis			X		
546	Rib					
686	Cranium			X		
704	Femur	468.3		X		
704	Pelvis	566.7	X*			
704	Rib	33.2		X*		

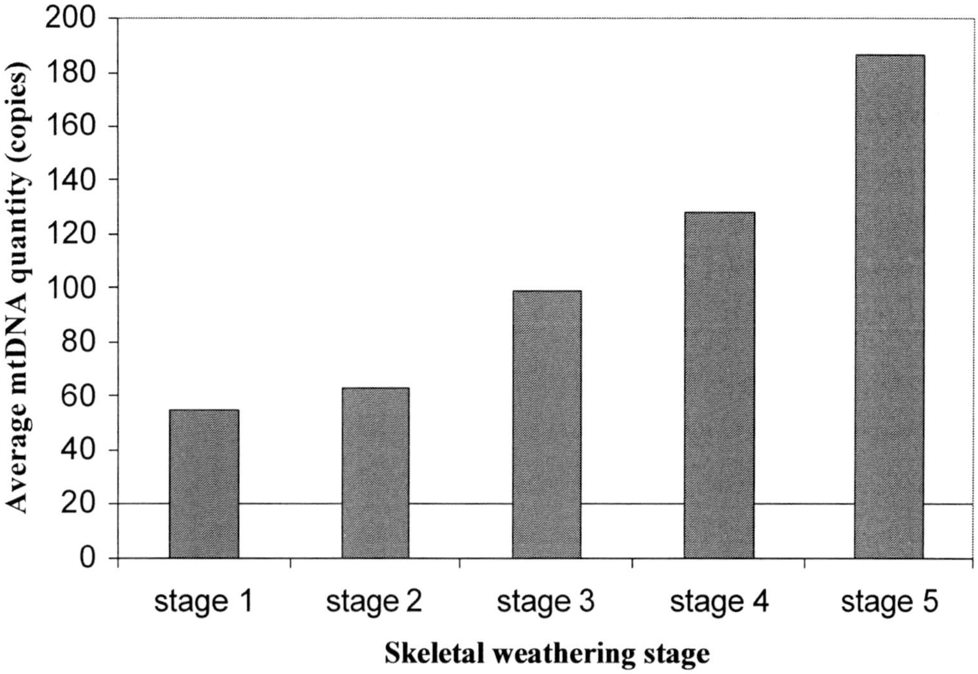

The average mtDNA quantity (given in copies of DNA) is on the y-axis, and the skeletal weathering skeletal stages range from 1 (least weathered) to 5 (most weathered) along the x-axis.

Figure 5. Average mtDNA quantity in each skeletal weathering stage

Table 4. Average mtDNA quantity in each skeletal weathering stage

Skeletal weathering stage	Average mtDNA quantity (copies/μl)	Number of samples
Stage 1	54.7	4
Stage 2	63.0	20
Stage 3	98.6	15
Stage 4	128.3	9
Stage 5	186.4	12

The average mtDNA quantities (in copies/μl) found in each skeletal weathering stage. There were no stage zero bones available for analysis.

Table 5. Average mtDNA quantity in rib samples categorized by skeletal weathering stage

Rib samples categorized by skeletal weathering stage	Average mtDNA quantity (copies/μl)	Number of samples
Stage 1	42.0	1
Stage 2	91.5	7
Stage 3	80.8	6
Stage 4	90.6	4
Stage 5	162.2	4

Table 6. Average mtDNA quantity in femur samples categorized by skeletal weathering stage

Femur samples categorized by skeletal weathering stages	Average mtDNA quantity (copies/μl)	Number of samples
Stage 1	60.3	2
Stage 2	56.3	7
Stage 3	130.0	5
Stage 4	195.8	3
Stage 5	157.5	6

Table 7. Average mtDNA quantity in pelvic samples categorized by skeletal weathering stage

Pelvic samples categorized by skeletal weathering stage	Average mtDNA quantity (copies/μl)	Number of samples
Stage 1	56.3	1
Stage 2	37.7	6
Stage 3	86.1	4
Stage 4	101.8	2
Stage 5	321.8	2

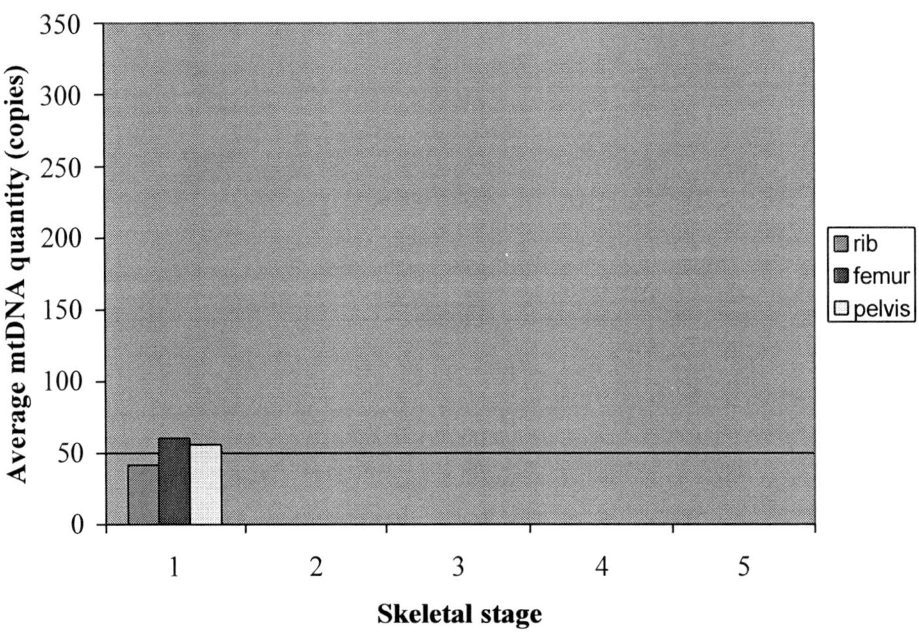

The average mtDNA quantity in each skeletal stage is given on the y-axis, and the skeletal weathering stages range from 1 (least weathered) to 5 (most weathered) along the x-axis. In each stage, the left column portrays rib samples, the middle column femur samples, and the right column pelvic samples.

Figure 6. Average mtDNA quantity in each skeletal weathering stage categorized by bone type

As is apparent, there is an upward trend in mtDNA yields in relationship to increasing levels of skeletal degradation. However, based on ANOVA there was no significant difference among the stages divided by bone type for ribs, femora, or pelves (p=0.78, p=0.31, and p=0.13 respectively), in part due to the much smaller samples sizes generated by the increasing number of categories.

Individual Bone Weathering Stage

If the level of degradation is predictive of the quality of DNA within the bone, a bone rating system might reveal a correlation that was masked when the whole skeleton rating system was used. A new four stage weathering classification system was created and applied to each bone. Reclassification of individual bones confirmed that the level of degradation of a skeleton was not consistent throughout the skeleton. In general, bones within a skeleton were reclassified into different stages, and only rarely were all three bones classified to the same stage.

Table 8. Average mtDNA quantity in each bone weathering stage

Bone weathering stage	Average mtDNA quantity (copies/μl)	Number of samples
Stage 1	129.6	15
Stage 2	100.7	25
Stage 3	103.1	14
Stage 4	90.7	6

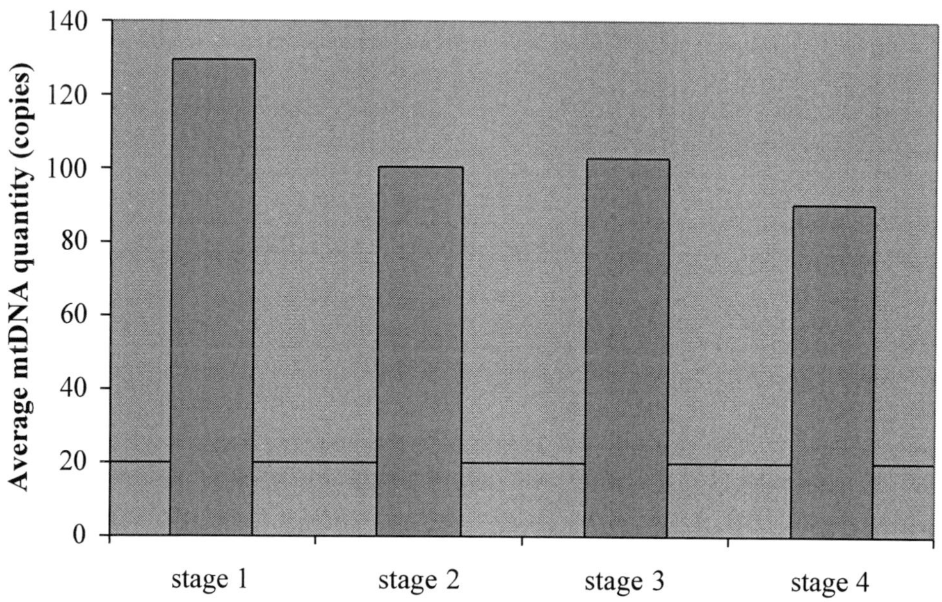

The average mtDNA quantity (in copies) is on the y-axis, and the bone weathering stages range from 1 (least weathered) to 4 (most weathered) along the x-axis.

Figure 7. Average mtDNA quantity for each bone weathering stage

MtDNA quantities were calculated based on the weathering level of individual bones (Table 8 and Figure 7). In contrast to skeletal weathering, there was no significant difference in the amount of mtDNA extracted across the bone weathering stages (p=0.91).

Bone Weathering Stage and Bone Type

The mtDNA quantities obtained for each bone type were also categorized into bone weathering stage for analysis (Tables 9, 10, and 11). As can be seen in Figure 8, there is no common trend among the three bone types. However, there were trends within bone types. Ribs showed a general increase in mtDNA yields with advanced weathering, while the opposite was true for pelves. Femora appeared to change little. This was borne out statistically in that there was no significant difference in fe mora (p=0.69), ribs (p=0.57), nor pelves (p=0.053) although pelves approached significance. This difference was due to one pelvic sample in stage 1 with a very high mtDNA yield. Note that there were no femur or pelvic samples graded as stage 4.

Table 9. Average mtDNA quantity for rib samples categorized by bone weathering stage

Rib samples categorized by bone weathering stage	Average mtDNA quantity (copies/μl)	Number of samples
Stage 1	9.5	1
Stage 2	78.9	7
Stage 3	137.6	8
Stage 4	90.7	6

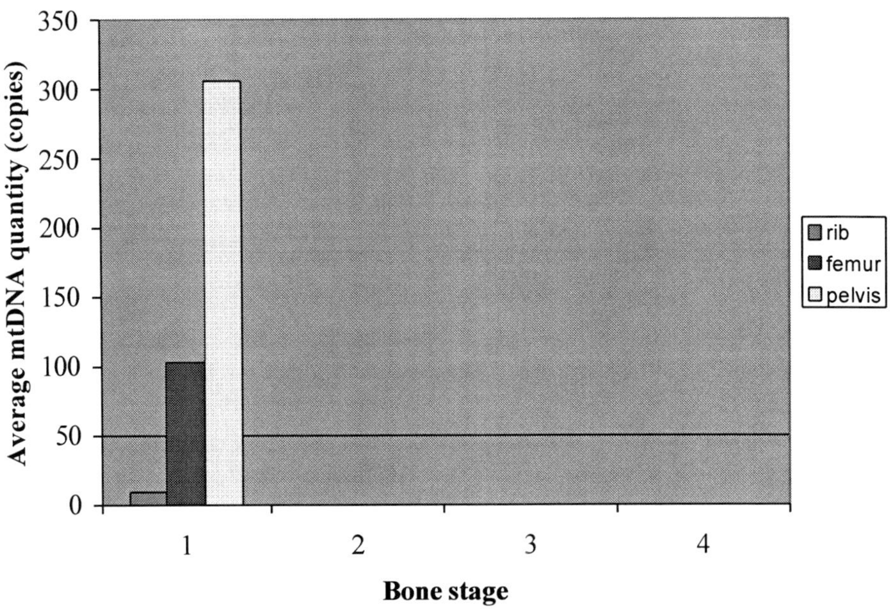

The average mtDNA quantity (in copies) in each bone stage is shown. The bone stages range from 1 (least weathered) to 4 (most weathered) along the x-axis. The high stage 1 results for pelves stemmed from a single high sample. No femur or pelvic samples were rated as stage 4.

Figure 8. Average mtDNA quantity versus bone stage categorized by bone type

Table 10. Average mtDNA quantity for femur samples categorized by bone weathering stage

Femur samples categorized by bone weathering stage	Average mtDNA quantity (copies/μl)	Number of samples
Stage 1	103.2	12
Stage 2	139.4	10
Stage 3	64.2	1

Table 11. Average mtDNA quantity for pelvic samples categorized by bone weathering stage

Pelvic samples categorized by bone weathering stage	Average mtDNA quantity (copies/μl)	Number of samples
Stage 1	306.3	2
Stage 2	72.9	8
Stage 3	55.6	5

MtDNA Quantity and Bone Type

MtDNA quantity was examined based on bone type (Table 12 and Figure 9). Femora were found to generate the highest mtDNA quantity, while ribs and pelves were quite similar. Statistical analysis showed no difference in the quantity of mtDNA obtained from each bone type ($p=0.84$).

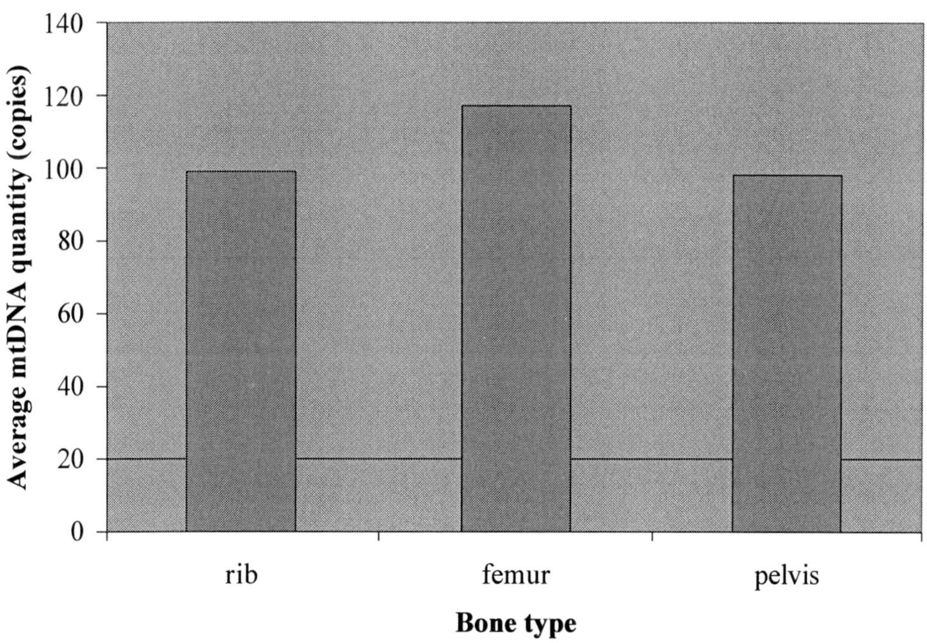

The average mtDNA quantity (in copies) in relation to bone type. MtDNA quantity is on the y-axis, and the bone type is on the x-axis.

Figure 9. Average mtDNA quantity versus bone type 0 20 40 60 80 100 120 140 Average mtDNA quantity (copies)

Table 12. Average mtDNA quantity in each bone type

Bone type	Average mtDNA quantity (copies/μl)	Number of samples
Ribs	99.0	22
Femora	117.2	23
Pelves	98.3	15

Sex Estimates and Average Mtdna Quantities

The average bone mtDNA yield was compared to the individual's sex estimated anthropologically; samples where the sex was not estimated were excluded from these analyses. If there were multiple bone results from an individual, average mtDNA quantity was used. The mtDNA quantity extracted from males (n=17) averaged 113.2 copies/μl, while the average from females (n=8) was 98.6 copies/μl (Figure 10). There was not a statistical difference in mtDNA quantity between the sexes (p=0.88).

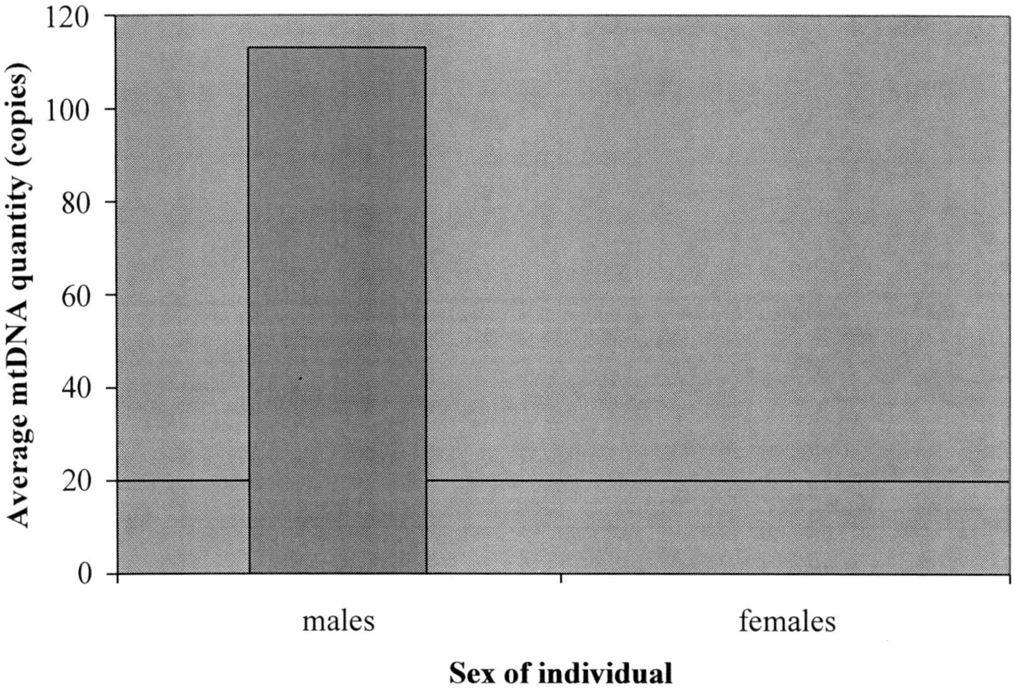

The average quantity of mtDNA for males and females. Sex of the individual is on the x-axis.

Figure 10. Average mtDNA quantity for each sex

Age at Death and DNA Quantity

The anthropologically estimated ages at death were put into six categories fo r analysis: infant (less than 1 year old), child (1–13 years), adolescent (14–17 years), young adult (18–24 years), adult (25–49 years), and older adult (50+ years); mtDNA quantities by age are shown in Table 13 and Figure 11. If there were multiple bone results from an individual, average mtDNA quantity was used. There was no apparent trend in DNA quantity with age, and there was no statistical difference in mtDNA yields from each of the age ranges (p= 0.97). It should be noted that the multiple categories made samples sizes very small in some cases.

Table 13. Average mtDNA quantity in each age range

Age ranges	Average mtDNA quantity (copies/µl)	Number of samples
Infant (<1 year)	64.9	1
Child (1–13)	108.8	5
Adolescent (14–17)	70.3	2
Young adult (18–24)	106.3	4
Adult (25–49)	103.0	15
Older adult (50+)	54.7	1

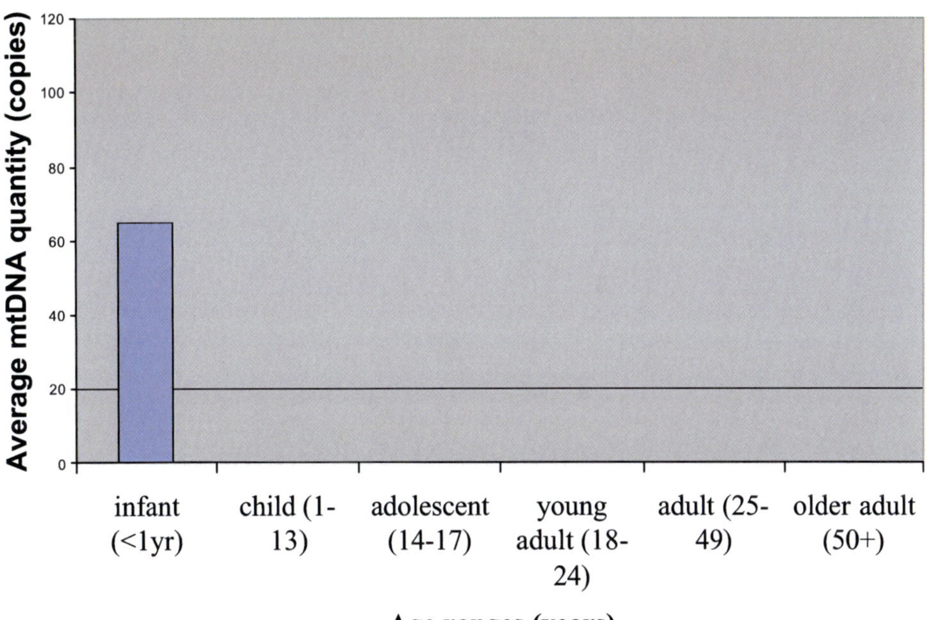

The average quantity of mtDNA for each age range is. The age ranges (in years) are along the x-axis.

Figure 11. Average mtDNA quantity in each age range

The Effects of PCR Inhibition on DNA Quantification

Samples that showed PCR inhibition (based on a lack of primer activity) were analyzed through addition of (spiking with) known amounts of target sequence, using 6,000,000 – 60 copies in 10-fold intervals. The same samples had either BSA or a commercial PCR enhancer added as well. Following QPCR, results among treatments were compared. An examp le, with 60,000 copies of target DNA added, is shown in Figure 12, with a graph of all results shown in Figure 13. The native samples all showed a high level of PCR inhibition (79% and above), as did the samples with the commercial PCR enhancer, (41% and above, although all but the sample containing 6,000,000 copies of added target were 85% inhibited and above). In contrast, samples with BSA added were not inhibited at high target DNA addition levels, and surprisingly even showed enhanced PCR. At lower target levels samples with BSA were inhibited. There were no statistical differences between native samples and those with the commercial enhancer at any added DNA concentration. Samples with BSA differed significantly from native DNA at all added DNA levels except at 6,000 and 60 copies.

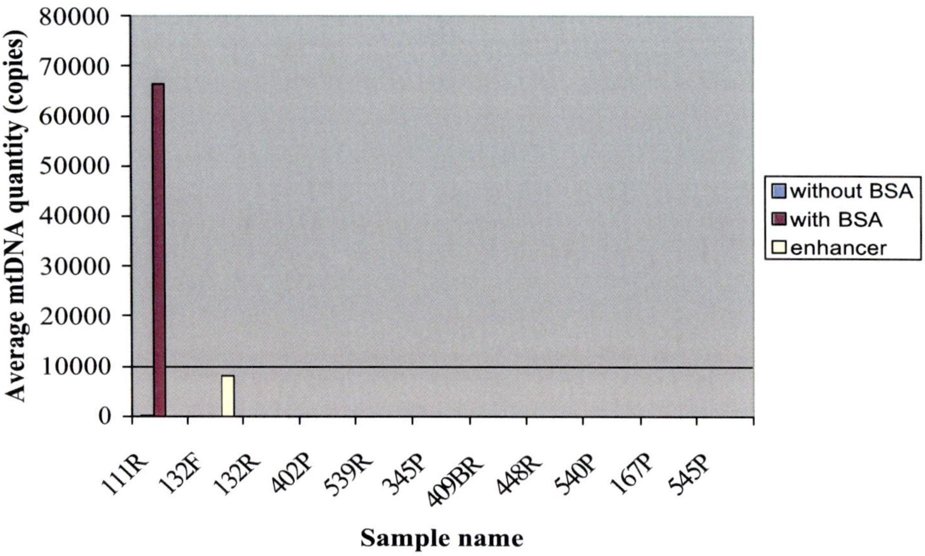

An example of QPCR measured inhibition in Voegtly bone samples amplified with and without reagents thought to reduce PCR inhibition. 60,000 copies of the target DNA was added to each sample. Sample name indicates the burial number and bone type (R=rib, F=femur, P=pelvis).

Figure 12. Samples spiked with 60,000 copies of control DNA

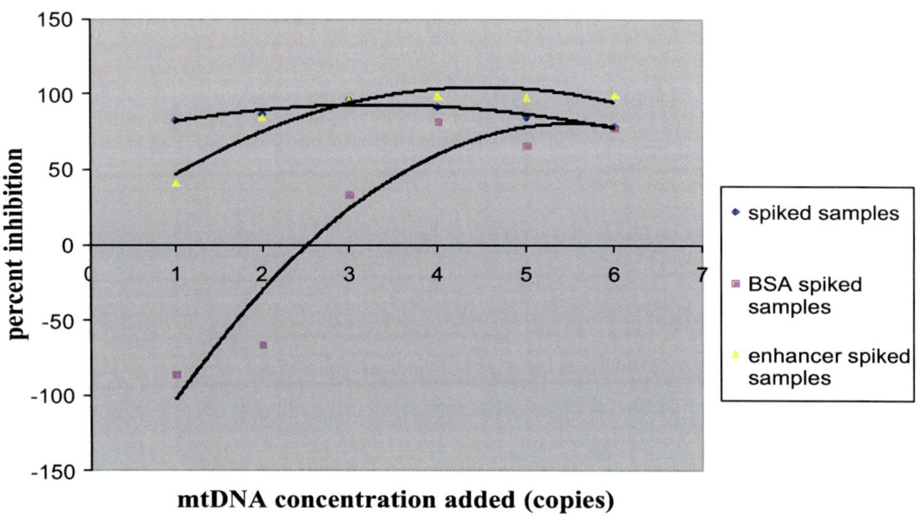

Average QPCR results for inhibited bone DNAs spiked with known amounts of target DNA. Spiked samples are numbered 1 – 6 on the X axis, indicating 6,000,000 – 60 copies of target. Percent inhibition ranges from close to 100 at the top of the figure, to excess DNA estimated below 0 on the Y axis for some samples containing BSA.

Figure 13. Percent PCR inhibition of bone samples containing known amounts of DNA

MtDNA Quality

The Voegtly Samples

Final mtDNA PCR results for the Voegtly Cemetery samples, arranged by burial number and bone type, are shown in Table 3. If amplification was successful, it was noted by the maximum fragment length obtainable. Samples that were subject to Microcon-100 processing are denoted by a star. Thirty-four samples (10 femora, 11 ribs, 6 pelves, 1 fibula, 1 cranium, and the 5 detailed below) produced the 220 bp amplicon, all of which were additionally analyzed using the 329 bp set of primers. Five samples (203 cranium, 164 femur and rib, and 345 rib 1 and 2) produced the 329 bp amplicon. PCR of those five samples with the 402 bp primers was carried out, but negative results were obtained from all. Of the 50 samples that did not produce a 220 bp band, but did not show PCR inhibition, 21 produced a 107 bp amplicon. Samples that had a maximum amplicon of 107 bp included 11 femora, 7 ribs, and three pelves.

When amplification product was available from two or more bones from any one individual, amplicons were sequenced to ensure that the DNA extracted from the different bones originated from the same source. For all bones sequenced from a skeleton, the sequencing results were consistent within an individual. In no instance was incongruent mtDNA sequence derived from bones from a single burial (Table 14).

Table 14. Mt DNA sequence in skeletons generating PCR products from more than one bone

Burial Number and Bone Type	Sequence Interval	Sequence Polymorphism
27 femur F rib F/R	16121-16232 16272-16376	16340C
164 femur F/R rib F/R	16173-16216 16247-16385	16267T
192 femur F/R pelvis F	16167-16390	None
203 fibula F/R cranium F/R	16167-16388	16270T
447 femur F/R rib F/R	16169-16260 16299-16378	16248T, 16340C
448 femur F rib R	16177-16382	None
529A femur F/R rib F/R	16169-16387	None
704 femur F/R rib F/R	16186-16378	None

The sequence interval available for comparison between at least two bones of an individual, with differences from the human mtDNA reference sequence noted. F=forward, R=reverse sequence.

Skeletal Weathering Stage

Amplification results broken down by skeletal weathering stage are displayed in Figure 14 and show that there was no obvious relationship between weathering stage and amplification success. Bones from stage five, the most weathered, amplified the most often at 70% (14 out of 20), followed by stage two at 69.57% (16 out of 23), stage one at 66.67% (4 out of 6), and stage four at 61.11% (11 out of 18). Samples from stage three amplified the least often, at 45.45% (10 out of 22). The difference in amplification among all weathering stage categories was not significant (p=0.460).

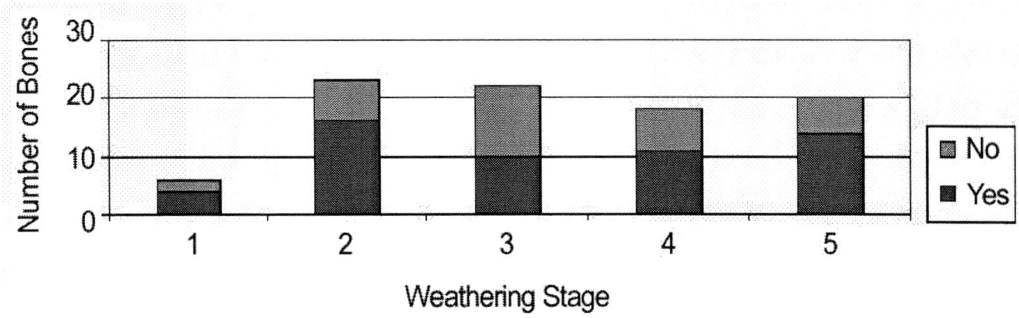

Graph depicting amplification success (yes) and failure (no) in relationship to the five skeletal weathering stages.

Figure 14. Amplification results in comparison to skeletal weathering stage

Amplification results were broken down further to examine if skeletal weathering had any influence on amplicon size. For each skeletal weathering stage, bones were categorized by the maximum amplicon length that was amplified. When compared across skeletal weathering stages, Figure 15 shows no relationship between stage and the maximum amplicon length. However, the largest amplicon produced, 329 bp, was only seen in the first three weathering stages. When compared, there was no significant difference between the size of the amplicon produced and skeletal weathering stage

Most skeletons from the Voegtly cemetery had more than one bone available for analysis, thus it was interesting to note if less weathered skeletons were more likely to have DNA from multiple bones amplify. Figure 16 displays the amplification success of these at each weathering stage. Amplification was determined in terms of the percentage of bone DNAs that amplified from a single individual (0%, 33%, 50%, 66% or 100%). There was no significant difference between how often multiple bones from a single individual could be amplified and weathering stage (p=0.679).

Skeletal Weathering Stage Categorized by Bone Type

To incorporate the potential influence of specific bone types on amplification success, each skeletal weathering stage was further divided by bone type. Amplification success is similar across the five weathering stages, with pelvis and rib samples amplifying the least often at stage one (0 out of 1 and 1 out of 2, respectively), while femur samples amplifying the least often at stage three (42.9%, 3 out of 7). There was no significant difference in the pelvis, rib, or femur data among the five stages (p =0.604, p=0.956, and p=0.076, respectively). This further indicates that staging based on skeletal weathering does not aid in the prediction of the quality of DNA that can be extracted from the bone, although due to the large number of categories, samples sizes became quite small.

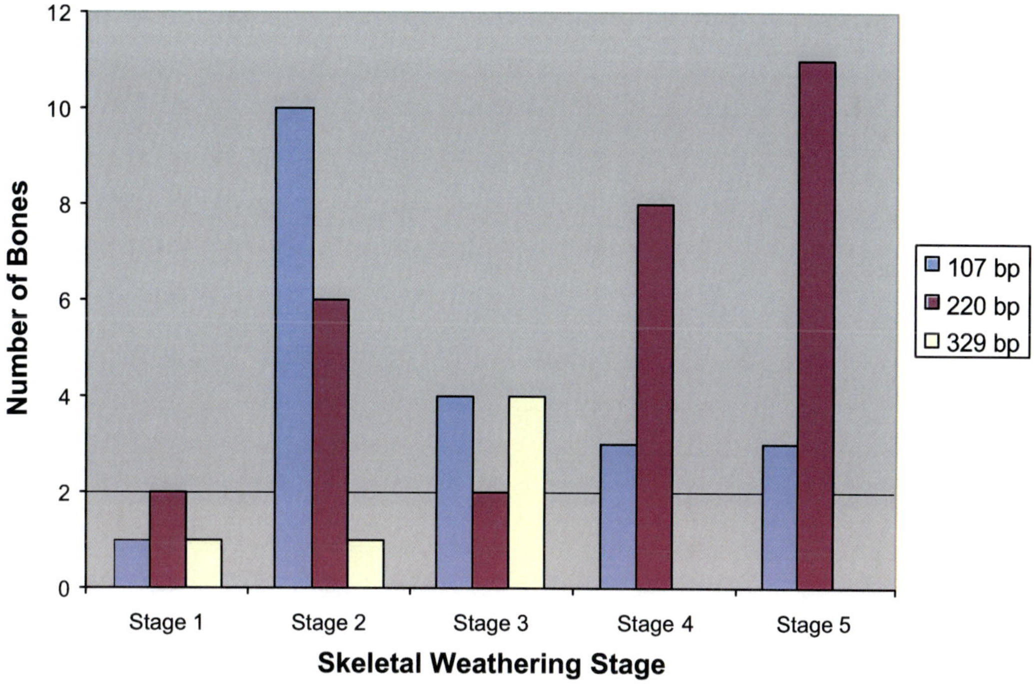

Graph depicting maximum amplicon length for bones at each skeletal weathering stage.

Figure 15. Maximum obtainable amplicon produced for each skeletal weathering stage

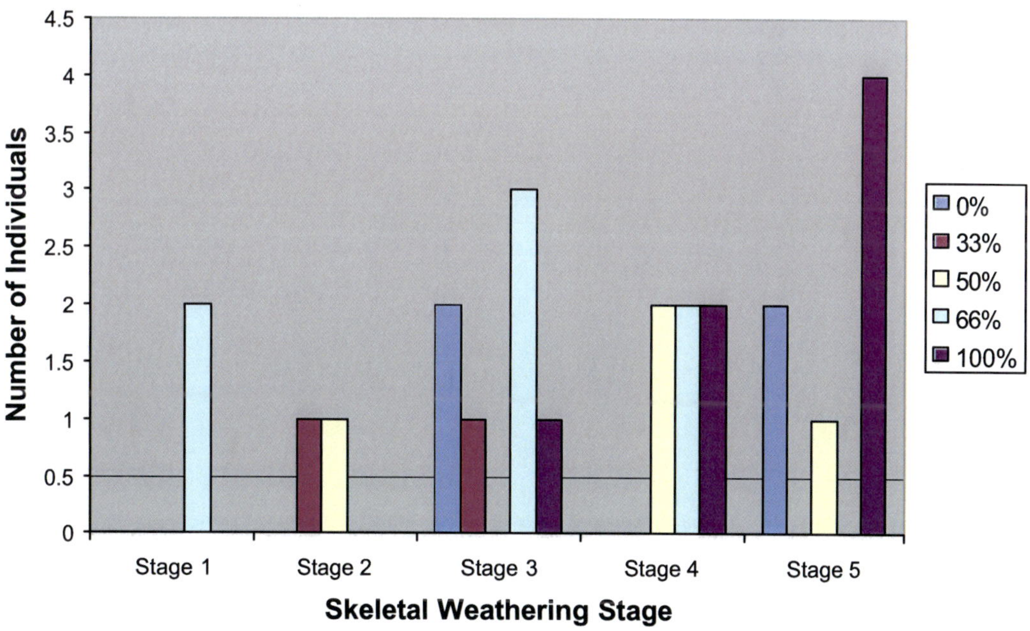

Graph depicting the success of bone DNA amplification for individuals with more than one bone available for analysis.

Figure 16. DNA amplification rate of multiple bones from individuals at each weathering stage

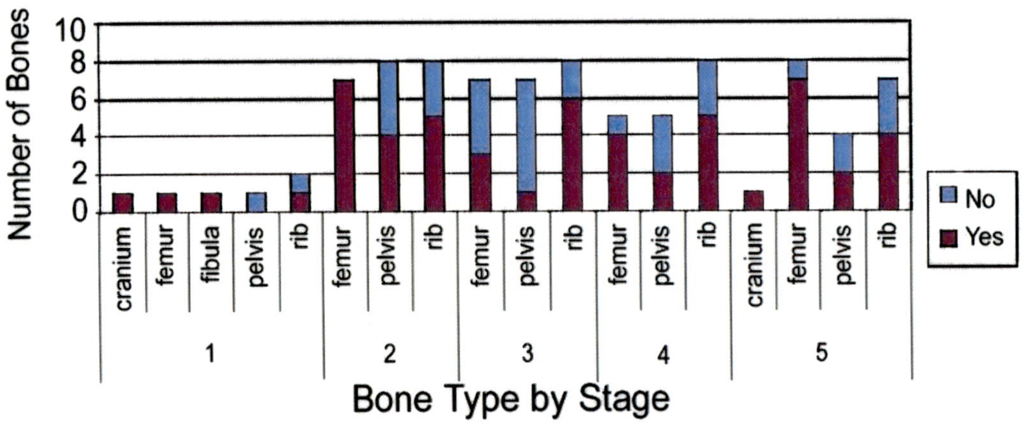

Graph depicting amplification success (yes) and failure (no) arranged by bone type within each of the five skeletal weathering stages.

Figure 17. Amplification results in comparison to skeletal weathering stage and bone type

Individual Bone Weathering Stage

Figure 18 shows amplification results based on the individual bone weathering criteria in which each bone was staged individually. Amplification success across the stages (without considering bone type) was similar, with the highest at stage two (71.4%, 25 out of 35) followed by stage four (63.6%, 7 out of 11), stage one (63.2%, 12 out of 19), and stage three (45.8%, 11 out of 24). Statistical analysis comparing all four weathering stages showed the variance in amplification success across the stages is not significantly different (p=0.269).

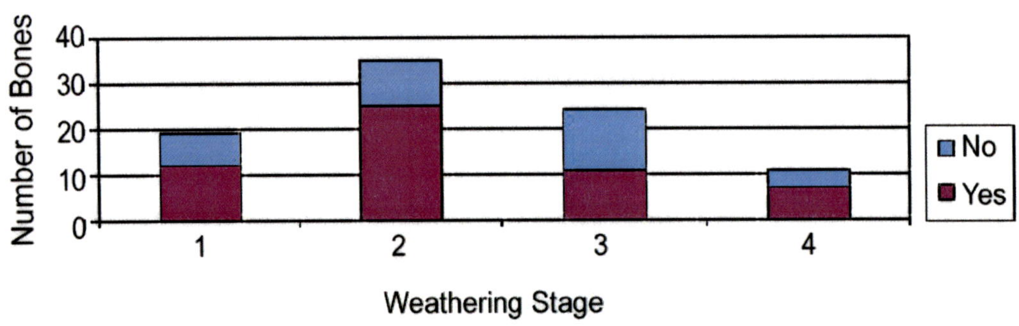

Graph depicting amplification success (yes) and failure (no) in relation to the four individual bone weathering stages.

Figure 18. Amplification results in comparison to individual bone weathering stage

It should be noted that as a consequence of reclassification, the sample sizes across the four weathering stages was not equal. Because of this unequal sampling, differences among the stages may be hard to uncover, particularly among the most weathered bones. Regardless, the data do not appear to follow a trend and indicate that individual bone weathering condition is not predictive of DNA quality.

Amplification results were broken down further to exa mine if individual bone weathering had any influence on maximum amplicon size. Figure 19 shows no apparent relationship between bone weathering stage and the maximum amplicon length

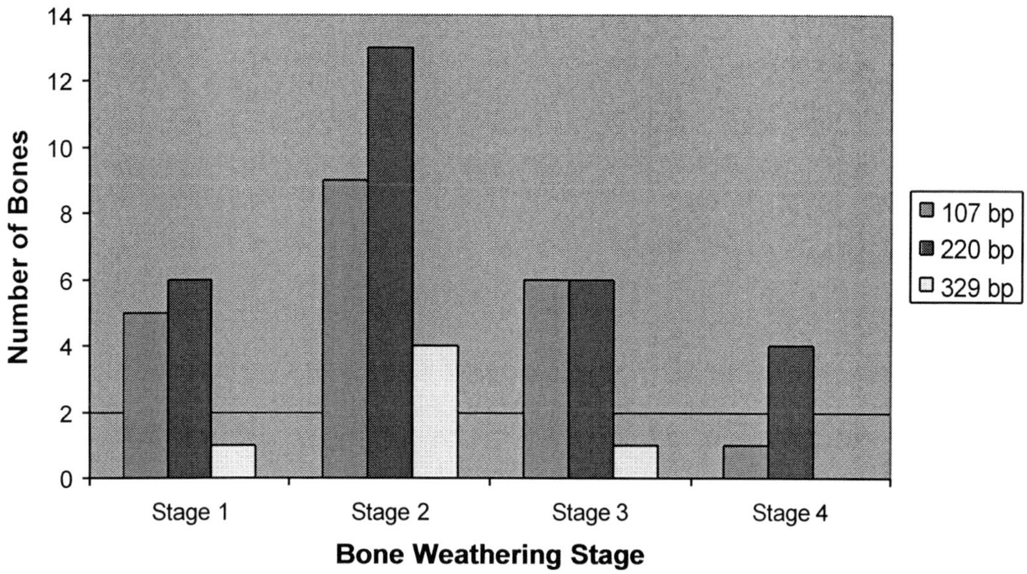

Figure 19. Maximum obtainable amplicon produced for each bone weathering stage

Amplification success of the different bone types varied across the four weathering stages (Figure 20), however the differences were not significant. For example, stage two femora had the highest amplification success at 90.9% (10 out of 11), followed by those at stage one at 76.9% (10 out of 13), and stage three at 50% (2 out of 4) ($p=0.213$). The pelvic samples showed a decrease in amplification success from stage one to stage three (as with femora, none of the pelvic samples were categorized as stage four) (66.7%, 2 out of 3; 46.2%, 6 out of 13; and 11.1%, 1 out of 9 for stages one, two, and three, respectively) ($p=0.130$). Rib samples had the highest amplification success at stage two (75%, 6 out of 8), followed by stage three (72.7%, 8 out of 11), stage four (63.6%, 7 out of 11), and stage one (0%, 0 out of 3) ($p=0.111$).

MtDNA Quality and Bone Type

The strongest influence on amplification success appeared to originate from bone type. The effect of bone type was analyzed on its own, showing a strong difference in amplification success among pelves, femora, and ribs. As shown in Figure 21, amplification occurred in the 2 crania samples (100%), 79.3% (23 out of 29) of the femur/fibula samples, 36% (9 out of 25) of the pelvis samples, and 63.6% (21 out of 33) of the rib samples.

Across bone types (excluding crania and fibula with their small sample sizes) there is strong statistical evidence ($p=0.006$) for a difference in amplification success, with the greatest difference between femora and pelves ($p=0.0009$), followed by ribs and pelves ($p=0.037$). There is no significant difference between ribs and femora ($p=0.181$).

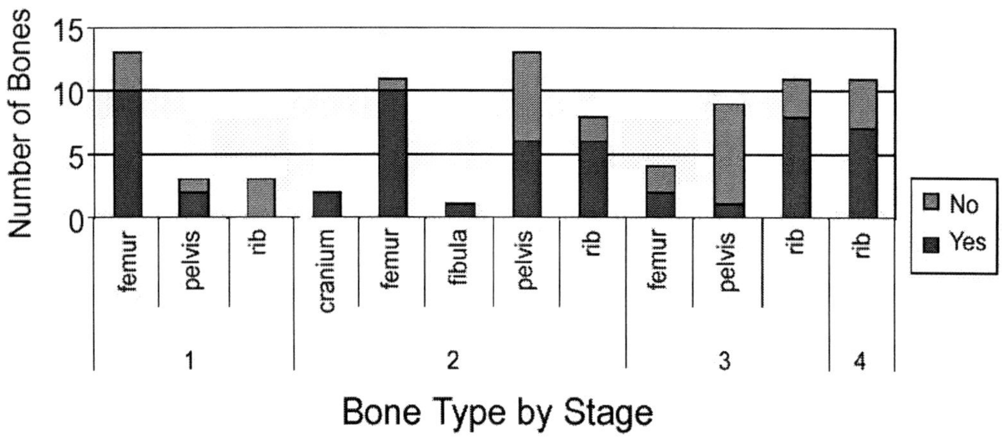

Graph depicting amplification success (yes) and failure (no) arranged by bone type within each of the four individual bone weathering stages.

Figure 20. Amplification results in comparison to individual bone weathering stage and bone type

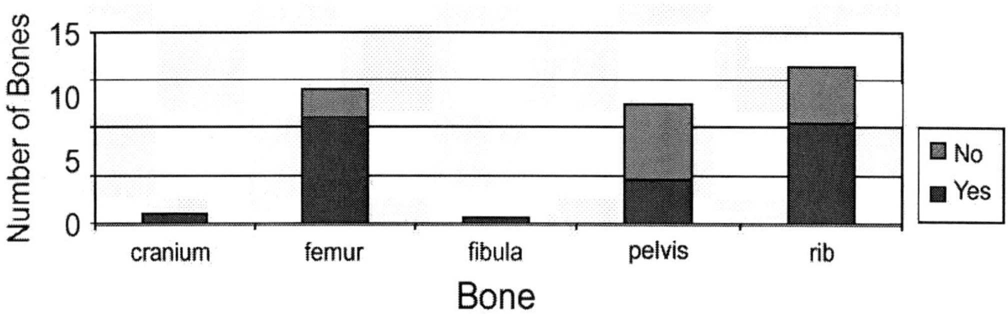

Graph depicting amplification success (yes) and failure (no) arranged by bone type.

Figure 21. Amplification results in comparison to bone type

In addition to amplification success for bones type, amplification was further broken down into largest amplicon size obtained for each bone type (Figure 22). Although femora had the overall highest amplification success rate, in many instances these were the smaller 107 bp amplicons. However, there is no significant difference between the maximum obtainable amplicon and bone type (p=0.44). Once again, crania and fibula were not included in the statistical analysis due to the small sample sizes.

Sex Estimates and mtDNA Quality

Amplification results are shown in Figure 23 by the four sex categories (female, male, "possible male", and undetermined). Amplification occurred in 57.1% (4 out of 7) of the undetermined individuals, 63.6% (7 out of 11) of the females, and 94.1% (16 out of 17) of the males. The one individual classified as "possibly male" (M?) also amplified. There was no significant difference in amplification success among the four categories (p=0.120). However, removing the undetermined individuals from the analysis revealed a significant difference in amplification success between males and females (p=0.041), with male samples amplifying more often. Adding the "possible male" to the male category dropped the p-value to 0.034.

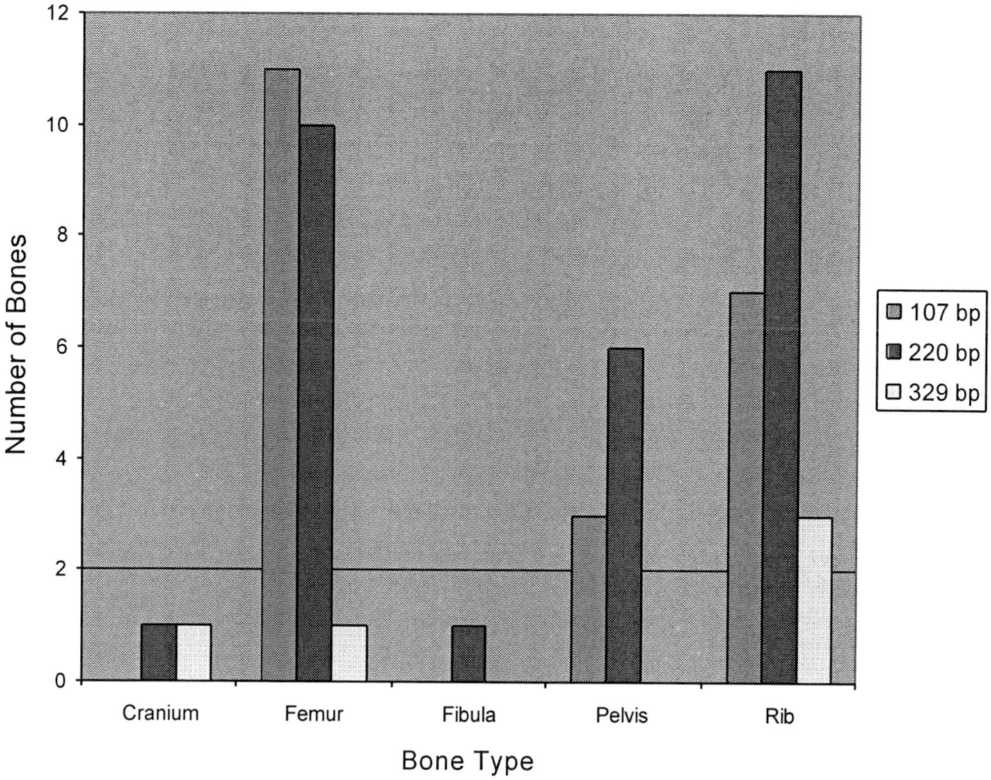

The largest amplicon size by bone is displayed. Note the far great number of femur, pelvis, and rib samples, which were the focus of this study.

Figure 22. Maximum obtainable amplicon in comparison to bone type

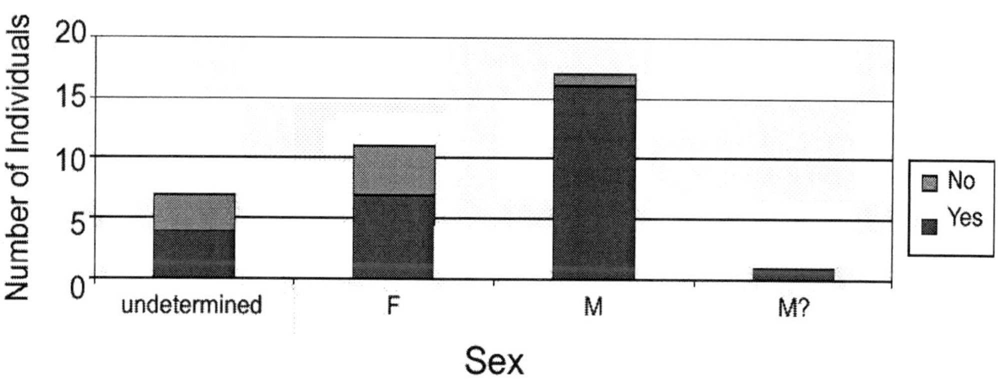

Graph depicting amplification success (yes) and failure (no) in relation to the anthropologically estimated sex of the individual. Four categories were used to describe the individuals sampled in this study: undetermined (sex of the individual could not be determined), female (F), male (M), and possible male (M?).

Figure 23. Amplification results in comparison to sex of the individual

Age at Death and DNA Quality

The effect of estimated age of the individual on amplification success is displayed in Figure 24. There was no significant difference in the amplification success across the five age categories (p=0.748). The amplification results of each age category are as follows: 6 out of 8 (75%) children, 2 out of 2 (100%) adolescents, 5 out of 5 (100%) young adults, 14 out of 19 (73.7%) adults, and 1 out of 1 (100%) older adult amplified. The age of one individual (from burial number 389) was not estimated at the time of recovery and therefore is not included in the statistical analysis.

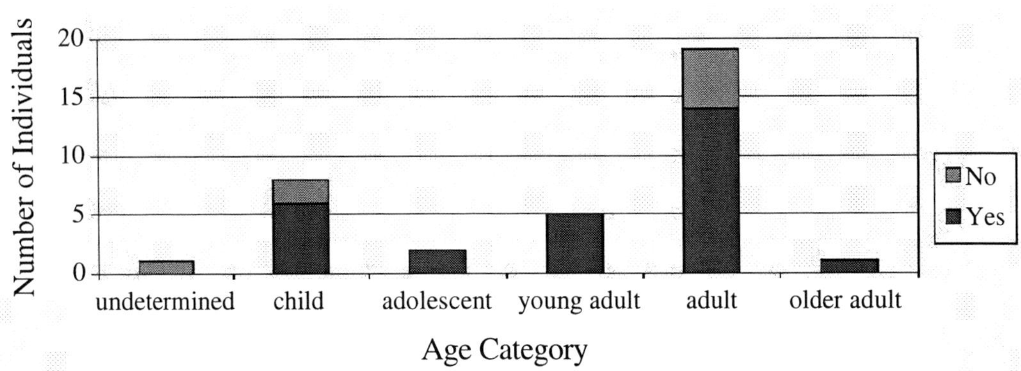

Graph depicts amplification success (yes) and failure (no) of each bone sampled in relation to the five age categories. The age of one individual was not estimated.

Figure 24. Amplification results in comparison to estimated age

The Relationship between DNA Quantity vs. DNA Quality

The ability/inability to amplify mtDNA (regardless of size) and DNA quantity from the Voegtly samples was examined. The mean quantity of mtDNA obtained from samples that were successfully amplified for sequencing was 114.9 copies/μl while the mean quantity from samples not amplified was 73.2 copies/μl. These did not differ statistically (p= 0.125) although this was likely due to the large variance in the quantitative data.

Voegtly Teeth Samples

Amplification and sequencing success was compared between the root and crown portions of tooth samples. Success rate using standard PCR was extremely low, thus a nested PCR procedure was used. When crown samples were amplified using semi-nested PCR, 30 out of the 31 were successfully amplified. Root samples showed the same results for amplification success, with 30 out of the 31 samples being amplified. For the crown samples, 26 of the thirty samples were successfully sequenced, while 24 out of 30 root samples could be sequenced. There was no relationship between skeletal weathering stage and tooth amplification success rates. It must be remembered that tooth appearance bore little relationship to overall skeletal appearance.

Albania Bone Samples

Bone Type and Amplification Success

Eight anthropologically sexed females, seven males, and one child whose sex could not be determined were analyzed. Among these 16 skeletons, DNA isolation was attempted from 62 different bones. These included 1 clavicle, 15 femora, 6 humeri, 11 petrous portions, 1 mandible, 1 metacarpal, 4 radii, 2 scapulae, 1 skull portion (nonpetrous), 5 tibiae, 13 teeth, and 2 ulnae. Femur samples were divided equally between females and males, the mandible belonged to a male skeleton, the metacarpal to a female skeleton, the radii were all from males, while the ulnae were from female skeletons.

A total of 52 bones (84%) produced DNA product that was successfully sequenced, while 10 (16%) did not. Of the 12 bone types, 6 produced sequences from all individuals, including clavicle, humerus, mandible, metacarpal, radius and scapula. The clavicle, mandible, metacarpal, radius, and scapula all had sample sizes of 4 or less. The femur, petrous, and tooth bones had sample sizes of 15, 11, and 13 respectively. The femur was next most successful at 87%; the petrous at 82% and the tibia at 80%. Seventy-eight percent of the teeth and 50% of the ulnae produced sequence, while the non-petrous skull portion resulted in none. Taking sample size into consideration, femora, petrous portions, and teeth were all bones that could reliably be amplified and sequenced.

Bone Integrity and Amplification Success

Albania bones were given an integrity rating based on appearance. Bones rated 3 produced the highest amplification rate; out of the 27 analyzed, 85% were successfully amplified and sequenced. This success was followed closely by a bone rating of 1 (84%), 2 (82%), and 4 (80%). However, the sample size of bones rated 4 was quite small with only five bones being analyzed. As with the Voegtly samples, there are no visible trends between the different bone integrity ratings and amplification/sequencing success.

Sex Estimates and Amplification Success

Sexual disparity between sequence production in HVI were investigated. Femur, humerus, petrous, tibia, and tooth were collected from both anthropologically estimated male and female skeletons. No trends were seen, in that femur and tibia both produced sequences slightly more often from female skeletons, while humerus and petrous produced sequence more often from males. Teeth produced similar results between the sexes.

Enhanced Techniques

Mini-STR Sets

The Mini-STR sets used for nuclear DNA analysis, both for CODIS loci obtained from NIST and the amelogenin primers designed in house, did not produce profiles for any loci tested (but see nested results below).

Nested PCR

Nested PCR of mtDNA was successful on the Voegtly tooth samples (see above). For nuclear DNA, 65 Voegtly samples that produced mtDNA results were analyzed using the newly designed primers for nested amelogenin amplification. Twelve produced an amelogenin profile. Likewise, 4 of 17 Albania bone samples produced profiles.

Two of the Voegtly bones that were successfully amplified using the amelogenin nested PCR technique were then tested with the Mini-STR sets. These samples were initially amplified for 40 cycles using the individual primer sets, along with mini A1, but no bands were present on a 2% agarose gel. Nested PCR was then attempted beginning with the Identifiler™ primer set followed by the Mini-STR sets. No amplification products were observed on a 2% gel. For more information on these experiments see Ramos, 2005.

Whole Genome Amplification

The 220 bp mtDNA amplification that was successfully cond ucted on Voegtly bones acted as the basis for assaying PCR following WGA. Five samples were tested (Table 15). Of the five I-PEP samples, one was successfully PCR amplified based on agarose gel electrophoresis. All PCR products following MDA WGA were unusable due to a high number of non-target bands on the gel. These results pointed to the general reduction in DNA size following WGA (see Discussion). For more information on these procedures see Barber, 2005.

Table 15. Amplification of mtDNA from whole genome amplified samples

Sample	No WGA*	I-PEP	MDA
27F	+	-	[+]
114F	+	-	[+]
349F	+	-	[+]
448F	+	-	[+]
704F	+	+	[+]

Treatment type is displayed on the top of each column. * indicates data were obtained from Misner (2004), + indicates successful amplification, - indicates amplification failure, [+] indicates sample amplification was successful, but multiple nonspecific bands were present.

Soil Analysis from the Voegtly Cemetery

The soil from all Voegtly burials were from the clay loam textural class, or were a combination of clay loam and sandy dry loam. The soil samples from the burials contained nearly equal amounts of sand, clay, and silt; specifically the soils were composed of approximately 30 – 40 % sand, 30 – 35% clay and 25 – 35% silt.

The soil collected from each burial was tested for levels of several inorganic and organic compounds, as well as soil pH (see Methods). Each soil element was compared to the weathering stage assigned by Ubelaker and Jones (2003). The only notable correlation between skeletal weathering and any of the factors tested was with the pH of the soil. In this case, skeletal weathering was more extensive at lower pHs, with an R2 value of 0.2064.

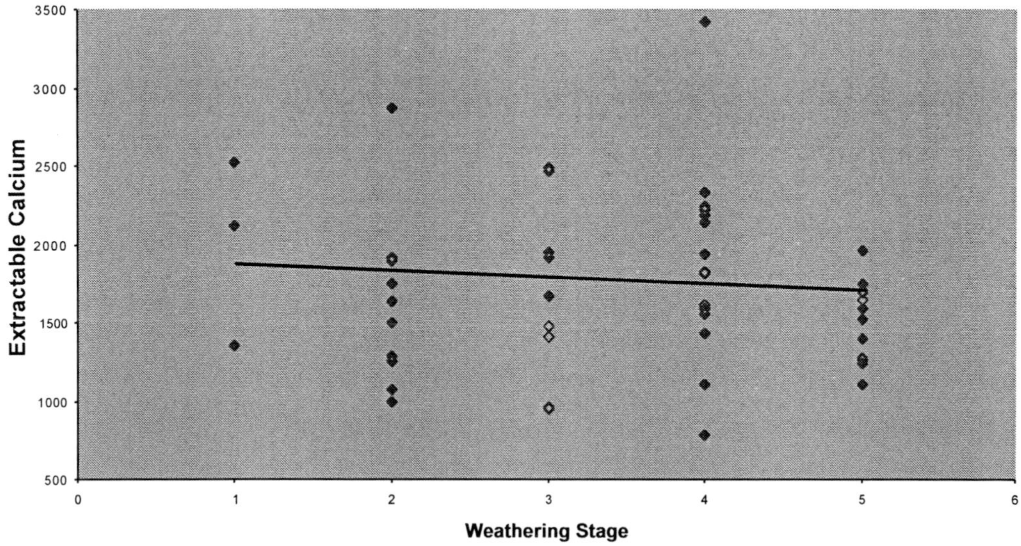

Graph depicting the relationship between skeletal weathering stage and the amount of calcium found in soil from the Voegtly burials. The two factors have an R2 value of 0.0108.

Figure 25. Skeletal weathering stage and the amount of extractable calcium from soil from Voegtly burials

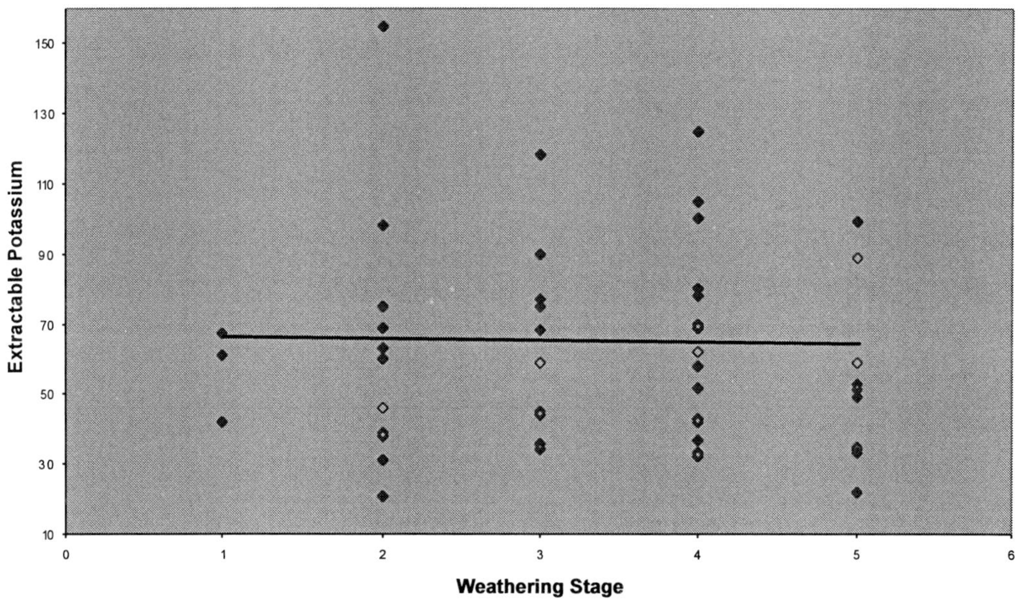

Graph depicting the relationship between skeletal weathering stage and the amount of potassium found in soil from the Voegtly burials. The two factors have an R2 value of 0.0007.

Figure 26. Skeletal weathering stage and the amount of extractable potassium from soil from Voegtly burials

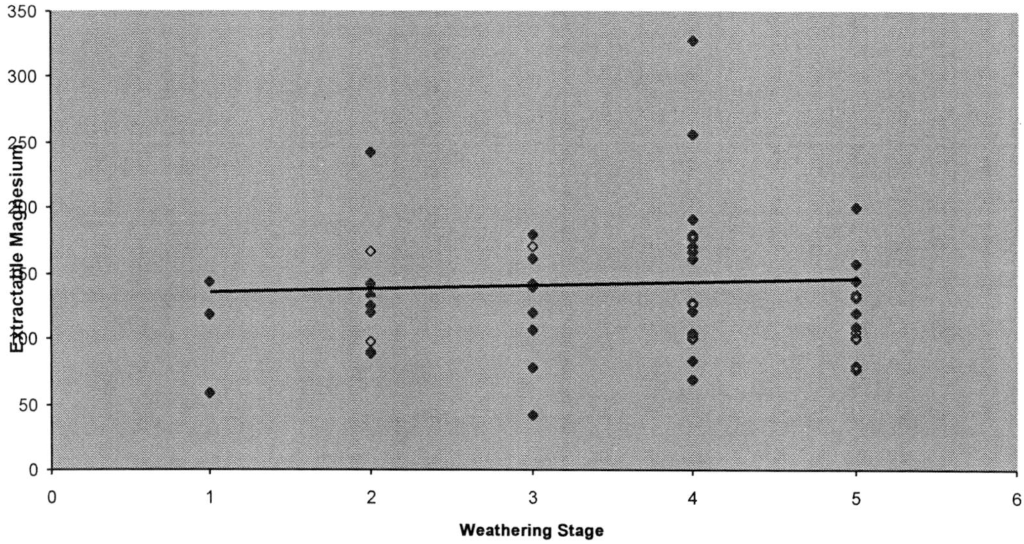

Graph depicting the relationship between skeletal weathering stage and the amount of magnesium found in soil from Voegtly burials. The two factors have an R2 value of 0.0033.

Figure 27. Skeletal weathering stage and the amount of extractable magnesium from soil from Voegtly burials

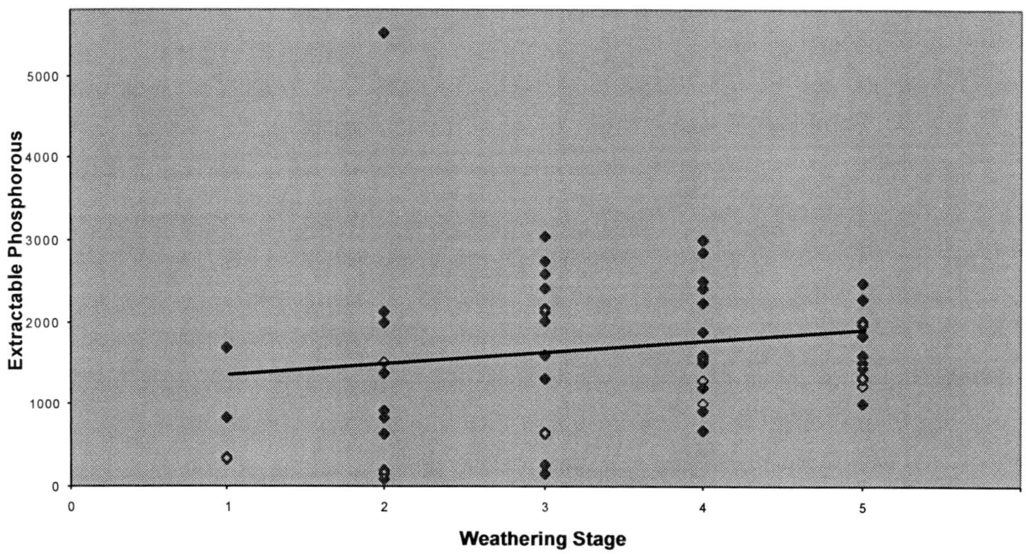

Graph depicting the relationship between skeletal weathering stage and the amount of phosphorus found in soil from Voegtly burials. The two factors have an R2 value of 0.0335.

Figure 28. Skeletal weathering stage and the amount of extractable phosphorus from soil from Voegtly burials

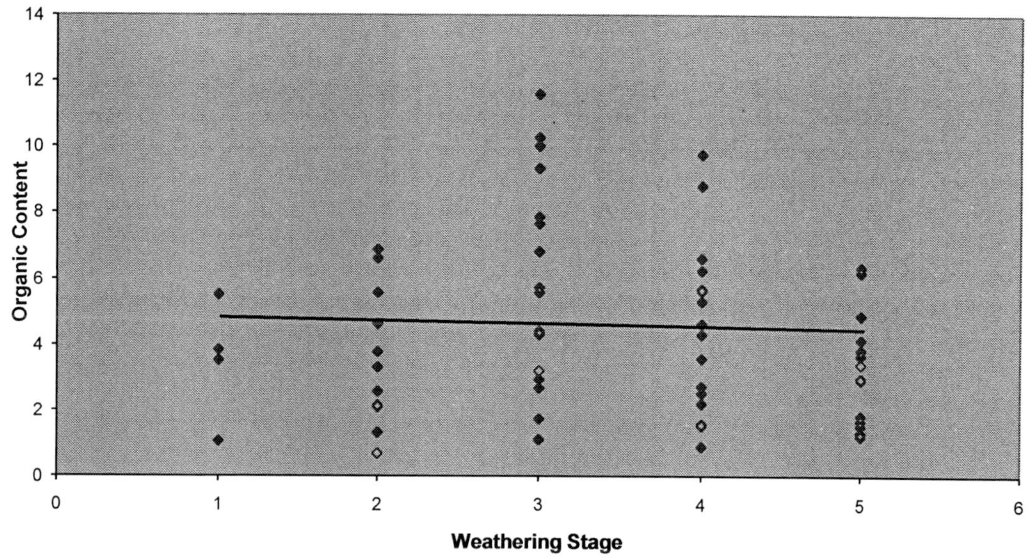

Graph depicting the relationship between skeletal weathering stage and the organic content found in soil from Voegtly burials. The two factors have an R2 value of 0.0018.

Figure 29. Skeletal weathering stage and the organic content from soil from Voegtly Burials

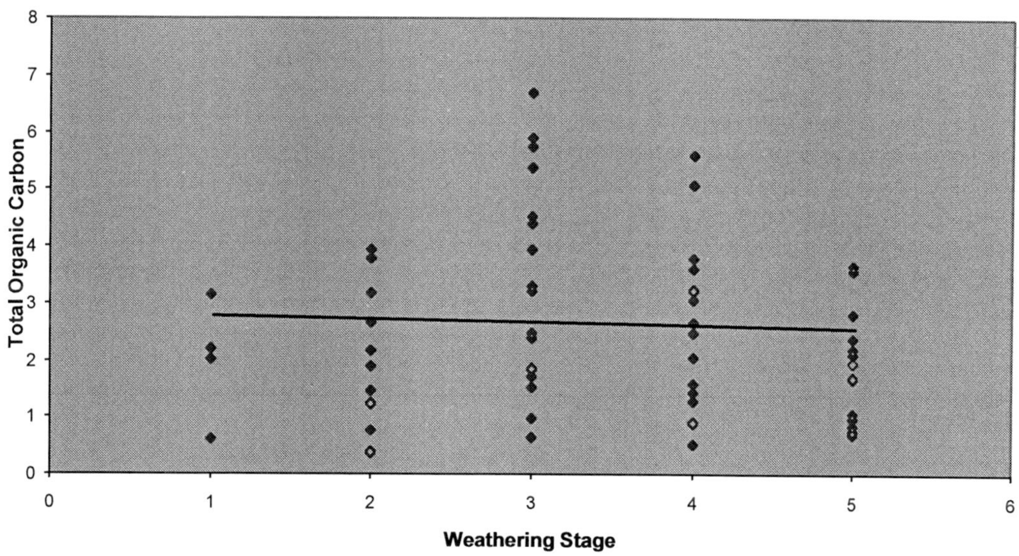

Graph depicting the relationship between skeletal weathe ring stage and the amount of organic carbon found in soil from Voegtly burials. The two factors have an R2 value of 0.0018.

Figure 30. Skeletal weathering stage and the amount of extractable organic carbon from soil from Voegtly burials

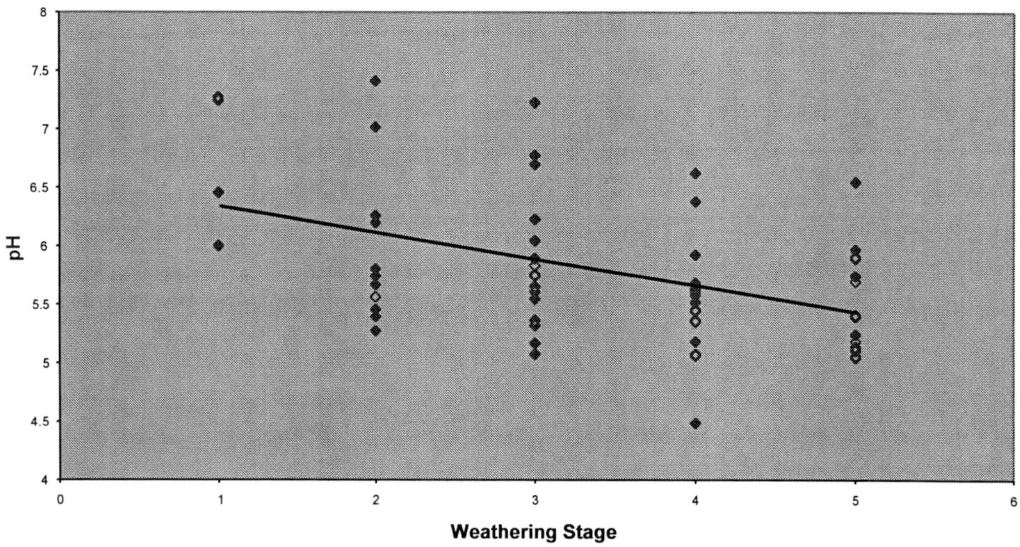

Graph depicting the relationship between skeletal weathering stage and the pH level of the soil from Voegtly burials. The two factors have an R2 value of 0.2064.

Figure 31. Skeletal weathering stage and pH level of soil from Voegtly burials

Discussion

The goal of this study was to determine if there is a relationship between the outward appearance of skeletal material (considering bone type and level of weathering) and the quantity and quality of the DNA within. Being able to predict the amount of obtainable DNA and its level of degradation has the potential to assist the forensic scientist in providing a more efficient and productive analysis of skeletal material. If the scientist can examine skeletal material visually and make a reasonable assessment of what sized fragment of DNA is likely to be successfully amplified, as well as how many PCR cycles may be required to generate analyzable product, both time and resources will be conserved. Likewise, if given an assortment of skeletal material, to know which is most likely to harbor analyzable DNA would also be useful. Further, if other variables, such as the anthropologically estimated age or sex of the remains have an influence on DNA results, these too would be worth knowing, as could being aware of soil characteristics from which the remains were recovered. Finally, if knowledge about skeletal remains can help predict when standard forensic DNA testing is likely to fail, while advanced techniques may prove successful, then identifications might be made that would otherwise be impossible.

The research detailed above ties together a large number of separate studies, perhaps eight in all, although even this number may expand with work being done on cellular features of the skeletal material. Key to this was having a standard set of skeletal remains to work with. In this regard the Voegtly Cemetery material was ideal: it provided a large number of skeletons from which different bones could be examined, that were located at a common site for a similar amount of time, thus removing environmental variables except at the micro-habitat level. Yet the Voegtly material displayed a remarkable variety of weathering, ranging from complete and rather sturdy skeletons to small bone fragments that could easily be crumbled by hand (indeed many burials in the Voegtly Church were never found). Access to such a large number of skeletons of common burial age and environment generated a robust dataset and a number of interesting findings.

Skeletal Weathering and DNA Quantity and Quality

First among these findings was the relationship between the weathering stage of a skeleton and the DNA found within. Intuitively one would expect good bone to yield good DNA, and highly degraded bone to little or no DNA. In contrast not only was such a relationship not found over the course of this research, the complete skeleton data point towards the opposite—more weathered samples generated more DNA ($p=0.036$). Likewise the most weathered skeletons had the highest PCR success rate (DNA quality), although these differences were not as strong as DNA quantity. In contrast, there was no correlation between skeletal weathering and the largest amplicon that could be generated, nor with the number of bones from an individual that produced amplifiable DNA.

The reason for the increase in DNA yield with increased skeletal weathering is not clear (and deserves further study) but several possibilities exist. The first is that DNA is simply easier to recover from degraded bone. There is little known on the cellular or sub-cellular level about how DNA, and particularly mtDNA, is stored or degrades in bone. A very reasonable hypothesis is that bone that is quick to crumble is also quick to release any DNA it contains, while bone that is firm will hold that DNA.

A second possibility is that whatever process acted to keep some bones from the Voegtly cemetery in relatively good shape (less weathered) was detrimental to DNA. Among the many chemicals that were tested from the soil, none were found to correlate greatly with skeletal preservation. Calcium levels were slightly higher among more preserved samples, although it does not seem likely that this would negatively impact DNA. Soil acidity did show a correlation with skeletal preservation, with more degraded remains found at lower pHs. Low pH is known to create nicks in DNA, however given the lowest ph found here (above 5) this may not have an influence on DNA while still affecting bone. In turn, at the higher pHs more conducive to bone preservations it is possible that microbial activity or other factors that degrade DNA could be more active. In that sense two related but different factors might be acting on the skeletons and their DNA, with low pH aiding in the degradation of bone, while more neutral pH allowing factors to degrade DNA.

The overall condition of a skeleton was the primary grading criterion used on the Voegtly remains, as it was conducted first by the anthropologists who characterized the remains. However, during the course of this study it became apparent that skeletal staging and the condition of an individual femur, rib, pelvis, etc., did not go hand-in-hand. This might be due to sampling bias, as workers at a site are likely to (and perhaps logically forced to) collect bones that are in the best condition. If all the ribs but one are in very poor shape and disintegrate upon handling, the single good rib will be collected, leading perhaps to a difference between skeletal staging and bone staging. (This should not affect forensic analyses tremendously, as the same would be true of any discovered remains, however it might bias the results obtained here.) Rarely in this study were individual restaged bones given the same classification as whole skeletons, and often different bones from a single skeleton did not fall into the same weathering category. In the long run this did not seem to matter ho wever; when the DNA yields results were compared to restaged bones, no significant correlation was seen. Further, there was no correlation between bone staging and the maximum amplicon size produced. Once again the appearance of a bone was not a good indicator of the DNA within.

The Influence of Bone Type

In contrast, the type of bone tested did seem to have an influence on both mtDNA quantity and DNA typing success. Amplification attempts among long bones, flat bones, and ribs, showed that long bones (femora and fibula) produced both the most DNA and the highest successful PCR rate (teeth are not considered here, as they required nested PCR for typing, a technique not widely used in crime labs currently and not directly comparable to the other bone preparations). These were followed by rib samples, and lastly by pelves. Pelves contained similar quantities of DNA as ribs, however their PCR success rate was much lower (36 vs. 64%). This PCR success differences among bone type was highly significant (p=0.006). Note that amplicon size was not influenced by bone type, in that femoral DNA often amplified at the smallest size class. Regardless, from these results it becomes clear that bone type is an important factor when considering samples to analyze.

Because bone type had a significant influence on successful mtDNA amplification as well as the amount of DNA present, it was interesting to note the correlation between the two of these. Indeed the average copy number for samples that amplified was 115 while for those that did not amplify it was 73 (this result was not significant due largely to the high level of variance in the quantitative data). However, there was no 'cutoff' for successful amplification; samples with the lowest copy number could be amplified, meaning that quantitative PCR results will likely not be a good indicator of downstream PCR success.

The Influence of Sex and Age at Death

Age of an individual at death did not seem to influence the quantity or quality of DNA recovered. One might expect that the very young, with poorly developed bones, would have increased bone/DNA degradation. This may be true, as few infant remains were recovered (see Introduction and History). Older individuals might also be expected to have poorer bone strength, but here again very few elderly individuals were recovered. Among other age groups no relationship was seen.

Sex did have an effect on DNA quality (though not quantity). While this result was significant, it should be viewed with come caution. The skeletal rema ins were often poorly preserved, and the pelvis, which is the best tool for sexing a skeleton, was frequently degraded. Sex was then estimated based on overall skeletal robusticity, a far weaker criterion. Also, a disproportionate number of estimated males was recovered. It is possible that this group of people, of southern German/Swiss descent, was particularly large, and that female skeletons were miscalled. It is also possible that males did preserve better, causing their bones to be recovered more often. However, experiments involving the amelogenin locus (see below) indicate some called male skeletons are likely female.

PCR Inhibition

Another factor that could readily influence both quantitative experiments and PCR amplification is inhibition. PCR inhibition was seen in several of the bone samples amplified for sequencing. In many instance it could be overcome with the addition of BSA or a commercial PCR enhancer, or through the use of a Microcon column. However, because standard PCR is not quantitative, it was impossible to tell if these positive samples still had some level of PCR inhibition, or if they were amplifying like pure DNA.

It then became of interest to understand how PCR inhibition might be influencing the results obtained. A series of eleven bone samples known to be inhibited from earlier experiments were tested using QPCR, with the addition of known amounts of the same DNA used for the quantitative standards (from 6 million to 60 copies as 10-fold dilution). If inhibition occurred in a 'standard way' (e.g., there was 20% inhibition) one would expect the spiked bone samples to all generate quantitative values approximately 20% lower than anticipated, with some correction for the bone DNA present. On the other hand, it is possible inhibitio n might be 'overcome' with the addition of large levels of DNA while having its greatest influence at the very dilute DNA levels expected in skeletal remains. The same experiment was then conducted in the presence of BSA or the enhancer, and the average percent inhibition for all eleven samples was determined for each quantity of spiked standard.

The results from these experiments were quite surprising (Figure 13). The samples without BSA or enhancer were inhibited at high levels at all spiked concentrations, from 79 – 96%. Addition of the enhancer did little to decrease inhibition, except at the most concentrated DNA level (6,000,000 copies added), where inhibition dropped to 41%. In contrast, BSA addition dramatically affected amplification, again most notable at the highest concentrations. At the two highest concentrations the quantification results were actually substantially higher than what was added, at 186% and 166%. At lower concentrations inhibition occurred and reached a level similar to untreated samples. The reason for this phenomenon is not directly apparent, and it is possible multiple phenomena are occurring. Certainly the samples are inhibited and this inhibition occurs regardless of spiked DNA quantity added. If addition of BSA simply binds up factors that would otherwise bind to and inhibit Taq, it seems it would work at all DNA concentrations, not only at the high concentrations seen in Figure 13.

In contrast, if an inhibitor binds to DNA it may be possible to out compete it with additional DNA. For instance, the hydroxyapatite found in bone binds DNA and could inhibit PCR. Adding thousands or hundreds of thousands of copies of target DNA could make numerous copies available for PCR. However, if this was solely the case, all samples with high amounts of DNA, not just those with BSA, should amplify. Thus, it seems as if a combination of factors are causing PCR inhibition in these samples, and that both BSA and high DNA quantity are required to overcome it. We are still left to wonder why the high DNA/BSA samples produced quantitative results surpassing the amount the samples were spiked with. Certainly the QPCR inhibition results open up new paths for research.

Other Skeletal Material Analyzed

The other skeletal samples utilized in this research, including teeth from the Voegtly Cemetery and skeletal materials from the Tumulus at Kamenica, Albania, were used to provide supporting information for the Voegtly burials. Teeth, generally molars, from the Voegtly graves did not follow the weathering scheme used for whole skeletons, as most were solid without caries. These were divided into root and crown to test if there were differences in PCR results between the two. It was not possible to obtain PCR products from these samples without using nested PCR, making them difficult to compare to the other skeletal remains discussed above, where this procedure was not used. No difference was found between root and crown amplification success.

The Albania tumulus bones were far older than the Voegtly material (2500 – 3000 year old vs. ca 150 years old). While many of the skeletons appeared to be in excellent condition (Figure 3), most of the bones fell apart during collection. In many instances pelves of the Albania skeletons had disintegrated, meaning this bone could not be compared to the Voegtly results. However, long bones and teeth were collected, as was the petrous portion of the temporal bone, the hardest bone in the human skeleton. Each of these bone types produced DNA results at a frequency similar to their counterparts in the Voegtly Cemetery. For instance, femora from Voegtly successfully produced PCR product 79% of the time, while the Albania samples resulted in product 87% of the time. The one important bone that was impossible to compare was the petrous, as these were not collected from the Voegtly remains. For the Albania samples the petrous led to PCR product 82% of the time, and should be considered when skeletal remains undergo DNA testing. The disadvantage of the petrous is that it is located on the inside of the skull and for practical purposes is impossible to reach if the skull is not open. Obviously in a forensic case it would be undesirable to damage an intact skull. On the other hand if skull sections are one of or the only bones available, the petrous may be the best target available. It would be interesting to conduct a complete study on skull bones and DNA typing success.

Enhanced Techniques

Three enhanced techniques were conducted during the study of the Voegtly material. While these were not part of the original proposal, because the Voegtly bones already had DNA extracted it seemed worthwhile to examine the effectiveness of each method on DNA know to be in limited quantity and/or degraded. The first of these, using nuclear DNA primer pairs that reduced amplicon size (both the Mini-STRs from NIST and amelogenin primers designed in house), had little effect on amplification success. Naturally this may simply have been due to a lack of DNA. When the amelogenin primers were used in nested experiments, with the first round of amplification producing amplicons just over 100 bp and the second round producing products approximately 70 bp, over 20% of the ancient remains produced a profile, showing the potential of this technique. However, when an Identifiler™ kit was used in combination with the NIST Mini-STRs, no products were produced. This is most likely due to the larger starting size of the Identifiler™ amplicons.

Finally, two methods of WGA were tested on the Voegtly samples. This work was part of a larger study on WGA, thus only a small sample of bones was tested. The findings, which are concordant with other degraded samples we have tested, is that WGA is not a functional technique when DNA is highly fragmented. This finding makes sense in that all methods of WGA will inherently shorten DNA as it is amplified, as the primers are unlikely to sit at the very end of the fragment they will replicate. Therefore, with each round of WGA the targets will become shorter and shorter. For instance, if a target strand of DNA is 400 bp in length, a primer may anneal at any point in the sequence. While some products may be larger and some may be smaller, the average amplified DNA will be approximately 200 bp. This 200 bp product will likely be shortened in the next round, etc. Methods of WGA will plainly need to be redesigned if they are to be used on degraded DNA.

Conclusions and Recommendations

The research presented here leads to a number of conclusions. 1) The overall appearance (level of weathering) of a skeleton is not likely to be useful in estimating if DNA testing will be possible. Likewise, the appearance of an individual bone does not make a worthwhile metric for subsequent DNA testing success. In this sense attempting DNA typing on skeletons/bones that appear to be in very poor shape may be prudent. 2) Bone type can offer substantial guidance as to the likelihood of successfully obtaining analyzable DNA. Long bone, teeth, and petrous portions, and to a lesser extent ribs, make good targets, while spongy bone does not. 3) DNA quantity, while related to PCR results, cannot act as a hard and fast assay for downstream PCR success; bones with the lowest level of DNA were capable of generating results. 4) DNA quality does not relate to bone/skeletal appearance; mtDNA at all stages was generally degraded down to sizes of about 200 bp. Attempts to produce amplicons larger than this were rarely successful, and if the forensic scientist is attempting to amplify larger regions, consideration should be given to assaying smaller segments of DNA. 5) Nested PCR can be a powerful tool when dealing with samples that contain very little DNA. Naturally, extreme caution needs to be used given the sensitivity of the technique, with appropriate blanks and nega tive controls run each time, and results replicated at a separate time. However it was only with this technique that we were able to obtain results from a number of samples.

ACKNOWLEDGEMENTS

This project was supported under award 2002-IJ-CX-K016 from the National Institute of Justice. Points of view in the document are those of the authors and do not necessarily represent the official view of the U.S. Department of Justice. We would like to gratefully acknowledge the Office of the Vice President for Research and Graduate Studies, the Graduate School, and the School of Criminal Justice at Michigan State University for support. We would also like to gratefully acknowledge collaborators Dr. Doug Ubelaker of The Smithsonian Institution and Dr. Todd Fenton from Michigan State University. The study involved the joint effort of the following individuals: Dr. David Foran, PI, Dr. Doug Ubelaker (The Smithsonian Institution), Dr. Todd Fenton (Michigan State University, Department of Anthropology), Lisa Misner, Andrea Halvorson, Virginia Clemmer, Lisa Ramos, Amy Barber, Rebecca Elk, Timothy Lange, Michael Mutolo, and Melissa Meyers (Forensic Science Graduate Program, Michigan State University).

BIBLIOGRAPHY

ABI 7700 Sequence Detector (TaqMan). *<http://ukl.uni-freiburg.de/core-facility/taqman/taqindex.html>* Accessed 2004 July 14.

ABI Sequence Detection System. 2001. *User Bulletin* #2.

Allard, M.W., K. Miller, M. Wilson, K. Monson, and Budowle B. 2002. Characterization of the Caucasian Haplogroups Present in the SWGDAM Forensic mtDNA Dataset for 1771 Human Control Region Sequences. *Journal of Forensic Sciences.* 47(6):1 – 9.

Alonso, A., P. Martin, C. Albarran, P. Garcia, O. Garcia, L. Fernandez de Simon, J. Garcia-Hirchfeld, M. Sancho, C. de la Rua, and J. Fernandez-Piqueras. 2004. Real-Time PCR designs to estimate nuclear and mitochondrial DNA copy number in forensic and ancient DNA studies. *Forensic Science International*. 139:141 – 149.

Amersham Biosciences. 2003 – 2004.*GenomiPhi DNA Amplification Kit: More from Less*. [Brochure].

Anderson, S., A.T. Bankier, B.G. Barrell, M.H.L. deBruijn, A.R. Coulson, J. Drouin, I.C. Eperon, D.P. Nierlich, B.A. Rose, F. Sanger, R.H. Schreier, A.J.H. Smith, R. Staden, and I.G. Young. 1981. Sequence and organization of the human mitochondrial genome. *Nature*. 290:457 – 465.

Andreasson, H. and M. Allen. 2003. Rapid Quantification and Sex Determination of Forensic Evidence Materials. *Journal of Forensic Science*. 48(6):1 – 8.

Applied Biosystems Corporation. 2003. GeneMapper™ ID Software Version 3.1 *Human Identification Analysis user's manual*. Foster City, CA.

Applied Biosystems Corporation. 2001. *AmpFlSTR® Identifiler™ user's manual*. Foster City, CA.

Applied Biosystems 2002. *TaqMan® Universal PCR Master Mix Protocol*.

Arismendi, J.L., L.E. Baker, and K.J. Matteson. 2004. Effects of processing techniques on the forensic DNA analysis of human skeletal remains. *Journal of Forensic Sciences*. 49(5): 1 – 5.

Armed Forces DNA Identification Laboratory. Armed Forces Institute of Pathology. 2005. *<http://www.afip.org/Departments/oafme/dna/>* Accessed 2005.

Barber, A.L. 2005. *The Utility of Whole Genome Amplification in Forensic DNA Analysis* (MS – thesis). East Lansing, MI: Michigan State University.

Bartram S., S. Halliday, R. Ptak, T. Fletcher III, R. Buckheit Jr., and A. Serquest. 2003. *High Throughput Screening of the Effects of Anti-Cancer Agents on Expression of Cancer Related Genes in Numerous Cell Lines*. Southern Research Institute.

Barker, D.L., M.S.T. Hansen, A.F. Faruqi, D. Giannola, O.R. Irsula, R.S. Lasken, M.Latterich, V. Makarov, A. Oliphant, J.H. Pinter, R. Shen, I. Sleptsova, W. Ziehler,and E. Lai. 2004. Two Methods of Whole-Genome Amplification Enable Accurate Genotyping Across a 2320-SP Linkage Panel. *Genome Research*. 14(5):901 – 907.

Bass, W. 1995. *Human Osteology: a laboratory and field manual*. 4th Edition. Columbia: Missouri Archaeological Society.

Behrensmeyer, A.K. 1978. Taphonomic and Ecologic Information from Bone Weathering. *Paleobiology*. 4(2):150 – 162.

Bejko, L. 1999-2000. Mortuary customs in the late bronze age of south-eastern Albania. *Iliria*. 29(1 – 2): 155 – 181.

Bejko, L. 1994. Some problems of the Middle and Late Bronze Age in southern Albania. *Bulletin of the Institute of Archeology*. 31:105 – 126.

Bell, L., M. Skinner, and S. Jones. 1996. The speed and of post mortem change to the human skeleton and its taphonomic significance. *Forensic Science International*. 82:129 – 140.

Blanco, L., A. Bernad, J.M. Lázaro, G. Marin, C. Garmendia, and M. Salas. 1989. Highly efficient DNA synthesis by the phage phi 29 DNA polymerase. Symmetrical mode of DNA replication. *Journal of Biological Chemistry*. 264(15):8935 – 8940.

Boles, T., C. Snow, and E. Stover. 1995. Forensic DNA testing of skeletal remains from mass graves: A pilot study in Guatemala. *Journal of Forensic Sciences*. 40:349 – 355.

Buikstra, J.E. and D.H. Ubelaker, editors, 1994. Standards for Data Collection from Human Skeletal Remains, *Proceedings of a Seminar at The Field Museum of Natural History*.

Arkansas Archeological Survey Research Series No. 44. Fayetteville: Arkansas Archeological Survey.

Butler JM. 2001. *Forensic DNA Typing: biology and technology behind STR markers.* London: Academic Press.

Butler, JM., Y. Shen, and B.R. McCord. 2003. The development of reduced size STR amplicons as tools for the analysis of degraded DNA. *Journal of Forensic Sciences.* 48(5): 1054 – 64.

Byers. S.N. 2001. *Introduction to Forensic Anthropology: a textbook.* Boston: Pearson Allyn and Bacon.

Cheung, V.G., and S.F. Nelson. 1996. Whole genome amplification using a degenerate oligonucleotide primer allows hundreds of genotypes to be performed on less than one nanogram of genomic DNA. *Proceedings of the National Academy of Science USA.* 93(25):14676 – 14679.

Christophersen, A.G., H. Jun, K. Jørgensen, and L.H. Skibsted. 1991. Photobleaching of astaxanthin and canthaxanthin: quantum-yields dependence of solvent, temperature, and wavelength of irradiation in relation to packaging and storage of carotenoid pigmented salmonoids. *Z. Lebensm. Unters. Forsch.* 192: 433 – 439.

Chung , D.T., J. Drábek, K.L. Opel, J.M. Butler, and B.R. McCord. 2004. A study on the effects of degradation and template concentration on the amplification efficiency of the STR miniplex primer sets. *Journal of Forensic Science.* 49(4): 1 – 8.

Clayton T.M., S.M. Hill, L.A. Denton, S.K. Watson and A. Urquhart. 2004. Primer binding site mutations affecting the typing of STR loci contained within the AMPFlSTR((R)) SGM plus (TM) kit. *Forensic Science International.* 139 (2 – 3): 255 – 259.

Clemmer, V. 2005. *Maternal Relatedness Within Double Burials of an Ancient Albanian Tumulus* (MS – thesis). East Lansing, MI: Michigan State University.

Cline, R.E., N.M. Laurent and D.R. Foran. 2003. The fingernails of Mary Sullivan: developing reliable methods for selectively isolating endogenous and exogenous DNA from evidence. *Journal of Forensic Sciences.* 48(2): 1 – 6.

Collins, M.J., C.M. Nielsen-Marsh, J. Hiller, C.I. Smith, J.P. Roberts, R.V. Prigodich, T.J. Wess, J. Csapo, A.R. Millard, and G. Turner-Walker. 2002. The survival of organic matter in bone: A review. *Archaeometry.* 44(3): 383 – 394.

Dean, F.B, S. Hosono, L. Fang, X. Wu, A.F. Faruqi, P. Bray-Ward, Z. Sun, Q. Zong, Y. Du, J. Du, , M. Driscoll, W. Song, S.F. Kingsmore, M. Egholm, and R.S. Lasken. 2002. Comprehensive human genome amplification using multiple displacement amplification. *Proceedings of the National Academy of Science U S A.* 99(8):5261 – 5266.

Dietmaier. W., A. Hartmann, S. Wallinger, E. Heinmoller, T. Kerner, E. Endl, K.W. Jauch, F. Hofstadter, and J. Ruschoff. 1999. Multiple mutation analyses in single tumor cells with improved whole genome amplification. *American Journal of Pathology.*154(1):83 – 95.

Dorak, M. 2004. Real-Time PCR. *<http://dorakmt.tripod.com/genetics/realtime.html>* Accessed 2004 July 4.

Dyes and Fluorescence Detection Chemistry in qPCR. *<http://dyes.gene-quantification.info/>* Accessed 2004 November 21.

Eng, B., P. Ainsworth, and J.S. Waye. 1994. Anomalous Migration of PCR Products Using Nondenaturing Polyacrylamide Gel Electrophoresis: The Amelogenin Sex Typing System. *Journal of Forensic Sciences.* 39(6): 1356 – 1359

Esteban, J.A., M. Salas, and L. Blanco. 1993. Fidelity of phi 29 DNA polymerase.Comparison between protein-primed initiation and DNA polymerization. *Journal of Biological Chemistry*. 268(4):2719 – 2726.

Garmendia, C., A. Bernad, J.A. Esteban, L. Blanco, and M. Salas. 1992. The bacteriophage phi 29 DNA polymerase, a proofreading enzyme. *Journal of Biological Chemistry*. 267(4):2594 – 2599.

Gaytmenn, R. and D. Sweet. 2003. Quantification of Forensic DNA from Various Regions of Human Teeth. *Journal of Forensic Sciences*. 48(3): 622 – 625.

Gehring, M.E. 2004. *The recovery and analysis of mitochondrial DNA from exploded pipe bombs* (MS – thesis). East Lansing, MI: Michigan State University.

Geigl, E.M. 2002. On the circumstances surrounding the preservation and analysis of very old DNA. *Archaeometry*. 44(3): 337 – 342.

Gilbert, M.T., A.J. Hansen, E. Willerslev, L. Rudbeck, I. Barnes, N. Lynnerup, and A. Cooper. 2003. Characterization of genetic miscoding lesions caused by postmortem damage. *American Journal of Human Genetics*. 72(1):48 – 61.

Gilbert, M.T., E. Willerslev, A.J. Hansen, I. Barnes, L. Rudbeck, N. Lynnerup, and A. Cooper. 2003. Distribution patterns of Postmortem Damage in Human Mitochondrial DNA. *American Journal of Human Genetics*. 72: 32 – 47.

Gotherstrom, A., M.J. Collins, A. Angerbjorn, and K. Liden. 2002. Bone preservation and DNA amplification. *Archaeometry*. 44(3):395 – 404.

Graffy, E.A. 2003. *Development and Validation of an Alkaline Extraction Method for Isolating Mitochondrial DNA from Human Hair Shafts* (MS – thesis). East Lansing, MI: Michigan State University.

Grant, S.F., S. Steinlicht, U. Nentwich, R. Kern, B. Burwinkel, and R. Tolle. 2002. SNP genotyping on a genome-wide amplified DOP-PCR template. *Nucleic Acids Research*. 30(22):e125.

Haas – Rocholz, H. and G. Weiler. 1997. Additional primer sets for an amelogenin gene PCR-based DNA-sex test. *International Journal of Legal Medicine*. 110: 312 – 315.

Hagelberg, E., I.C. Gray, and A.F. Jeffreys. 1991. Identification of the skeletal remains of a murder victim by DNA analysis. *Nature*. 352:427 – 429.

Haglund, W., and M. Song. 1997. *Forensic Taphonomy: The Postmortem Fate of Human Remains*. Boca Raton: CRC.

Hall, T.A. BioEdit: a user-friendly biological sequence alignment editor and analysis program for Windows 95/98/NT. *Nucl. Acids. Symp.*. 41:95 – 98.

Hall, T. 2004. BioEdit sequence alignment editor for Windows 95/98/NT/2K/XP. Homepage. *<http://www.mbio.ncsu.edu/BioEdit/bioedit.html>* Accessed 2004 July 13.

Halvorson, A. 2005. *Quantification of Mitochondrial DNA from Aged Skeletal Material* (MS – thesis). East Lansing, MI: Michigan State University.

Hedges, R.E.M. 2002. Bone diagenesis: an overview of processes. *Archaeometry*. 44(3): 319 – 328.

Hofreiter, M., V. Jaenicke, D. Serre, Av. A. Haeseler, and S. Paabo. 2001. DNA sequences from multiple amplifications reveal artifacts induced by cytosine deamination in ancient DNA. *Nucleic Acids Research*. 23:4793 – 4799.

Holland, M.M. and T.J. Parsons. 1999. Mitochondrial DNA sequence analysis— validation and use for forensic casework. *Forensic Science Review*. 11: 22 – 49.

Holland, M.M., C.A. Cave, C.A. Holland, and T.W. Bille. 2003. Development of a quality, high throughput DNA analysis procedure for skeletal samples to assist with the identification of victims from the World Trade Center attacks. *Croation Medical Journal.* 44(3):264 - 272.

Hosono, S., A.F. Faruqi, F.B. Dean, Y. Du, Z. Sun, X. Wu, J. Du, S.F. Kingsmore, M. Egholm, and R.S.Lasken. 2003. Unbiased whole-genome amplification directly from clinical samples. *Genome Res.* 13(5):954 – 964. Epub 2003 Apr 14.

Höss, M., P. Jaruga, T.H. Zastawny, M. Dizdaroglu, and S. Pääbo. 1996. DNA damage and DNA sequence retrieval from ancient tissues. *Nucleic Acids Research.* 24(7): 1304 – 1307.

Kalmar, T., C.Z. Bachrati, A. Marcsik, and I. Rasko. 2000. A simple and efficient method for PCR amplificable DNA extraction from ancient bones. *Nucleic Acid Research.* 28(12):e67.

Kelman, Z., and L. Moran.1996. Degradation of ancient DNA. *Current Biology.* 6(3): 223.

Kimpton, C., P. Gill, A. Walton, A. Urquhart, E. Milican, and M. Adams. 1993. Automated DNA Profiling Employing Multiplex Amplification of Short Tandem Repeat Loci. PC*R Methods and Applications.* 3: 13 – 22.

Klein, D. 2002. Quantification using real-time PCR technology: applications and limitations. *Trends in Molecular Medicine.* 8(6)257 – 260.

Kuivaniemi, H., S. Yoon, H. Shibamura, M. Skunca, S. Vongpunsawad, and G. Tromp. 2002. Primer-extension preamplified DNA is a reliable template for genotyping. *Clinical Chemistry.* 48(9):1601 – 1604.

Langmore, J.P. 2002. Rubicon Genomics, Inc. *Pharmacogenomics.* 3(4):557 – 560.

Lasken, R.S., and M. Egholm. 2003. Whole genome amplification: abundant supplies of DNA from precious samples or clinical specimens. *Trends in Biotechnology.* 21(12):531 – 525.

Latham, K. 2003. Using amplification of bacteriophage lambda DNA to detect PCR inhibitors in skeletal DNA. *Proceedings of the American Academy of Forensic Sciences.* 9:264.

Lightcycler Principles. Principles and Applications: Parameter-specific Applications for the LightCycler® System. *<http://www.roche-applied-science.com/lightcycler online/lc_ principles>* Accessed 2004 July 4.

Macaulay, V., M. Richards, E. Hickey, E. Vega, F. Cruciani, and V. Guida. 1999. The emerging tree of West Eurasian mtDNAs: a synthesis of control region sequences and RFLPs. *American Journal of Human Genetics.* 64:232 – 249.

Martell, M., J. Gomez, J. Esteban, S. Sauleda, J. Quer, B. Cabot, R. Esteban, and J. Guardia J. 1999. High-Throughput Real-Time Reverse Transcription-PCR Quantification of Hepatitis C Virus RNA. *Journal of Clinical Microbiology.* 37(2):327 – 332.

McCutchen, L. 2003 Fall. Biology 2401: Human anatomy and physiology. Homepage. *<http://blc1.kilgore.cc.tx.us/kcap1/practical_2_photos.htm>* Accessed 2004 July

Micozzi, M. 1991. *Postmortem changes in human and animal remains: A systematic approach.* Springfield: Charles C. Thomas.

Misner, L.M. 2004. *Predicting mtDNA quality based on bone weathering and type (MS - thesis).* East Lansing, MI: Michigan State University.

MITOMAP: A Human Mitocho ndrial Genome Database. 2005. *<http://www.mitomap.org>* Accessed 2005.

Molecular Probes: invitrogen detection technologies. Schematic representation of real time PCR with Scorpion primers. 2002. <*http://www.probes.com/handbook/figures/0711.html*> Accessed 2004 July 5.

Monson, K.L., K.W.P. Miller, M.R. Wilson, J.A. DiZinno, and B. Budowle. 2002. The mtDNA population database: an integrated software database resource for forensic comparison. *Forensic Science Communications*. 4(2). <*http://www.fbi.gov/hq/lab/fsc/backissu/april2002/miller1.htm*> Accessed 2004 August 12.

Nakahori, Y., O. Takenaka, and Y. Nakagome. 1991. A human X-Y homologous region encodes "amelogenin". *Genomics*. 9(2):264 – 269.

Nicholls, H. 2005. Ancient DNA comes of age. *PLoS Biology*. 3(2): 192 – 196.

O'Rourke, D.H., G. Hayes, and S.W. Carlyle. 2000. Ancient DNA Studies in Physical Anthropology. *Annual Review of Anthropology*. 29:217 – 242.

Ott, R., and M. Longnecker. 2001. *An Introduction to Statistical Methods and Data Analysis*. 5th Ed. Pacific Grove, CA: Duxbury Thomson Learning.

Pääbo, S., R.G. Higuchi, and A.C. Wilson. 1989. Ancient DNA and the polymerase chain reaction: The emerging field of molecular archaeology. *Journal of Biological Chemistry*. 264: 9709 – 9712.

Paez, J.G., M. Lin, R. Beroukhim, J.C. Lee, X. Zhao, D.J. Richter, S. Gabriel, P. Herman, H. Sasaki, D. Altshuler, C. Li, M. Meyerson, and W.R. Sellers. 2004. Genomecoverage and sequence fidelity of phi29 polymerase-based multiple strand displacement whole genome amplification. *Nucleic Acids Research*. 32(9):e71.

Parsons, T.J. and V.W. Weedn. 1997. Preservation and recovery of DNA in postmortem specimens and trace samples. In *Forensic taphonomy: the postmortem fate of human remains*, ed. W.D. Haglund and M.H Sorg. Boca Raton: CRC.

Powledge, T. Breakthroughs in Science. The Polymerase Chain Reaction. <*http://www.faseb.org/opar/bloodsupply/pcr.html*> Accessed 2004 November 21.

Primorac, D., S. Andelinovic, M. Definis-Gojanovic, I. Drmic, B. Rezic, M.M. Baden, M.A. Kennedy, M.S. Schanfield, S.B. Skakel, and H.C. Lee. 1996. Identification of war victims from mass graves in Croatia, Bosnia, and Herzegovina by the use of standard forensic methods and DNA testing. *Journal of Forensic Sciences*. 41: 891 – 894.

Prince, J. 2004. Optimization of PCR Markers for the Detection and Study of Eutypa Infections in Grapevine. *CSU Agricultural Research Initiative (ARI) Final Report*.

Public Health Research Institute. Introduction to Molecular Beacons. <*http://www.molecular-beacons.org*> Accessed 2004 July 5.

Ramos, L.M. 2005. *The Use of Enhanced PCR Techniques for Nuclear DNA Analysis of Compromised Forensic Samples* (MS – thesis) [In Prep]. East Lansing, MI: Michigan State University.

Real-time PCR Goes Prime Time. Ambion TechNotes 8:1. <*http://www.ambion.com/techlib/tn/81/813.html*> Accessed 2004 July 7.

Rennick, S., Fenton, T., and D Foran. 2005. The Effects of Skeletal Preparations on Subsequent DNA Analysis. *Journal of Forensic Sciences*. 50:1016 – 1019.

Richard, M., R. Frappier, and J. Newman. 2003. Developmental Validation of a Real Time Quantitative PCR Assay for Automated Quantification of Human DNA. *Journal of Forensic Sciences*. 48(5):1041 – 1046.

Roche Applied Science. Elliminate Errors. 2003. *<http://www.roche-applied-science.com/fst/amplification.htm?/sis/amplification/pifs/enzymes/pwo.htm>* Accessed 2004 March 14.

Roche Applied Sciences. 2003. *Important Note: Expand High Fidelity PCR System*. [Product Update].

Roffey, P.E., C.I. Eckhoff, and J.L Kuhl. 2000. A rare mutation in the amelogenin gene and its potential investigative ramifications. *Journal of Forensic Sciences*. 45(5): 1016 – 1019.

Rogan, P.K. and J.J. Salvo. 1990. Study of Nucleic acids isolated from ancient remains. *Yearbook of Physical Anthropology*. 33:195 – 214.

Rozen, S., and H. Skaletsky. 2000. Primer3 on the WWW for general users and for biologist programmers. In: Krawetz S, Misener S (eds) *Bioinformatics Methods and Protocols: Methods in Molecular Biology*. Totowa, NJ: Humana Press.

Saferstein, R. 2002. *Forensic Science Handbook* Volume I 2nd Edition. New Jersey: Pearson Education.

Saiki, R.K., D.H. Gelfand, S. Stofel, S.J. Schar, R. Higuchi, G.T. Horn, K.B. Mullis, and H.A. Erlich. 1988. Primer directed enzymatic amplification of DNA with athermostable DNA polymerase. *Science*. 239: 487 – 491.

Shackleford, J.M. 1966. The ultrastructure of Mississippian and Archaic Indian bones from various soil and drainage conditions. *American Journal of Phys. Anthro.* 25:291 – 298.

Sinha, S.K., B. Budowle, S.S. Arcot, S.L. Richey, R. Chakraborty, M.D. Jones, P.W. Wojtkiewicz, D.A. Schoenbauer, A.M. Gross, S.K. Sinha, and J.G. Shewale. 2003. Development validation of a multiplexed Y-chromosome STR genotyping system, Y-PLEX™ 6, for forensic casework. *Journal of Forensic Sciences*. 48(1): 1 – 11.

Smith, C.I., A.T. Chamberlain, M.S. Riley, C. Stringer, and M.J. Collins. 2003. The thermal history of human fossils and the likelihood of successful DNA amplification. *Journal of Human Evolution*. 45:203 – 217.

Solomon, C.D., and N. Hasse. 1967. Histological and histochemical observations of decalcified sections of ancient bones from excavations in Israel. *Israel Journal of Medical Science*. 3:747 – 754.

Stout, S.D., and S.L. Teitelbaum. 1976. Histological analysis of undecalcified thin sections of archaeological bone. *American Journal of Physical Anthropology*. 44:263 – 269.

Strom, C.M., and S. Rechitsky. 1998. Use of nested PCR to identify charred human remains and minute amounts of blood. *Journal of Forensic Sciences*. 43(3): 696 – 700.

Sullivan, K.M., A. Mannucci, C.P. Kimpton, and P. Gill. 1993. A rapid and quantitative DNA sex test: fluorescence-based PCR analysis of X – Y homologous gene amelogenin. *Biotechniques*. 15(4): 636 – 641.

Telenius, H., N.P. Carter, C.E. Bebb, M. Nordenskjold, B.A. Ponder, and A. Tunnacliffe. 1992. Degenerate oligonucleotide-primed PCR: general amplification of target DNA by a single degenerate primer. *Genomics*. 13(3):718 – 725.

Tichopad, A., A. Didier, and M. Pfaffl. 2004. Inhibition of real-time PCR quantification due to tissue-specific contaminants. *Molecular and Cellular Probes*. 18:45 – 50.

Tuross, N. 1994. The biochemistry of ancient DNA in bone. *Experentia*. 50:530 – 535.

Tzvetkov, M.V., C. Becker, B. Kulle, P. Nurnberg, J. Brockmoller, and L. Wojnowski. 2005. Genome-wide single-nucleotide polymorphism arrays demonstrate high fidelity of multiple displacement-based whole-genome amplification. *Electrophoresis.* 26(3):710 – 715.

Ubelaker, D.H. and EB Jones, Editors. Diane Beynon Landers, Associate Editor for Archaeology. 2003. *Human remains from Voegtly Cemetery, Pittsburgh, Pennsylvania. Smithsonian Contributions to Anthropology Series*, Number 46, Smithsonian Institution Press, Washington, D.C.

Von Wurmb-Schwark, N., R. Higuchi, A.P. Fenech, C. Elfstrom, C. Meissner, M. Oehmichen, and G.A. Cortopassi. 2002. Quantification of human mitochondrial DNA in real time PCR. *Forensic Science International.* 126:34 – 39.

Wickenheiser, R.A. 2002. Trace DNA: a review, discussion of theory, and application of the transfer of trace quantities of DNA through skin contact. *Journal of Forensic Sciences.* 47(3): 442 – 450.

Wilson, I. 1997. Inhibition and Facilitation of Nucleic Acid Amplification. *Applied and Environmental Microbiology*. 63(10): 3741 – 3751.

Whitaker, J.P., T.M. Clayton, A.J. Urquhart, E.S. Millican, and C.P. Kimpton. 1995. Short tandom repeat typing of bodies from a mass disaster: high success rate and characteristic amplification patterns in highly degraded sample. *BioTechniqes.* 18(4):670 – 677.

Zhang, L., X. Cui, K. Schmitt, R. Hubert, W. Navidi, and N. Arnheim. 1992. Whole genome amplification from a single cell: implications for genetic analysis. *Proceedings of the National Academy of Science U S A.* 89(13):5847 – 5851.

In: Forensics in Law Enforcement
Editor: M. V. Shoester, pp. 123-131
ISBN 1-60021-164-X

Chapter 3

Decreased Turn-Around Time for Forensic Genetic Testing*

Barry Duceman
New York State Police;
Forensic Investigation Center; Albany, NY 12226

Project Objective

At the time of the initial CLIP grant application, the Biological Science Section of the New York State Police Forensic Investigation Center was in the process of implementing a program with dual objectives which were to 1.) eliminate a current forensic DNA analysis casework backlog and 2.) decrease average casework turn – around time from approximately three months to thirty days.

Project Overview

The DNA casework backlog and turn-around period at the time of application are provided in Table 1. As indicated in that table, the two objectives described for this project have not yet been fully achieved. All aspects of the program must be implemented before it will be possible to fairly assess the success of our approach. We are continuing to make progress in each of the components that were recognized as essential to our overall strategy and have implemented additional measures toward achieving those goals. Our current progress and the contribution of the funds available through the CLIP grant to that progress are described below.

* Excerpted from http://www.ncjrs.gov/pdffiles1/nij/grants/211978.pdf.

Table 1. Comparison of Casework Production Status Currently and at CLIP Grant 2002 Application

DNA CASEWORK PRODUCTIVITY					
Productivity Measure	Initial	Current	Initial	Current	Productivity Measure
				Last Quarter	Total
Backlog (Cases)	801	1205	N/A	N/A	N/A
Turnaround – average (days)	N/A	N/A	82	37	142
Turnaround – range (days)	N/A	N/A	11 minimum 342 maximum	4 minimum 69 maximum	4 minimum 697 maximum

Table 1. indicates the total backlog of all cases pending analysis in the Biological Science Section currently and at the time of the original grant application. The turn – around time at the time of application (2002) is the average for the 455 items analyzed from March 1, 2002 to May 31, 2002. The current turn-around is available in greater detail due to the implementation of our LIMS system during the tenure of the CLIP 2003 grant. Two measures are given: 1.) DNA casework turn-around for cases that were both submitted and closed during the third quarter of 2005 (45 "priority" cases); 2.) DNA casework turn-around for all other cases closed during the third quarter of 2005 (191 cases). The lengthiest (maximum) and shortest (minimum) duration for case turn-around times are given for each measure

PROJECT AIMS

The overall goal of the project plan of The Biological Science Section of the New York State Police Forensic Investigation Center as described in the Crime Laboratory Improvement Grant (FY 2003) has been to increase DNA casework productivity. The plan had four components which together constituted a comprehensive strategy to eliminate projected casework production bottlenecks and to support a shift to more automated processes. The aims that constitute the plan of action to attain the objectives presented in this proposal are described below.

AIM 1. ACCELERATED STAFF TRAINING

One response of the New York State Police to the challenge of higher throughput and backlog reduction was to increase the number of competent DNA analyst / examiners in the Biological Science Section. At the time of Grant application, the Section had completed a round of hiring that provided as additional 20 Forensic Scientists and 15 supporting Senior Laboratory Technicians. (The job title Forensic Scientist in the New York State Police Crime

Laboratory System is equivalent to the position of DNA examiner/analyst described in the current federal DNA Advisory Board Guidelines). Without exception, these new forensic scientists and technicians were hired with no prior forensic DNA casework experience. In the past, an experienced competent mentor would have trained these new staff over an extended period of time. As can be expected, such an approach negatively impacts the casework output of the mentor and extends the training period far beyond the applicable guidelines.

To facilitate training of these new employees, the NYSP renovated a training facility on the East Campus of the State University of New York in East Greenbush, NY. This facility, dubbed the *NYSP Forensic DNA Training Laboratories*, was a working model of a modern forensic genetic training laboratory and held much of the equipment necessary to examine and identify biological stains on simulated casework samples and then perform forensic Short Tandem Repeat DNA analysis.

During the duration of the grant, equipment purchased with grant funds allowed the Biological Science section to position key items, including thermacyclers and capillary electrophoresis genetic analyzers, at the training facility. Grant funds also provided equipment, such as computers, micro-centrifuges, and a microscope, which helped alleviate major bottlenecks in the training program. The availability of a well-equipped training facility effectively reduced the duration of training from thirteen months to approximately seven months.

In total, fourteen Forensic Scientists completed STR DNA analysis training at the East Greenbush facility and subsequently successfully passed appropriate competency examinations. Eighteen Forensic Scientists also trained and established competency in a curriculum intended to impart DNA evidence recognition, collection and handling skills as well as a solid knowledge base in body fluid stain identification (Forensic Serology). At the facility, we also were able to train three Senior Laboratory Technicians in the extraction, species determination and quantification of DNA from casework samples. Table 2 is a summary table showing the number of forensic scientists and senior laboratory technicians that successfully established these core competencies during the grant period. Grant funds were also applied to provide specialized in-depth training to staff Forensic Scientist through attendance at a full day workshop in capillary electrophoresis at the Northeast Association of Forensic Scientist annual meeting.

The duration of training for the latest training cycles has been reduced to seven months as measured from the beginning of training until internal certification of competency in Forensic DNA analysis. Based on this, the training period for a Biological Science staff member to achieve competency in forensic DNA analysis has been decreased to essentially the minimum six-month period required by the federal DNA Advisory Board Standards. Updated training modules, a dedicated training facility, modern equipment, skilled instructors and an emphasis on important performance measures [moot court, oral boards, examinations] has allowed the Biological Science section to achieve this aim without sacrificing the quality of the training provided to the staff.

Table 2.

Training Topic	Staff Competent
Forensic Scientist -Serology	18
Forensic Scientist -DNA Analysis	14
Technicians – DNA Extraction and	3

Table 2. Staff Training at the NYSP DNA Training Labs Table 2 shows the total number of Biological Science Staff trained in forensic DNA related specialties during the tenure of the CLIP 2003 grant.

Even with the initial staff expansion described above, the need for additional casework forensic scientists and supporting laboratory technicians became clear. The goal has been to support rather than limit the enthusiasm of law enforcement for DNA testing technology. Further staff expansion has thus been achieved in two ways:

1. Increased efficiency in the NYS Convicted Offender DNA Databank yielded excess testing capacity which, in turn, allowed that facility to re-assign five Forensic Scientists to the casework unit of the Biological Science Section.
2. Senior Laboratory Technician positions were converted to Forensic Scientist job classification. The converted positions have recently been re-instituted and are in the process of being filed from an applicant pool.

Aim 1 Future

At the end of the grant period the NYSP decided to close the training facility because the main contingent of new hires had completed training. Future training will be carried out both in-house and through training opportunities available through the Northeast Forensic Training Institute which is located on the University at Albany campus near to the Forensic Investigation Center.

Aim 1 Performance Measure

The availability of a well-equipped training facility successfully reduced the duration of training from thirteen months to approximately seven months. The fourteen new analysts are expected to provide capacity for analysis of at least 1000 additional DNA cases each year.

Aim 2. Elimination of Production Bottlenecks

Approximately 3,100 sq. ft. of laboratory space was renovated to support casework by the staff of newly trained Forensic Scientists (described above). Obviously, bringing such a large number of staff on-line at once threatened to result in significant equipment bottlenecks. The items in the list below were identified by the Biological Science Section supervisory staff and were described in the original budget narrative as necessary to ensure that the new staff could be integrated smoothly into the section with out incurring delays in casework analysis.

1. ABI Prism 3100-Avant Capillary Electrophoresis Genetic Analyzer
2. Nikon Eclipse E400 Microscopes (7)
3. Applied Biosystems GeneAmpR PCR System 9700 (2)

Electrophoresis Genetic Analyzer is a high-throughput 4 capillary instrument which is upgradeable to 16 capillaries. This device thus allows 4 samples to be analyzed during a single 40-minute run of the instrument. This run time compares very favorably with the turn-around-time on the ABI Prism 310 Capillary Electrophoresis Genetic Analyzer (CE310) which is the instrument currently employed by the Biological Science Section for casework STR DNA analysis. Run time for a single sample on the CE310 typically requires twenty-six (26) minutes. To date, the validation of the four capillary instrument has been completed according to federal guidelines for casework. The validation study is undergoing review before approval to be used to support the efforts of the Biological Science Section to implement automated processes (see specific aim 3).

Equipment items have been purchased, using funds available through the CLIP 2003 grant, to alleviate bottlenecks in the production of STR DNA profiles for casework evidentiary and reference specimens. These items include three Nikon Eclipse E400 Microscopes. These scopes are employed for sperm identification and for assessment of the success of differential sperm / epithelial cell extraction. These evaluations are labor intensive and time-consuming. Previously, the Biological Science Section had only five [5] microscopes for a staff of 21 Forensic Scientists performing identification of biological stains. Without the grant funds, 26 forensic scientists would have been vying to use this equipment creating an obvious bottleneck.

Personal computers have been procured for the interpretation of STR DNA data from the ABI analytical platforms and for data quality review. These additional computers provide increased data interpretation throughput which, in our experience, has proven to be a critical need in order to avoid a production bottleneck. Three of the four requested computers were intended to avoid this limitation; the fourth was intended to replace a currently inoperable computer.

Grant funds have also been applied to connect a wireless computer system on all forensic scientists' laptops at the Forensic Investigation Center in order to provide portability and continual access to our Laboratory Information Management system during DNA evidence examination and analysis. A paperless documentation system is being developed to expedite and increase efficiency of evidence logging, tracking, analysis and reporting. The system will speed-up report generation and facilitate production of accurate productivity statistics. Deployment of the wireless network also has allowed for greater standardization of our analytical processes as newly Forensic Scientist come on-line. The entire Biological Science Section is now using a LIMS on laptop computers for recording notes while evaluating and isolating evidence for downstream DNA analysis. This capability has endowed the process with efficiency through greater portability and ease of access to case-related information. The availability of LIMS on laptop has conferred the ability to work without accessing a desktop computer which, in turn, has remover space constraints.

Additional funds were used to provide two Applied Biosystems GeneAmp PCR System 9700 thermacyclers to update and replace the same number of aging PCR System 9600 thermacyclers in use in the Biological Science Section. In addition to updating these instruments, the new thermacyclers also provide increased DNA amplification throughout in support of a more automated approach. The section has completed validation of these equipment items for forensic DNA casework applications and, on the basis of that experience, has switched to exclusive use of the 9700 thermacyclers.

Aim 2. Performance Measure

The performance measures for AIM 2 are elapsed casework turn – around time and backlog reduction. The data for these measures are given in Table 1.

AIM 3. FORENSIC CASEWORK AUTOMATION

The Biological Science Section has made steady progress implementing high throughput, automated forensic genotyping. We have established a high-throughput facility and validated liquid handling systems [robotics] to extract, quantitative and normalize samples for downstream DNA amplification. We have introduced bar coding and sample tracking into the process and are presently completing the integration of the high-throughput system into our newly implemented Laboratory Management System. We have provided staff for the facility and are also currently integrating the output of our analytical platforms with the Cybergenetics Inc. TrueAllele system for data quality review and interpretation. This is an important enabling sub-project with Cybergenetics, Inc., a Pennsylvania – based genetic analysis firm. As designed, the entire system can be configured to produce 200 STR DNA profiles in a 5-day workweek. This capacity, which is in excess of 10,000 profiles annually, would alone triple our current casework output (4,600 STR patterns produced annually).

The funds available through the CLIP grant have provided two key components of this project. The first is the high-throughput genetic analyzer, the ABI Avant Model 3100 Genetic Analyzer, described in Aim 2. This instrument has been installed in the Biological Science Section and, upon review and approval of the corresponding forensic validation, will be placed on-line for batch processing of casework.

The second key component was system integration with the Porter-Lee Beast Laboratory Information Management System that is being custom-installed in the Biological Science Section. The Beast LIMS system handles evidence-receiving functions for the Forensic Investigation Center. The CLIP award provided funds for detailed planning of expanded LIMS System functionality and the preparation of a documented Statement of Work. This planning document laid the groundwork for the Biological Science Section's automation program. The expected outcomes of an automated process can include decreased throughput times, enhanced process quality, improved reproducibility, and superior data traceability.

According to that program, an integrated LIMS system serves as the "backbone" that will support batch processing, enhanced sample flow and an entire automated process. The thoughtful design and development of this custom software solution has been foremost in achieving out goals of backlog elimination and 30-day turn-around times. The critical need for this second integration component derives from its multi-functional capabilities. The system will provide the capability to manage "work lists" that can be used to assign samples to instrument plates or other tests. The software system provides the user with the capability to track sample plates or other containers throughout the analytical process and to view information associated with the samples in the wells of a plate. Barcode labels can be printed for specimen containers, plates and storage containers to allow the analyst to quickly and accurately scan information into forms. The system will also provide instrument sample sheet generation for the high-throughput capillary electrophoresis device. The system will also provide tools for generating laboratory management reports. Reports can be written to summarize, for example the number of samples processed through the laboratory by analyst, instrument or sample type. These types of reports, which form the basis for important performance measures, are currently manually compiled.

The status of the modules designated for STR DNA analysis is described in the accompanying Table 4. In general, the downstream amplification of template and subsequent production of DNA patterns already involve little user intervention and can be considered semi-automated.

Table 3. Current Status of Implementation of Automated Forensic STR DNA Analysis

Module	Status
Evidence Preparation	Staffing of the facility is complete. Training in progress
DNA Extraction	Liquid Handling System validation completed. Not on line.
DNA Quantitiation	Validation completed. On line.
STR Data Production	ABI Prism 3100-Avant Capillary Electrophoresis Genetic Analyzer validation completed. Not on line
LIMS System Integration	Software development completed. In acceptance testing November 2005.
STR Data Quality Review	Software in development.
STR Data Interpretation	Software in development

Aim 3 Future

Once the essential component steps for enhancing productivity through the process has been integrated into the controlling LIMS; it will be possible to implement additional upgrades. For example, once the modules for performing extraction, quantization and PCR are implemented, it will then be possible to add robotic arms for moving microtiter plates from extraction / quantization platform to a PCR set-up and then to a thermacycler. In terms of overall process, the automation of these sample movements is not critical to reliability, reproducible results or sample throughput but, rather, can enhance user convenience and walk away time. Ideally, the system should also be developed to incorporate a quality control matrix to ensure compliance with federal guidelines and laboratory accreditation standards.

The automation of technical aspects of forensic DNA analysis can only be considered a partial solution to resolving casework backlogs and achieving reasonable turn-around times.

The main challenges to achieving those goals are those steps in the analysis which remain as bottlenecks. In forensic DNA tests, there are still components of the process which are not currently amenable to automation. Identifiable bottlenecks without an easy or inexpensive solution include the identification and isolation of probative stains; a task which, for the foreseeable future, will depend on the talent of forensic scientists. This issue is especially critical since full efficiency of an automated or semi-automated genotyping system will require a steady stream of evidence into the process flow. This supply bottleneck can be somewhat addressed by forensic scientists freed from DNA extraction and quantization tasks. Also, time spent sifting through large submissions of many items can be reduced because of the capacity of the automated system. Instead of screening evidence, the analyst will simply submit the items for DNA analysis and use the final data interpretation step to determine relevance to the ongoing investigation.

In the current automation strategy, then, the key bottleneck becomes the interpretation of analytical result and the technical review process. Fortunately, although these processes are currently dependent upon manual applications, software solution are emerging that can be implement and integrated into an automated approach.

Aim 3. Performance Measure

The performance measures AIM 3 are elapsed casework turn – around time and backlog reduction. The date for these measures is given in Table 1.

AIM 4. APPLICATION OF BACKLOG REDUCTION FUNDS

The Biological Science Section has established an effective process for providing analysis, by commercial DNA testing laboratories, of several hundred cases from our non-suspect case backlog. The aim has been to help control the growth of the number of cases pending analysis while the Biological Science Section simultaneously 1.) trained a large cadre of *new* staff, 2). validated *new* high-throughput equipment, 3.) implemented *new* automated STR DNA analysis. The funding for this enabling subproject has been supplied by *NIJ No Suspect Casework DNA Backlog Reduction Grants* to the NY State Division of Criminal Justice Services. Personnel overtime funds have been applied to provide processing of submitted evidentiary items in preparation for shipping to vendor laboratories for subsequent analysis and, also, to provide technical review of vendor results.

The availability of the backlog reduction funds did impact significantly upon the backlog of cases with no identified suspect and, also, provided expedited entry of the corresponding perpetrator's DNA patterns into CODIS. The program is stopgap, however, and will not impact the remaining cases in the backlog nor, by itself, have a long-term effect on the section's turn-around time.

Aim 4 Future

The Biological Science Section will continue to submit casework to commercial DNA testing laboratories with funds from NIJ DNA Backlog Reduction Grants FY2004 and FY2005.

Aim 4. Performance Measure

To date, the Biological Science Section has sent 559 non-suspect DNA cases to vendor labs using funds available through the CLIP grant, and tallied 30 CODIS convicted offender and 11 forensic hits against the resultant DNA patterns.

In: Forensics in Law Enforcement
Editor: M. V. Shoester, pp. 133-171
ISBN 1-60021-164-X

Chapter 4

FORENSIC APPLICATIONS OF Y CHROMOSOME STRS AND SNPS*

Michael Hammer and Alan J. Redd

I. ABSTRACT

We identified and characterized 20 novel STRs on the non-recombining portion of the Ychromosome (NRY) that are robust and informative for forensic casework. These Y-STRs,comprised of tetranucleotide, pentanucleotide, and hexanucleotide repeats, greatly improveresolution among paternal lineages above levels obtained with previously used Y-STRs.Multiplex protocols were optimized to amplify 41 Y-STRs in 5 PCR reactions (an additional 2Y-STRs were typed in uniplex assays). A total of 38 Y-STRs was typed in a panel of 2,517 U.S.samples representing African-Americans, European-Americans, Hispanics, Native Americans,and Asian Americans, as well as a large worldwide database. The entire U.S. Y-STR database is available for online searches to estimate frequencies of Y chromosome haplotypes determined from crime scene material. Comparisons of commercially available kits revealed that AppliedBiosystems Yfiler©, which contains three of our novel Y-STRs, is superior to others. The 11"core" Y-STRs recommended by the Scientific Working Group on DNA Analysis Methods wereanalyzed to estimate the extent of population structure within and among ethnic groups in theU.S. The analyses support the creation of separate African-American, European-American,Hispanic-American, and Asian-American databases in which samples of the same ethnic groupfrom different geographic regions within the U.S can be pooled. We recommend that separatedatabases be constructed for different Native American groups. A set of 61 Y chromosome single-nucleotide-polymorphisms (Y-SNPs) was also typed in the U.S. database to infer thegeographic origins of Y chromosomes in the U.S. and to test for paternal admixture among U.S.ethnic groups. Admixture estimates vary greatly among populations and ethnic groups. A series of analyses was performed to test for the effects of inter-ethnic admixture on the structure of Y-STR diversity in the U.S. Results indicated that low levels of genetic heterogeneity betweenpairs of Hispanic-American populations disappear when African-derived chromosomes areremoved from the analysis. This is not the case for an unusual sample of European-Americansfrom New York City

* Excerpted from http://www.ncjrs.gov/pdffiles1/nij/grants/211979.pdf.

when its African-derived chromosomes were removed, or for NativeAmerican populations when European-derived chromosomes were removed. We infer that both inter-ethnic admixture and population structure in ancestral source populations contributed tofine scale Y-STR heterogeneity within U.S. ethnic groups. Finally, empirical tests of associationbetween Y-chromosome and autosomal markers are presented and a theoretical framework fordetermining a joint match probability is recommended. A conservative estimate of the jointprobability is obtained by multiplying the largest value of the group autosomal matchprobabilities by the estimated matching probability for the Y chromosome.

II. Executive Summary

This award funded a project to develop DNA markers on the Y-chromosome for forensic applications. The specific aims of the grant were to: 1) develop a DNA typing system that targets the male-specific portion of the human genome (the non-recombining portion of the Y chromosome or NRY), 2) identify a set of informative NRY markers that are robust in forensic analysis (Y-SNPs and Y-STRs), 3) develop detailed protocols for PCR-based multiplex genotyping kits, and 4) construct a database of Y chromosome markers in U.S. populations. We identified and characterized 20 novel Y-STRs on the NRY (Note: some STRs are duplicatedsuch that 15 STR sequences map to 20 locations; in this report we refer to each location as a Y-STR). These Y-STRs are comprised of tetranucleotide repeats (DYS449, DYS453, DYS454,DYS455, DYS456, DYS458, DYS459ab, DYS464abcd, and DYS724ab), pentanucleotide repeats (DYS446, DYS447, DYS450, DYS452, and DYS463), and hexanucleotide repeats(DYS448). These novel Y-STRs greatly improve resolution among paternal lineages beyondlevels obtained with previously used Y-STRs. After discussions with Applied Biosystems, threeof our markers (DYS448, DYS456, DYS458) were incorporated in their Yfiler kit. Multiplexprotocols were developed to amplify 41 Y-STRs in 5 PCR reactions (an additional 2 Y-STRs were typed in uniplex assays). A total of 38 Y-STRs was typed in a panel of 2,517 U.S. samplesrepresenting African-Americans, European-Americans, Hispanics, Native Americans, and AsianAmericans. An additional 5 Y-STRs were typed in a subset (1,000) of these samples. The resolution of commercially available kits was compared using these markers. The Yfiler kit showed greater capacity to resolve paternal lineages than the standard U.S. core Y-STRs or thePromega PowerPlex Y kit in all ethnic groups, although the complete set of 38 Y-STRs hadhigher capacity to resolve paternal lineages, especially in Native American populations. The entire Y-STR database is available for online searches to estimate frequencies of Y chromosome haplotypes determined from crime scene material.

The 11 core U.S. loci recommended by the Scientific Working Group on DNA AnalysisMethods were analyzed in our U.S. database of 2,517 individuals from 38 populations toestimate the extent of population structure within and among ethnic groups in the U.S. A multidimensional scaling (MDS) plot placed the populations into four discrete clusters (African-Americans, European-Americans, Hispanic-Americans, and Asian-Americans) and one dispersedcluster of Native Americans. An analysis of molecular variance (AMOVA) indicated that a largeproportion of the total genetic variance is partitioned among ethnic groups (24.8%); while only asmall amount (1.5%) is found among populations within ethnic groups. Separate AMOVAanalyses within each ethnic group showed that only the sample of Native Americans containsstatistically significant among-population variation. Pair-wise population differentiation tests diduncover heterogeneity among European-American and among Hispanic-American populations;however, this was due to only a single sample within each group. For example, only the NYCEuropean-American sample and the Mesa Arizona Hispanic-American sample differed infrequency of Y-haplotypes when compared with a subset of populations within their respectiveethnic groups.

In sum, analyses of Y-STRs indicated a lack of significant geographic structure among African-American and Asian-American populations, minor heterogeneity among European-American and Hispanic-American populations, and broad-scale subdivision among Native American populations. The extremely consistent patterns of genetic structure observed in this study and two others of similar scope [1, 2] lead us to make the following recommendations for the construction of U.S. databases of Y-STRs: 1) it is good policy to continue gathering more data from additional regional populations, especially those not represented in existing databases, 2) there is no evidence at present that pooling samples from different geographic regions will lead to strong biases in the estimation of Y-STR haplotype frequencies for African-American, European-American, Hispanic-American and Asian-American populations, and 3) separate, larger databases from Native American subpopulations (tribal groups) are needed. Methods to correct for very low levels of structure within European-American and Hispanic-Americans may need to be considered [3].

A set of 61 Y chromosome single-nucleotide-polymorphisms (Y-SNPs) was typed in the samedatabase (i.e., 2,517 individuals from 38 populations) to infer the geographic origins of Ychromosomes and to test for paternal admixture among African-Americans, European-Americans, Hispanic-Americans, Asian-Americans, and Native-Americans. Admixture estimates varied greatly among populations and ethnic groups. The frequencies of non-European(3.4%) and non-Asian (4.5%) Y chromosomes were generally low in European-American andAsian-American populations, respectively. The frequencies of European Y chromosomes inNative-American populations ranged widely (i.e., 7-89%) and followed a West to East gradient,whereas they were relatively consistent in African-American populations (26.4% ± 8.9%) fromdifferent locations. The European (77.8% ± 9.3%) and Native American (13.7% ± 7.4%)components of the Hispanic paternal gene pool were also relatively constant among geographicregions; however, the African contribution was much higher in the Northeast (10.5% ± 6.4%)than in the Southwest (1.5% ± 0.9%) or Midwest (0%).

To test for the effects of inter-ethnic admixture on the structure of Y-STR diversity in the U.S.,we performed "subtraction" analyses in which Y chromosomes inferred to be admixed by Y-SNP analysis were removed from the database and pairwise population differentiation (PPD) tests were implemented on the remaining Y-STR haplotypes. Results indicated that low levels of heterogeneity observed between pairs of Hispanic American populations (see above)disappeared when African-derived chromosomes were removed from the analysis. This was not the case for an unusual sample of European-Americans from New York City (see above) whenits African-derived chromosomes were removed, or for Native American populations whenEuropean-derived chromosomes were removed.

The highly similar admixture rates among African-American samples from different locales is consistent with the absence of statistically significant PPD tests based on our Y-STR data. Likewise, the similarly high frequencies of European-derived Y chromosomes in our Hispanic-American samples may account for low levels of Hispanic Y-STR heterogeneity in this survey, as well as in the surveys of Kayser et al. [1] and Budowle et al. [2]. The finding of frequencies of 6-18% African-derived Y chromosomes in Hispanic-American samples from the eastern seaboard suggests that broader regional patterns of African admixture in Hispanic-American populations should be investigated. The Y-SNP analysis provides insights into why Native American samples show such high levels of heterogeneity based on Y-STR AMOVA, MDS, and PPD tests. From West to East there is a pronounced admixture gradient, ranging from ~10%-90% European Y chromosomes, respectively. These results suggest that regional variation in inter-ethnic admixture, as well as population structure in ancestral European, Hispanic and Native American source populations, are important factors leading to population substructure within an ethnic group.

Empirical tests of association between Y-chromosome and autosomal markers are presented anda theoretical framework for determining a joint match probability is recommended. Statistical analyses of association were performed in sixteen U.S. populations between the autosomalgenotypes from loci CSF1PO, FGA, THO1, TPOX, vWA, D3S1358, D5S818, D7S820,D8S1179, D13S317, D16S539, D18S512, D21S11 and Y chromosome haplotypes from lociDYS19, DYS385ab, DYS389I, DYS389II, DYS390, DYS391, DYS392, DYS393, DYS438, andDYS439. The sample populations include individuals of European-American, African-American, Hispanic-American, Native-American, and Asian-American ancestry. The results are consistentwith independence of Y and autosomal markers. Hence, it is appropriate to compute joint-matchprobability by multiplying the Y haplotype frequency with the appropriately-corrected autosomalfrequency. Since two individuals sharing the same Y haplotype are more recently related thantwo randomly-chosen individuals, the autosomal frequencies have to be corrected to account forthis, and we develop this correction here. Likewise, one must also compute these probabilitiesfor each appropriate subpopulation. A conservative estimate of the joint probability is obtainedby multiplying the largest value of the group autosomal match probabilities by the estimatedmatching probability for the Y chromosome. Finally, we suggest an approach for presenting asingle match probability (as opposed to separate values for each major ethnic group) that is basedon weighting the major ethnic groups by the appropriate census sizes.

III. Overview

During the past ten years there has been a dramatic increase in the use and reliance on forensic DNA analysis. This has been especially true in sexual assault cases that routinely consist of evidentiary stains that are a mixture of body fluids from the victim and assailant. Current DNA differential analysis techniques permit the separation of the male and female components of these mixed stains [4]; however, a complete separation is not always possible due to the size and condition of the stain and the percentage of each component present [5-10]. In addition, mixed semen stains from vasectomized or azoospermic individuals cannot be relied upon to yield DNA information with current techniques. Because of the limitations of the separation process, forensic scientists are faced with the challenge of interpreting the significance of a mixed profile consisting of two or more contributors. This has become an increasingly important issue with the ability to analyze smaller samples through the use of Polymerase Chain Reaction (PCR) techniques. In many circumstances the application of

PCR-based DNA typing methods results in the failure to amplify the minor (e.g., male) component of DNA mixtures due to competition with alleles from the major (e.g., female) component.

One approach to resolving this issue is to target male-specific polymorphisms on the non-recombining portion of the Y chromosome (NRY). By genotyping markers on the NRY, DNA typing will become more useful in cases involving 1) unsuccessful differential lysis separations of male and female cells as a result of the age and/or quality of semen stains, 2) azoospermic men, 3) the presence of other body fluid mixtures from victims and suspects of different sex, and 4) two or more male semen donors [5, 7, 9, 11, 12]. Thus, the ability to target polymorphisms on the NRY expands the application of DNA technology to samples that were previously difficult to interpret and/or yielded no results.

Two classes of NRY markers are short tandem repeats (Y-STRs) and single nucleotide polymorphisms (Y-SNPs). The combination of alleles at multiple Y-STRs on a single Y chromosome defines a Y-STR haplotype, whereas the combination of alleles at multiple SNPs defines a NRY haplogroup [13]. The high geographic specificity of many NRY haplogroups [14, 15] provides forensic scientists with clues to the source of the male genetic material left at a crime scene. The forensic utility of Y-STRs results from their high levels of polymorphism in human populations [16], their small size in base pairs (~100-400 bp), and the ability to type multiple Y-STRs in a single PCR reaction [5, 11, 17, 18]. One limitation of Y-STRs in forensic and paternity applications is the lack of independence of these markers on the NRY (*i.e.*, the lack of recombination). The difficulty in distinguishing paternally related males in a population means that Y-STR haplotypes will have reduced inclusion probabilities compared with autosomal STRs. However, Y-STRs provide a valuable addition to the forensic scientist's tool kit, especially as more variable markers are discovered and the potential to distinguish Y-chromosomes in a population increases.

The major questions to be addressed in this report are 1) what is the best way to construct a Y-STR database for forensic purposes, 2) what is the degree of Y chromosome population structure among U.S. ethnic groups and among populations within U.S. ethnic groups, 3) can population samples from different geographic regions within the U.S. be pooled in forensic databases, 4) how much admixture is there among U.S. ethnic groups and how do admixture rates vary regionally, 5) what is the effect of admixture on levels of population structure, and 6) how do we calculate a Y chromosome-autosome joint match probability? One must be wary of the possibility that different U.S. groups will have different levels of sub-structure (e.g., Native American populations that have a history of partial isolation). Because U.S. populations are composed of diverse immigrant groups it is also necessary to consider the effects of recent admixture. The degree to which these factors affect U.S. population groups and the impact they might have on statistical analyses of Y chromosome data can only be understood through the establishment of detailed databases of well-defined U.S. sub-populations and their parental populations in Europe, Africa, and Asia. Here we analyze both Y-STRs and Y-SNPs in a sample of 2,517 Y chromosomes from 5 U.S. ethnic groups: African-Americans (AA), European-Americans (EA), Hispanic-Americans (HA), Asian-Americans (SA), and Native Americans (NA).

IV. MAIN FINDINGS

A. Forensic Value of Novel STRs on the Human Y Chromosome

1. Background and Significance

At the time we began this work, approximately 35 STRs had been described on the Ychromosome. In total, these Y-STRs include: 5 dinucleotide (YCAI, YCAIIab, YCAII, andDYS288) 6 trinucleotide (DYF371, DYS388, DYS392, DYS425, DYS426, DYS436), 24tetranucleotide (DYS19, DYS385ab, DYS389I, DYS389AB, DYS390, DYS391, DYS393,DYS434, DYS435, DY437, DYS439, DYS441, DYS442, DYS443, DYS444, DYS445,DYS460, DYS461, DYS462, G10123, A10, C4, and H4), and 2 pentanucleotide repeats(DXYS156, and DYS438). Most of the Y-STR primer pairs amplify one PCR product, whilesome Y-STR primer pairs amplify two or more PCR products (YCAI, YCAII, YCAIII, DYF371,DYS385, G10123). With the exception of one multicenter-study using 13 Y-STRs [11], globalpopulation screens using the majority of the published Y-STRs had not been performed;although much progress had been made in establishing a large database of European populationsusing the following Y-STRs: DYS19, DYS385ab, DYS389I, DYS389II-I, DYS390, DYS391,DYS392, and DYS393. These Y-STRs define the "minimal haplotype", while the addition ofYCAIIab to the these Y-STRs has been termed the "extended haplotype" [11, 19, 20].

The identification of additional Y-STRs was warranted for several reasons. First and foremost,increasing the number of highly polymorphic markers would improve the ability to distinguishpaternal lineages. There are shared Y-STR haplotypes in populations because either males shareidentity by descent or because a particular set of Y-STRs does not distinguish closely related, but different, paternal lineages. In a sample of 41 European populations the discriminationcapacities were 52% (n = 4,688 individuals) and 71% (n = 1,957 individuals) using the minimaland extended sets of Y-STRs, respectively [20]. The sharing of paternal lineages is likely to bemore common in isolated populations where there is a higher degree of genetic drift, such asNative American populations. Second, there is a need to identify more Y-STRs that have longerrepeats units. For example, YCAII is a polymorphic dinucleotide marker that suffers from"stutter" products during the PCR process due to polymerase slippage [21]. Stutter products arepronounced in dinucleotide repeats. Stutter bands are often reduced in longer repeat motif STRs,these loci can provide additional resolution in sample mixtures of multiple-male DNA profiles[22]. Third, a large pool of Y-STRs would provide a diverse sample of markers from which onecan select tailored sets of STRs with distinct characteristics for multiplex design for particularapplications. A small multiplex of the most informative Y-STRs could more efficientlydistinguish Y-chromosome lineages than a set of a dozen or more less informative Y-STRs.Finally, increasing the number of Y-STRs will improve the estimation of the time to the mostrecent common ancestor (TMRCA). The TMRCA between two Y-STR haplotypes provides anatural metric to describe the relatedness between two individuals and could be used to make exclusions in forensics [23]. By including more Y-STRs, estimates of the TMRCA becomemore precise [23, 24] and the ability to exclude paternal relatives increases.

2. Results

In our first publication [25], we identified and characterized 14 novel Y-STRs mapping to 18 locations on the NRY and typed them in two samples, a globally diverse panel of 73 cell lines, and 148 individuals from a European-American population. These Y-STRs include 12 tetranucleotide repeats (DYS449, DYS453, DYS454, DYS455, DYS456, DYS458, DYS459ab, and DYS464abcd), 5 pentanucleotide repeats (DYS446, DYS447, DYS450, DYS452, and DYS463), and 1 hexanucleotide repeat (DYS448). Sequence data were obtained to designate a repeat number nomenclature. Multiplex PCR assays were designed in our lab, as well in collaboration with John Butler's lab [18], incorporating both previously described and novel Y-STRs. Gene diversities of an additional 26 Y-STR locations, including the most commonly used in forensic databases, were directly compared in the cell line DNAs. Six of the 10 most polymorphic markers include the newly identified Y-STRs. Furthermore, these novel Y-STRs greatly improved the resolution of paternal lineages, above the level obtained with commonly used Y-STRs, in the European-American population.

More recently, we identified and characterized additional novel Y-STRs (DYS724ab) and extensively genotyped an additional four Y-STRs (DYS442, DYS570, DYS576, DYS607) [26, 27]. We typed a total of 38 Y-STRs in a database of 2,718 U.S. individuals from 38 populations representing 5 U.S. ethnic groups (see below), and a global database of 2,500 samples from Europe, Africa, and Asia. We also typed a total of 43 Y-STRs (Figure 1) in a *subset* of this database (n = ~1,0000). Our multiplex assays are shown schematically in Figure 2. The rank order of diversities of single copy Y-STRs are given in Table 1.

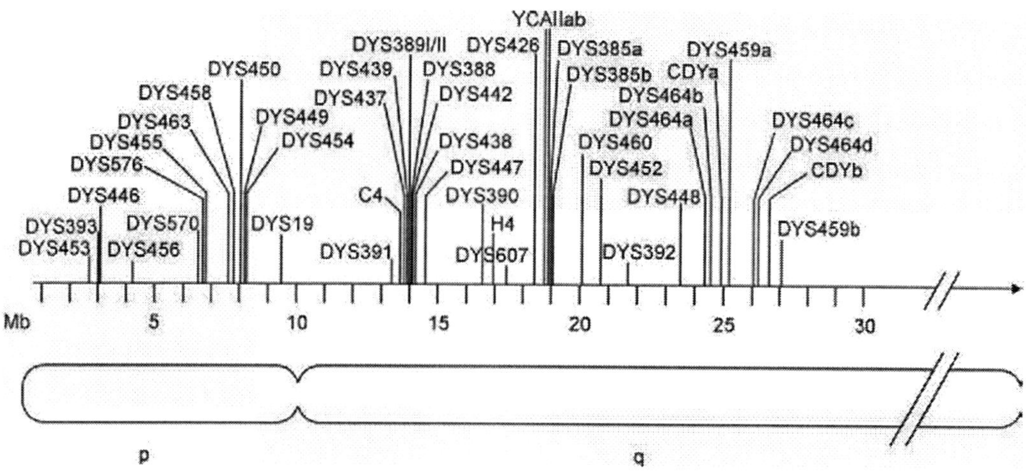

Figure 1. Locations of 43 Y-STRs typed in the Hammer lab. Approximate positions of Y-STR on megabase (Mb) scale shown above schematic of Y chromosome.

3. Conclusions

The novel Y-STRs discovered and characterized in this research are extremely useful forforensic casework for two reasons: 1) they provide additional power to resolve Y chromosomehaplotypes, and 2) they are all tetra-, penta- and hexa-nucleotide repeats. The novel Y-STRs have more than doubled the number of known pentanucleotide markers and they include the firsthexanucleotide repeat on the NRY (DYS448). These longer repeat motif STRs may be usefulfor improving the interpretation of sample mixtures [12, 28]. Depending on the particular STR,the stutter peak heights of dinucleotide and trinucleotide repeats can be higher than 30% of theircorresponding STR allele, while stutter products of tetranucleotides are approximately 15%, andpentanucleotide repeats may have stutter products of less than 1-2% [22]. These novel Y-STRs with longer repeat motifs should be evaluated for use in mixture studies.

Table 1. Diversity rank and Rst in U.S. populations of Y-STRs*

DYS	#Alleles	Het	Rst
449	13	0.842	0.089
570	12	0.794	0.043
576	12	0.791	0.081
458	9	0.772	0.036
463	12	0.765	0.289
607	9	0.764	0.221
390	8	0.760	0.335
447	13	0.754	0.068
448	9	0.714	0.172
19	8	0.709	0.190
446	13	0.702	0.030
438	7	0.698	0.067
932	9	0.676	0.319
439	7	0.664	0.101
456	9	0.660	0.012
389II	7	0.659	0.125
452	10	0.635	0.056
442	8	0.617	0.103
H4	6	0.600	0.041
460	7	0.588	0.071
389I	5	0.587	0.030
437	6	0.582	0.132
391	5	0.528	0.029
426	4	0.520	0.232
393	5	0.503	0.098
450	5	0.467	0.287
388	9	0.416	0.026
453	6	0.238	0.059
455	6	0.198	0.024
454	5	0.173	0.024

*not including multicopy STRs; U.S. Core loci are bolded.

Interestingly, these results suggest that different Y-STRs may vary in their gene diversitydepending on the particular population sample under investigation, and perhaps the length of thealleles. While most of the variation in diversity was Y-STR dependent, there was some variationamong different geographic groups in the rank order of Y-STR diversity. Our comparativeanalysis of Y-STR diversity indicates that 5 of our novel Y-STRs (DYS449, DYS458, DYS463,DYS447, and DYS448) are among the 10 most polymorphic single-copy

Y-STRs (Table 1),while one multicopy Y-STR (DYS464abcd) appears to be the most polymorphic Y-STR yetdescribed (data not shown).

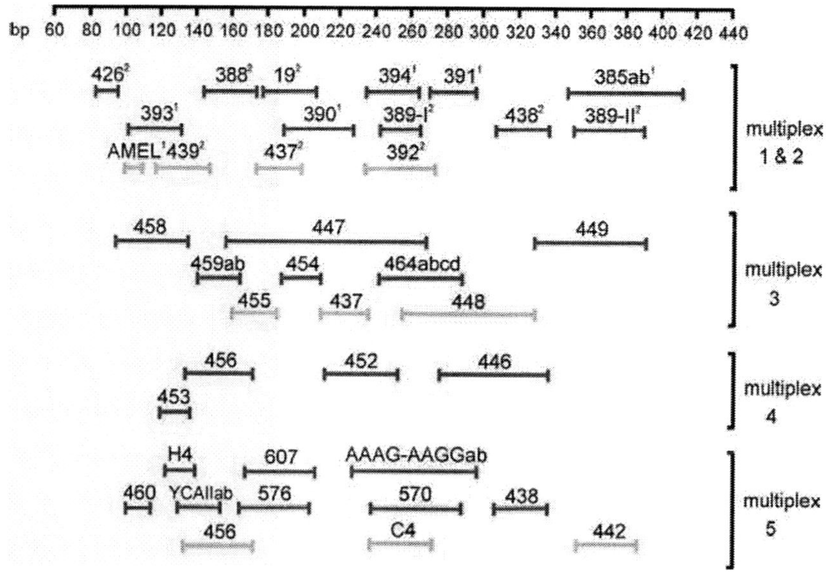

Figure 2. Size and color schemes for 43 Y-STRs in 5 multiplex reactions.

The addition of novel Y-STRs to the minimal haplotype improves the ability to distinguish Y chromosomes in European-American samples. The most common European haplotype, 14-[11,14]-13-16-24-11-13-13, is found in 3.1% of 9,972 individuals in the Y-STR HRDatabase [20]. This haplotype was found at 5.4% in the European-American sample. DYS464 alone distinguishes 75% of these haplotypes in the European-American sample. The remaining shared haplotypes are distinguished using only three additional Y-STRs. Thus, these European-American Y chromosomes are not identical by descent, as the minimal haplotype suggested. When the Bayesian method of Walsh [23] was used to estimate the TMRCA between pairs of Y chromosomes that are not resolved with 36 Y-STRs, assuming a mutation rate of 2.0 x 10-3 we found a TMRCA of only 11.8 generations (95% C.I. = 1.7-39.2 generations). Future studies of Y-chromosomes from well-characterized pedigrees could test the potential to distinguish between patrilineal relatives of various degrees using highly variable Y-STRs.

B. A Novel, Searchable, Online Database—USAYSTR—for Estimating Y Chromosome Haplotype Frequencies in the U.S.

1. Background and Significance

As in any DNA analysis, in the event of a match between the Y-STR haplotypes for a case sample and a suspect sample, it is desirable to have an estimate of the probability that a match would occur by chance. Multiplication of single locus allele frequencies to obtain estimated Y-STR haplotype frequencies is not appropriate since all STRs are from the NRY and hence are completely linked. As with mitochondrial DNA, databases of complete Y-STR haplotypes have to be generated as a source for estimating frequencies. Because of the much higher diversity of combined Y-STR haplotypes compared with single Y-STR loci, such a database has to be much larger in order to be able to serve as a reliable representation of the underlying population haplotype frequencies. Also, since the NRY is more sensitive to genetic drift as a result of its haploid and paternal mode of inheritance, populations are more likely to show statistically significant differences with regard to Y-STR haplotype frequencies [29]. The potential for population structure must therefore be considered when generating Y-STR haplotype databases.

Recently, a large Y-STR haplotype reference database (YHRD) for U.S. populations was made available [3]. However, this database contains only 9-locus Y-STR haplotypes, which are determined by what is commonly referred to as the minimal haplotype loci [20]. Here we describe a novel U.S. Y chromosome database based on the 11 "core" U.S. Y-STR loci recommended by the Scientific Working Group on DNA Analysis Methods (SWGDAM) and now used in forensic casework in the U.S. We make this database available to the U.S. forensic DNA community, along with tools for obtaining Y-STR haplotype frequencies needed for calculating matching or paternity probabilities in cases of non-exclusions in forensic analysis and paternity testing.

2. Results

An online (http://amadeus.biosci.arizona.edu/~kcaldero/str.php) Y-chromosome DNA database called *USAYSTR* is constructed to aid forensic scientists estimate Y chromosome haplotype frequencies (Figure 3). *USAYSTR* consists of genotypes at 38 Y-STR markers in 2,517 individuals from 38 populations currently living in 10 states (Figure 4). The 38 Y-STRs include the 11 core U.S. Y-STRs (DYS19, DYS385ab, DYS389I, DYS389II, DYS390, DYS391, DY392, DYS393, DYS438, and DYS439), STRs found in commercial Y-chromosome multiplexes (DYS437, DYS448, DYS456, DYS458, H4, and C4), as well as many additional Y-STRs (DYS388, DYS426, DYS442, DYS446, DYS447, DYS449, DYS450, DYS452, DYS453, DYS454, DYS455, DYS459ab, DYS460, DYS463, DYS464a-d, DYS570, DYS576, DYS607, DYS724ab, YCAIIab) (Table 2). Features of *USAYSTR* include: (1) flexibility in sorting the match results alphabetically or numerically, (2) the ability to include or exclude populations, (3) haplotype frequency estimation with either a standard 95% confidence interval (CI) or a bootstrap 95% CI, (4) a printout of the results, and (5) flexibility in the choice of STR markers with the potential to query haplotypes composed of up to 43 Y-STRs.

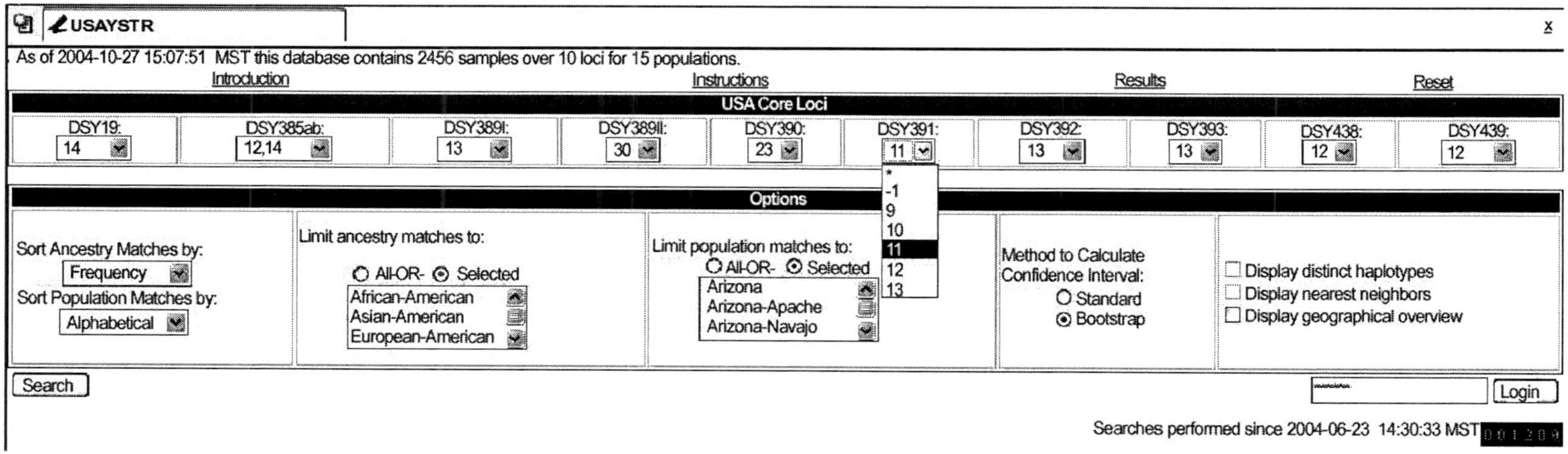

Figure 3. An example of a view of the online USAYSTR database. Our purpose is to provide a web-based, open access, searchable Y-STR database for estimating haplotype frequencies in the USA. Search for a Y-haplotype

SIO (NA)
SD (AA, EA, HA, NA)
VT (AA, EA, HA, NA)
CT (AA, EA, HA)
NYC (AA, EA, HA, SA)
OH (AA, EA, HA)
VA (AA, EA, HA)
NC (AA, EA)
FL (AA, EA, HA)
Navajo (NA)
Apache (NA)
AZ1-Phoenix (AA, EA, HA)
AZ2-Mesa (AA, EA, HA)
Pima (NA)
Tucson (SA)

Figure 4.

Table 2. Populations and haplotype diversity based on 11 U.S. core Y-STRs

Ethnic Group/population	sample size	number of haplotypes	haplotype resolution	haplotype diversity (± SE)
African-Americans (AA)				
Arizona-Phoenix (AZ 1)	76	71	93.4	0.9982± 0.0025
Arizona-Mesa (AZ 2)	52	49	94.2	0.9977± 0.0043
Connecticut (CT)	89	89	100.0	1.0000± 0.0017
Florida (FL)	20	20	100.0	1.0000± 0.0158
North Carolina (NC)	84	83	98.8	0.9997± 0.0019
New York City (NYC)	42	41	97.6	0.9988± 0.0055
Ohio (OH)	103	99	96.1	0.9992± 0.0015
South Dakota (SD)	57	57	100.0	1.0000± 0.0033
Virginia (VA)	77	71	92.2	0.9976± 0.0027
Vermont (VT)	51	49	96.1	0.9984± 0.0043
Total	**651**	**564**	**86.6**	0.9994± 0.0002
European-Americans (EA)				
Arizona-Phoenix (AZ 1)	56	54	96.4	0.9987± 0.0037
Arizona-Mesa (AZ 2)	43	41	95.3	0.9978± 0.0056
Connecticut (CT)	85	76	89.4	0.9955± 0.0032
Florida (FL)	37	36	97.3	0.9985± 0.0067
North Carolina (NC)	87	81	93.1	0.9984± 0.0020
New York City (NYC)	42	42	100.0	1.0000± 0.0052
Ohio (OH)	99	87	87.9	0.9965± 0.0023
South Dakota (SD)	182	149	81.9	0.9968± 0.0012
Virginia (VA)	97	87	89.7	0.9970± 0.0022
Vermont (VT)	199	163	81.9	0.9958± 0.0015
Total	**927**	**664**	**71.6**	0.9972± 0.0004
Hispanic-Americans (HA)				
Arizona-Phoenix (AZ 1)	109	104	95.4	0.9992± 0.0014
Arizona-Mesa (AZ 2)	47	44	93.6	0.9972± 0.0051
Connecticut (CT)	90	80	88.9	0.9973± 0.0022
Florida (FL)	20	18	90.0	0.9895± 0.0193
New York City (NYC)	38	32	84.2	0.9986± 0.0065
Ohio (OH)	24	24	100.0	1.0000± 0.0120
South Dakota (SD)	42	38	90.5	0.9954± 0.0063
Virginia (VA)	92	86	93.5	0.998 1± 0.002 1
Vermont (VT)	17	17	100.0	1.0000± 0.0202
Total	**479**	**386**	**80.6**	0.9981± 0.0004
Native Americans (NA)				
Apache	86	43	50.0	0.9436± 0.0141
Cheyenne	29	27	93.1	0.9951± 0.0106
Navajo	88	56	63.6	0.9804± 0.0059
Pima	19	17	89.5	0.9883± 0.02 10
South Dakota	112	91	81.3	0.9924± 0.003 5
South Dakota-Sioux	45	39	86.7	0 .9909± 0.0080
Vermont	19	19	100.0	1.0000± 0.0171
	398	**259**	**65.1**	0.9938± 0.0010
Asian-Americans (SA)				
Arizona-Tucson (AZ)	25	24	96.0	0.9967± 0.0125
New York City (NYC)	37	37	100.0	1.0000± 0.0063
Total	**62**	**61**	**98.4**	0 .9995± 0.0030

*DYS19 ,DYS385ab,DYS389I,DYS389II,DYS390,DYS391 ,DYS392,DYS393 DYS438,DYS439

Based on the 11 U.S. core loci, we find that the number of haploypes (corrected for sample size) varies by ethnic group (Table 2). Haplotype resolution is highest in Asian-Americans (98%) and African-Americans (87%), followed by Hispanic-Americans (81%) and European-Americans (72%). Haplotype resolution in pooled Native American samples is much lower (65%). The frequency of common haplotypes, as well as the number of haplotypes observed two or more times, also vary by ethnic group. The most common haplotype is found at the following frequencies for African-American, European-American, Hispanic-American, Asian-American, and pooled Native Americans: 0.7%, 2.8%, 2.3%, 3.2%, and 3.5%. When we included a total of 38 Y-STRs, haplotype resolution is near 100% for all ethnic groups, except Native Americans, which has a value of 90%. The Y-Filer kit (AB), which includes three of the loci discovered during this research (DYS448, DYS456, DYS458), produces higher haplotype resolution (average for all ethnic groups = 93.4%) than either the Power-Plex (Promega) (82.6%) or the 11 core U.S. loci (82.2%) (Figure 5).

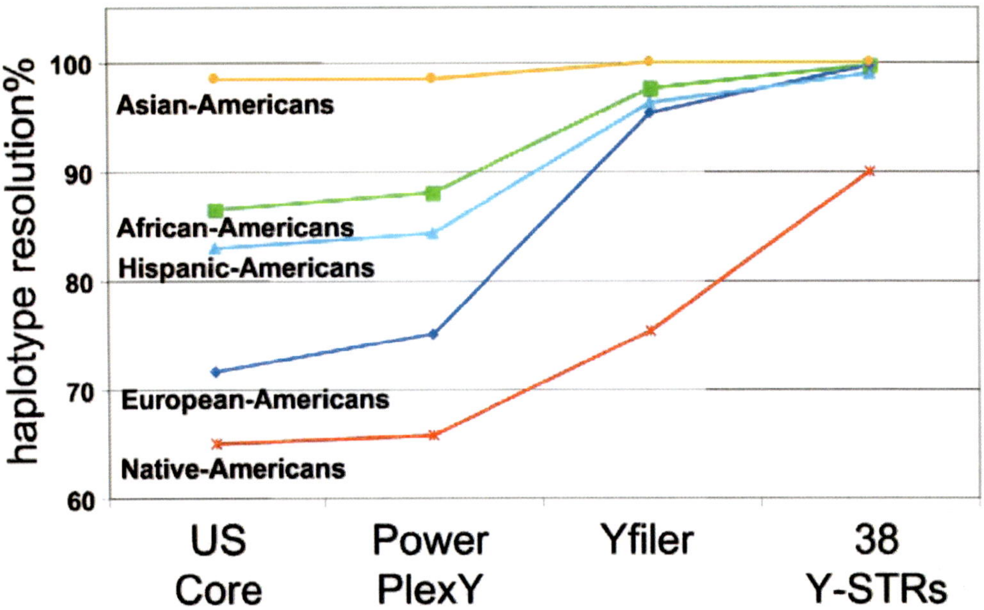

Figure 5. Comparison of haplotype resolution in 5 ethnic groups when using 11 U.S. core loci, 2 commercially available kits, and 38 Y-STRs.

3. Conclusions

USYSTR provides the DNA forensic community the ability to estimate Y-STR haplotype frequencies with associated 95% confidence intervals. Common Y chromosome haplotypes using the 11 U.S. core loci can be resolved by adding additional informative markers. Forensic labs that have validated the AB Y-Filer kit will achieve excellent resolution. For labs that have access to custom multiplex assays, we recommend using the following high-resolution markers to be used as a supplement to the 11 core U.S. loci: DYS449, DYS464, DYS570, DYS576, DYS463, and DYS607.

It is important to note (see below) that we do not endorse pooling of Native American populations for population genetic analyses. When considering individual Native American populations, haplotype resolution tend to be much lower and the frequency of common haplotypes much higher. For example, in our Apache sample, haplotype resolution is only 44.8% and the frequency of the most common haplotype is 16.7% (data not shown). In the following sections we explore reasons for the observed patterns of Y chromosome diversity in Native American and other U.S. populations.

C. Genetic Structure Among 38 Populations from the United States Based on 11 U.S. Core Y Chromosome STRs

1. Background and Significance

A key consideration for the proper scientific use of Y-STRs in DNA forensics is the creation of an appropriate population database. A large population database is necessary to help estimate the probability that two or more unrelated males share the same Y-STR haplotype [19]. To obtain an accurate estimate of a haplotype's frequency the database should represent the range ethnic groups within a population [30]. Otherwise, the frequency of a Y-STR haplotype of an individual whose ethnic group is not represented in the database is likely to be underestimated. Analyses of patterns of population subdivision can provide a means for determining the appropriate structure of a database. Given limitations in the number of individuals that can be sampled, it is important to assess whether data can be pooled for populations from the same ethnic group that have been collected from different geographic regions in the U.S. Because Y chromosome haplotypes have been shown to exhibit large frequency differences among populations from different regions of the world [31, 32], and because U.S. populations are composed of individuals with ancestry deriving from many parts of the world, empirical studies are required to measure the proportion of variation within and among populations of different ethnic groups [33]. Here we estimate the extent of U.S. population structure with an analysis of 11 Y-STRs in a sample of 2,517 individuals representing 38 U.S. populations.

2. Results

Polymorphism data are collected from an analysis of the 11 Y-STRs recommended by SWGDAM for use in the U.S. The population samples include individuals of self-described ancestry from five ethnic groups (African-Americans, European-Americans, Hispanic-Americans, Asian-Americans, and Native Americans) currently living in 10 Western (AZ, NM), Midwestern (SD, OH), Northeastern (VT, CT, NY, VA), and Southern states (NC, FL) (Figure 4). Population structure is examined using multidimensional scaling (MDS), analysis of molecular variance (AMOVA), and pairwise-population differentiation (PPD) tests. A MDS plot places the populations into four discrete clusters (African-American, European-American, Hispanic-American, and Asian-American) and one dispersed cluster of Native American populations (Figure 6). AMOVA indicates that most of the genetic variance

(73.7%) is found within populations; a notable amount (24.8%) is found between ethnic groups; while only a small amount (1.5%) is found among populations within ethnic groups (Table 3). Separate AMOVA analyses within each ethnic group show that only Native Americans contain statistically significant among population variation, while no statistically significant variation is found among populations within other ethnic groups (Table 3). PPD tests uncover no statistically significant differences among the 45 comparisons of pairs of African-American samples (Table 4A). For European-American samples, 3 out of 45 comparisons (NYC-CT, NYC-VA, and NYC-NC) are found to be statistically significant at $\alpha = 0.01$ level (Table 4B). Similarly, 2 of 36 comparisons among pairs of Hispanic-American samples reject panmixia (Mesa-CT, Mesa-VA) (Table 4C). Notably, this heterogeneity is due to only a single sample within each group (NYC and Mesa). For Native American samples, 13 out of 21 comparisons are statistically significant (Table 4D). Because multiple comparisons are made with the PPD tests, caution should be exercised in the interpretation of the results without a multiple test correction.

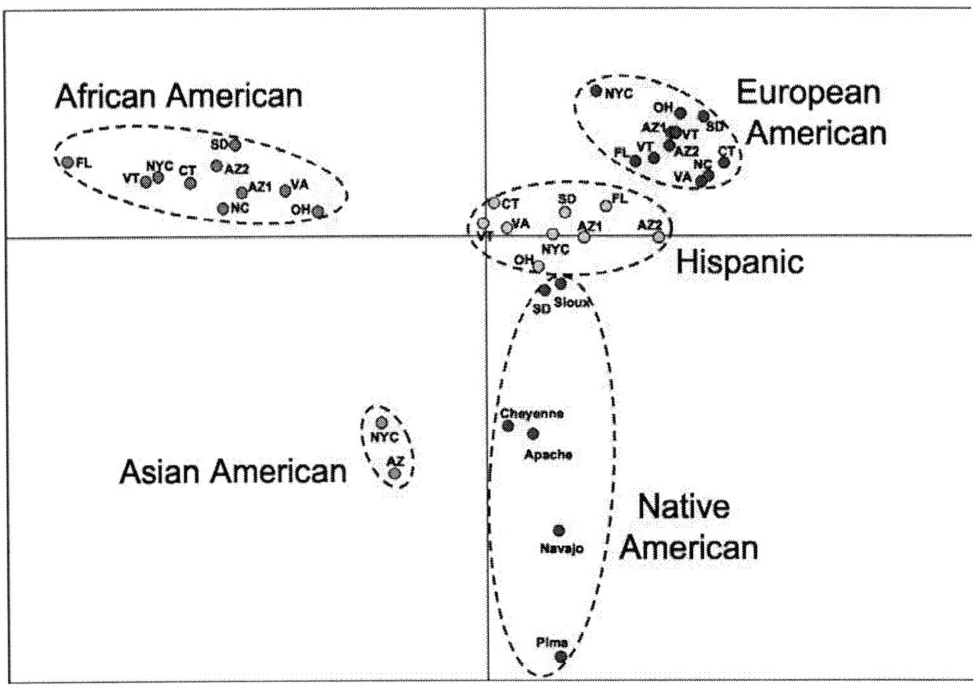

Figure 6.

3. Conclusions

This is the third large-scale study of the structure of Y-STR diversity in multiple U.S.populations [1, 2], and only the second that we are aware of that screens the 11 core locirecommended by SWDAM [2]. We find that levels of diversity based on the 11 U.S. core Y-STR loci (Table 2) are similar to those in Budowle et al.'s [2] 12 Y-STR analysis and consistently higher than those found by Kayser et al. [1] based on 9 Y-STRs. For example, discrimination capacity for Kayser et al.'s [1] African-American, European-American, andHispanic-American samples were on average 8% lower than for our samples. Our survey differs from the other two published studies in that it examines multiple Native American populations.The results indicate that Native American populations have lower levels of Y chromosome diversity than other U.S. ethnic groups. This is reflected in a higher percentage of shared haplo types and higher random match probabilities, both of which are important to take into consideration in forensic casework.

Table 3. Y-STR AMOVA

Comparison	Number of populations	Number of groups**	Among groups	Among populations within groups	Within populations
African-American (AA)	10	1	-	0.7	99.3
	10	4	0.2	0.5	99.3
European-American (EA)	10	1	-	0.2	99.8
	10	4	0	0.2	99.8
Hispanic-American (HA)	9	1	-	0.8	99.2
	9	4	0.4	0.4	99.2
Native-American (NA)	7	1	-	9.5	90.5*
	7	3	11.1*	1.8*	87.1*
Asian-American (SA)	2	Na	-	0	100
All groups except NA	31	4	27.55*	0.42	72.03*
All groups	38	5	24.8*	1.5*	73.7*

* $P < 0.01$
** SW, MW, NE, & S

Similar to the results of Kayser et al. [1] we find that Y chromosomes are significantly differentiated among U.S. ethnic groupings, but not among populations within ethnic groups from different geographic regions in the U.S. The proportion of among ethnic group variancereported here is almost identical to that found (24.9%) in the three ethnic groups (African-American, European-American, and Hispanic-American) sampled by Kayser et al. [1], and higher (15.4%) than that reported in the 5 ethnic groups (African-American, European-American, Hispanic-American, Asian-American, and Native American) sampled by Budowle etal. [2]. Our AMOVA results differ somewhat from those in previous studies in that the proportion of variance among-populations-within- groups is not significant for African-Americans, European-Americans, or Hispanic-Americans, either when placing all geographic populations into a single ethnic grouping, or when subdividing populations within each ethnic group into geographic regions in the U.S. (Table 3). Kayser et al. [1] found that the very small proportion of among-populations-within-groups variance in both their European-American and Hispanic-American samples (e.g., 1.8% and 2.6%, respectively) was statistically significant. The among-populations-within-groups variance (1.6%) for Budowle et al.'s [2] European-American sample was statistically significant, but not for their Hispanic-American sample (0.9%). Here,the only ethnic group with a statistically significant proportion of among-populations-within-group variance is Native Americans, where we find 9.5% of the total variance partitioned among 7 populations (tribes) (Table 3). Budowle et al. [2] found 3.0% of the total variance partitioned between their Navajo and Apache samples. The average among-populations-within-groups variance in the three studies is 1.2%. When we remove

Native Americans from our analysis, the among-populations-within-groups variance is only 0.4% (not statistically significant; data not shown).

Despite the lack of significant differentiation among regional African-American, European-American, Hispanic-American, and Asian-American populations in AMOVA, when multiple differentiation tests are performed among all pairs of populations some comparisons between European-American and Hispanic-American populations are statistically significant. The question we face is whether these comparisons are significant by chance or as a result of true biological differences. Our results are very similar to those of Kayser et al. [1], who did not find different frequencies of Y-STR haplotypes among their African-American samples, but did find heterogeneity within their European-American and Hispanic-American samples in pair-wise population differentiation tests. As is the case here, this heterogeneity was attributed to a single sample within each group. Because they could not identify an obvious reason why either of the samples was an outlier, they concluded that their result reflected chance [1]. We concur that a single outlier does not support a pattern of broad-scale geographic structuring (e.g., as observed for Native American populations) and the combined results provide no compelling evidence for incorporating geographic structure within African-American, European-American, and Hispanic-American Y-STR databases at present. One implication of these results is that independent databases can be combined for each of these ethnic groups. Still, it would be prudent to continue sampling from additional populations to further assess the structure of U.S. populations.

The extent to which we expect significant population structure within an ethnic group depends mainly on four factors: levels of subdivision in the ancestral source populations, the extent of non-random migration to the U.S., migration rates among geographic regions after arrival in theU.S., and the degree to which inter-ethnic admixture varies regionally. Kayser et al. [1]suggested that the lack of geographic heterogeneity among their African-American samples maybe a by-product of extensive migration from rural to urban areas during and after World War I. However, not enough is yet known about the structure of Y-STR haplotype variation among African source populations, or the extent of mixing among source populations in the process offorced migration to the U.S. The finding of relatively high levels of population structure in Native Americans is not unexpected given a long history of small effective population sizes,endogamy, isolation, and founder effects [34]. Perhaps it is more surprising that Hispanic-American populations do not show stronger geographic structure given that the term Hispanicdoes not refer to a defined geographic region, but can refer to individuals of Mexican, PuertoRican, Cuban, Central/South American, or other Spanish culture ancestry. In fact, Hispanic-American populations are known to have differing degrees of Spanish, Native American, and African ancestry in different U.S. regions [1, 35]. For example, Eastern Hispanics are expected to have more Afro-Caribbean ancestry than Hispanic populations from the Southwest, which are expected to have more Native American ancestry [36]. However, our Eastern Hispanic-American populations do not seem to cluster closer to the African-American populations than do the southwest Hispanic-American populations (Figure 6).

In conclusion, the extremely consistent patterns of genetic structure observed in this study and previous studies [1, 2] suggest that pooling samples from different geographic regions will not lead to strong biases in the estimation of Y-STR haplotype frequencies for African-American, European-American, Hispanic-American, and Asian-American populations. On the other hand, separate larger databases from Native American subpopulations are needed to infer match probabilities for different tribal groups. Finally, the continued collection of core Y-STR data from additional populations is needed to ensure that we construct databases that most accurately reflect the structure of U.S. populations.

D. Population Structure of Y Chromosome SNP Haplogroups in the United States and Forensic Implications for Constructing Y Chromosome STR Databases

1. Background and Significance

The MDS and AMOVA analyses of Y-STRs indicate low levels of population structure withinAfrican-American, European-American, Hispanic-American, and Asian-American groups. However, the more sensitive PPD test detected heterogeneity in our European-American and Hispanic-American samples. The fact that a single sample within each of the European-American (NYC) and Hispanic-American (Mesa) ethnic groups accounts for all of the statistically significant PPD tests argues against a broad-scale pattern of geographic structuring within these ethnic groups. One possibility is that the heterogeneity results from chance rather than any true biological differentiation [1]. Additional inquiry into the ways that populations were sampled, the extent of admixture in each sample, and the gathering of additional samples from these and other regions may help to pinpoint the underlying causes of these observations.

A major component of population structure in the U.S. may be determined by admixture among ethnic groups. Because the largest proportion of among-group genetic variation in the U.S. is partitioned between ethnic groups, and only a small proportion is found among populations within ethnic groups [1, 2, 37], it is imperative to examine the extent to which there is regional variation in the rates of inter-ethnic admixture. There is a body of literature indicating that substantial mixing among some U.S. ethnic groups has occurred [35, 38-43]. If inter-ethnic admixture rates do, in fact, vary regionally, then there could be a need for regional forensic databases.

In this study we employ a set of 61 Y-SNPs to estimate levels of population structure and rates of admixture among U.S. populations. Our estimates of population heterogeneity are then compared with similar estimates based on Y-STRs. The advantage of Y-SNPs for estimating admixture rates is that they permit direct estimates of admixture deriving from *multiple* parental source populations. This is due to the high geographic specificity of Y-SNPs, which makes these markers a powerful tool for inferring the ancestral source population(s) of paternal lineages. Through use of a large database of SNP haplogroup frequencies in samples collected from many regions of the world, we are able to infer the geographic provenance of Y chromosomes in the U.S. population; i.e., whether they originated in African, European, Asian, or Native American source populations.

2. Results

A set of 61 Y-SNPs is typed in 2,517 individuals from 38 populations in the U.S. The 61 Y-SNPs mark all 18 major haplogroups (A-R) on the Y chromosome tree, as well as several sub-lineages providing key information on the continental origins of Y chromosomes (Figure 7). While there is general correspondence between estimates of population structure based on Y-STRs and Y-SNPs, AMOVA indicates a greater proportion of SNP variation partitioned among ethnic groups (32.3%) than for Y-STRs (24.8%). Most of the genetic variance (65.8%) is found within populations and only a small amount (2.0%) is found among populations within ethnic groups (Table 5). Separate AMOVA analyses within each ethnic group show that only the Native Americans contain high levels of among population variation (17.9%), while ≤1% of the total variation is partitioned among populations within other ethnic groups (Table 5). A MDS plot reflects these patterns, placing African-Americans, European-Americans, Hispanic-Americans, and Asian-Americans into discrete clusters, with Native Americans being more dispersed. Patterns of admixture vary dramatically across ethnic groups (Figure 8). All European-American (Figure 9) and Asian-American (data not shown) samples have very low levels of admixture. Approximately 30% of African-American Y chromosomes have European ancestry, and this proportion is relatively constant across the sampled geographic regions. Hispanic-American Y chromosomes descend mainly from European ancestors (79%). The proportion of Native American Y chromosomes is surprisingly consistent among Hispanic-American samples (averaging ~12%), while the African contribution (~7%) is clearly higher on the eastern seaboard (~16%) (Figure 9). Native Americans exhibit the largest regional variation in admixture rates, with European-derived Y chromosomes in Southwestern, Midwestern, and Eastern populations at frequencies of ~9%, 44%, and 90%, respectively.

3. Conclusions

These results support the conclusion that Y chromosomes are significantly differentiated among U.S. ethnic groupings, but not among populations within ethnic groups from different geographic regions within the U.S. Hence, with the exception of Native Americans, geographic origin of samples within a U.S. ethnic database is not critical. There is general correspondence betweenestimates of population structure parameters based on these 61 Y-SNPs and 11 core Y-STRstyped in the same samples [37]. However, the Y-SNP results indicate a greater proportion of total variation partitioned among ethnic groups (32.3%) than for Y-STRs (24.8%). This may be due to higher geographic specificity of Y-SNPs [14] and higher mutation rates of Y-STRs [44,45], which lead to much higher discrimination capacities and measures of Y chromosome diversity for Y-STR haplotypes [12] compared with Y-SNP haplogroups (Table 4). Similar to the case for Y-STRs [37], separate AMOVA analyses within each ethnic group show that only Native Americans contain high levels of among population SNP haplogroup variation (Table 5).In contrast, ≤1% (n.s.) of the total SNP variation is partitioned among-populations-within-groups when considering only African-American, European-American, Hispanic-American, and Asian-American samples (data not shown).

Table 4A. P values resulting from pairwise population differentiation tests on African-American samples

AA	Phoenix	Mesa	CT	FL	NC	NYC	OH	SD	VA	VT
Phoenix	*									
Mesa	0.829	*								
CT	0.789	0.546	*							
FL	0.088	0.122	0.106	*						
NC	0.792	0.602	0.639	0.095	*					
NYC	0.554	0.382	0.875	0.173	0.373	*				
OH	0.213	0.112	0.048	0.011	0.125	0.056	*			
SD	0.542	0.705	0.333	0.065	0.211	0.271	0.103	*		
VA	0.481	0.273	0.140	0.019	0.269	0.119	0.868	0.218	*	
VT	0.360	0.544	0.562	0.343	0.500	0.644	0.028	0.145	0.067	*

Table 4B. P values resulting from pairwise population differentiation tests on European-American samples

EA	Phoenix	Mesa	CT	FL	NC	NYC	OH	SD	VA	VT
Phoenix	*									
Mesa	0.968	*								
CT	0.541	0.805	*							
FL	0.797	0.813	0.260	*						
NC	0.436	0.636	0.943	0.474	*					
NYC	0.159	0.155	**0.004**	0.176	**0.004**	*				
OH	0.504	0.547	0.091	0.522	0.170	0.018	*			
SD	0.939	0.963	0.279	0.574	0.270	0.011	0.633	*		
VA	0.343	0.458	0.384	0.589	0.896	**0.007**	0.335	0.197	*	
VT	0.532	0.879	0.208	0.773	0.340	**0.017**	0.736	0.817	0.337	*

Table 4C. P values resulting from pairwise population differentiation tests on Hispanic-American samples

HA	Phoenix	Mesa	CT	FL	NYC	OH	SD	VA	VT
Phoenix	*								
Mesa	0.116	*							
CT	0.036	**0.006**	*						
FL	0.738	0.817	0.165	*					
NYC	0.479	0.142	0.219	0.479	*				
OH	0.804	0.084	0.282	0.5 12	0.630	*			
SD	0.657	0.070	0.256	0.3 99	0.370	0.467	*		
VA	0.138	**0.007**	0.686	0.215	0.271	0.693	0.333	*	
VT	0.234	0.030	0.734	0.3 13	0.417	0.645	0.263	0.743	*

Table 4D. P values resulting from pairwise population differentiation tests on Native American samples

NA	APA	CHY	NAV	PIM	SD	SIO	VT
APA	*						
CHY	0.547	*					
NAV	0.047	0.104	*				
PIM	**0.001**	**0.001**	**0.006**	*			
SD	**0.000**	0.022	**0.000**	**0.000**	*		
SIO	**0.001**	0.021	**0.000**	**0.000**	0.714	*	
VT	**0.000**	**0.000**	**0.000**	**0.000**	0.018	0.038	*

The set of 61 Y-SNPs employed here mark all 18 major haplogroups (A-R) on the Ychromosome haplogroup tree, as well as several sub-lineages providing information on thecontinental origins of Y chromosomes (Figure 7). The geographic specificity of Y-SNP haplogroups allows direct estimates of the proportion of paternal genetic ancestry or admixture rates deriving from multiple source populations. We find that the proportion of chromosomes with African, European, Asian, and Native American ancestry varies among populations within groups (Figure 9). Regional variation in the proportion of European Y chromosomes in African-American populations is apparent in the MDS plot in Figure 8 (with OH as the most admixed population on the far left and FL as the least admixed population on the far right), as is regional variation in the frequency of African Y chromosomes in Hispanic-American populations (with VA, CT, VT being placed on the right side of the Hispanic-American cluster closest to the African-Americans). Native Americans exhibit the largest regional variation in admixture rates,with European-derived Y chromosomes in Southwestern, Midwestern, and Eastern (VT) populations at frequencies of 8.5% ± 1.8%, 44.1% ± 23.7%, and 89.5%, respectively. The finding of high frequencies of European Y chromosomes in the VT, SD, and SIO Native-American samples helps to explain their position on the MDS plot.

It is interesting that the European and Native American paternal contribution to Hispanic-American populations is so consistent given that the term Hispanic does not refer to a defined geographic region, but can refer to individuals of Mexican, Puerto Rican, Cuban, Central/SouthAmerican, or other Spanish culture ancestry. In fact, Hispanic-American populations are known to have differing degrees of Spanish, Native American, and African ancestry in different regionsof the U.S. [1, 35]. The higher frequency of African-derived Y chromosomes in the East is consistent with a greater contribution of Puerto Rican and Cuban Hispanics to East Coast U.S.populations, compared with a higher Mexican presence in the West [46]. In contrast to these Y chromosome results, both mt DNA and autosomal systems point to a much higher frequency of Native American maternal lineages in Hispanic-American populations, especially in Mexican Americans, and higher frequencies of African maternal lineages in Puerto Ricans and Cubans [1,35, 36, 47]. The larger European paternal contribution to Hispanic-American populations likely reflects sex-specific biases in admixture rates for Hispanics, not necessarily while in the U.S. but in their source populations (e.g., [48]). Despite this regional variation, there were low levels of Hispanic Y-STR haplotype heterogeneity in our previous survey [37], as well as in the surveys of Kayser et al. [1] and

Budowle et al. [2]. Thus, geographic origin of samples is not a critical factor in the construction of U.S. Hispanic Y-STR databases.

Table 5. Diverity statistics for Y chromosome haplogroups (Hg)

Ethnic Group/population	Sample size	Number of Hgs	Discrimination capacity (%)	diversity (+/- SE)
African-Americans (AA)	**651**	**24**	**3.7**	**0.585± 0.020**
Arizona-Phoenix	76	8	10.5	0.564± 0.05 8
Arizona-Mesa	52	8	15.4	0.554± 0.076
Connecticut (CT)	89	13	14.6	0.514± 0.061
Florida (FL)	20	5	25.0	0.442± 0.133
North Carolina (NC)	84	10	11.9	0.595± 0.054
New York City (NYC)	42	5	11.9	0.440± 0.088
Ohio (OH)	103	13	12.6	0.671± 0.038
South Dakota (SD)	57	11	19.3	0.666± 0.066
Virginia (VA)	77	10	13.0	0.635± 0.050
Vermont (VT)	51	10	19.6	0.522± 0.083
European-Americans (EA)	**927**	**30**	**3.2**	**0.637± 0.017**
Arizona-Phoenix	56	12	21.4	0.688± 0.062
Arizona-Mesa	43	10	23.3	0.713± 0.067
Connecticut (CT)	85	13	15.3	0.578± 0.060
Florida (FL)	37	11	29.7	0.673± 0.085
North Carolina (NC)	87	12	13.8	0.568± 0.060
New York City (NYC)	42	13	31.0	0.818 ± 0.044
Ohio (OH)	99	15	15.2	0.660 ± 0.05 1
South Dakota (SD)	182	17	9.3	0.641 ± 0.036
Virginia (VA)	97	13	13.4	0.548± 0.058
Vermont (VT)	199	14	7.0	0.626± 0.037
Hispanic-Americans (HA)	**479**	**27**	**5.6**	**0.786± 0.018**
Arizona-Phoenix	109	15	13.8	0.792± 0.035
Arizona-Mesa	47	12	25.5	0.662± 0.076
Connecticut (CT)	90	19	21.1	0.792± 0.03 8
Florida (FL)	20	8	40.0	0.700± 0.109
New York City (NYC)	38	12	31.6	0.757± 0.067
Ohio (OH)	24	11	45.8	0.815± 0.072
South Dakota (SD)	42	13	31.0	0.812± 0.053
Virginia (VA)	92	20	21.7	0.817± 0.037
Vermont (VT)	17	9	52.9	0.868± 0.068
Native Americans (NA)	398	18	4.5	0.775± 0.010
Apache	86	6	7.0	0.667± 0.032
Cheyenne	29	4	13.8	0.677± 0.069
Navajo	88	9	10.2	0.597± 0.03 1
Pima	19	3	15.8	0.608± 0.070
South Dakota	112	15	13.4	0.789± 0.025

Table 5. Diverity statistics for Y chromosome haplogroups (Hg) (continued)

Ethnic Group/population	Sample size	Number of Hgs	Discrimination capacity (%)	diversity (+/- SE)
South Dakota-Sioux	45	11	24.4	0.711± 0.058
Vermont	19	6	31.6	0.597± 0.122
Asian Americans (SA)	62	12	19.4	0.848± 0.025
Arizona-Tucson	25	8	32.0	0.840± 0.038
New York City	37	11	29.7	0.857± 0.040

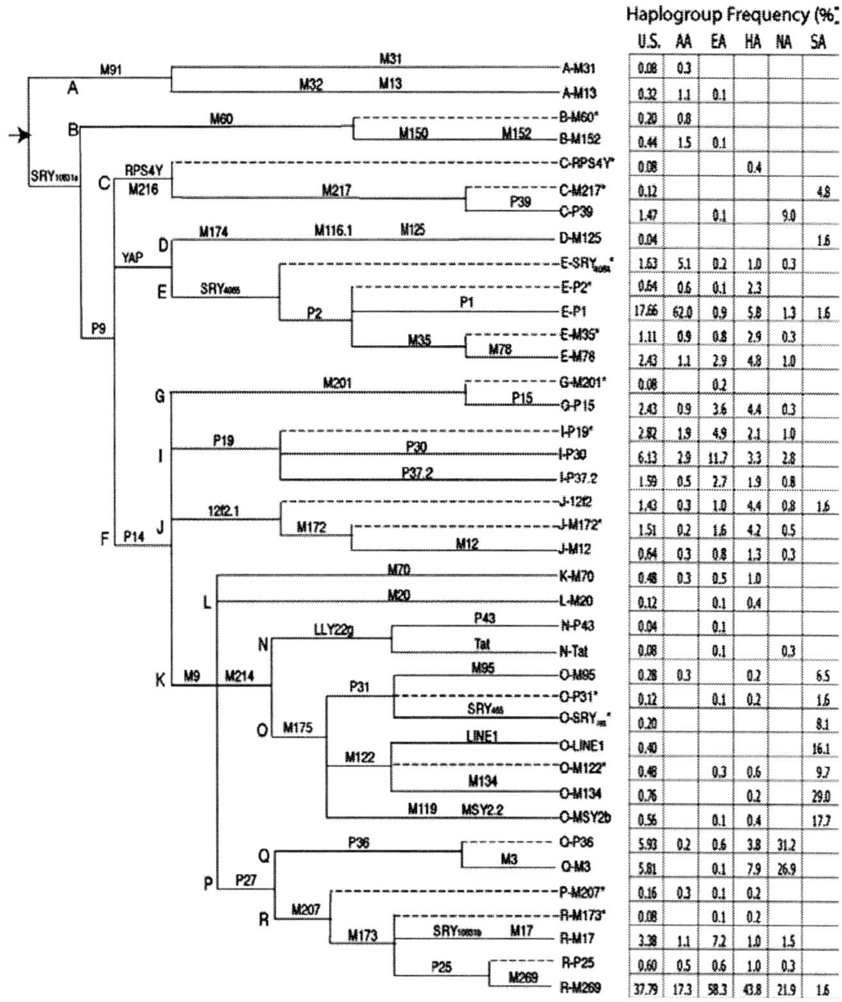

Figure 7. Maximum-parsimony tree of 39 Y chromosome haplogroups present in this surveyalong with their frequencies in five ethnic groups from the U.S. The root of the tree is denoted by an arrow. Major clades (i.e., A-R) are labeled with large capital letters to the left of eachclade. Mutation names are given along the branches. The length of each branch is notproportional to the number of mutations or the age of the mutation. Dotted lines refer to internalnodes not defined by downstream markers (i.e., paragroups). The names of the 39 haplogroupsobserved in the present study are shown to the right of the branches. Haplogroup frequencies areshown on the far right for the total sample (n = 2,517), African Americans (AA, n = 651),European Americans (European-American, n = 927), Hispanic Americans (HA, n = 479), NativeAmericans (NA, n = 398), and Asian Americans (SA, n = 62).

Y-SNP MDS population plot

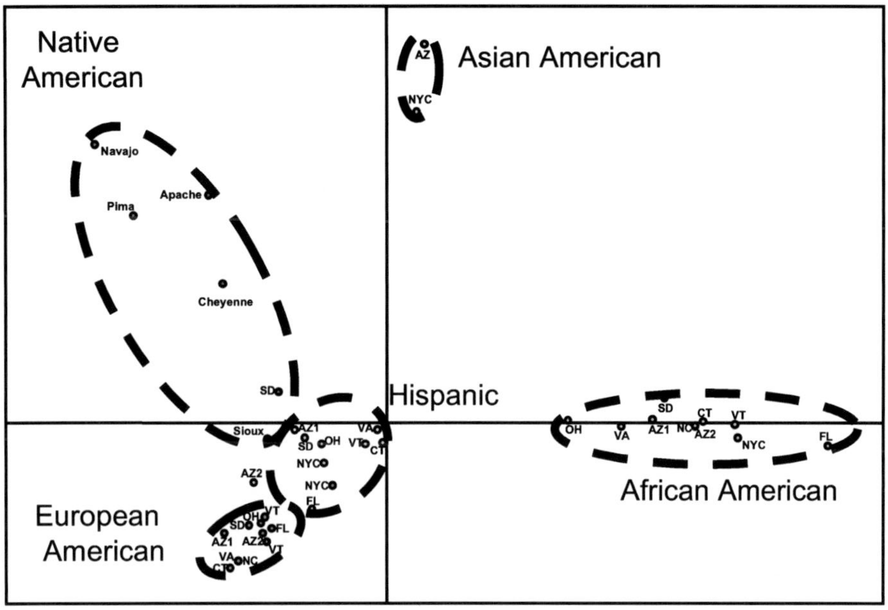

Figure 8. MDS plot of 38 populations based on ΦST genetic distances. Population codes are thesame as in Table 2. Note that the NYC and the VT samples are outliers with respect to thedotted circles placed around the European American and Native American samples, respectively.

Table 6. Y-SNP AMOVA

Populations	number of chromosomes	number of populations	number of groups	% variance		
				among groups	among populations within groups	within populations
African-Americans	651	10	1	-	1.4	98.6
		10	4a	0.4	1.0	98.6
European-Americans	927	10	1	-	0.2	99.8
		10	4a	-0.1	0.3	99.9
Hispanic-Americans	479	9	1	-	1.0	99.0
		9	4a	1.0	0.1	98.9
Native-Americans	398	7	1	-	**16.0**	**84.0**
		7	3b	17.9	**2.9**	**79.2**
Asian-Americans	62	2	1	-	0.0	100.0
five ethnic groups	2718	38	5	**32.3**	**2.0**	**65.8**

bolded numbers, P < 0.00 1

a Southwest, Midwest, Northeast, and South

b Southwest, Midwest, East

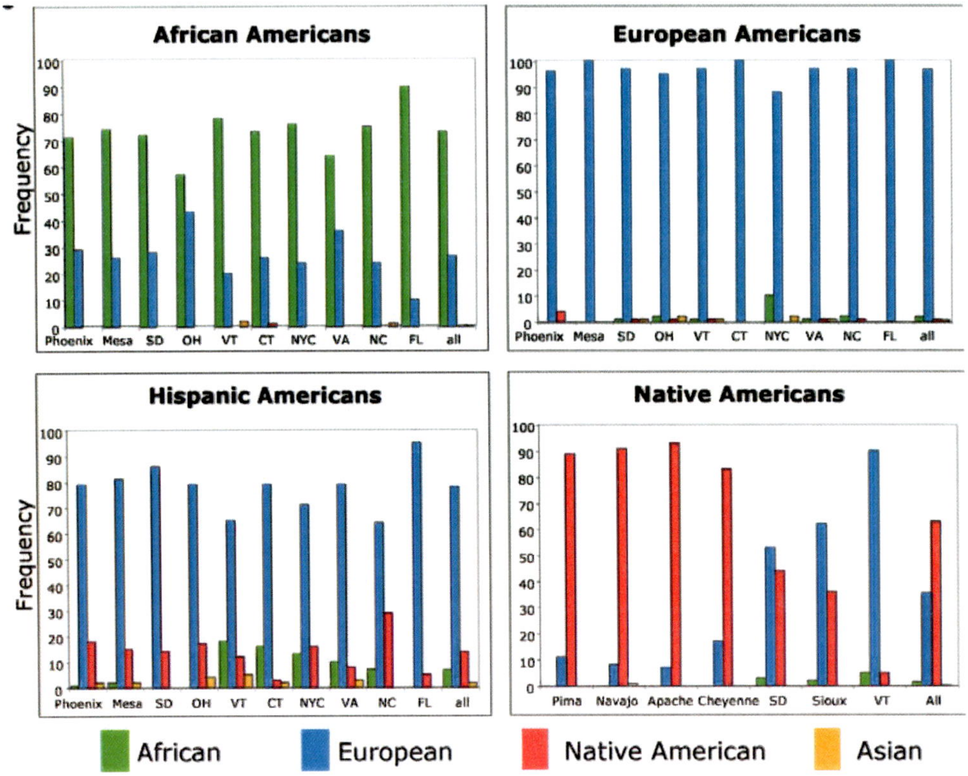

Figure 9. Bar chart showing the relative proportions of Y chromosomes with African (greenbar), European (blue bar), Native American (pink bar), and Asian ancestry (orange bar). (A)African Americans, (B) European Americans, (C) Hispanic Americans, and (D) NativeAmericans. Population codes are the same as in Table 2. A small sample of Hispanics from North Carolina (n = 15) that was not included in other analyses is shown here.

One of our main objectives is to examine the extent to which variation in inter-ethnic admixture contributes to observed heterogeneity in Y-STR haplotype frequencies. As noted above, regional variation in the proportion of paternal ancestry may not always be due to local differences in rates of admixture (i.e., gene flow between ethnic groups after their arrival in the U.S.), but to different rates of inter-ethnic admixture in ancestral source populations, or to ancestral population structure in combination with non-random migration to the U.S. While previous studies revealed very little heterogeneity in Y-STR haplotype frequencies among populations within ethnic groups [1, 2, 37], cases of statistically significant differences between particular pairs of populations were observed in pairwise population differentiation (PPD) tests [1, 37]. For example, in our Y-STR database [37], 3 of 45 comparisons between pairs of European-American samples, and 2 of 36 comparisons between pairs of Hispanic-American samples, were statistically significant. All three European-American comparisons involved our sample fromNew York City, which differed from our Connecticut, Virginia, and North Carolina European-American samples. Both Hispanic-American comparisons involved our Mesa (Arizona) sample, which differed from our Connecticut and Virginia Hispanic-American samples. Similarly, PPD tests performed by Kayser et al. [1] on their database of 1,705 haplotypes based on 9 Y-STR srevealed heterogeneity between their Texas European-American sample and other European-Americans, and between their Texas Hispanic-

American sample and other Hispanic-Americans. They concluded that the significant heterogeneity involving these two samples reflected chance rather than any true biological differences.

We test whether the statistically significant PPD tests involving Y-STR haplotypes in our Hispanic samples [37] can be explained by variable frequencies of African Y chromosomes. When we remove the 36 African Y chromosomes identified by Y-SNPs from our Hispanic-American Y-STR database and repeat the PPD tests, we find no significant difference between any of the 36 pairs of Hispanic-American samples (data not shown). This suggests that regional variation in settlement patterns of Hispanics, for example, from the Caribbean or from Mexico, could cause regional heterogeneity in frequencies of Y-STR haplotypes. However, current data reveal only minor effects on Y chromosome variation [1, 2, 37].

Next, we test whether variable frequencies of African Y chromosomes in European-American populations leads to the significant heterogeneity in Y-STR haplotypes in our NYC, CT, NC, and VA samples [37]. Upon removal of t[1, 37] European-American samples) and I-P30 (4.8% for NYC *versus* 11.3% ± 2.8% for other European-American samples), and the highest frequency of the Eastern European signature haplogroup, R-M17 (23.8% for NYC *versus* 7.4% ± 4.7% for other European-American samples). Thus, we hypothesize that descent from a structured European source population (with non-random migration to the U.S.) underlies the observed Y-STR heterogeneity. To address this hypothesis, we analyze four western (England, Ireland, France, and Germany) and three eastern (Poland, Hungary, and Russia) European population samples that are potential sources for the European-American population. We find statistically significant population structure in Europe, with 10.9% of the total Y-STR haplotype variance partitioned between Western and Eastern European samples (data not shown). Interestingly, our NYC sample itself is differentiated from three of the four Western European samples (England, Ireland, and France) and not from any of the three Eastern European samples. Therefore, we conclude that population structure in Europe is a potential factor leading to heterogeneity among European-Americans.

Finally, we wanted to know whether regional variation in admixture among Native American populations plays an important role in structuring Native American Y chromosome variation. When we remove the 124 European-derived Y chromosomes from our Native American database, we find that AMOVA still results in significant differences in Y-STR haplotype frequencies among Western, Midwestern, and Eastern Native American populations (data not shown). The percent of among group variance (9.4%) is only slightly lower than in the case when all (i.e., admixed and indigenous) Y-STR haplotypes are included in the analysis (11.1%).We conclude that Native American Y chromosomes are differentiated with respect to geography and/or tribal affiliation, regardless of the degree of admixture with European-American males.This is consistent with a long history of genetic drift as a result of small effective population sizes of Native American tribal groups, endogamy, isolation, and founder effects [34].

E. JOINT MATCH PROBABILITIES FOR Y CHROMOSOME AND AUTOSOMAL MARKERS

1. Background and Significance

In several forensic settings, one may need to obtain a joint match probability for a set of autosomal and Y chromosome markers. The ability to combine data from the autosomes and the Y chromosome is particularly important in cases where the signal from the male autosomal markers is largely obscured by the overwhelming amount of the victim's DNA, such that only a subset of the tested autosomal markers can be detected in the resulting mixture [10, 49]. In these cases Y-linked markers might be easily amplied, resulting in an *n*-locus haplotype for the perpetuator's Y chromosome. How can we estimate the joint match probabilities for autosomal and Y chromosome markers with a random draw from the reference population?

Following the 1996 National Research Council recommendations [3], the product rule is typically used to compute the match probability for autosomal markers, multiplying the single locus genotype frequencies (suitably corrected for population structure and differences in allele frequencies among distinct subpopulations) of the *m* scored markers to obtain the *m*-locus genotype frequency. The product rule does not apply for obtaining the frequency of a particular Y haplotype from estimates of individual marker allele frequencies. Y-linked markers (i.e., from the non-recombining region) are typically in strong linkage disequilibrium. Thus, the frequency of the particular haplotype must be estimated from a reference database. Here we test for a Y-autosomal association and provide some theoretical recommendations for obtaining a joint match probability.

Because the Y chromosome and autosomes are unlinked, this might suggest using the product of the autosomal and Y match probabilities for the joint matching probability. There are some concerns with this assumption. First, disequilibrium between the mitochondrial DNA and the autosomes is known to exist in many hybrid zones in natural populations of various organisms [50, 51]. Y-autosomal disequilibria should be empirically quantified in population samples rather than assumed. Sinha et al. [52] tested for associations between seven Y-STRs and thirteen autosomal STRs in an African-American and a European-American sample from Louisiana. We suggest that the appropriate test is between Y haplotypes and autosomal genotypes. Second, Y chromosome haplotypes can be highly informative as to which subpopulation an individual belongs, and this in turn potentially changes the autosomal allele frequencies used to compute the autosomal match probabilities.

2. Results

Empirical tests of association between Y chromosome and autosomal markers are presented and a theoretical framework for determining a joint match probability is recommended. Statistical analyses of association are performed in sixteen U.S. populations between the autosomal genotypes from loci CSF1PO, FGA, THO1, TPOX, vWA, D3S1358, D5S818, D7S820, D8S1179, D13S317, D16S539, D18S512, D21S11 and Y chromosome haplotypes determined from loci DYS19, DYS385ab, DYS389I, DYS389II, DYS390,

DYS391, DYS392, DYS393, DYS438, and DYS439. The sample populations include individuals of African-American,European-American, Hispanic-American, Asian-American, and Native American ancestry. The results are consistent with independence of Y and autosomal markers (Figure 10). A more complete account of our approach to computing the joint Y-autosomal matching probability is described in APPENDIX A. This approach includes weighting the major ethnic groups by the appropriate census sizes and a correction for population structure. A conservative estimate of the joint probability is obtained by multiplying the largest value of the group autosomal match probabilities by the estimated matching probability for the Y chromosome (see APPENDIX A).

	N		CSF1PO 1	FGA 2	THO1 3	TPOX 4	vWA 5	D3S1358 6	D5S818 7	D7S820 8	D8S1179 9	D13S317 10	D16S539 11	D18S512 12	D21S11 13
	137	Yhap	-	-	-	-	-	-	-	-	-	-	-	-	-
NYC	43	Yhap	-	-	-	-	-	-	-	-	-	-	-	-	-
NC	94	Yhap	-	-	-	-	-	-	-	-	-	-	-	-	-
	137	Yhap	-	-	-	-	-	-	-	-	-	-	-	-	-
NYC	41	Yhap	-	-	-	-	-	-	-	-	-	-	-	-	-
NC	96	Yhap	-	-	-	-	-	-	-	-	-	-	-	-	-
	53	Yhap	-	-	-	-	-	-	-	-	-	-	-	-	-
NYC	38	Yhap	-	-	-	-	-	-	-	-	-	-	-	-	-
NC	15	Yhap	-	-	-	-	-	-	-	-	-	-	-	-	-
	168	Yhap	-	-	-	-	-	+	-	-	-	-	-	-	-
Apac he	85	Yhap	-	-	-	-	-	-	-	-	-	-	-	-	-
Naaj o	83	Yhap	-	-	-	-	-	-	-	-	-	-	-	-	-

Figure 10. Exact test of non-random association between Y haplotype and CODIS loci. A minus sign means not statistically significant.

3. Conclusions

Analysis of existing data show that the product rule can be safely applied in computing joint autosomal genotype/Y haplotype match probabilities. A conservative estimate of the joint probability is obtained by multiplying the largest value of the group autosomal match probabilities by the estimated matching probability for the Y chromosome. We also suggest that an alternative approach to the current reporting of match probabilities by ethnic group is (given a defined reference population) to weight the ethnic match probabilities by the census values for ethnic groups, providing a much more natural probability.

V. Final Thoughts and Recommendations

The population of the U.S. is comprised of people with ancestry tracing to Africa, Europe, Asia, the Pacific, and the Americas. The results presented here indicate that continental origin rather than current location in the U.S. determines major patterns of Y chromosome variation for most ethnic groups. Presently, intermarriage among groups has not eliminated inter-ethnic genetic structure. Despite the potential for admixture to erode population structure, the 2000 U.S.Census revealed that only 2.4% of all respondents reported being derived from two or more "racial" groups (excluding Hispanics; [46]). Nonetheless, there is a body of literature indicating substantial mixing among some U.S. ethnic groups [35, 38-42]. Continuing migration and admixture among ethnic groups may eventually reduce population structure to the point wherewe will no longer need to construct separate forensic databases in the U.S. In the meantime, more research is needed for several reasons. While simple methods for adjusting for minor levels of population structure among Hispanic populations should be sufficient for correcting haplotype frequency estimates [3], the finding of significant differences in frequencies of African-derived Y chromosomes among Hispanic samples raises potential concerns for the proper construction of Hispanic databases. In addition, more analyses of European-American samples from various parts of the U.S. that are known to have different ethnic compositions will help to determine how frequent we expect outliers (such as NYC) in Y chromosome databases. While African-American populations seems to show the least amount of among population within group variation of any ethnic group surveyed, additional research should help to understand the underlying causes for the apparent homogeneity [1]. Additional Y-STR surveys of putative African source populations will help to determine whether a lack of structure in the putative source population, along with similar admixture rates in the U.S., can explain the observed homogeneity among African-American sub-populations. Finally, more work is needed to construct appropriate Y-STR databases of Native American populations.

Summary of Notable Results that Impact Forensic Casework

1) An increase in the number of highly informative markers on the Y chromosome that are useful for forensic casework. Some of these markers are already included in a commercially available Y-typing kit (Applied Biosystems Yfiler), while many others may eventually be available in particular labs after testing on non-probative samples in forensic crime labs.

2) An online searchable database of these and many previously available markers already in use in forensic casework. This database includes 38 Y-STRs typed in over 2,500 samples representing the major U.S. population groups. An additional 5 Y-STRs have been typed in a subset of these samples, and 61 Y-SNPs have been typed in all samples. This database can be used by forensic laboratories to establish match statistics.

3) Demonstration of independence between Y haplotypes and autosomal markers for most surveyed populations and recommendations for a statistical approach on how to combine Y haplotype and autosomal marker frequencies to estimate joint match probabilities.

4) Demonstration that data from different regional areas in the U.S. can be pooled without leading to strong biases in the estimation of Y-STR haplotype frequencies. While this is true for four of the major U.S. ethnic groups, larger databases of Native Americans are needed for proper estimation of Native American Y chromosome haplotypes.

Publications

Hammer MF, TM Karafet, AJ Redd, H. Jarjanazi H, S. Santachiara-Benerecetti, H. Soodyall, and S.L. Zegura. 2001. Hierarchical patterns of global human Y chromosome diversity. *Molecular Biology and Evolution* 18:1189-1203.

Redd AJ, AB Agellon, VA Kearney, VA Contreras, T Karafet, H Park, P de Knijff, JM Butler, and MF Hammer. 2002. Forensic value of fourteen novel STRs on the human Y chromosome. *Forensic Science International.* 130:97-111.

Butler JM, R Schoske, PM Vallone, MC Kline, AJ Redd, and MF Hammer. 2002. A novel multiplex for simultaneous amplification of 20 Y chromosome STR markers. *Forensic Science International* 129:10-24.

Redd AJ, J Roberts-Thomson, T Karafet, M Bamshad, LB Jorde, JM Naidu, B Walsh, and MF Hammer. 2002. Gene flow from the Indian subcontinent to Australia: evidence from the Y chromosome. *Current Biology* 12:673-677.

The Y chromosome Consortium: M Hammer , ME Hurles, MA Jobling, T Karafet, TE King, P de Knijff, A Pandya, A Redd, FR Santos, C Tyler-Smith, P Underhill, E Wood, M Thomas, L Cavalli-Sforza, N Ellis, T Jenkins, J Kidd, K Kidd, P Forster, S Zegura, and M Kaplan. 2002. A nomenclature system for the tree of human Y-chromosomal binary haplogroups. *Genome Research* 12:339-348.

Bonne-Tamir B, M Korostishevsky, AJ Redd, Y Pel-Or, ME Kaplan, MF Hammer. 2003. Maternal and paternal lineages of the samaritan isolate: mutation rates and time to most recent common male ancestor. *Annals of Human Genetetics* 67:153-64.

Redd AJ, VA Contreras, VA Kearney, D Stover, T Karafet, and MF Hammer. 2006. Genetic structure among 38 populations from the United States based on 11 U.S. core Y chromosome STRs. *Journal of Forensic Science*: in press

Hammer MF, VA Contreras, VA Kearney, D Stover, G Zhang, T Karafet, and Redd AJ. 2006. Population structure of Y chromosome SNP haplogroups in the United States and forensic implications for constructing Y chromosome STR databases. *Journal of Forensic Science*: in press.

In Progress

Walsh JB, AJ Redd, MF Hammer. Joint match probabilities for Y and autosomal markers. To be submitted to *Int. J. Leg. Med.*

Calderon K, AJ Redd, and MF Hammer. New, searchable, online database—*USAYSTR*—for estimating haplotype frequencies in the U.S. To be submitted to *Genomics.*

References

[1] M. Kayser, S. Brauer, H. Schadlich, M. Prinz, M. Batzer, P. Zimmerman, B. Boatin, and Stoneking, Y chromosome STR haplotypes and the genetic structure of U.S. M. populations of African, European, and Hispanic ancestry. *Genome Res 13* (2003) 624-634.

[2] B. Budowle, M. Adamowicz, X. G. Aranda, C. Barna, R. Chakraborty, D. Cheswick, B.Dafoe, A. Eisenberg, R. Frappier, A. M. Gross, C. Ladd, H. S. Lee, S. C. Milne, C.Meyers, M. Prinz, M. L. Richard, G. Saldanha, A. A. Tierney, L. Viculis, and B. E.Krenke, Twelve short tandem repeat loci Y chromosome haplotypes: genetic analysis on populations residing in North America. Forensic Sci Int 150 (2005) 1-15.

[3] NRC. *The Evaluation of Forensic DNA Evidence.* 1996. Washington, D.C.: National Academy Press.

[4] P. Gill, A. J. Jeffreys, and D. J. Werrett, Forensic application of DNA 'fingerprints'. Nature 318 (1985) 577-9.

[5] M. Prinz, K. Boll, H. Baum, and B. Shaler, Multiplexing of Y chromosome specific STRs and performance for mixed samples. Forensic Sci Int 85 (1997) 209-18.

[6] K. Honda, L. Roewer, and P. de Knijff, Male DNA typing from 25-year-old vaginal swabs using Y chromosomal STR polymorphisms in a retrial request case. *J Forensic Sci 44* (1999) 868-72.

[7] A. Betz, G. Bassler, G. Dietl, X. Steil, G. Weyermann, and W. Pflug, DYS STR analysis with epithelial cells in a rape case. Forensic Sci Int 118 (2001) 126-30.

[8] M. Prinz and M. Sansone, Y chromosome-specific short tandem repeats in forensic casework. *Croat Med J 42* (2001) 288-91.

[9] M. Prinz, A. Ishii, A. Coleman, H. J. Baum, and R. C. Shaler, Validation and casework application of a Y chromosome specific STR multiplex. *Forensic Sci Int 120* (2001) 177- 88.

[10] W. Parson, H. Niederstatter, S. Kochl, M. Steinlechner, and B. Berger, When autosomal short tandem repeats fail: optimized primer and reaction design for Y-chromosome short tandem repeat analysis in forensic casework. *Croat Med J 42* (2001) 285-7.

[11] M. Kayser, A. Caglia, D. Corach, N. Fretwell, C. Gehrig, G. Graziosi, F. Heidorn, S.Herrmann, B. Herzog, M. Hidding, K. Honda, M. Jobling, M. Krawczak, K. Leim, S. Meuser, E. Meyer, W. Oesterreich, A. Pandya, W. Parson, G. Penacino, A. Perez-Lezaun,A. Piccinini, M. Prinz, C. Schmitt, L. Roewer, and et al., Evaluation of Y-chromosomal STRs: a multicenter study. *Int J Legal Med 110* (1997) 125-33.

[12] P. Gill, R. Sparkes, R. Pinchin, T. Clayton, J. Whitaker, and J. Buckleton, Interpretingsimple STR mixtures using allele peak areas. *Forensic Sci Int 91* (1998) 41-53.

[13] P. de Knijff, Messages through bottlenecks: on the combined use of slow and fastevolving polymorphic markers on the human Y chromosome. *Am J Hum Genet* 67 (2000) 1055-61.

[14] M. A. Jobling and C. Tyler-Smith, Fathers and sons: the Y chromosome and humanevolution. *Trends Genet 11* (1995) 449-56.

[15] M. F. Hammer, T. M. Karafet, A. J. Redd, H. Jarjanazi, S. Santachiara-Benerecetti, H.Soodyall, and S. L. Zegura, Hierarchical patterns of global human Y-chromosomediversity. *Mol Biol Evol 18* (2001) 1189-203.

[16] L. Roewer, M. Kayser, P. Dieltjes, M. Nagy, E. Bakker, M. Krawczak, and P. de Knijff,Analysis of molecular variance (AMOVA) of Y-chromosome-specific microsatellites intwo closely related human populations. *Hum Mol Genet* 5 (1996) 1029-33.

[17] A. J. Redd, S. L. Clifford, and M. Stoneking, Multiplex DNA typing of short-tandem-repeat loci on the Y chromosome. *Biol Chem* 378 (1997) 923-7.

[18] J. Butler, R. Schoske, P. Vallone, M. Kline, A. Redd, and M. Hammer, A novel multiplexfor simultaneous amplification of 20 Y chromosome STR markers. *Forensic Sci Int 129 (*2002) 10-24.

[19] P. de Knijff, M. Kayser, A. Caglia, D. Corach, N. Fretwell, C. Gehrig, G. Graziosi, F.Heidorn, S. Herrmann, B. Herzog, M. Hidding, K. Honda, M. Jobling, M. Krawczak,

K.Leim, S. Meuser, E. Meyer, W. Oesterreich, A. Pandya, W. Parson, G. Penacino, A.Perez-Lezaun, A. Piccinini, M. Prinz, L. Roewer, and et al., Chromosome Ymicrosatellites: population genetic and evolutionary aspects. *Int J Legal Med 110* (1997)134-49.

[20] L. Roewer, M. Krawczak, S. Willuweit, M. Nagy, C. Alves, A. Amorim, K. Anslinger, C. Augustin, A. Betz, E. Bosch, A. Caglia, A. Carracedo, D. Corach, A. F. Dekairelle, T. Dobosz, B. M. Dupuy, S. Furedi, C. Gehrig, L. Gusmao, J. Henke, L. Henke, M.Hidding, C. Hohoff, B. Hoste, M. A. Jobling, H. J. Kargel, P. de Knijff, R. Lessig, E.Liebeherr, M. Lorente, B. Martinez-Jarreta, P. Nievas, M. Nowak, W. Parson, V. L.Pascali, G. Penacino, R. Ploski, B. Rolf, A. Sala, U. Schmidt, C. Schmitt, P. M.Schneider, R. Szibor, J. Teifel-Greding, and M. Kayser, Online reference database ofEuropean Y-chromosomal short tandem repeat (STR) haplotypes. Forensic Sci Int 118 (2001) 106-13.

[21] P. S. Walsh, N. J. Fildes, and R. Reynolds, Sequence analysis and characterization ofstutter products at the tetranucleotide repeat locus vWA. *Nucleic Acids Res 24* (1996)2807-12.

[22] J. M. Butler, Forensic DNA Typing. Academic Press, San Diego (2001).

[23] B. Walsh, Estimating the time to the most recent common ancestor for the Ychromosome or mitochondrial DNA for a pair of individuals. *Genetics 158* (2001) 897-912.

[24] M. P. Stumpf and D. B. Goldstein, *Genealogical and evolutionary inference with thehuman Y chromosome. Science 291* (2001) 1738-42.

[25] A. Redd, A. Agellon, V. Kearney, V. Contreras, T. Karafet, H. Park, P. de Knijff, J.Butler, and M. Hammer, Forensic value of 14 novel STRs on the human Y chromosome. *Forensic Sci Int 130* (2002) 97-111.

[26] M. Kayser, R. Kittler, A. Erler, M. Hedman, A. C. Lee, A. Mohyuddin, S. Q. Mehdi, Z.Rosser, M. Stoneking, M. A. Jobling, A. Sajantila, and C. Tyler-Smith, A comprehensivesurvey of human Y-chromosomal microsatellites. *Am J Hum Genet 74* (2004) 1183-97.

[27] Y. Ogata, T. Yamaba, K. Sawazaki, R. Iida, E. Tsubota, H. Takatsuka, T. Matsuki, T.Yasuda, and K. Kishi, Improvement of a multiplex PCR system for DYS441, DYS442,DYS443, DYS444 and DYS445, and a population study in 340 Japanese males. *Leg Med(Tokyo) 7* (2005) 183-9.

[28] T. M. Clayton, J. P. Whitaker, R. Sparkes, and P. Gill, Analysis and interpretation ofmixed forensic stains using DNA STR profiling. *Forensic Sci Int 91* (1998) 55-70.

[29] M. Kayser, M. Krawczak, L. Excoffier, P. Dieltjes, D. Corach, V. Pascali, C. Gehrig, L. F. Bernini, J. Jespersen, E. Bakker, L. Roewer, and P. de Knijff, An extensive analysis of Y-chromosomal microsatellite haplotypes in globally dispersed human populations. *Am J Hum Genet 68* (2001) 990-1018.

[30] R. Lewontin and D. Hartl, Population genetics in forensic DNA typing. Science 20(1991) 1745-1750.

[31] J. Wilder, S. Kingan, Z. Mobasher, M. Pilkington, and M. Hammer, Global patterns ofhuman mitochondrial DNA and Y-chromosome structure are not influenced by highermigration rates of females versus males. *Nat Genet 36* (2004) 1122-1125.

[32] M. F. Hammer and S. L. Zegura, The role of the Y chromosome in human evolutionarystudies. *Evol Anthropol 5* (1996) 116-134.

[33] L. Zhivotovsky, S. Ahmed, W. Wang, and A. Bittles, The forensic DNA implications ofgenetic differentiation between endogamous communities. *Forensic Sci Int 119* (2001) 269-272.

[34] S. L. Zegura, T. M. Karafet, L. A. Zhivotovsky, and M. F. Hammer, High-resolutionSNPs and microsatellite haplotypes point to a single, recent entry of Native American Ychromosomes into the Americas. Mol Biol Evol 21 (2004) 164-75.

[35] D. Merriwether, S. Huston, S. Iyengar, R. Hamman, J. Norris, S. Shetterly, M. Kamboh,and R. Ferrell, Mitochondrial versus nuclear admixture estimates demonstrate a pasthistory of directional mating. Am J Phys *Anthropol. 102* (1997) 153-159.

[36] B. M. Chakraborty, M. E. Fernandez-Esquer, and R. Chakraborty, Is being Hispanic arisk factor for non-insulin dependent diabetes mellitus (NIDDM)? *Ethn Dis 9* (1999) 278- 83.

[37] A. J. Redd, V. F. Chamberlain, V. C. Kearney, D. Stover, T. M. Karafet, K. Calderon,and M. F. Hammer, Genetic structure among 38 populations from the United States basedon 11 U.S. core Y-chromosome STRs. *J Foren Sci in press* (2006).

[38] E. Foster, M. Jobling, P. Taylor, P. Donnelly, P. de Knijff, R. Mieremet, T. Zerjal , and C. Tyler-Smith, Jefferson fathered slave's last child. *Nature 396* (1998) 27-8.

[39] E. Parra, R. Kittles, G. Argyropoulos, C. Pfaff, K. Hiester, C. Bonilla, N. Sylvester, D.Parrish-Gause, W. Garvey, L. Jin, P. McKeigue, M. Kamboh, R. Ferrell, W. Pollitzer,and M. Shriver, Ancestral proportions and admixture dynamics in geographically definedAfrican Americans living in South Carolina. *Am J Phys Anthropol 114* (2001) 18-29.

[40] E. Parra, A. Marcini, J. Akey, J. Martinson, M. Batzer, R. Cooper, T. Forrester, D.Allison, R. Deka, R. Ferrell, and M. Shriver, Estimating African American admixtureproportions by use of population-specific alleles. *Am J Hum Genet 63* (1998) 1839-1851.

[41] C. Bonilla, E. J. Parra, C. L. Pfaff, S. Dios, J. A. Marshall, R. F. Hamman, R. E. Ferrell,C. L. Hoggart, P. M. McKeigue, and M. D. Shriver, Admixture in the Hispanics of theSan Luis Valley, Colorado, and its implications for complex trait gene mapping. *Ann Hum Genet 68* (2004) 139-53.

[42] C. Bonilla, M. Shriver, E. Parra, A. Jones, and J. Fernandez, Ancestral proportions andtheir association with skin pigmentation and bone mineral density in Puerto Rican women from New York city. *Hum Genet 115* (2004) 57-68.

[43] E. Lander and J. Ellis, Founding father. *Nature 396* (1998) 13-14.

[44] B. Bonne-Tamir, M. Korostishevsky, A. J. Redd, Y. Pel-Or, M. E. Kaplan, and M. F.Hammer, Maternal and paternal lineages of the Samaritan isolate: mutation rates and timeto most recent common male ancestor. *Ann Hum Genet 67* (2003) 153-64.

[45] L. Jin and R. Chakraborty, Population structure, stepwise mutations, heterozygotedeficiency and their implications in DNA forensics. *Heredity 74* (Pt 3) (1995) 274-85.

[46] U. S. C. Bureau.2000, http://www.census.gov/main/www/cen2000.html.

[47] C. L. Hanis, D. Hewett-Emmett, T. K. Bertin, and W. J. Schull, Origins of U.S.Hispanics. Implications for diabetes. *Diabetes Care 14* (1991) 618-27.

[48] N. R. Mesa, M. C. Mondragon, I. D. Soto, M. V. Parra, C. Duque, D. Ortiz-Barrientos, L. F. Garcia, I. D. Velez, M. L. Bravo, J. G. Munera, G. Bedoya, M. C. Bortolini, and A. Ruiz-Linares, Autosomal, mtDNA, and Y-chromosome diversity in Amerinds: pre-

and post-Columbian patterns of gene flow in South America. *Am J Hum Genet 67* (2000)1277-86.

[49] N. Cerri, U. Ricci, I. Sani, A. Verzeletti, and F. De Ferrari, Mixed stains from sexual assault cases: autosomal or Y-chromosome short tandem repeats? *Croat Med J 44* (2003) 289-92.

[50] Z. Redenbach and E. B. Taylor, Evidence for bimodal hybrid zones between two speciesof char (Pisces: Salvelinus) in northwestern North America. *J Evol Biol 16* (2003) 1135- 48.

[51] A. L. Roca, N. Georgiadis, and S. J. O'Brien, Cytonuclear genomic dissociation inAfrican elephant species. *Nat Genet 37* (2005) 96-100.

[52] S. K. Sinha, B. Budowle, R. Chakraborty, A. Paunovic, R. D. Guidry, C. Larsen, A. Lal,M. Shaffer, G. Pineda, E. Schneida, H. Nasir, and J. G. Shewale, Utility of the Y-STRtyping systems Y-PLEX 6 and Y-PLEX 5 in forensic casework and 11 Y-STR haplotypedatabase for three major population groups in the United States. J Forensic Sci 49 (2004) 691-700.

APPENDIX A

As shown in Figure 10, the results are consistent with independence of Y and autosomal markers within each subpopulation. Thus our concern of lack of independence within a subpopulation does not appear to be an issue, at least for the populations examined here. Thus, within a particular subpopulation the joint match probability is simply obtained by multiplying the subpopulation-speci.c autosomal and Y match probabilities. However, this leads to a second potential concern, namely that a Y chromosome haplotype may be highly informative as to which subpopulation an individual belongs, and this in turn potentially changes the autosomal allele frequencies used to compute the autosomal match probabilities. To formally see this, express the joint match probability by conditioning on the observed Y haplotype *y*,

$$\Pr(y, \text{autosomal genotype}) = \Pr(\text{autosomal genotype}|y)\,\Pr(y) \qquad (1)$$

As we detail below, there are several approaches for obtaining the autosomal match probabilities conditional on the Y haplotype. We start with two simple approaches before moving to a more complex approach that allows for population substructure conditioned on the Y haplotype.

For purposes of discussion, suppose we have the following match probabilities for the Y and autosomes using appropriate databases for various ethic populations:

Caucasian		African	Hispanic	Native America
Y match	3/1,500	1/1,500	5/800	0/300
Y match freq	0.0020	0.0007	0.00625	0
Autosomal match	1/40,000	1/20,000	1/30,000	1/50,000

Further, suppose that the appropriate male reference population from which we sample a random individual consists of 45% Caucasian, 30% Africans, 20% Hispanics, and 5% Native Americans. While one might use as our estimate of the Y chromosome match probability the overall frequency of the haplotype in the database (9/4100 = 0.0022), it is more appropriate to weight by the actual fraction of ethnicity on the reference population, as opposed to the sample. In this case, the match probability for the Y haplotype becomes

$$0.45\ 0.002 + 0.30\ 0.0007 + 0.20\ 0.00625 + 0.05\ 0.00 = 0.00235$$

Clearly this Y haplotype is more frequent in Hispanic (0.625%, as opposed to 0.20% in Caucasian and 0.070% in individuals of African extraction), and this suggests that the appropriate autosomal conditional match probability to use is that for Hispanics, giving a match probability of

$$0.00235\ (1/30,\ 000) = 7.83 \text{ x } 10^{8}$$

However, this same Y haplotype is also (albeit more rarely) found in individuals of Caucasian and Africa extraction. A more careful approach would be to use a weighted match probability, conditioning on autosomal matches over the probability of the y haplotype indicating membership in dierent ethnic groups,

$$\begin{aligned}&\text{Pr(autosomal genotype}|\text{Y haplotype)}\\&= \text{Pr(autosomal genotype}|\text{Group } i)\ \text{Pr(Group } i|\ \text{Y haplotype)}\end{aligned} \tag{2}$$

From Bayes' theorem, we can estimate the group probabilities as follows:

$$\text{Pr(Group } i\,|\text{Y haplotype}) = \frac{\text{Pr(Y haplotype} \mid \text{Group } i)\,\text{Pr(Group } i)}{\sum_i \text{Pr(Y haplotype} \mid \text{Group } i)\,\text{Pr(Group } i)} \tag{3}$$

For example, for our above hypothetical match probabilities,

$$\text{Pr(Caucasian}\,|\text{Y haplotype}) = \frac{0.002 \cdot 0.45}{0.002 \cdot 0.45 + 0.0007 \cdot 0.3 + 0.00625 \cdot 0.20} = 0.383,$$

while the resulting weights for Africans and Hispanics are 0.085 and 0.532, respectively. The resulting match probability using Equation (2) becomes

$$0.00235\ [0.383(1/40000) + 0.085(1/20000) + 0.532(1/30000)] = 7.42 \text{ x } 10^{8}$$

Finally, the most conservative approach is to chose the largest autosomal match probabilities over ethnic groups within which the haplotype occurs. In our example, this occurs in individuals of African extraction, giving a conservative match probability of

0.00235 (1/20000) = 1.18 x 10^7

Accounting for Autosomal Subpopulations

It remains to specify how to compute the probability of two matching autosomal genotypes given that two individuals share the identical Y haplotype. As mentioned above, the Y haplotype may be rather informative as to ethnic group, which in turn suggests the appropriate group from which to compute allele frequencies. However, an additional correction may be in order beyond simply computing these probabilities for the different ethnic groups. Two individuals with identical Y haplotypes are likely more related to each other than are two random individuals. In a population-genetics framework, we expect the time back to the common (Y-contributing) ancestor of two individuals with identical Y haplotypes to be more recent than the time back to a common ancestor for two randomly-chosen individuals. In essence, the common Y haplotype imparts a subgroup structure and we need to account for this. Balding and Nichols (1994) show that the correct single-locus expressions for match probabilities when individuals come from the same subpopulation is a function of the average coecient of coancestry θ , with

$$\Pr(A_iA_i \mid A_iA_i) = \frac{[2\theta + (1-\theta)p_i][3\theta + (1-\theta)p_i]}{(1+\theta)(1+2\theta)} \qquad (4a)$$

6

$$\Pr(A_iA_j \mid A_iA_j) = \frac{2[\theta + (1-\theta)p_i][\theta + (1-\theta)p_j]}{(1+\theta)(1+2\theta)} \qquad (4b)$$

How do we compute the expected value of θ given two individuals are identical at all n tested Y chromosome markers? We do this by conditioning on the distribution of time back to a common (Y) ancestor given the number of identical markers scored on the Y. This uses the results of Walsh (2001), who developed Bayesian estimators for the distribution of the time back to this most recent common ancestor (MRCA) given the marker dierences between two Y haplotypes.

If the mutation rate per marker is μ , then the chance that two haplotypes are identical at n markers given they last shared a common (Y) ancestor t generations ago is just

$$\Pr(n \text{ marker match } t \text{ generations to MRCA}) = (1 \mid u)^{2nt} \qquad (5)$$

This is the likelihood function for t given the mutation rate and number of markers. A more detailed analysis under the stepwise mutation model in Walsh (2001) shows that, when all n markers match, that this simple expression based on the innite alleles model is essentially equivalent to the more exact analysis under a stepwise model that allows for back mutations.

Population genetics theory provides the prior distribution for the time to MRCA for two randomly-drawn Y chromosomes in the absence of any marker information (Walsh 2001). The time back to MRCA follows a geometric distribution with parameter λ $=1/Ne$, the reciprocal of the eective population size (since the Y chromosome is haploid). Hence, the prior becomes

$$\Pr(\tau \text{ generations to MRCA}) = \lambda\ (1\ \lambda\ )^{\tau\ \ 1} \qquad (6)$$

The resulting posterior distribution (from Equations 5 and 6) becomes

$$\Pr(\tau \text{ generations to MRCAn-marker match}) = C(1 \mid u)^{2n\tau}\ \lambda\ (1\ \lambda\ )^{\tau\ \ 1} \qquad (7)$$

where the constant C assures that the probabilities sum to one.

In particular, the posterior distribution for the time to MRCA given two individuals exactly match at n markers is

$$p(t \mid t \geq k) = \frac{(1-u)^{2nt} \cdot (1-\lambda)^{t-1}}{\sum_{\tau=k}^{\infty} (1-u)^{2n\tau} \cdot (1-\lambda)^{\tau-1}} \qquad (8)$$

We have invoked the conditioning of the MRCA being at least a certain number k of generations because good practice with Y chromosome data would involve testing both the father/son and any paternal sibs (full or half) of a suspect, and hence these individuals are removed from consideration.

Since the coecient of coancestry for two individuals that shared a common ancestor τ generations ago is just $(1/2)2\tau\ +1$, the expected coecient of coancestry θ thus becomes

$$\begin{aligned} E[\theta \mid t \geq k] &= \sum_{t=k}^{\infty} \left(\frac{1}{2^{2t+1}}\right) p(t \mid t \geq k) \\ &= \frac{\sum_{t=k}^{\infty} (1/2)^{2t+1} (1-u)^{2nt} \cdot (1-\lambda)^{t-1}}{\sum_{t=k}^{\infty} (1-u)^{2nt} \cdot (1-\lambda)^{t-1}} \\ &= \frac{2^{1-2k}[1-(1-\lambda)(1-\mu)^{2n}]}{4-(1-\lambda)(1-\mu)^{2n}} \end{aligned} \qquad (9)$$

For $k = 2$ (the typical case in Forensic settings), this simplies to

$$E[\theta\,|\,t \geq 2] = \frac{1-(1-\lambda)(1-\mu)^{2n}}{32-8(1-\lambda)(1-\mu)^{2n}} \tag{10a}$$

$$\simeq \frac{\lambda+2n\mu}{24-8(\lambda+2n\mu)} \tag{10b}$$

For a test of $n = 11$ STR markers, Equation (10a) gives the following values for $E[\theta]$ for dierent mutation rates μ ,

Ne	μ =0.001	μ =0.002	μ =0.004
∞	0.00090	0.00177	0.003426
5,000	0.00091	0.00178	0.00343
500	0.00098	0.00185	0.00349
100	0.00130	0.00216	0.00378
50	0.00170	0.00254	0.00414

Given that we except the eective population sizes from most ethnic groups to exceed 100, and most estimates of STR mutation rates are around 0.002, taking $E(\theta)$=0.002 is expected to be conservative. With allele frequencies of 0.02 or higher, this value for θ in Equations (4a) and (4b) essentially recovers Hardy-Weinberg proportions (*p*2 for homozygotes, 2*pipj* for heterozygotes).

Recommendation

A conservative approach to computing the joint Y-autosomal matching probability is thus as follows. For each of the major ethnic groups, compute the autosomal match probability using the product of single-locus genotype frequencies obtained from using Equations (4a) and (4b) with θ =0.002 and the allele frequencies appropriate for each group. A consevative estimate of the joint probability is obtained by multipling the largest value of these group autosomal match probabilities by the estimated matching probability for the Y. Finally, as to the issue of estimating the y match probability from a database, we favor a conservative modication of the simple counting method,

$$\widehat{\Pr}(y) = \frac{i+2}{n+2}$$

where there are *i* matches in an initial data base of *n* haplotypes. Making the converative (favoring a suspect) assumption that a crime sample came from a dierent individual than the suspect, we have two more samples (hence *n* + 2 total samples) and matches for the suspect, the crime sample and *i* matches from the databases (hence *i* + 2 matches).

In: Forensics in Law Enforcement
Editor: M. V. Shoester, pp. 173-181
ISBN 1-60021-164-X

Chapter 5

VALIDATION OF A DNA METHOD FOR THE INDIVIDUALIZATION OF PLANT EVIDENCE*

Heather Miller Coyle[1], Gary Shutler[2], Lois Tully[3], Elaine Pagliaro[4], Albert Harper[5], Timothy Palmbach[1] and Henry C. Lee[1,4]
[1] Forensic Science Program, University of New Haven,
300 Boston Post Road, West Haven, CT 06516
[2] Washington State Patrol; [3] National Institute of Justice
[4] Division of Scientific Services, 278 Colony Street, Meriden, CT 06451
[5] Henry C. Lee Institute of Forensic Science University of New Haven,
300 Boston Post Road, West Haven, CT 06516

INTRODUCTION

Many forensic cases involve plant evidence that may be useful to link a suspect, a victim, a weapon, a vehicle and crime scenes. Currently, most plant evidence is identified to the Genus or species level by class characteristics such as leaf morphology, color, size, geographic distribution and any special structures such as shape and presence of trichomes or inclusion bodies [1-4]. These characteristics may be observed macroscopically or microscopically but rarely can confirm the source of the plant unless a good physical match is obtained. With the advent of new DNA technologies, however, plant material may be chemically extracted for DNA, and typed using a multilocus detection method called amplified fragment length polymorphism (AFLP).

The AFLP method was developed in 1995 by Vos et al. and has been used for numerous years in research laboratories and for patent applications [5]. For the samples tested, DNA was extracted from single source plant material, digested into fragments with two different restriction enzymes, amplified by polymerase chain reaction (PCR) and finally detected using a DNA sequencer. Customized computer macros aid in determining a candidate match and for

* Excerpted from http://www.ncjrs.gov/pdffiles1/nij/grants/211999.pdf.

searching a reference population database by converting DNA fragment patterns into binary code [6].

As a model system, *Cannabis sativa* (marijuana) was selected due to its wide geographic distribution and close association with forensic casework. Sourcing of marijuana is not only useful for drug cases and for tracking distribution networks but also for providing additional evidence in many burglaries and homicides. Previous work [6] demonstrated that consistency in DNA profiles was obtained from different somatic tissues of a *Cannabis* plant, that the presence of resin on leaf surfaces was not inhibitory to PCR, and that plants suspected of clonal propagation did indeed have identical DNA patterns and unrelated marijuana samples had different patterns. Additional studies presented here further define the appropriate use of the AFLP method for plant testing.

MATERIALS AND METHODS

A. Reproducibility Studies

All of the DNA extraction, PCR amplification and analytical steps for evaluation of AFLP data were executed as previously described [6]. The following studies were performed:

Different analysts-AFLP profiles were generated for five different marijuana samples by two individuals with molecular biology experience. Each analyst processed identical DNA extracts in duplicate using the same reagents and equipment. In addition, a set of plant samples was co-extracted and processed to compare the effect of different DNA extractions on the AFLP pattern.

Different thermal cyclers-PCR amplifications were performed on two different models of thermal cyclers (9600 and 9700; PE Corporation) by two different analysts; one analyst performed this experiment extensively with multiple experiments.

Different laboratories-To establish the difficulty in potentially training an analyst without prior molecular biology experience, DNA extracts were sent to a student at Florida International University for duplicate processing along with a set being processed at the Connecticut State Forensic Science Laboratory. A set of work instructions and equipment specifications were included with the samples. Data was co-reviewed by each facility.

Effect of drying plant material-Since marijuana is frequently purchased as dried leaf and stem fragments, fresh and dried material was processed and compared for DNA patterns. Two live plants were removed from the ground during a seizure operation and inverted to air dry in a dark room at 25C and relative humidity at the Connecticut State Forensic Laboratory.

Effect of time-A substantial amount of time may intervene between when a fresh plant is harvested and when it is purchased and used by the consumer. Therefore, the dried plants were sampled for an extended period of time (0, 1, 2, 3, 5, 7 days; 2, 3, 4, 8, 12, 16, 20, 25 and 32 weeks) to determine the effect of drying and potential DNA degradation on the DNA patterns.

Effect of DNA degradation-DNA from a single fresh plant was digested into fragments with an enzyme, DNase I (Gibco BRL). Aliquots of the same DNA stock were removed and incubated with the enzyme for the following time points: 0, 0.5, 1, 1.5, 2, 4, 6, 9, 15, 23 and 35 minutes. The samples were then visualized for the level of degradation by electrophoresis on a 1% agarose gel stained with ethidium bromide. In addition, a ten year old plant sample (*Jacaranda*) was processed multiple times and the DNA patterns compared.

Effect of DNA template concentration-Starting DNA concentration in the PCR reaction may have an effect on the resultant AFLP profile. To test this hypothesis, different amounts of DNA (450, 200, 100, 50, 20, 10, 5, 2, 0.5 and 0.2ng) were processed in duplicate and the DNA patterns compared. In addition, single seeds of marijuana and tomato (*Lycopersicon* spp.) were extracted for DNA to determine if sufficient quantity and quality DNA could be obtained from a single seed for AFLP testing.

B. Ability to discriminate between related plant samples and street seizure samples: Half-sibling and seed stocks-Three marijuana seizure samples were obtained with different case numbers. Each had a female flower from a single plant that contained a few seeds. The seeds were dissected into two components: the embryo and the pericarp. DNA was also extracted from the parental somatic tissue. Each sample was processed separately and the patterns compared. Several bags of labeled seeds were seized from one case by the Royal Canadian Mounted Police (RCMP). Representative samples were extracted and processed for DNA patterns from several bags that were labeled with genetic breeding information. The number of fragments that differed between parent and seed and the different seed samples were compared.

Random street seizures-A population database of donated marijuana street seizure samples from multiple states was generated to gain a better understanding of how similar or different one might expect marijuana samples to be based on unknown genetic heritage. The donated samples were acquired from a variety of locations where plants were being grown outdoors in fields, indoors in soil or as hydroponic operations [6-8]; also as drug samples packaged for individual use.

RESULTS AND DISCUSSION

A. Reproducibility

No differences in AFLP profiles were observed between the duplicate samples that were processed by two trained analysts at the Division of Scientific Services in Connecticut. In fact, multiple students on internship were also trained to perform this DNA testing method, most with complete success in obtaining reproducible results. The most frequent sources of error that were identified as affecting test result reproducibility both within a laboratory and between laboratories based on individual analysts were the following: pipetting skills, attention to protocol details, lack of mixing of samples prior to PCR amplification, incorrect dilutions of restriction enzymes to the recommended concentrations for AFLP and computer errors. Appropriate training and prior molecular biology experience were the two most significant factors in analysts achieving reproducible DNA patterns.

The use of different models of thermal cyclers for PCR amplification may affect AFLP patterns based on ramp speeds which can alter the manner in which PCR primers anneal to the DNA template. Most significantly, one analyst observed single peak drop out between samples that should have been identical when using two different models of thermal cyclers. This same observation was made when a ten-year old plant sample (with marginal quality

DNA) was processed by the AFLP method. Both types of observations can be best explained by a similar mechanism (Figure 1). In the case of the different ramp speeds on thermal cyclers, PCR primers may not anneal efficiently to the DNA fragment and peaks may drop out of a profile due to inefficient amplification. This same issue has been noted for RAPD markers [9] and can be corrected by using comparable equipment and testing known standards prior to performing tests on the evidence. The ten year old plant sample contained degraded DNA based on a visual exam on an agarose gel. This test case and the enzymatic digestion studies both indicate that if the starting DNA for AFLP is badly damaged, some fragments will not amplify by PCR. To avoid this situation, only DNA that is of sufficient quality (>1Kb) should be used for AFLP analysis (Figure 2).

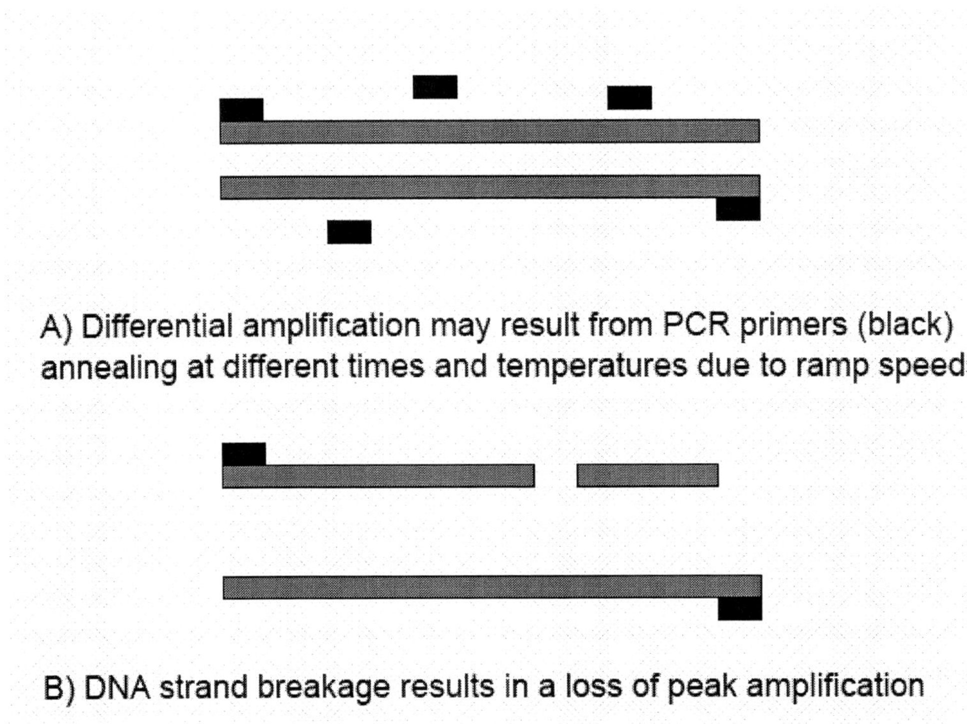

Figure 1. Two different mechanisms can result in a DNA fragment dropping out of an AFLP profile. First, differential annealing of PCR primers to the DNA template due to thermal cycler ramp speed differences can result in loss or reduction of a fragment. Secondly, a break in a DNA fragment can result in loss of amplification and a peak being absent from an AFLP profile.

No differences in AFLP patterns were observed when comparing fresh and dried marijuana samples even over an extended time period of thirty-two weeks. In addition, a wide range of DNA template concentrations resulted in comparable AFLP profiles as long as the relative peak heights were within approximately two-fold of each other (Figure 3). In other words, duplicate samples that were on a similar scale for relative fluorescence have identical DNA patterns. Samples that were more than two-fold different in relative fluorescence units may exhibit minor peak drop-out. The peaks that dropped out of the profile could be detected again once the samples were processed and detected within the same scale. These results agree with that of Vos et al. (1995). High quality and sufficient quantity of DNA was obtained from both single marijuana and single tomato seeds indicating this method may be very useful for sourcing trace seed evidence from clothing or stomach contents [3].

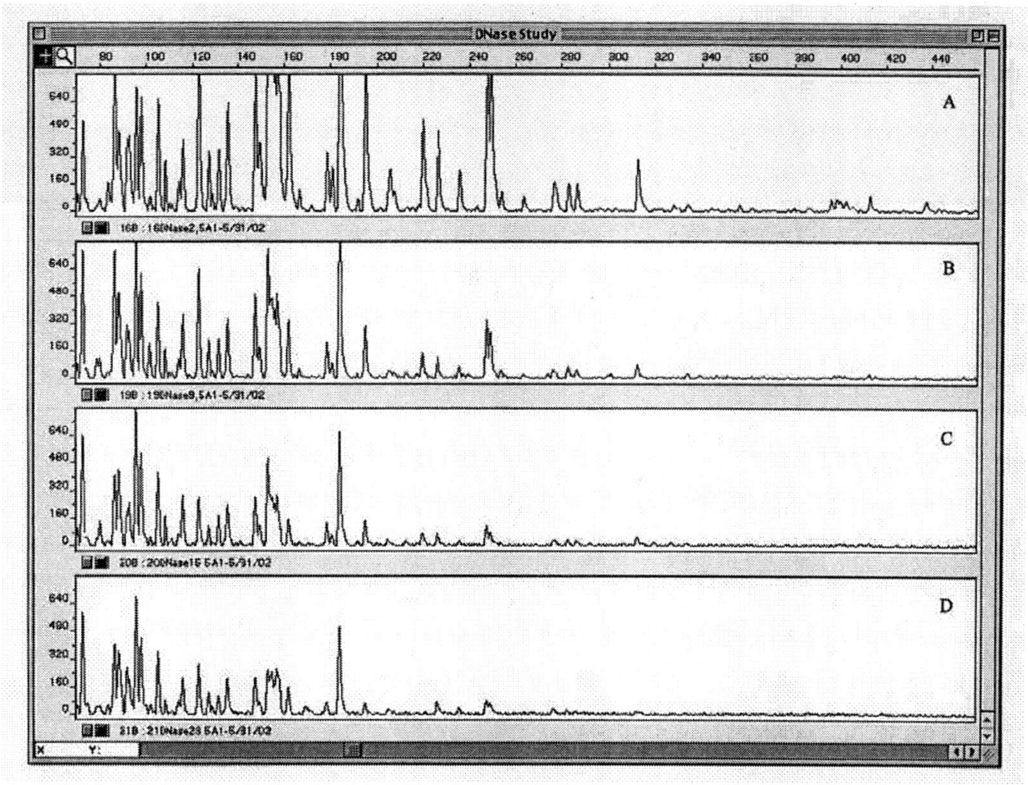

Figure 2. The AFLP profiles generated from four treatments with DNaseI to determine the effect of degradation of template DNA on AFLP profiles. A) 2 minutes with DNA fragments >1Kb, B) 9 minutes with DNA fragments 500-50bp, C) 15 minutes with DNA fragments 300-50bp, D) 23 minutes with DNA fragments 200-50bp. The effect of DNaseI-induced degradation indicates larger fragments do not amplify well as DNA becomes increasingly more fragmented and reduced in size. DNA fragments greater than 1Kb yield a highly reproducible AFLP profile.

B. Population Studies

The seeds collected from the marijuana flowers represent half-siblings since they all share at least the female parent. It was unknown whether they were pollinated from one or more male plants. When their DNA patterns were compared for multiple PCR primer sets, they averaged between two and ten peak differences between parent and seed. When compared to each other, the seeds averaged between one and seven peak differences for three different PCR primer sets. For the seeds collected from the RCMP, it was expected that they may be any one of the following based on the label: siblings, half-siblings, or individuals of the same variety; however, the variety was not specifically designated. In all cases, a single PCR primer set was sufficient to distinguish between the seed samples.

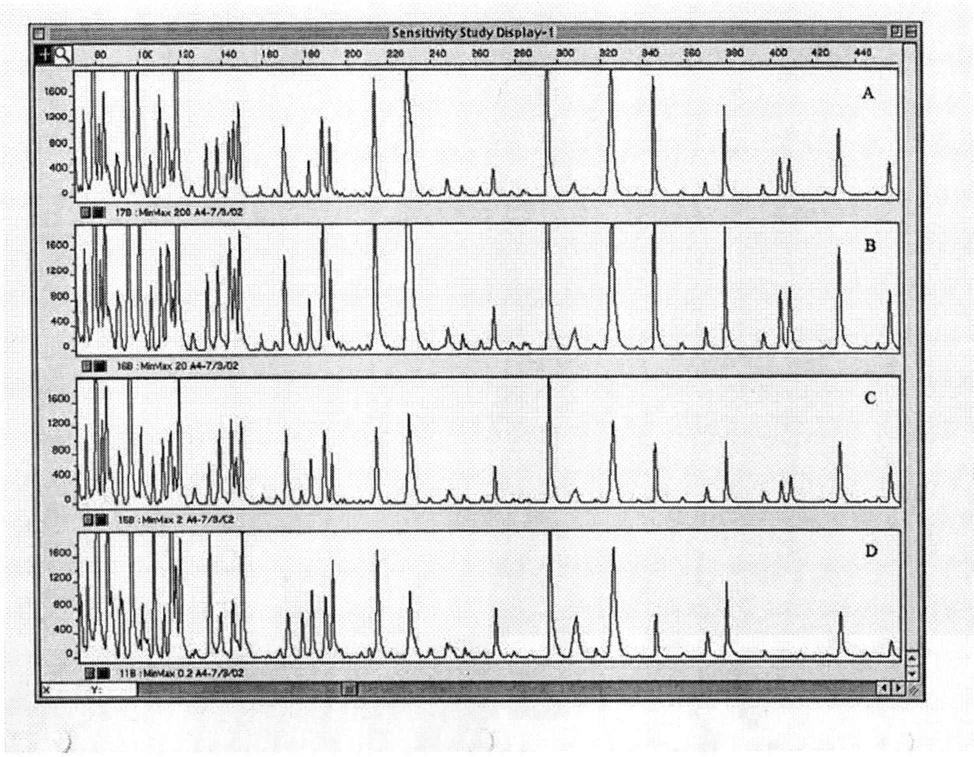

Figure 3. Varying the starting DNA template concentration shows no difference in the AFLP profiles (A-C; 200, 20 and 2 ng, respectively) unless the starting concentration is low (D, 0.2ng). In panel D, some minor peak drop out can be observed.

A survey of existing street seizures of marijuana with unknown cultivar designations revealed some interesting results. In one case from Iowa, an entire field of marijuana samples (approximately 500 plants) had identical DNA profiles indicating they were propagated clonally and then planted outdoors. In another case in Connecticut, multiple cultivars were being expanded clonally in an indoor hydroponic grower operation. For most of the random street seizures from across the United States, the DNA profiles were unique indicating either that the marijuana samples were generated by seed or the sampling was random enough that clonal marijuana samples were not encountered repeatedly except when in local geographic regions. For example, two samples from the Northeast that were collected from different states had identical DNA profiles suggesting they originated from a common clonal population.

The validation of the AFLP method for plant evidence has defined the conditions for when plant evidence can be appropriately processed for DNA comparisons between evidentiary samples and known reference samples. The quantity and quality of the DNA needs to be sufficient for an accurate comparison; otherwise a false exclusion may result due to peak drop out during the PCR amplification steps. The DNA template concentration has relatively little effect on the DNA profile as the same profiles were observed for 200, 20 and 2 nanograms of DNA in the AFLP reaction. The generation of a marijuana DNA database of approximately three hundred unrelated cases contained both unique and clonally propagated samples and gave a relative estimate of the extent of genetic diversity one might expect from marijuana seizure samples.

The AFLP method is a useful technique for any single source plant sample since it can be applied to any organism without prior knowledge of the target segments of DNA. The DNA fragment patterns generated by AFLP are considered multilocus in nature and genetic linkages between fragments are unknown. For this reason, when reference population databases are generated for comparative purposes, it is suggested that a modified counting method be used to determine random match probability estimates.

Although this may decrease the power of discrimination of the test method, a conservative statistical approach and the use of a generally applicable method for all forms of plant evidence should increase its usage in forensic casework.

ACKNOWLEDGEMENTS

Thank you to the National Institute of Justice for funding this project (NIJ 2001-IJ-CX-K011). The results and any manufacturers mentioned within this manuscript do not imply an endorsement by the authors, their affiliated institutions or NIJ. Thanks to all who donated samples for this project and to the following persons for their helpful assistance: Captain Pete Warren and the CT State Narcotics Task Force, Richard Pinders, Carll Ladd, Cheng-Lung Lee, Eric Carita, Joselle Germano-Presby, Jose Almirall, Sabrina Frank, Suzanne Neylon Thompson, Elizabeth McClure Baker, Edward Jachimowicz, III, Shane Lumpkins, Laura Kushner, Matthew Cimino, Khartika Divakaran, Michelle Irvin.

REFERENCES

[1] Bock JH, Norris DO. Forensic botany: an under-utilized resource. *J Forensic Sci* 1997;42:364-7.

[2] Hall, DW. The contributions of the forensic botanist to crime scene investigations. *The Prosecutor* 1988;22:35-8.

[3] Miller Coyle H. (Ed) Forensic botany: principles and applications to criminal casework. Florida: *CRC Press,* 2005.

[4] Mertens J. Forensics follows foliage. *Law Enforcement Technology* 2003;62:1-7.

[5] Vos P, Hogers R, Bleeker M, Reijans M, van de Lee T, Hornes M et al. AFLP: a new technique for DNA fingerprinting. *Nucleic Acids Res* 1995;23(21):4407-4414.

[6] Miller Coyle H., Germano-Presby J., Ladd C., Palmbach T. and H.C. Lee. Tracking clonal marijuana using amplified fragment length polymorphism (AFLP) analysis: an overview. Proceedings 13th International Symposium on Human Identification 2002;Phoenix, AZ.

[7] Miller Coyle H, Ladd C, Palmbach T, Lee HC. The green revolution: botanical contributions to forensics and drug enforcement. *Croatian Medical Journal* 2001;42(3):340-5.

[8] Miller Coyle H, et al. An overview of DNA methods for the identification and individualization of marijuana. *Croatian Medical Journal* 2003;44:250.

[9] Yoon CK (1993) Forensic science: botanical witness for the prosecution. *Science* 260:894-895

Final Report: "Plant DNA Typing by Amplified Fragment Length Polymorphism (AFLP)"; Grant # NIJ 2001-IJ-CX-K011

Grant Participants

University of New Haven, Forensic Science Program

Timothy Palmbach, Director, MS, JD
Henry C. Lee, Full Professor
Heather Miller Coyle, PhD
Cheng-Lung Lee, MS, PhD candidate
Eric Carita, Research Assistant
Joselle Germano/Presby, Research Assistant

Henry C. Lee Institute for Forensic Sciences

Albert Harper, PhD, Director
Theresa Misuraca
Peter Massey

Division of Scientific Services, CT State Forensic Science Laboratory

Henry C. Lee, PhD, Chief Emeritus
Elaine Pagliaro, Director, MS, JD
Carll Ladd, PhD
Suzanne Neylon/Thompson, MS
Elizabeth McClure Baker, student intern
Edward Jachimowicz, III, student intern
Shane Lumpkins, student intern
Matthew Cimino, student intern
Khartika Divakaran, student intern
Michelle Irvin, student intern

Agencies Providing Cooperative Assistance

Gary Shutler, PhD, Washington State Patrol

Captain Peter Warren, CT Statewide Narcotics Task Force Eric Buel, PhD, Vermont Crime Laboratory Margaret Sanger, PhD, Kentucky State Police Laboratory

Jose Almirall, PhD, Sabrina Frank, MS candidate, Florida International University Robert Bever, PhD, The BODE Technology Group

Relevant Scientific Publications

H. Miller Coyle, C.-L. Lee, T. Palmbach and H.C. Lee. 2005. Collection and preservation of plant evidence. Manuscript in preparation.

C.-L. Lee, H. Miller Coyle, E. Carita, C. Ladd, N. Yang, T.M. Palmbach, I. C. Hsu and H.C. Lee. 2004. DNA analysis of digested tomato seeds in stomach contents. American Journal of Forensic Medicine and Pathology (in press).

H. Miller Coyle, T. Palmbach, N. Juliano, C. Ladd and H.C. Lee. 2003. An overview of DNA methods for the identification and individualization of marijuana. Croatian Medical Journal 44(3): 315-321.

H. Miller Coyle, G. Shutler, S. Abrams, J. Hanniman, S. Neylon, C. Ladd, T. Palmbach and H.C. Lee. 2003. A simple DNA extraction method for marijuana samples used in amplified fragment length polymorphism (AFLP) analysis. J. Forensic Sciences 48(2): 343-347.

H. Miller Coyle, J. Germano-Presby, C. Ladd, T. Palmbach and H.C. Lee. 2002. Tracking clonal marijuana using amplified fragment length polymorphism (AFLP) analysis: an overview. Conference proceedings: 13th International Symposium on Human Identification. Phoenix, AZ. Available on-line at www.promega.com.

H. Miller Coyle, C. Ladd, T. Palmbach and H.C. Lee. 2001. The Green Revolution: botanical contributions to forensics and drug enforcement. Croatian Medical Journal 42(3): 340-345.

Scientific Presentations

2002- J. Germano, H. Miller Coyle, T. Palmbach, E. Pagliaro, C. Ladd and H.C. Lee. Development of a national AFLP DNA database for marijuana (*Cannabis sativa*). 13th International Symposium on Human Identification, Phoenix, AZ.

2002- H. Miller Coyle, S. Neylon, C. Ladd, T. Palmbach and H.C. Lee. Validation of the AFLP technique for the individualization of marijuana samples. American Academy of Forensic Sciences, Atlanta, GA.

2001- H. Miller Coyle, K. Divakaran, E. Jachimowicz, C. Ladd and H.C. Lee. Individualization of marijuana (*Cannabis sativa*) samples for forensic applications and narcotics enforcement. American Academy of Forensic Sciences, Seattle, WA.

2000- H. Miller Coyle, C. Secore, C. Ladd and H.C. Lee. Plant DNA typing: applications to forensics. American Academy of Forensic Sciences, Reno, NV.

Transfer of Technology Workshops

(2) Laboratory based training sessions for workshop attendees sponsored by the Henry C. Lee Institute for Forensic Sciences

In: Forensics in Law Enforcement
Editor: M. V. Shoester, pp. 183-208

ISBN 1-60021-164-X

Chapter 6

USING DNA TO SOLVE COLD CASES*

Shirley S. Abrahamson, John Ashcroft[1], Deborah J. Daniels[2] and Sarah V. Hart[3]

U.S. Department of Justice; Office of Justice Programs; 810 Seventh Street N.W.; Washington, DC 20531; [1] Attorney General; [2] Assistant Attorney General; [3] Director, National Institute of Justice

NATIONAL COMMISSION ON THE FUTURE OF DNA EVIDENCE

In 1995, the National Institute of Justice (NIJ) began research that would attempt to identify how often DNA had exonerated wrongfully convicted defendants. After extensive study, NIJ published the report Convicted by Juries, Exonerated by Science: Case Studies in the Use of DNA Evidence to Establish Innocence After Trial, which presents case studies of 28 inmates for whom DNA analysis was exculpatory.

On learning of the breadth and scope of the issues related to forensic DNA, the Attorney General asked NIJ to establish the National Commission on the Future of DNA Evidence as a means to examine the most effective use of DNA in the criminal justice system. The Commission was appointed by the NIJ Director and represented the broad spectrum of the criminal justice system. Chaired by the Honorable Shirley S. Abrahamson, Chief Justice of the Wisconsin Supreme Court, the Commission consisted of representatives from the prosecution, the defense bar, law enforcement, the scientific community, the medical examiner community, academia, and victims' rights organizations.

The Commission's charge was to submit recommendations to the Attorney General that will help ensure the best use of DNA as a crimefighting tool and foster its use throughout the entire criminal justice system. Other focal areas for the Commission's consideration included crime scene investigation and evidence collection, laboratory funding, legal issues, and research and development. The Commission's working groups, consisting of commissioners and other experts, researched and examined various topics and reported back to the Commission.

---

* Excerpted from http://www.ncjrs.gov/pdffiles1/nij/194197.pdf.

The working groups' reports were submitted to the full Commission for approval, amendment, or further discussion and provided the Commission with background for its recommendations to the Attorney General.

By nature of its representative composition and its use of numerous working groups, the Commission received valuable input from all areas of the criminal justice system. The broad scope of that input enabled the Commission to develop recommendations that both maximize the investigative value of the technology and address the issues raised by its application.

COMMISSION MEMBERS

Chair
The Honorable Shirley S. Abrahamson
Chief Justice
Wisconsin Supreme Court

Members
Dwight E. Adams
Director
Federal Bureau of Investigation Laboratory

Jan S. Bashinski
Chief
Bureau of Forensic Services
California Department of Justice
Sacramento, California

George W. Clarke
Deputy District Attorney
San Diego, California

James F. Crow
Professor
Department of Genetics
University of Wisconsin

Lloyd N. Cutler
Wilmer, Cutler and Pickering
Washington, D.C.

Joseph H. Davis
Former Director
Miami-Dade Medical Examiner Department

Paul B. Ferrara
Director
Division of Forensic Sciences
Commonwealth of Virginia

Norman Gahn
Assistant District Attorney
Milwaukee County, Wisconsin

Terrance W. Gainer
Executive Assistant Chief
Metropolitan Police Department
Washington, D.C.

Terry G. Hillard
Superintendent of Police
Chicago Police Department
Chicago, Illinois

Aaron D. Kennard
Sheriff
Salt Lake County, Utah

Philip Reilly
Interleukin Genetics
Waltham, Massachusetts

Ronald S. Reinstein
Associate Presiding Judge
Superior Court of Arizona
Maricopa County, Arizona

Darrell L. Sanders
Chief
Frankfort Police Department
Frankfort, Illinois

Barry C. Scheck
Professor
Cardozo Law School
New York, New York

Michael Smith
Professor
University of Wisconsin Law School

Jeffrey E. Thoma
Public Defender
Mendocino County, California

Kathryn M. Turman
Director
Office for Victim Assistance
Federal Bureau of Investigation

William Webster
Milbank, Tweed, Hadley and McCloy
Washington, D.C.

James R. Wooley
Baker and Hostetler
Cleveland, Ohio

Commission staff
Christopher H. Asplen
Executive Director

Lisa Forman
Deputy Director

Robin W. Jones
Executive Assistant

Crime Scene Investigation Working Group

The Crime Scene Investigation Working Group is a multidisciplinary group of criminal justice professionals from across the United States who represent both urban and rural jurisdictions. Working group members and contributors were recommended and selected for their experience in the area of criminal investigation and evidence collection from the standpoints of law enforcement, prosecution, defense, the forensic laboratory, and victim assistance.

DNA has proven to be a powerful tool in the fight against crime. DNA evidence can identify suspects, convict the guilty, and exonerate the innocent. Throughout the Nation, criminal justice professionals are discovering that advancements in DNA technology are breathing new life into old, cold, or unsolved criminal cases. Evidence that was previously unsuitable for DNA testing because a biological sample was too small or degraded may now yield a DNA profile. Development of the Combined DNA Index System (CODIS) at the State and national levels enables law enforcement to aid investigations by effectively and efficiently identifying suspects and linking serial crimes to each other. The National Commission on the Future of DNA Evidence made clear, however, that we must dedicate more resources to empower law enforcement to use this technology quickly and effectively.

Using DNA to Solve Cold Cases is intended for use by law enforcement and other criminal justice professionals who have the responsibility for reviewing and investigating unsolved cases. This report will provide basic information to assist agencies in the complex process of case review with a specific emphasis on using DNA evidence to solve previously unsolvable crimes. Although DNA is not the only forensic tool that can be valuable to unsolved case investigations, advancements in DNA technology and the success of DNA database systems have inspired law enforcement agencies throughout the country to reevaluate cold cases for DNA evidence. As law enforcement professionals progress through investigations, however, they should keep in mind the array of other technology advancements, such as improved ballistics and fingerprint databases, which may substantially advance a case beyond its original level.

Chair
Terrance W. Gainer
Executive Assistant Chief
Metropolitan Police Department
Washington, D.C.

Members
Susan Ballou
Office of Law Enforcement Standards
National Institute of Standards and Technology
Gaithersburg, Maryland

Jan S. Bashinski
Chief
Bureau of Forensic Services
California Department of Justice
Sacramento, California

Sue Brown
INOVA Fairfax Hospital
SANE Program
Falls Church, Virginia

Lee Colwell
Director
Criminal Justice Institute
University of Arkansas System
Little Rock, Arkansas

Thomas J. Cronin
Chief
City of Coeur d'Alene Police Department
Coeur d'Alene, Idaho

Terry G. Hillard
Superintendent of Police
Chicago Police Department
Chicago, Illinois

Mark Johnsey
Master Sergeant (Ret.)
Division of Forensic Services
Illinois State Police Department
Springfield, Illinois

Christopher Plourd
Attorney at Law
San Diego, California

Darrell L. Sanders
Chief
Frankfort Police Department
Frankfort, Illinois

Clay Strange
Assistant District Attorney
Travis County District Attorney's Office
Austin, Texas

Contributors
Cheryl May
Assistant Director
Forensic Sciences Education Center
Little Rock, Arkansas

William McIntyre
Detective Sergeant (Ret.)
Atlantic County Prosecutor's Office
Homicide Unit
Hammonton, New Jersey

INTRODUCTION

In 1990, a series of brutal attacks on elderly victims occurred in Goldsboro, North Carolina, by an unknown individual dubbed the "Night Stalker." During one such attack in

March, an elderly woman was brutally raped and almost murdered. Her daughter's early arrival home was the only thing that saved the woman's life. The suspect fled, leaving behind materials intended to burn the residence and the victim in an attempt to conceal the crime. In July 1990, another elderly woman was brutally raped and murdered in her home. Three months later, a third elderly woman was raped and stabbed to death. Her husband was also murdered. Their house was burned in an attempt to cover up the crime, but fire/rescue personnel pulled the bodies from the house before it was engulfed in flames.

When DNA analysis was conducted on biological evidence collected from vaginal swabs from each victim, authorities concluded that the same perpetrator had committed all three crimes. However, there was no suspect.

For 10 years, both the Goldsboro Police Department and the crime laboratory refused to forget about these cases. With funding from the National Institute of Justice, the crime laboratory retested the biological evidence in all three cases with newer DNA technology and entered the DNA profiles into North Carolina's DNA database. This would allow the DNA profile developed from the crime scene evidence to be compared to thousands of convicted offender profiles already in the database.

In April 2001, a "cold hit" was made to the perpetrator's convicted offender DNA profile in the database. The perpetrator had been convicted of shooting into an occupied dwelling, an offense that requires inclusion in the North Carolina DNA database. The suspect was brought into custody for questioning and was served with a search warrant to obtain a sample of his blood. That sample was analyzed and compared to the crime scene evidence, thereby confirming the DNA database match. When confronted with the DNA evidence, the suspect confessed to all three crimes.

Mark Nelson, special agent in charge of the North Carolina State Crime Laboratory, said, "Even though these terrible crimes occurred more than 10 years ago, we never gave up hope of solving them one day."

Every law enforcement department throughout the country has unsolved cases that could be solved through recent advancements in DNA technology. Today, investigators who understand which evidence may yield a DNA profile can identify a suspect in ways previously seen only on television. Evidence invisible to the naked eye can be the key to solving a residential burglary, sexual assault, or murder. The saliva on the stamp of a stalker's threatening letter, the perspiration on a rapist's mask, or the skin cells shed on the ligature of a strangled child may hold the key to solving a crime.

In Austin, Texas, for example, an investigator knowledgeable about DNA technology was able to solve the rape of a local college student. Having read about the potential for obtaining DNA evidence from the ligature used to strangle a victim, the investigator requested DNA testing on the phone cord used to choke the victim in his case. He realized that in the course of choking someone, enough force and friction is applied to the rope or cord that the perpetrator's skins cells may rub off his hands and be left on the ligature.

The investigator's request paid off in an unanticipated way. In spite of the attacker's attempt to avoid identification through DNA evidence by wearing both a condom and rubber gloves, a reliable DNA profile was developed from the evidence. During the struggle, the attacker was forced to use one hand to hold the victim down, leaving only one hand to pull the phone cord tight. The attacker had to grab the remaining end of the cord with his mouth, thereby depositing his saliva on the cord. Although the developed profile came from saliva rather than skin, DNA not only solved the case in Austin, but also linked the perpetrator to a similar sexual assault in Waco.

Without the investigator's understanding of DNA technology and where DNA might be found, the case may have gone unsolved. The successful review and investigation of unsolved cases require the same basic elements as the investigation of new cases: cooperation among law enforcement, the crime laboratory, and the prosecutor's office. Investigators should be aware of technological advances in DNA testing that may yield profiles where previous testing was not performed or was unsuccessful. The crime laboratory can be essential to the preliminary review of unsolved cases, for example, by providing investigators with laboratory reports from previous testing and consultation regarding the investigative value of new DNA analysis techniques and DNA database search capabilities. Additionally, the prosecutor's office should be involved as soon as a case is reopened so that legal issues are addressed appropriately. It is also extremely important that case reconstruction considers the victim or victim's family and the importance of finality to closing a case.

Although DNA is not the only forensic tool available for the investigation of unsolved cases, advancements in DNA testing and the success of DNA database systems have inspired law enforcement agencies throughout the country to reevaluate cases previously thought unsolvable. The purpose of this report is to provide law enforcement with a practical resource for the review of old, cold, or unsolved cases that may be solved through DNA technology and DNA databases. "The Long and Short of DNA" and "How Can DNA Databases Aid Investigations?" will educate the reader about the science and technology of DNA testing and DNA databases. "Practical Considerations" provides important background information on legal and practical considerations regarding the application of DNA technology to old, cold, or unsolved cases. Finally, a step-by-step process is provided to help investigators select cases that would most likely be solved with DNA evidence. As investigators advance through this process, they should also keep in mind the array of other technology advancements, such as improved ballistics and fingerprint databases, that may benefit their investigation.

Advancements in DNA Technology

Advancements in DNA analysis, together with computer technology and the Combined DNA Index System (CODIS),[1] have created a powerful crimefighting tool for law enforcement. CODIS is a computer network that connects forensic DNA laboratories at the local, State, and national levels.

DNA database systems that use CODIS contain two main criminal indexes and a missing persons index. When a DNA profile is developed from crime scene evidence and entered into the forensic (crime scene) index of CODIS, the database software searches thousands of convicted offender DNA profiles (contained in the offender index) of individuals convicted of offenses such as rape and murder. Similar to the Automated Fingerprint Identification System (AFIS), CODIS can aid investigations by efficiently comparing a DNA profile generated from biological evidence left at a crime scene against convicted offender DNA profiles and forensic evidence from other cases contained in CODIS. CODIS can also aid investigations by searching the missing persons index, which contains DNA profiles of unidentified remains and DNA profiles of relatives of those who are missing. Because of the recidivistic nature of violent offenders, the power of a DNA database system is evident not only in the success of solving crimes previously thought unsolvable, but perhaps more importantly, through the prevention of crime.

When properly documented, collected, and stored, biological evidence can be analyzed to produce a reliable DNA profile years, even decades, after it is collected. Just as evidence collected from a crime that occurred yesterday can be analyzed for DNA, today evidence from an old rape kit, bloody shirt, or stained bedclothes may contain a valuable DNA profile. These new analysis techniques, in combination with an evolving database system, make a powerful argument for the reevaluation of unsolved crimes for potential DNA evidence.

Knowledgeable law enforcement officers are taking advantage of powerful DNA analysis techniques by investigating crime scenes with a keener eye toward biological evidence. The same new approach being applied to crime scene processing and current case investigation can be applied to older unsolved cases. Law enforcement agencies across the country are establishing cold-case squads to systematically review old cases for DNA and other new leads. This report will serve as a resource to assist law enforcement with maximizing the potential of DNA evidence in unsolved cases by covering the basics of DNA analysis and its application to forensic casework. The report will also demonstrate how DNA database systems, advancing technology, and cooperative efforts can enhance unsolved case investigative techniques.

New Laws

Advancements in DNA technology have led to significant changes in many States' statutes, which may affect the manner in which unsolved cases are investigated, filed, and prosecuted. Advancements in the technology have been so significant that laws are being created, amended, and even repealed to take advantage of its ability to identify and convict the guilty and exonerate the innocent. Laws regarding DNA admissibility in court, its use in postconviction appeals, the creation and expansion of databases, and the extension or elimination of statutes of limitation are examples of the quickly evolving impact of DNA on the criminal justice system. Given the legal changes occurring throughout the country, constant contact and consultation with the local prosecutor is critical not only for the investigation of older cases but for all cases in which DNA may be relevant evidence.

Statutes of Limitation

Statutes of limitation may be one of the most difficult issues to overcome when examining older cases. Statutes of limitation establish time limits under which criminal charges can be filed for a particular offense. These statutes are rooted in the protection of individuals from the use of evidence that becomes less reliable over time. For example, witnesses' memories fade as time goes by.

However, although some evidence, such as eyewitness accounts, can lose credibility over time, DNA evidence has the power to determine truth 10, 15, even 20 years after an offense is committed. States are beginning to realize that the reliability of DNA technology may necessitate the reevaluation of statutes of limitation in the filing of cases.

Database Expansion

The use of DNA evidence and convicted offender DNA databases has expanded significantly since the first U.S. DNA database was created in 1989.

Although State and local DNA databases established in the early 1990s contained only DNA profiles from convicted murderers and sex offenders, the undeniable success of DNA databases has resulted in a national trend toward database expansion. All States require at least some convicted offenders to provide a DNA sample to be collected for DNA profiling and, in 2000, the Federal Government began requiring certain offenders convicted of Federal or military crimes to also provide a DNA sample for the criminal DNA database.

Recognizing that the effectiveness of the DNA database relies on the volume of data contained in both the forensic index (crime scene samples) and the convicted offender index of CODIS, many States are changing their database statutes to include less violent criminals. Many States are enacting legislation to require all convicted felons to submit a DNA profile to the State database. The tendency for States to include all convicted felons in their databases dramatically increases the number of convicted offender DNA profiles against which forensic DNA evidence can be compared, thus making the database system a more powerful tool for law enforcement.

New Legal Approaches

DNA technology and DNA databases have encouraged the development of new approaches to old cases. One such approach is the filing of charges by "John Doe" warrant. These warrants are based on the unique DNA profile obtained from the analysis of unsolved crime scene evidence. Although John Doe warrants are traditionally filed based on the physical description or alias of an unnamed suspect, investigators and prosecutors are now filing charges using the suspect's DNA profile as the identifier. This innovative approach has allowed charges to be filed that toll and permit old cases to be prosecuted when the person matching the John Doe DNA profile is identified. John Doe DNA warrants are one way to permit cases to remain active, allowing them the chance to be solved through the DNA database in the future.

THE LONG AND SHORT OF DNA

DNA is the fundamental building block for an individual's entire genetic makeup. It is a component of virtually every cell in the human body, and a person's DNA is the same in every cell. That is, the DNA in a person's blood is the same as the DNA in his skin cells, saliva, and other biological material.

DNA analysis is a powerful tool because each person's DNA is unique (with the exception of identical twins). Therefore, DNA evidence collected from a crime scene can implicate or eliminate a suspect, similar to the use of fingerprints. It also can analyze unidentified remains through comparisons with DNA from relatives. Additionally, when evidence from one crime scene is compared with evidence from another using CODIS, those crime scenes can be linked to the same perpetrator locally, statewide, and nationally.

DNA is also a powerful tool because when biological evidence from crime scenes is collected and stored properly, forensically valuable DNA can be found on evidence that may be decades old. Therefore, old cases that were previously thought unsolvable may contain valuable DNA evidence capable of identifying the perpetrator.

Similar to Fingerprints

DNA is often compared with fingerprints in the way matches are determined.

When using either DNA or fingerprints to identify a suspect, the evidence collected from the crime scene is compared with a "known" standard. If identifying features are the same, the DNA or fingerprint can be determined to be a match. However, if identifying features of the DNA profile or fingerprint are different from the known standard, it can be determined that it did not come from that known individual.

DNA Technology Advancements

Recent advancements in DNA technology have improved law enforcement's ability to use DNA to solve old cases. Original forensic applications of DNA analysis were developed using a technology called restriction fragment length polymorphism (RFLP). Although very old cases (more than 10 years) may not have had RFLP analysis done, this kind of DNA testing may have been attempted on more recent unsolved cases. However, because RFLP analysis required a relatively large quantity of DNA, testing may not have been successful. Similarly, biological evidence deemed insufficient in size for testing may not have been previously submitted for testing. Also, if a biological sample was degraded by environmental factors such as dirt or mold, RFLP analysis may have been unsuccessful at yielding a result. Newer technologies could now be successful in obtaining results.

Newer DNA analysis techniques enable laboratories to develop profiles from biological evidence invisible to the naked eye, such as skin cells left on ligatures or weapons. Unsolved cases should be evaluated by investigating both traditional and nontraditional sources of DNA. Valuable DNA evidence might be available that previously went undetected in the original investigation.

If biological evidence is available for testing or retesting in unsolved case investigations, it is important that law enforcement and the crime laboratory work together to review evidence. Logistical issues regarding access to and the cost of DNA analysis will be a factor, as well as issues that relate to the discriminating power of each technology and that might affect the outcome of the results. Laboratory personnel can also provide a valuable perspective on which evidence might yield valuable and probative DNA results. Finally, if previously tested biological evidence produced a DNA profile but excluded the original suspect, revisiting those "exclusion" cases in the context of comparing them with DNA databases might prove to be very valuable to solving old cases.

PCR Analysis

PCR (polymerase chain reaction) enhances DNA analysis and has enabled laboratories to develop DNA profiles from extremely small samples of biological evidence. The PCR technique replicates exact copies of DNA contained in a biological evidence sample without affecting the original, much like a copy machine. RFLP analysis requires a biological sample about the size of a quarter, but PCR can be used to reproduce millions of copies of the DNA contained in a few skin cells. Since PCR analysis requires only a minute quantity of DNA, it can enable the laboratory to analyze highly degraded evidence for DNA. On the other hand, because the sensitive PCR technique replicates any and all of the DNA contained in an evidence sample, greater attention to contamination issues is necessary when identifying, collecting, and preserving DNA evidence. These factors may be particularly important in the evaluation of unsolved cases in which evidence might have been improperly collected or stored.

STR Analysis

Short tandem repeat (STR) technology is a forensic analysis that evaluates specific regions (loci) that are found on nuclear DNA. The variable (polymorphic) nature of the STR regions that are analyzed for forensic testing intensifies the discrimination between one DNA profile and another. For example, the likelihood that any two individuals (except identical twins) will have the same 13-loci DNA profile can be as high as 1 in 1 billion or greater.

The Federal Bureau of Investigation (FBI) has chosen 13 specific STR loci to serve as the standard for CODIS. The purpose of establishing a core set of STR loci is to ensure that all forensic laboratories can establish uniform DNA databases and, more importantly, share valuable forensic information. If the forensic or convicted offender CODIS index is to be used in the investigative stages of unsolved cases, DNA profiles must be generated by using STR technology and the specific 13 core STR loci selected by the FBI.

Mitochondrial DNA Analysis

Mitochondrial DNA (mtDNA) analysis allows forensic laboratories to develop DNA profiles from evidence that may not be suitable for RFLP or STR analysis. While RFLP and PCR techniques analyze DNA extracted from the nucleus of a cell, mtDNA technology analyzes DNA found in a different part of the cell, the mitochondrion (see exhibit 1). Old remains and evidence lacking nucleated cells--such as hair shafts, bones, and teeth--that are unamenable to STR and RFLP testing may yield results if mtDNA analysis is performed. For this reason, mtDNA testing can be very valuable to the investigation of an unsolved case. For example, a cold case log may show that biological evidence in the form of blood, semen, and hair was collected in a particular case, but that all were improperly stored for a long period of time. Although PCR analysis sometimes enables the crime laboratory to generate a DNA profile from very degraded evidence, it is possible that the blood and semen would be so highly degraded that nuclear DNA analysis would not yield a DNA profile. However, the hair shaft could be subjected to mtDNA analysis and thus be the key to solving the case. Finally, it is important to note that all maternal relatives (for example, a person's mother or maternal grandmother) have identical mtDNA.

This enables unidentified remains to be analyzed and compared to the mtDNA profile of any maternal relative for the purpose of aiding missing persons or unidentified remains investigations. Although mtDNA analysis can be very valuable to the investigation of criminal cases, laboratory personnel should always be involved in the process.

Y-Chromosome Analysis

Several genetic markers have been identified on the Y chromosome that can be used in forensic applications. Y-chromosome markers target only the male fraction of a biological sample. Therefore, this technique can be very valuable if the laboratory detects complex mixtures (multiple male contributors) within a biological evidence sample. Because the Y chromosome is transmitted directly from a father to all of his sons, it can also be used to trace family relationships among males. Advancements in Y-chromosome testing may eventually eliminate the need for laboratories to extract and separate semen and vaginal cells (for example, from a vaginal swab of a rape kit) prior to analysis.

Cooperative efforts with the crime laboratory are essential to deciding which analysis methods will be most valuable in a particular case. It is important to note, however, that while RFLP and mtDNA testing may be valuable to the investigation of an old case, current DNA databases are being populated with DNA profiles that are generated using STR analysis. RFLP and mtDNA profiles are not compatible with the convicted offender or forensic indexes of CODIS.[2]

HOW CAN DNA DATABASES AID INVESTIGATIONS?

The development and expansion of databases that contain DNA profiles at the local, State, and national levels have greatly enhanced law enforcement's ability to solve cold cases with DNA. Convicted offender databases store hundreds of thousands of potential suspect DNA profiles, against which DNA profiles developed from crime scene evidence can be compared.

Given the recidivistic nature of many crimes, such as sexual assault and burglary, a likelihood exists that the individual who committed the crime being investigated was convicted of a similar crime and already has his or her DNA profile in a DNA database that can be searched by CODIS. Moreover, CODIS also permits the cross-comparison of DNA profiles developed from biological evidence found at crime scenes. Even if a perpetrator is not identified through the database, crimes may be linked to each other, thereby aiding an investigation, which may eventually lead to the identification of a suspect.

What is CODIS?

CODIS is a computer software program that operates local, State, and national databases of DNA profiles from convicted offenders, unsolved crime scene evidence, and missing persons. Every State in the Nation has a statutory provision for the establishment of a DNA database that allows for the collection of DNA profiles from offenders convicted of particular crimes. CODIS software enables State, local, and national law enforcement crime laboratories to compare DNA profiles electronically, thereby linking serial crimes to each other and identifying suspects by matching DNA profiles from crime scenes with profiles from convicted offenders. The success of CODIS is demonstrated by the thousands of matches that have linked serial cases to each other and cases that have been solved by matching crime scene evidence to known convicted offenders.

The missing persons index consists of the unidentified persons index and the reference index. The unidentified persons index contains DNA profiles from recovered remains, such as bone, teeth, or hair. The reference index contains DNA profiles from related individuals of missing persons so that they can be periodically compared to the unidentified persons index. All samples for this index are typed using mtDNA and STR DNA analysis (if possible) to maximize the power of advancing technology.

How Does CODIS Work?

CODIS uses two indexes to generate investigative leads in crimes for which biological evidence is recovered from a crime scene. The convicted offender index contains DNA profiles of individuals convicted of certain crimes ranging from certain misdemeanors to sexual assault and murder. Each State has different "qualifying offenses" for which persons convicted of them must submit a biological sample for inclusion in the DNA database. The forensic index contains DNA profiles obtained from crime scene evidence, such as semen, saliva, or blood. CODIS uses computer software to automatically search across these indexes for a potential match.

A match made between profiles in the forensic index can link crime scenes to each other, possibly identifying serial offenders. Based on these "forensic hits," police in multiple jurisdictions or States can coordinate their respective investigations and share leads they have developed independent of each other.

Matches made between the forensic and convicted offender indexes can provide investigators with the identity of a suspect(s). It is important to note that if an "offender hit" is obtained, that information typically is used as probable cause to obtain a new DNA sample from that suspect so the match can be confirmed by the crime laboratory before an arrest is made.

LDIS, SDIS, and NDIS

CODIS is implemented as a distributed database with three hierarchical levels (or tiers)--local, State, and national. All three levels contain forensic and convicted offender indexes and a population file (used to generate statistics).

The hierarchical design provides State and local laboratories with the flexibility to configure CODIS to meet their specific legislative and technical needs.

A description of the three CODIS tiers follows (see exhibit 2).

- Local. Typically, the Local DNA Index System (LDIS) installed at crime laboratories is operated by police departments or sheriffs' offices. DNA profiles originated at the local level can be transmitted to the State and national levels.
- State. Each State has a designated laboratory that operates the State DNA Index System (SDIS). SDIS allows local laboratories within that State to compare DNA profiles. SDIS also is the communication path between the local and national tiers. SDIS is typically operated by the agency responsible for implementing and monitoring compliance with the State's convicted offender statute.
- National. The National DNA Index System (NDIS) is the highest level of the CODIS hierarchy and enables qualified State laboratories that are actively participating in CODIS to compare DNA profiles. NDIS is maintained by the FBI under the authority of the DNA Identification Act of 1994.

Limitations of Using the DNA Database

The more data contained in the forensic and offender indexes of CODIS, the more powerful a tool it becomes for law enforcement, especially in its application to unsolved case investigation. However, because many jurisdictions are in the process of developing and populating their DNA databases, convicted offender and forensic casework backlogs have been created over time and continue to grow for several reasons. First, as States recognize the crime-solving potential of DNA databases, they continue to expand the scope of their convicted offender legislation, which increases the number of samples to be collected and analyzed by the DNA laboratory. As a result, more than 1 million uncollected convicted offender DNA profiles are "owed" to the system.

An equally important but more difficult problem to quantify is that of unprocessed casework that contains biological evidence. This casework backlog may include nonsuspect or unsolved cases that could be analyzed and solved as a result of advancements in DNA technology.

Convicted Offender Backlogs

Although all 50 States have passed DNA database legislation, many States have backlogs of convicted offender samples that have been collected but have not yet been analyzed. Although Federal funding has played an important role in reducing existing backlogs, the crimefighting potential of DNA has prompted many States to revise their statutes to require nonviolent convicted offenders to provide a DNA sample for analysis and upload into CODIS. The trend toward expanding convicted offender DNA statutes to include nonviolent offenders has significantly increased the number of DNA samples requiring collection and analysis. Although the success of using the DNA database as a crime-solving and crime-prevention tool can easily be demonstrated once convicted offender backlogs are reduced, it should be recognized that new backlogs are instantly created by the passage of expanded DNA legislation laws. Convicted offender backlogs are an ongoing logistical issue that can compound the complexity of investigating cold cases by using the DNA database.

Forensic Casework Backlogs

Addressing issues that affect the efficient and effective use of DNA databases in the United States is complicated further by the existence of casework backlogs. This refers to biological evidence in perhaps tens of thousands of criminal cases, including violent and nonviolent crimes, that has not been tested or retested for DNA.

Unprocessed rape kits are a clear example of this kind of backlog. Despite the established fact that rape typically yields biological evidence, as of October 1999, at least 180,000 rape kits remained on shelves across the country, unprocessed, because no suspects have been identified. The DNA evidence from these and other criminal cases often is not analyzed and entered into the DNA database because forensic laboratories have to prioritize their work and cases scheduled for trial take precedence over cases in which no suspect is known. In most jurisdictions, nonsuspect criminal cases that contain biological evidence are not being analyzed and entered into the DNA database. In many jurisdictions, DNA from crime scenes is still primarily used to prosecute offenders, not to investigate crimes. The convicted offender backlog and limited resources for casework going to trial preclude State forensic laboratories from analyzing all biological evidence for DNA, which in turn prevents law enforcement from being able to realize the full crime-solving potential of CODIS.

The backlog of forensic cases has practical consequences for most law enforcement agencies in the United States. Laboratory capacity limitations result in the ability to process crime scene samples from only the most serious of offenses. More and more, however, agencies such as those in the United Kingdom are discovering the value of DNA technology in solving property crimes. Blood left on a broken apartment window or saliva found on a discarded beer bottle can be used to identify burglars, and the skin cells rubbed off onto the steering wheel of a stolen vehicle can solve car thefts. However, as long as forensic laboratories remain able to process only the most serious cases, the full potential of DNA technology to solve crime will remain untapped.

Practical Considerations

A broad range of considerations must be made long before any DNA testing is actually attempted in older, unsolved cases. These include

- Legal considerations, such as the application or expiration of statutes of limitation.
- Technological considerations, such as the nature and condition of the evidence as originally collected, stored, and in some instances, subjected to other forensic tests.
- Practical considerations, such as the availability of witnesses in the event DNA testing would identify a suspect and lead to an arrest and a trial.

- Resource issues, such as the time and money available for investigation and forensic analysis.

The nature and scope of these issues require that any approach to reexamining old cases for potential DNA evidence be collaborative, whether by an individual investigator or by a specialized unit developed specifically for cold case review. Local prosecutors can provide valuable insight into legal issues that might prevent or help a future prosecution. Victim/witness units or advocates can provide valuable assistance with locating, educating, and encouraging witnesses. Consultation with representatives from the crime laboratory is critical to ensuring that potential DNA evidence can be successfully analyzed.

Evidence Considerations

When collecting unsolved case evidence from storage facilities, the case investigator should be ready to handle all types of packaging disasters. Evidence may be stored in heavy-duty plastic bags, stapled shut as the past form of "sealing." Multiple items may be sealed in one plastic bag, or even unpackaged in large, open, cardboard boxes. Unprotected microscope slides from medical facilities might also be found as a result of investigating old cases.

No attempt should be made on the part of the investigator to separate and repackage evidence. The condition and position that the evidence has been stored in could provide valuable clues to the forensic scientist for testability of evidence. Only when evidence is found unpackaged should the investigator properly package and label the item(s) to minimize the possibility for contamination from that point forward. It is important that any evidence items are handled minimally and only by individuals wearing disposable gloves. As always, it is also very important that all actions taken as a result of opening, evaluating, packaging, or repackaging evidence are documented thoroughly in the case folder.

Degraded Evidence

Prior to the frequent use of DNA technology, biological evidence may have been collected and stored in ways that were not necessarily the best methods for preserving samples for future DNA testing. For example, evidence containing biological fluids that were originally collected for ABO Blood Typing analysis or other serology methods may have been packaged or stored in ways that can limit DNA testing. Some methods of collection and storage may promote the growth of bacteria and mold on the evidence. Bacteria can seriously damage or degrade DNA contained in biological material and inhibit the ability to develop a DNA profile; however, evidence can still sometimes yield DNA results. For example, PCR technology can allow the laboratory to develop profiles from some moldy biological samples, whereas other evidence may fail to yield a usable DNA profile, even when no mold is visible. Therefore, close consultation with the laboratory is important to determine the type of DNA testing most likely to yield results on the available evidence.

Contamination Issues

Because of the particularly sensitive nature of DNA technology, the potential contamination of evidence should be carefully considered. Technologies used to analyze evidence prior to the forensic application of DNA were not always sensitive to contaminants. Evidence in older cases may have been collected in ways that lacked appropriate contamination or cross-contamination safeguards, which can make the DNA results less useful or even misleading. In these cases, clarifying results by identifying the contributor of an additional profile can determine whether the DNA results may now be used. When a mixture is detected, a careful reconstruction of the evidence collection, storage, and analysis process must be undertaken. It may be determined that DNA profiles will be required from on-scene officers, evidence technicians, or laboratory scientists who had access to the evidence for comparison with evidence results.

In these instances, proper chain-of-custody reconstruction is critical. It is also important to avoid contamination when handling biological evidence during the course of the current review. If evidence that may contain biological material is already sealed, do not reopen it before sending it to the laboratory. (See Evidence Handling Recommendations.)

Legal Considerations

Numerous legal issues might arise when examining older cases for potential DNA evidence. These issues are most likely jurisdictionally specific and may differ from State to State. Although most jurisdictions maintain no statute of limitation for filing charges in a homicide case, States can vary widely in the time allowed for filing charges in other cases, such as rape and other sexual assault crimes. Furthermore, in recognition of DNA technology's ability to solve old cases, many States are extending or even eliminating statutes of limitation for certain crimes.

Chain of Custody

When a case remains unsolved for a long period of time, evidence is usually handled by an increased number of individuals. Many unsolved cases to be reviewed for DNA evidence may have been previously reinvestigated or handled by several different investigators as a result of new leads or periodic, systematic reviews. Furthermore, as cases age, the likelihood increases that evidence may be moved to new or remote storage locations as evidence from newer cases fills police department shelves.

Many cases may also have had evidence submitted to the laboratory for various forms of forensic testing. Evidence in older cases may have been submitted for standard serological testing, but can now be tested for DNA with much greater success. Hair previously submitted for standard microscopic hair analysis may now be submitted for mtDNA testing. As with all criminal investigations, chain-of-custody issues are critical to maintaining the integrity of the evidence.

In all cases, the ultimate ability to use DNA evidence will depend on the ability to prove that the chain of custody was maintained.

Statutes of Limitation

One of the first issues to address when reviewing an unsolved case is whether the statutes of limitation on a case have run out. Several considerations arise when addressing a statute of limitation issue. Good communication between law enforcement and local prosecutors is critical when examining these legal questions.

Changes in statutes. Advances in DNA technology and the creation of DNA databases are leading many criminal justice professionals to rethink time limits placed on the filing of criminal charges. Because biological evidence can yield reliable DNA analysis results years after the commission of a crime, many State legislatures have begun to extend, and in some cases eliminate, the statutes of limitation for some crimes and in certain circumstances. Many States have extended the length of time for which a complaint can be filed, other States have eliminated statutes of limitation for certain crimes, and some legislation is retroactive.

Exceptions to statutes. Exceptions often exist under existing and new statutes. Under such exceptions, time can be added to the statute of limitation, giving police the legal authority to arrest even if it appears as though the statute has run out. For example, many jurisdictions have exceptions for a suspect's flight from jurisdiction. In a case for which there is a 5-year statute of limitation, if the government can prove that the suspect has been absent from the jurisdiction for 2 years, the State can still file against the suspect for up to 7 years after the commission of the crime. Exceptions also exist for cases in which child victims are assaulted by a family member, which can be valuable in the context of a current investigation.

Victim and Witness Considerations

Another important consideration to be made early in the process is the willingness of victims and witnesses to proceed. Although many victims may continuously monitor the progress of their investigations, some choose to detach from the process over time. Reinvestigating a case may cause renewed psychological trauma to the victim and victim's family. It should not be assumed that victims and witnesses, even if they were eager to pursue the case when it occurred, are still interested in pursuing the case. A phone call from an investigator years later may not be a welcome event. Whenever possible, enlist the aid of victim service providers. If a new officer is handling the investigation, enlisting the assistance of the original investigator to make the first contact with the victim may also be helpful.

The older a case is, the more difficult it may be to locate witnesses. However, early identification of victim and witness availability may ultimately save significant resources. Consultation with prosecutors is mandatory when considering whether a witness would be necessary at trial.

Identifying, Analyzing, and Prioritizing Cases

Whether the process of reviewing unsolved cases is initiated by a single officer or by a specialized unit, it must ultimately be a team effort. At all stages of the process, investigators should avail themselves of the scientific advice of the laboratory and the legal expertise of the local prosecutor's office. Close consultation with the laboratory can ensure that evidence integrity is maintained and that limited laboratory resources are allocated effectively. Similarly, prosecutors can help identify issues that might occur at trial if a suspect is identified and arrested upon successful DNA testing. Good communication between police, laboratories, and prosecutors can help identify and convict serious offenders and save valuable time and resources.

Identify Potential Cases for Review

An initial step in the DNA review of unsolved cases is to identify cases that might be amenable to DNA testing. While the cases considered for this kind of review will vary from jurisdiction to jurisdiction, it is important to define minimum requirements that will likely benefit from this approach. Issues such as statutes of limitation and solvability factors should be thoroughly examined in cooperation with a prosecutor and the forensic laboratory to establish guidelines for case selection. It also will be important to identify the ultimate goals of the program so that the selection criteria can be tailored to meet those specific goals.

Cases that could benefit from a review for potential DNA evidence can be identified from numerous sources. In some instances a single police officer or investigator may remember an unsolved case from years ago. In some departments a formalized cold-case unit may systematically review cases for the potential of DNA testing. Other cases may be identified by coordinated, interdepartmental efforts, victims or witnesses who have heard about the potential of DNA evidence, and laboratories taking inventory of their storage facilities. If a department is pursuing a systematic review of cases, either by one or two officers or by a formal unit, there are many sources that can be consulted for valuable investigative information, such as

- Autopsy, laboratory, prosecutor, and local agency logbooks.
- Retired investigators.
- Computer databases.

Identify Statute of Limitation Issues

Statute of limitation issues might affect the ultimate ability to prosecute a case. Cases should be preliminarily reviewed by investigators in conjunction with the prosecutor's office to identify which prosecutions would be barred by the statutes of limitation. If the goal of the unsolved case review program is to obtain convictions and statutes of limitation have expired on a particular case, a department may wish to save its resources for cases likely to yield convictions.

However, if the goal of the program is to solve and close unsolved cases regardless of whether a conviction could be obtained, a jurisdiction may decide to review all cases that qualify under its guidelines. This is an important consideration in the context of investigating serial offenders whose criminal acts might span the course of years or decades.

Define Categories of Cases--Solvability Factors

Because the number of cases that qualify for reinvestigation might be very large, it may be beneficial for a jurisdiction to define cases according to several solvability factors. Solvability factors include facts and circumstances of a case that influence the likelihood that it might be solved through advancements in DNA technology. For example, a high probability exists that analysis of nonsuspect rape kits will yield valuable DNA results. Profiles generated as a result of DNA analysis can now be entered into CODIS, which can solve a case by matching to a convicted offender, or aid investigations by linking serial rapes to each other. Additionally, if an unsolved murder case contains biological evidence foreign to the victim that did not produce viable results from ABO blood typing or RFLP DNA analysis, evidence could be reanalyzed with the more discriminating and powerful STR technology. It is also important to recognize and sort out cases that might not be as likely to be solved with DNA technology. An example might be an unsolved drive-by homicide because the perpetrator most likely would not have left biological evidence at this kind of crime scene.

Case Review-Establish Priorities

Once solvability factors and statute of limitation issues are addressed, it is important to continue the process by identifying the cases to be reviewed first. To preserve investigative resources when considering a larger number of unsolved cases for review, jurisdictions may prioritize according to the likelihood that cases will be solved or the likelihood that investigations will be aided. In establishing this priority, the following criteria can be considered:

- How many qualifying cases are there?
- Where are the case files located?
- Are case summaries available?
- How many cases will be assigned to an investigator?

To establish an investigative hierarchy, qualifying cases should be reviewed by experienced, proficient investigators. A checklist can be used throughout the review process so that managers can decide which cases will be worked first. A checklist can also provide review process consistency throughout the agency. (See Sample Checklist at the end of this report.) The following categories may serve as a model for a hierarchy in prioritizing cases:

- There is a known suspect and physical evidence appears to have been preserved in a manner consistent with successful DNA testing and use of CODIS.
- There is no known suspect but physical evidence has been preserved in a manner consistent with successful DNA testing and use of CODIS.
- There is no known suspect and evidence was collected and preserved in a manner that may make it difficult to obtain a DNA profile.

Locating Case Files, Obtaining Evidence Logs, and Other Documentation

Locating the case file and original evidence for the investigation may be a challenging endeavor. Changes in personnel, procedure, and facilities and the passage of time may complicate the process. When searching for a case file or evidence, an investigator may need to look in numerous places. Potential locations include, but are not limited to, the following:

- Police department property rooms (case files, evidence logs, whole evidence).
- Property warehouses (case files, evidence logs, whole evidence).
- Public crime laboratories (previously tested/submitted evidence, lab reports).
- Private laboratories (previously tested evidence, lab reports).
- Hospital/medical facilities (rape kits, medical reports, slides).
- Coroner/medical examiners' offices (autopsy reports).
- Courthouse property rooms.
- Prosecutors' offices (previous trial or suspect investigation).
- Retired investigators' files (case notes and details not contained in file).
- Other investigating agency offices (investigative leads--serial offender).

Forensic Testing Reports and Previously Tested Evidence

Because advancements in DNA technology enable laboratories to successfully analyze old evidence that might have been improperly stored or subjected to previous forensic analysis, it will be very valuable to locate any and all forensic reports that were produced as a result of previous analysis and/or testing. ABO blood typing, microscopic hair analysis, RFLP DNA analysis, or fingerprint analysis (among others) might have been performed in the course of the original investigation. The original case file should indicate whether and which types of forensic analysis were attempted. These reports also serve to memorialize proper chain of custody. Cooperation with the crime laboratory is crucial to locate and interpret existing forensic reports and to determine whether evidence would be amenable to reanalysis with new DNA techniques.

Many combinations of options are available to investigators and laboratory personnel if biological evidence was available and previously tested. Exhibit 3 may serve to help investigators as they work with the laboratory to discuss options throughout the course of the investigation.

Locate Biological Evidence

When reviewing the case file for potential DNA evidence, it is important to know what kinds of evidence may yield a DNA profile. Given the power and sensitivity of newer DNA testing techniques, DNA can be collected from virtually anywhere. Only a few cells can be sufficient to obtain useful DNA information to help solve a case. Exhibit 4 identifies some common items of evidence that may have been collected previously but not analyzed for the presence of DNA evidence. Remember, if a stain is not visible it does not mean that there are not enough cells for DNA typing. Further, DNA does more than just identify the source of the sample; it can place a known individual at a crime scene, in a home, or in a room where the suspect claimed not to have been. It can refute a claim of self-defense and put a weapon in the suspect's hand. It can also provide irrefutable evidence that can change a suspect's story from an alibi to one of consent.

Evaluate for Probative DNA Evidence

On completion of reviewing the case file, reports, and evidence in consultation with the laboratory, it will be necessary to identify which evidentiary items will be amenable to DNA analysis. Consultation with the laboratory will be essential to determine the likelihood of obtaining results from DNA analysis, and consultation with a prosecutor is very important to determine which evidence will be probative to the case. Building the new investigation on cooperative efforts between the laboratory and prosecutor can save valuable resources, develop leads, and identify previously overlooked evidence that may yield a DNA profile.

Continue Investigative Protocol

If DNA analysis is to be conducted, it may be important to obtain reference samples from prior suspects, and it might be necessary to be creative when obtaining these samples. While a biological sample in the form of blood or saliva can be obtained voluntarily through a consent form, a standard reference sample might already exist if previous forensic analysis, such as serological testing, was performed during the course of the original investigation.

Additionally, elimination samples from anyone who had lawful access to the crime scene, such as family members, may be required if the laboratory determines that there is more than one DNA profile present in the evidence sample. Early identification of the location and status of persons who might be requested to submit an elimination sample could save valuable time and resources if the laboratory needs such information. Consultation with the laboratory is essential to properly coordinating this process.

Follow Agency Procedures for Submitting the DNA Profile to CODIS

On successful laboratory analysis resulting in a DNA profile developed from crime scene evidence, existing and/or new suspect DNA profiles should be compared with the evidence profile. If the laboratory determines a match between a suspect and the evidence, the prosecutor's office should be consulted on how to proceed. However, if a match is not found, agency procedures should be followed, in accordance with the crime laboratory, to submit the crime scene evidence DNA profile into CODIS.

Because CODIS contains hundreds of thousands of convicted offender DNA profiles, it is possible that the person who committed the unsolved crime being investigated was convicted of a qualifying offense that required submission of a DNA profile to the database. If that person has not previously been convicted of a qualifying offense, especially in light of expanding database law, it is possible that they will be convicted in the future. Further, because the forensic index of CODIS contains thousands of crime scene evidence profiles, the investigation could be aided if a match is made to another forensic DNA profile already in the database. Finally, an investigator should not assume that a new DNA profile generated from unsolved case evidence and submitted to the laboratory for entry into CODIS will be compared with every possible convicted offender or crime scene index profile. The investigator may need to proactively request that his CODIS administrator search the new profile against the local, State, and national DNA databases.

Prepare a John Doe Warrant

CODIS is a powerful crime-solving and crime-prevention tool, but many cases will not be solved as a result of entering a DNA profile into the forensic index of the database. Additionally, many cases will have statute of limitation issues that might prevent the prosecution of the case if a match is not determined in a timely manner. Therefore, if no offender match occurs in cases in which statutes of limitation are an issue, consideration may be given, in consultation with the prosecutor, to preparing a John Doe warrant. These types of warrants can identify the perpetrator according to his or her DNA profile. The 13-loci profile generated by the crime laboratory should be clearly printed on the face of the warrant. The John Doe warrant is not novel; however, the unconventional method of describing an individual by his or her DNA profile may allow for prosecution of a case if a DNA match is determined in the course of future investigations or as a result of the CODIS system being populated with more convicted offender and forensic DNA profiles.

Notes

1. CODIS uses two indexes--the forensic index and the offender index—to generate investigative leads in crimes where biological evidence is recovered from crime scenes. The forensic index contains DNA profiles of biological crime scene evidence and the offender index contains DNA profiles of individuals convicted of a qualifying offense.

2. CODIS has a missing persons index that exclusively contains mtDNA profiles; the convicted offender and forensic indexes of CODIS exclusively contain STR DNA profiles.

The successful review and investigation of unsolved cases require cooperation among law enforcement, the crime laboratory, and the prosecutor's office.

The power of a DNA database system is evident not only in the success of solving crimes previously thought unsolvable, but through the prevention of crime.

The reliability of DNA technology may necessitate the reevaluation of statutes of limitation.

If biological evidence is available for testing or retesting in unsolved case investigations, it is important that law enforcement and the crime laboratory work together to review evidence.

If the convicted offender or forensic index of CODIS is to be used in the investigative stages of an unsolved case, DNA profiles must be generated using STR analysis.

Success Story

A "forensic hit" occurred in the National DNA Index System (NDIS) that linked a dead Florida man's DNA profile to eight serial unsolved rapes in Washington, D.C. and three offenses in Florida.

In 1999, Leon Dundas was killed in a drug deal. Investigators remembered Dundas refusing to give a blood sample in connection with a rape investigation in 1998. They were able to obtain Dundas' blood sample through the medical examiner's office and forwarded it to the DNA lab at the Florida Department of Law Enforcement. Dundas' DNA profile was compared with the national forensic index and a match was made between Dundas and DNA evidence from a rape victim in Washington, D.C.

The FBI then entered DNA evidence from additional unsolved rapes committed in Washington. Dundas' DNA matched seven additional rapes in Washington and three more in Jacksonville, Florida. Police in Washington said that without DNA, they would have never identified Dundas, who had no prior recorded history of violent crime.

The offender index contains DNA profiles of individuals convicted of certain crimes. The forensic index contains DNA profiles obtained from crime scene evidence.

Local prosecutors can provide valuable insight into legal issues. Victim/witness units or advocates can help locate, educate, and encourage witnesses. Consultation with representatives from the crime laboratory is critical.

Evidence Handling Recommendations

- Wear gloves. Change them between handling each item of evidence.
- Use disposable instruments or clean instruments thoroughly before and after handling each evidence sample.
- Avoid touching the area where you believe DNA may exist.
- Avoid touching your face, nose, and mouth when examining and repackaging evidence.
- Put dry evidence into new paper bags or envelopes; do not use plastic bags.
- Do not use staples.
- If repackaging of evidence is necessary, consult with laboratory personnel.

Statute of Limitation Recommendations

- Know the original statute of limitation.
- Determine whether the law has changed regarding time limits for filing. If so, is the law retroactive?
- Determine whether there are exceptions to the statute.
- Consult with the prosecutor.

It should not be assumed that victims and witnesses are still interested in pursuing the case. Whenever possible, enlist the aid of victim service providers.

Good communication between police, laboratories, and prosecutors can help identify and convict serious offenders and save valuable time and resources.

DNA Can Do More . . .

. . . than identify a suspect. It can also--

- Place a known individual at a crime scene.
- Refute a claim of self-defense.
- Put a weapon in a suspect's hand.
- Change a suspect's story from an alibi to one of consent.

Sample Checklist

- Identify potential cases.
  - Identify any statute of limitation issues (consult with prosecutors).
  - Define case categories according to solvability factors.
- Prioritize cases (consider solvability factors).
- Locate and review the case file; obtain evidence logs and other documentation such as laboratory and autopsy reports.
- Locate previous forensic testing reports and location of previously tested evidence. For example--
  - Blood previously ABO typed.
  - Hair analyzed microscopically.
  - Fingerprint evidence.
- Locate crime scene evidence containing biological material.
- Evaluate the case and evidence for potential probative DNA. Be sure to--
  - Consider all evidentiary possibilities.
  - Take appropriate precautions against contamination.
- In consultation with the laboratory and prosecutors, submit appropriate (probative) evidence to the laboratory for testing.
- Continue investigative protocol. If needed, obtain reference samples from suspects--
  - Voluntarily using a consent form.
  - By using a previously obtained sample (e.g., if a reference sample was used for standard serological testing).
- Identify witness issues
  - Legal availability.
  - Willingness to proceed.
  - Location.
- If a profile does not match suspect profiles, follow agency procedures for submitting the evidence profile to CODIS.
- If no offender match occurs in cases in which statutes of limitation are an issue, prepare a John Doe warrant.

About the National Institute of Justice

NIJ is the research, development, and evaluation agency of the U.S. Department of Justice and is solely dedicated to researching crime control and justice issues. NIJ provides objective, independent, nonpartisan, evidence-based knowledge and tools to meet the challenges of crime and justice, particularly at the State and local levels. NIJ's principal authorities are derived from the Omnibus Crime Control and Safe Streets Act of 1968, as amended (42 U.S.C. Sections 3721-3722).

NIJ's Mission

In partnership with others, NIJ's mission is to prevent and reduce crime, improve law enforcement and the administration of justice, and promote public safety. By applying the disciplines of the social and physical sciences, NIJ--

- Researches the nature and impact of crime and delinquency.
- Develops applied technologies, standards, and tools for criminal justice practitioners.
- Evaluates existing programs and responses to crime.
- Tests innovative concepts and program models in the field.
- Assists policymakers, program partners, and justice agencies.
- Disseminates knowledge to many audiences.

NIJ's Strategic Direction and Program Areas

NIJ is committed to five challenges as part of its strategic plan: 1) rethinking justice and the processes that create just communities; 2) understanding the nexus between social conditions and crime; 3) breaking the cycle of crime by testing research-based interventions; 4) creating the tools and technologies that meet the needs of practitioners; and 5) expanding horizons through interdisciplinary and international perspectives. In addressing these strategic challenges, the Institute is involved in the following program areas: crime control and prevention, drugs and crime, justice systems and offender behavior, violence and victimization, communications and information technologies, critical incident response, investigative and forensic sciences (including DNA), less-than-lethal technologies, officer protection, education and training technologies, testing and standards, technology assistance to law enforcement and corrections agencies, field testing of promising programs, and international crime control. NIJ communicates its findings through conferences and print and electronic media.

NIJ's Structure

The NIJ Director is appointed by the President and confirmed by the Senate. The NIJ Director establishes the Institute's objectives, guided by the priorities of the Office of Justice

Programs, the U.S. Department of Justice, and the needs of the field. NIJ actively solicits the views of criminal justice and other professionals and researchers to inform its search for the knowledge and tools to guide policy and practice.

NIJ has three operating units. The Office of Research and Evaluation manages social science research and evaluation and crime mapping research. The Office of Science and Technology manages technology research and development, standards development, and technology assistance to State and local law enforcement and corrections agencies. The Office of Development and Communications manages field tests of model programs, international research, and knowledge dissemination programs. NIJ is a component of the Office of Justice Programs, which also includes the Bureau of Justice Assistance, the Bureau of Justice Statistics, the Office of Juvenile Justice and Delinquency Prevention, and the Office for Victims of Crime.

To find out more about the National Institute of Justice, please contact:

National Criminal Justice Reference Service
P.O. Box 6000
Rockville, MD 20849-6000
800-851-3420
e-mail: askncjrs@ncjrs.org

In: Forensics in Law Enforcement
Editor: M. V. Shoester, pp. 209-221
ISBN 1-60021-164-X

Chapter 7

ADVANCING JUSTICE THROUGH DNA TECHNOLOGY*

United States Department of Justice

EXECUTIVE SUMMARY

DNA technology is increasingly vital to ensuring accuracy and fairness in the criminal justice system. DNA can be used to identify criminals with incredible accuracy when biological evidence exists, and DNA can be used to clear suspects and exonerate persons mistakenly accused or convicted of crimes.

The current federal and state DNA collection and analysis system needs improvement. In many instances, public crime labs are overwhelmed by backlogs of unanalyzed DNA samples. In addition, these labs may be ill-equipped to handle the increasing influx of DNA samples and evidence. The problems of backlogs and the lack of up-to-date technology result in significant delays in the administration of justice. More research is needed to develop faster methods for analyzing DNA evidence. Professionals involved in the criminal justice system need additional training and assistance in order to ensure the optimal use of DNA evidence to solve crimes and assist victims. And the criminal justice system needs the means to provide DNA testing in appropriate circumstances for individuals who assert that they have been wrongly convicted.

President Bush believes we must do more to realize the full potential of DNA technology to solve crime and protect the innocent. The President has proposed $232.6 million in federal funding in FY 2004 for his initiative, Advancing Justice Through DNA Technology, and calls for continuing this level of funding for five years – a total commitment of over $1 billion. Under the President's initiative, the Attorney General will improve the use of DNA in the criminal justice system – especially in federal, state, and local forensic laboratories – by providing funds, training and assistance to ensure that this technology reaches its full potential. The President's initiative promotes:

---

* Excerpted from http://www.whitehouse.gov/infocus/justice/dna_initiative-toc.html

Using DNA to Solve Crimes: When used to its full potential, DNA technology will permit the criminal justice system to identify criminals quickly and accurately. More crimes will be solved and persons mistakenly accused or convicted of crimes will be cleared if the criminal justice system is provided with the necessary funding, technology, and assistance it needs to reap the benefits of DNA technology. Under the President's initiative, the Attorney General will:

Eliminate Backlogs: The initiative provides funding to eliminate, within five years, the current backlogs of unanalyzed DNA samples for the most serious violent offenses – rapes, murders, and kidnappings – and for convicted offender samples needing testing.

Strengthen Crime Laboratory Capacity: The initiative provides funding to improve the analysis capacity of federal, state, and local crime labs so they can process DNA samples efficiently and cost-effectively and help prevent future backlogs.

Stimulate Research and Development: The initiative provides resources to stimulate innovative research in order to develop, among other things, more rapid and less costly methods of DNA analysis and the ability to analyze smaller and more degraded samples.

Provide Training: The initiative provides training on the collection and use of DNA evidence to the wide variety of professionals involved in using DNA evidence in the criminal justice system – police officers, prosecutors, defense attorneys, judges, forensic scientists, medical personnel, victim service providers, corrections officers, and probation and parole officers.

Using DNA to Protect the Innocent: Under the President's initiative, the Attorney General will advance the use of DNA technology to protect the innocent from wrongful prosecution. The initiative supports providing access to post-conviction DNA testing in appropriate circumstances for state or federal inmates who may have been wrongly convicted, and establishes a grant program to assist states in providing post-conviction testing.

Using DNA to Identify Missing Persons: The events of September 11, 2001 demonstrated on a national scale the potential for anguish when the remains of a missing person go unidentified. In order to help provide closure for families of missing persons, the President's initiative provides education and outreach to medical examiners, coroners, law enforcement officers, and victims' families on the use of DNA to identify missing persons.

USING DNA TO SOLVE CRIMES

The past decade has seen great advances in a powerful criminal justice tool: deoxyribonucleic acid, or DNA. DNA can be used to identify criminals with incredible accuracy when biological evidence exists. By the same token, DNA can be used to clear suspects and exonerate persons mistakenly accused or convicted of crimes. In all, DNA technology is increasingly vital to ensuring accuracy and fairness in the criminal justice system.

News stories extolling the successful use of DNA to solve crimes abound. For example, in 1999, New York authorities linked a man through DNA evidence to at least 22 sexual assaults and robberies that had terrorized the city. In 2002, authorities in Philadelphia, Pennsylvania, and Fort Collins, Colorado, used DNA evidence to link and solve a series of crimes (rapes and a murder) perpetrated by the same individual. In the 2001 "Green River" killings, DNA evidence provided a major breakthrough in a series of crimes that had remained unsolved for years despite a large law enforcement task force and a $15 million investigation.

DNA is generally used to solve crimes in one of two ways. In cases where a suspect is identified, a sample of that person's DNA can be compared to evidence from the crime scene. The results of this comparison may help establish whether the suspect committed the crime. In cases where a suspect has not yet been identified, biological evidence from the crime scene can be analyzed and compared to offender profiles in DNA databases to help identify the perpetrator. Crime scene evidence can also be linked to other crime scenes through the use of DNA databases.

For example, assume that a man was convicted of sexual assault. At the time of his conviction, he was required to provide a sample of his DNA, and the resulting DNA profile was entered into a DNA database. Several years later, another sexual assault was committed. A Sexual Assault Nurse Examiner worked with the victim and was able to obtain biological evidence from the rape. This evidence was analyzed, the resulting profile was run against a DNA database, and a match was made to the man's DNA profile. He was apprehended, tried, and sentenced for his second crime. In this hypothetical case, he was also prevented from committing other crimes during the period of his incarceration.

DNA evidence is generally linked to DNA offender profiles through DNA databases. In the late 1980s, the federal government laid the groundwork for a system of national, state, and local DNA databases for the storage and exchange of DNA profiles. This system, called the Combined DNA Index System (CODIS), maintains DNA profiles obtained under the federal, state, and local systems in a set of databases that are available to law enforcement agencies across the country for law enforcement purposes. CODIS can compare crime scene evidence to a database of DNA profiles obtained from convicted offenders. CODIS can also link DNA evidence obtained from different crime scenes, thereby identifying serial criminals.

In order to take advantage of the investigative potential of CODIS, in the late 1980s and early 1990s, states began passing laws requiring offenders convicted of certain offenses to provide DNA samples. Currently all 50 states and the federal government have laws requiring that DNA samples be collected from some categories of offenders.

When used to its full potential, DNA evidence will help solve and may even prevent some of the Nation's most serious violent crimes. However, the current federal and state DNA collection and analysis system needs improvement:

1. In many instances, public crime labs are overwhelmed by backlogs of unanalyzed DNA samples.
2. In addition, these labs may be ill-equipped to handle the increasing influx of DNA samples and evidence. The problems of backlogs and lack of up-to-date technology result in significant delays in the administration of justice.
3. More research is needed to develop faster methods for analyzing DNA evidence.
4. Professionals working in the criminal justice system need additional training and assistance in order to ensure the optimal use of DNA evidence to solve crimes and assist victims.

President Bush believes we must do more to realize the full potential of DNA technology to solve crime and protect the innocent. Under the President's initiative, the Attorney General will improve the use of DNA in the criminal justice system by providing funds and assistance to ensure that this technology reaches its full potential to solve crimes.

1. Eliminating Backlogs Top

One of the biggest problems facing the criminal justice system today is the substantial backlog of unanalyzed DNA samples and biological evidence from crime scenes, especially in sexual assault and murder cases. Too often, crime scene samples wait unanalyzed in police or crime lab storage facilities. Timely analysis of these samples and placement into DNA databases can avert tragic results. For example, in 1995, the Florida Department of Law Enforcement linked evidence found on a rape-homicide victim to a convicted rapist's DNA profile just eight days before he was scheduled for parole. Had he been released prior to being linked to the unsolved rape-homicide, he may very well have raped or murdered again.

By contrast, analysis and placement into CODIS of DNA profiles can dramatically enhance the chances that potential crime victims will be spared the violence of vicious, repeat offenders. The President's initiative calls for $92.9 million to help alleviate the current backlogs of DNA samples for the most serious violent offenses – rapes, murders, and kidnappings – and for convicted offender samples needing testing. With this additional federal backlog reduction funding, the funding provided by this initiative to improve crime laboratory capacity, and continued support from the states, the current backlogs will be eliminated in five years.

Understanding the Backlog

The state and local backlog problem has two components: (1) "casework sample backlogs," which consist of DNA samples obtained from crime scenes, victims, and suspects in criminal cases, and (2) "convicted offender backlogs," which consist of DNA samples obtained from convicted offenders who are incarcerated or under supervision. The nature of the DNA backlog is complex and changing, and measuring the precise number of unanalyzed DNA samples is difficult.

Casework Sample Backlogs: In a 2001 survey of public DNA laboratories, the Bureau of Justice Statistics (BJS) found that between 1997 and 2000, DNA laboratories experienced a 73% increase in casework and a 135% increase in their casework backlogs. Many casework samples go unanalyzed for lack of a suspect to which to compare the biological evidence from the crime scene. These are often referred to as "no-suspect" cases. Based on an ongoing assessment of crime laboratories and law enforcement agencies, the National Institute of Justice (NIJ) estimates that the current backlog of rape and homicide cases is approximately 350,000. The initiative calls for $76 million in FY 2004 to help eliminate these backlogs over five years.

Convicted Offender Backlogs: States are increasing the number of convicted offenders required to provide DNA samples. Currently, 23 states require all convicted felons to provide DNA samples. Preliminary estimates by NIJ place the number of collected, untested convicted offender samples at between 200,000 and 300,000. NIJ also estimates that there are between 500,000 and 1,000,000 convicted offender samples that are owed, but not yet collected. The initiative calls for $15 million in FY 2004 to help eliminate convicted offender backlogs over five years.

The federal government also faces a high demand for analysis of casework and convicted offender DNA samples. The FBI has two DNA casework analysis units (see page 5). The first unit, which focuses on analyzing nuclear DNA, has a backlog of approximately 900 cases. The second unit, which focuses on analyzing mitochondrial DNA (mtDNA), has a backlog of roughly 120 cases.

The federal government also collects DNA samples from persons convicted of offenses in certain categories, including crimes of violence or terrorism. The FBI currently has a backlog of approximately 18,000 convicted offender samples. The initiative calls for $1.9 million in FY 2004 to fund the federal convicted offender program; some of these funds will be devoted to eliminating the federal convicted offender backlog.

Effect of Clearing the Backlog

The results of addressing backlogs are dramatic, as the two examples below illustrate:

In September 1993, a married couple was attacked on a jogging trail in Dallas by a man with a gun who sexually assaulted the woman after shooting the man. No suspect was ever positively identified, although police investigated over 200 leads and 40 potential suspects. In August 2000, evidence from the case was analyzed using current DNA technology. Then, in February 2001, the DNA sample was matched to an individual who was already serving a five-year sentence for an unrelated 1997 sexual assault of a child. The man has since been convicted of capital murder and aggravated sexual assault.

In March 1992, an Alexandria, Virginia shop owner was stabbed more than 150 times in her home. There were no witnesses to the crime. For years, detectives had no leads, but they did have traces of someone's blood, apparently from the fierce struggle between the victim and the killer. Meanwhile, in 1996, a man pleaded guilty to robbing a gas station, and his DNA was collected for analysis and inclusion in the Virginia DNA database. Because of the backlog, the man's sample was not immediately analyzed. In the summer of 2000, the sample was analyzed and matched through the database to the evidence from the Alexandria woman's murder. In April 2001, almost nine years after the commission of this brutal crime, the man was sentenced to life in prison.

Several law enforcement agencies, prosecutors' offices, and crime labs across the country have established innovative programs to review old cases. Often called "cold case units," these programs have enabled criminal justice officials to solve cases that have languished for years without suspects. Most frequently, DNA evidence has been the linchpin in solving these cases. For instance, this past July, a California man was found guilty of the 1974 rape-homicide of a 19 year-old pregnant woman – a case that was solved through DNA evidence nearly thirty years after the crime was committed.

Prior Federal Support of State DNA Backlog Reduction

In recent years, the federal government has strongly supported states in their efforts to eliminate backlogs of convicted offender and casework DNA samples. Since the creation in 2000 of the Department of Justice's (DOJ's) Convicted Offender DNA Backlog Reduction Program, more than 493,600 offender samples from 24 states have been analyzed. Since the creation in 2001 of the No Suspect Casework DNA Backlog Reduction Program, federal funds have been provided to support the analysis of approximately 24,800 cases. States have analyzed evidence in an additional 18,000 "no-suspect" cases as a result of a match requirement of Convicted Offender DNA Backlog Reduction funding.

In 2002 and 2003 combined, the President requested and Congress appropriated $70.8 million to fund these DNA backlog reduction programs. Additionally, Attorney General John Ashcroft also made available $25 million in Asset Forfeiture funds to address the backlog of convicted offender and "no suspect" casework samples. Thus, the Bush Administration already has devoted more than $95 million to reducing DNA backlogs.

2. Strengthening Crime Laboratory Capacity Top

At present, many of our Nation's crime laboratories do not have the capacity necessary to analyze DNA samples in a timely fashion. Many have limited equipment resources, outdated information systems, and overwhelming case management demands. As a result, the criminal justice system as a whole is unable to reap the full benefits of DNA technology. The President's initiative will provide federal funding to further automate and improve the infrastructure of federal, state, and local crime labs so they can process DNA samples efficiently and cost-effectively. These infrastructure improvements are critical to preventing future DNA backlogs, and to helping the criminal justice system realize the full potential of DNA technology.

Increasing the Analysis Capacity of Public Crime Labs

The President's initiative will provide significant support to public crime labs so that these labs can update their infrastructure, automate their DNA analysis procedures, and improve their retention and storage of forensic evidence. The initiative calls for $60 million in FY 2004 funding, which will be dedicated to:

Providing Basic Infrastructure Support: Some public crime laboratories still need assistance to help them obtain equipment and material to conduct the basic processes of DNA analysis – extraction, quantitation, amplification and analysis – and to help them meet various accreditation requirements.

Building Infrastructure through Laboratory Information Management Systems: Laboratory Information Management Systems, or "LIMS," are designed to automate evidence handling and casework management, to improve the integrity and speed of evidence handling procedures, and to ensure proper chain of custody. DOJ estimates that only 10 percent of the public DNA laboratories have LIMS systems.

Providing Automation Tools to Public DNA Laboratories: To streamline aspects of the DNA analysis procedure that are labor and time-intensive, crime laboratories should have automated systems, such as robotic DNA extraction units. Automated DNA analysis systems increase analyst productivity, limit human error and reduce contamination.

Providing Support for the Retention and Storage of Forensic Evidence: Forensic evidence must be stored in a manner that ensures its integrity and maintains its availability throughout criminal investigations and judicial proceedings. Appropriate evidence storage conditions require costly equipment such as security systems, environmental control systems, ambient temperature monitors, and de-humidifiers. The initiative will support the improvement of evidence storage capabilities.

Funding the FBI Forensic Analysis Programs

The FBI Laboratory runs several different programs for the analysis of DNA information. The Nuclear DNA Program supports federal, state, local, and international law enforcement agencies by providing advanced technical assistance within the forensic biology discipline and sub-disciplines through interrelated capabilities and expertise. The Mitochondrial DNA (mtDNA) Analysis Program is responsible for performing mtDNA analysis of forensic evidence containing small or degraded quantities of DNA on items of evidence submitted from federal, state, and local law enforcement agencies. Mitochondrial DNA is a powerful tool available for investigating cases of kidnapping, missing persons, and skeletal remains where nuclear DNA is not present. The initiative will provide funds to these two existing programs to permit them to continue their important work. In addition, the initiative will provide funds to the FBI to further expand regional mtDNA labs that will provide an alternative source for mtDNA analysis to state and local law enforcement, and allow the FBI laboratory to concentrate more of its efforts on federal cases. The initiative calls for $20.5 million in FY 2004 to fund these programs.

Funding the Combined DNA Index System

The Combined DNA Index System (CODIS), administered by the FBI, maintains DNA profiles obtained through federal, state, and local DNA sample collection programs, and makes this information available to law enforcement agencies across the country for law enforcement identification purposes. Currently, the National DNA Index System (NDIS) of CODIS contains about 1.7 million DNA profiles. The President's initiative includes funding to complete a general redesign and upgrade of CODIS, which will increase the system's capacity to 50 million DNA profiles, reduce the search time from hours to microseconds for matching DNA profiles, and enable instant, real□time (as opposed to weekly) searches of the database by participating forensic laboratories. The initiative calls for $9.9 million in FY 2004 to fund this program.

3. Stimulating Research and Development Top

In order to improve the use of DNA technology to advance the cause of justice, the Attorney General will stimulate research and development of new methods of analyzing DNA samples under the President's initiative. Also, the President has asked the Attorney General to establish demonstration projects under the initiative to further study the public safety and law enforcement benefits of fully integrating the use of DNA technology to solve crimes. Finally, the President has directed the Attorney General to create a National Forensic Science Commission to study rapidly evolving advances in all areas of the forensic sciences and to make recommendations to maximize the use of the forensic sciences in the criminal justice system. In all, the President's initiative will devote $24.8 million in FY 2004 to fund advances in the use of DNA technology.

Improving DNA Technology

Forensic DNA analysis is rapidly evolving. Research and development of tools that will permit crime laboratories to conduct DNA analysis quickly is vital to the goal of improving the timely analysis of DNA samples. Smaller, faster, and less costly analysis tools will reduce capital investments for crime laboratories while increasing their capacity to process more cases. Over the course of the next several years, DNA research efforts will focus on the following areas:

The development of "DNA chip technology" that uses nanotechnology to improve both speed and resolution of DNA evidence analysis. This technology will reduce analysis time from several hours to several minutes and provide cost-effective miniaturized components.

The development of more robust methods to enable more crime labs to have greater success in the analysis of degraded, old, or compromised items of biological evidence.

Advanced applications of various DNA analysis methods, such as automated Short Tandem Repeats (STRs), Single Nucleotide Polymorphisms (SNPs), mitochondrial DNA analysis (mtDNA), and Y-chromosome DNA analysis.

The use of animal, plant, and microbial DNA to provide leads that may link DNA found on or near human perpetrators or victims to the actual perpetrator of the crime.

Technologies that will enable DNA identification of vast numbers of samples occasioned by a mass disaster or mass fatality incident.

Technologies that permit better separation of minute traces of male sexual assailant DNA from female victims.

The initiative devotes $10 million in FY 2004 funding to benefit the state and local criminal justice community through DNA research and development. It also requests $9.8 million in FY 2004 funding to further expand the FBI's DNA research and development program.

Establishing DNA Demonstration Projects

To further research the impact of increased DNA evidence collection on public safety and law enforcement operations, the Attorney General will conduct rigorous scientific research through demonstration projects on the use of DNA evidence under the initiative. This research will help determine the scope of public safety benefits that result when police are trained to more effectively collect DNA evidence and prosecutors are provided with training to enhance their ability to present this evidence in court.

Several jurisdictions will be selected to incorporate core training and evidence collection requirements in their daily operations. At each site, one or more law enforcement agencies will be chosen to implement extensive training on the collection of DNA evidence and to increase the resources devoted to the investigation and prosecution of these cases. Prosecutors will also receive training on how to more effectively present DNA evidence and how forensic DNA technology may be used to solve current and "cold" cases. Jurisdictions that received increased training and resources will be compared with jurisdictions that did not receive these benefits.

The resulting comparison will measure the impact of increased DNA evidence collection on public safety and law enforcement operations. For example, projects will examine whether there are increased crime clearance rates, whether DNA aided investigations, the number of cases successfully prosecuted, the number of cases where guilty pleas were obtained due to the presence of DNA evidence, any financial savings resulting from the use of forensic evidence, and increased responsiveness to victims. The information obtained will allow state and local governments to make more informed decisions regarding investment in forensic DNA as a crime-fighting tool. The initiative calls for $4.5 million in FY 2004 to fund these projects.

Creating a National Forensic Science Commission

To facilitate the ability of policymakers to assess the needs of the forensic science community, and to stimulate public awareness of the uses of forensic technology to solve crimes, the President has directed the Attorney General to create a National Forensic Science Commission. The Commission will be charged with two primary responsibilities: (1) developing recommendations for long-term strategies to maximize the use of current forensic technologies to solve crimes and protect the public, and (2) identifying potential scientific breakthroughs that may be used to assist law enforcement.

The Attorney General will appoint Commission members from professional forensic science organizations and accreditation bodies and from the criminal justice community. These individuals will have broad knowledge and in-depth expertise in the criminal justice system and in various areas of the forensic sciences such as analytical toxicology, trace evidence, forensic biology, firearms and toolmark examinations, latent fingerprints, crime scene analysis, digital evidence, and forensic pathology, in addition to DNA. Judges, prosecutors, attorneys, victim advocates, and other members of the criminal justice system will also be represented on the Commission.

The Commission will study advances in all areas of the forensic sciences and make recommendations on how new and existing technologies can be used to improve public safety. The Commission will also serve as an ongoing forum for discussing initiatives and policy, and may issue recommendations that will assist state and local law enforcement agencies in the cost-effective use of these technologies to solve crimes. The initiative devotes $500,000 in FY 2004 to the establishment of the Commission.

4. Training the Criminal Justice Community Top

In order to maximize the use of DNA technology, under the President's initiative, the Attorney General will develop training and provide assistance regarding the collection and use of DNA evidence to the wide variety of professionals involved in the criminal justice system, including police officers, prosecutors, defense attorneys, judges, forensic scientists, medical personnel, victim service providers, corrections officers, and probation and parole officers.

Key players in the criminal justice system should receive additional training in the proper collection, preservation, and use of DNA evidence. Fundamental knowledge of the capabilities of DNA technology is essential for police officers to collect evidence properly, prosecutors and defense attorneys to introduce and use it successfully in court, and judges to rule correctly on its admissibility. Victim service providers and medical personnel likewise need to understand DNA technology in order to encourage more successful evidence collection and to be fully responsive to the needs of victims.

Law Enforcement Training

As the first responders to crime scenes, law enforcement officers should be able to identify, collect and preserve probative biological evidence for submission to crime laboratories. Improper collection can mean that valuable evidence is missed or rendered unsuitable for testing. The initiative devotes $3.5 million in FY 2004 to assist law enforcement in meeting the following training needs:

- Basic "awareness training" on DNA evidence for patrol officers and other first-responders;
- Intensive training on identifying, collecting, and preserving potential DNA evidence for evidence technicians, investigators, and others processing crime scenes;
- Training and education for investigators and responding officers on DNA databases and their potential to provide leads in current and "cold" cases; and
- Training and information for law enforcement leadership and policymakers to facilitate more informed decisions about effective DNA evidence collection and testing.
- Training Prosecutors, Defense Attorneys, and Judges

In order to achieve just results in cases involving DNA evidence, prosecutors, defense attorneys, and judges should receive proper training on the use and presentation of DNA evidence. The initiative devotes $2.5 million in FY 2004 to support:

- Training and technical assistance for prosecutors to learn about solving "cold cases" with DNA evidence, responding to post-conviction DNA testing requests, and developing innovative legal strategies to optimize the power of forensic DNA technology. Grant funds will be available for state and local prosecutors' organizations for the development and delivery of training materials to assist prosecutors in presenting this evidence before courts and juries, and in understanding more about the value of DNA evidence in particular cases.
- Training for defense counsel handling cases involving biological evidence on the applications and limitations of DNA evidence. Grant funds will be made available to continuing legal education programs or bar associations to provide training and resources on forensic DNA technology.
- Training for judges, who must be equipped with sufficient technical and scientific knowledge to make appropriate rulings in cases involving DNA evidence. Grant funds will be available to national judicial conferences and organizations.

Training for Probation and Parole Officers and Corrections Personnel

Probation and parole officers play a critical role in ensuring that offenders are complying with their statutory obligations to provide DNA samples. Corrections personnel often are responsible for obtaining DNA samples from inmates required by law to submit such samples. Through training and education programs, these professionals will be better equipped to ensure that samples are taken from all individuals who are required by law to provide them. The initiative calls for $1 million in FY 2004 to support this training.

Training for Forensic Scientists

The forensic science community has a critical need for trained forensic scientists in public crime laboratories. The initiative will assist the development of comprehensive training programs for a new generation of forensic scientists, enabling new forensic scientists to receive in-depth training to prepare them for analyzing actual casework in a crime laboratory. The initiative calls for $3 million in FY 2004 to support this training.

Training for Medical Personnel

The initiative will also provide $5 million in FY 2004 to support the development of training and educational materials for doctors and nurses involved in treating victims of sexual assault. Trained medical personnel are needed to effectively collect usable DNA evidence, while safeguarding the privacy rights and addressing the needs of rape victims requiring sexual assault exams. These programs will specifically target underserved areas of the country. Funding may also be used to support the development of SANE (Sexual Assault Nurse Examiner), SAFE (Sexual Assault Forensic Examiner), and SART (Sexual Assault Response Team) programs.

Training for Victim Service Providers

Victims and those who advocate on their behalf must have access to information about the investigative and courtroom uses of forensic DNA evidence. Victims should be properly informed about how DNA evidence may impact their cases. In situations involving post-conviction DNA testing, victim service providers must be able to assist victims through the often-painful process of newly-ordered DNA tests and re-opened court proceedings. To address the concerns of victims, the initiative would develop additional DNA education and training programs for victim advocates and victim service providers so that they may better assist victims in all cases involving DNA evidence. The initiative calls for $5 million in FY 2004 to support this training.

USING DNA TO PROTECT THE INNOCENT

DNA technology is increasingly vital to ensuring fairness in the criminal justice system. Every effort that is made to reduce backlogs of untested evidence, to better equip forensic laboratories, to develop faster methods of analyzing samples, and to better train professionals in the use of DNA technology, will improve the accuracy of the criminal justice system. Accordingly, the measures described in the previous sections will not only help solve crimes and keep dangerous offenders off the streets, but will also help minimize the risk that innocent individuals are wrongly accused or convicted.

Post-conviction DNA testing has received considerable attention in recent years. Since the advent of forensic DNA analysis, a number of individuals convicted of crimes have been subsequently exonerated through DNA analysis of crime scene evidence that was not tested at the time of trial. The following are two recent reported examples:

In February 2003, a Hampton Roads, Virginia man was released from prison after post-conviction DNA tests proved that he did not rape a nursing student in 1981. The man had spent two decades in prison after being convicted of breaking into the woman's apartment and raping her. Two juries failed to reach a verdict, but a third jury found him guilty. From the time of his arrest, however, the man maintained his innocence. Last year, a Virginia crime lab located evidence in the man's case in a file maintained by a forensic scientist who had since died. DNA tests conducted on this evidence proved that he was not the perpetrator, and have preliminarily linked the crime scene evidence to a felon whose DNA sample was maintained in the Virginia DNA database. The Norfolk Commonwealth Attorney supported the man's immediate release from prison after learning of the DNA test result. Law enforcement authorities are following up on the "cold hit."

A Maryland man served 20 years of a 30-year sentence after being convicted of a 1982 home invasion rape of a schoolteacher. Through post-conviction DNA testing, the man was exonerated in 2002. When the crime scene profile was uploaded to CODIS, it was preliminarily linked to a felon whose DNA profile was maintained in a DNA database. This man has subsequently been arrested and charged for the 1982 crime, and is awaiting trial later this year. The original defendant was pardoned in January 2003.

Many states have already enacted provisions that allow convicted offenders in certain cases to seek post-conviction DNA testing of evidence collected in those cases. Currently, 31 states have enacted special statutory provisions providing post-conviction DNA testing, and additional states make post-conviction testing available through other procedures. Federal law also should provide for post-conviction DNA testing in appropriate cases.

To demonstrate support for appropriate post-conviction testing of DNA evidence, the Attorney General will create a $5 million grant program under the President's initiative to help states defray the costs of post-conviction DNA testing. In order to receive this funding, state programs will be required to meet criteria established by the Department of Justice. These criteria will require that DNA testing be performed by an accredited forensic laboratory, and will encourage states to develop plans that ensure prompt DNA testing of persons who may be wrongly convicted and discourage frivolous testing that may cause unnecessary expense and needless harm to crime victims.

Using DNA to Identify Missing Persons

Families of missing persons who are presumed dead face tremendous emotional turmoil when they are unable to learn about the fates of their loved ones. The events of September 11, 2001 demonstrated on a national scale the potential for anguish when the remains of a missing person go unidentified. In the wake of this tragedy, the Department of Justice brought together DNA experts from across the country to develop improved DNA analysis methods identifying the World Trade Center victims.

Despite tremendous scientific advancements, DNA technology is not routinely used in missing persons cases. According to statistics maintained by the FBI's National Crime Information Center (NCIC), there are nearly 5,000 reported unidentified persons in the United States. This element of the President's initiative will help identify the missing, and in doing so, will provide an increased sense of closure to their families.

The FBI's Missing Persons DNA Database Program currently provides the essential infrastructure for identifying human remains. This database maintains two indices of DNA samples. The first index contains DNA profiles of relatives of missing persons and the second contains DNA profiles of unidentified human remains. Successful identifications require that both profiles be entered. Currently, this database is not used to its full potential. States have only recently begun to conduct DNA analysis on human remains and to submit the results to the FBI for inclusion in its database. Many unidentified human remains continue to be disposed of without the collection of DNA samples. Further, even when the samples are collected, many crime labs lack the capacity to conduct timely analysis, especially where the biological sample is old or degraded. In addition, many family members and law enforcement officials lack sufficient information about the existence of the program and how to participate.

The President's initiative will help ensure that DNA forensic technology is used to its full potential to identify missing persons. The initiative will:

- Provide outreach and education to medical examiners, coroners, and law enforcement officers about the use of DNA to identify human remains and to aid in missing persons cases;
- Make DNA reference collection kits available to these state and local officials;
- Support the development of educational materials and outreach programs for families of missing children and adults;
- Encourage states to collect DNA samples before any unidentified remains are disposed;
- Strengthen crime lab capacity (see page 4) to enable more state and local labs to conduct timely DNA analysis of biological samples from unidentified human remains;
- Provide for the analysis of degraded and old biological samples through the FBI's Mitochondrial DNA Analysis Program ;
- Provide technical assistance to state and local crime labs and medical examiners on the collection and analysis of degraded remains through the FBI and the National Institute of Justice; and
- Support research and development of more robust methods for analyzing degraded, old, or compromised biological samples.

In: Forensics in Law Enforcement
Editor: M. V. Shoester, pp. 223-235
ISBN 1-60021-164-X

GLOSSARY OF TERMS

A

A.F.I.S. - Automated Fingerprint Identification System

ABO blood typing - A commonly used genetic typing test that uses antibodies to detect variations on the surface of human red blood cells. Individuals are typed as having A, B, O, or AB type blood by testing liquid or stains from body fluids (e.g., blood, saliva, vaginal secretions). One out of every three randomly selected pairs of people have the same ABO blood type.

Allele - A different form of a gene at a particular locus. The characteristics of a single copy of a specific gene, or of a single copy of a specific location on a chromosome. For example, one copy of a specific STR region might have 10 repeats, while the other copy might have 11 repeats. These would represent two alleles of that STR region.

Allele Frequencies - term used to characterize genetic variation of a species population.

Allelic dropout - Failure to detect an allele within a sample or failure to amplify an allele during PCR.

Alternate light source (ALS) - Equipment used to produce visible and invisible light at various wavelengths to enhance or visualize items of evidence (fluids, fingerprints, clothing fibers, etc.). The light will cause possible biological stains to change color or fluoresce assisting in the location process.

Amelogenin - A gene present on the X and Y sex chromosomes that is used in DNA identification testing to determine the gender of the donor of the DNA in a biological sample.

Amplification - Producing multiple copies of a chosen DNA region, usually by PCR (Polymerase Chain Reaction).

Analytical Threshold - An acceptable "Relative Fluorescence Units" (RFU) level determined to be appropriate for use in the PCR/STR DNA typing process. A minimum threshold for data comparison is identified by the specific forensic laboratory doing the testing through independent validation studies.

Artifact - Any non-allelic product of the amplification process (Stutter or Minus A) or anomaly of the detection process (Pull-up or Spike).

ASCLD - American Society of Crime Lab Directors

ASCLD-LAB - The American Society of Crime Lab Directors – Laboratory Accreditation Board. ASCLD-LAB is a crime lab accreditation program organized to review and inspect the quality assurance of forensic laboratories and insure that specified standards are followed. Accreditation is only available to forensic laboratories who perform casework.

Autosomal - Chromosomes which are not sex chromosomes.

B

Base Pairing - A,T,C and G are molecular building blocks of DNA that only continue in specific "base" pairs, e.g.,A only pairs with T, and C only pairs with G

Bases - The four building blocks of DNA are called bases. The building blocks are Cytosine, Guanine, Thymine, Adenine and are commonly referred to as C, G, T, A.

Bench notes - A laboratory analyst's recorded notes.

Biallelic - Pertaining to both alleles, e.g. single nucleotide polymorphisms display two alternate forms and are biallelic.

Bindle paper - Clean paper folded for the containment of trace evidence, sometimes included as part of the packaging for collecting trace evidence.

Biohazard bag - A container for materials that have been exposed to blood or other biological fluids and have the potential to be contaminated with hepatitis, AIDS, or other contagions.

Biological Evidence - Evidence commonly recovered from crime scenes in the form of hair, tissue, bones, teeth, blood or other bodily fluids.

Biological fluids - Fluids that have human or animal origin, most commonly encountered at crime scenes (e.g., blood, mucous, perspiration, saliva, semen, vaginal fluid and urine).

Blind testing - In a blind test analysts do not know they are being tested. In most forensic DNA laboratories, blind tests are not used.

In practice, it is almost impossible to design and implement an effective blind PT program in forensic science. Most attempts have failed because they could not produce an effective case scenario with realistic representation of the pre-laboratory steps. Others failed because the analyst recognized that the supposed "evidence" was a manufactured artifact. Overall, it has proven impossible to realize the theoretical extra benefits of blind testing and resources have been devoted to promoting better quality external open tests.

Boundaries - The perimeter or border surrounding potential physical evidence related to the crime.

C

Cambridge Reference Sequence (CRS) - A "master template" of the HVR-1 region of mitochondrial DNA.

Capillary Electrophoresis (CE) - The platform for CE uses narrow silica capillaries (or tubes) containing a polymer solution through which the negatively charged DNA molecules migrate under the influence of a high voltage electric field. Important advantages of the CE technique, compared to slab gel electrophoresis, include quicker and more easily automated analyses

Case file - The collection of documents comprising information concerning a particular investigation. (This collection may be kept in case jackets, file folders, ring binders, boxes, file drawers, file cabinets or rooms. Sub-files are often used within case files to segregate and group interviews, media coverage, laboratory requests and reports, evidence documentation, photographs, videotapes, audiotapes, and other documents.)

Case Identifier - The alphabetic and/or numeric characters assigned to identify a particular case.

Cell - The smallest component of life capable of independent reproduction and from which DNA is isolated for forensic analysis.

Chain of Custody - A record of individuals who have had physical possession of the evidence and the process used to maintain and document the chronological history of the evidence. (Documents can include, but are not limited to- name or initials of the individual collecting the evidence, each person or entity subsequently having physical possession of it, dates the items were collected or transferred, where the item(s) were collected from, agency and case number, victim's or suspect's name (if known), and a brief description of the item.)

Chromosome - The biological structure by which hereditary information is physically transmitted from one generation to the next. Located in the cell nucleus, it consists of a tightly coiled thread of DNA with associated proteins and RNA. The genes are arranged in linear order along the DNA.

Clean/sanitize - The process of removing biological and/or chemical contaminants from tools and/or equipment.

CODIS - Combined DNA Index System. A collection of databases of DNA profiles obtained from evidence samples from unsolved crimes and from known individuals convicted of particular crimes. Contributions to this database are made through State crime laboratories and the data are maintained by the FBI.

CODIS core loci - Thirteen STR (short tandem repeat) sequences that have been selected for the Combined DNA Index System (CODIS).

Cold hit - When CODIS recognizes a match between an offender and forensic profile, it is referred to as a "cold hit".

Collect/collection - The process of identifying, documenting, gathering and packaging or retaining physical evidence.

Competency - The combination of demonstrated knowledge, skills and abilities.

Contamination - The undesirable transfer of material to physical evidence (DNA) from another source.

Control Samples - Cuttings, swabbings, etc. from unstained adjacent material. A control sample is material of a known source that presumably was uncontaminated during the commission of the crime (e.g., a sample to be used in laboratory testing to ensure that the surface on which the sample is deposited does not interfere with testing. For example, when a bloodstain is collected from a carpet, a segment of unstained carpet must be collected). The control sample should be taken adjacent to the biological stain being collected.

Controls - Tests designed to demonstrate that a procedure worked correctly and performed in parallel with experimental samples.

Cross Contamination - The undesirable transfer of material between two or more sources of physical evidence.

Cytoplasm - The viscid, semifluid matter contained within the plasma membrane of a cell, excluding the nucleus.

D

Degradation - The fragmenting, or breakdown of DNA by chemical or physical means.

Dideoxy sequencing - Dideoxynucleotide sequencing, also known as the 'Sanger method,' is a technique which uses dideoxyribose instead of deoxyribose to stop the synthesis of a complementary DNA strand at various points when sequencing.

Differential extraction - A procedure in which sperm cells are separated, or extracted, from all other cells in a sample.

Disposable instruments - Items that will be used only once to collect evidence, such as biological samples, then discarded to minimize contamination (e.g., tweezers, scalpel blades, droppers).

DNA (Deoxyribonucleic acid) - Often referred to as the "blueprint of life," DNA is the genetic material present in the nucleus of cells which is inherited half from each biological parent. DNA is a chemical substance contained in cells, which determines each person's individual characteristics. An individual's DNA is unique except in cases of identical twins.

DNA Analysis - The process of testing to identify DNA patterns or types. In the forensic setting, this testing is used to exclude or include individual's as possible sources of body fluid stains (blood, saliva, semen) and other biological evidence (bones, teeth, hair). This testing can also be used to indicate parentage.

DNA fingerprinting - Analyses of the lengths of the fragments reveal that when looking at multiple VNTRs within and between individuals, no two people have the same assortment of lengths. This technique became known to the public as "DNA fingerprinting" because of its powerful ability to discriminate between unrelated individuals.

DNA mixtures - A sample that contains the DNA of more than one individual.

DNA Profile - The result of determining the relative positions of DNA sequences at several locations on the molecule. Each person (except identical twins) has a unique DNA profile when used in the context of the CODIS database, which evaluates 13 specific DNA locations.

Documentation - Written notes, audio/videotapes, printed forms, sketches and/or photographs that form a detailed record of the scene, evidence recovered, and actions taken during the search of the crime scene, including chain of custody information.

Double Helix - The shape the DNA assumes after it replicates during cell life.

E

Electropherogram - The graphic representation of the separation of molecules by electrophoresis or other means of separation.

Electrophoresis - A method of separating large molecules (such as DNA fragments) from a mixture of similar molecules. An electric current is passed through a medium at a different rate, depending on its electrical charge and size. Separation of DNA markers is based on these differences.

Elimination/Reference samples - A term used to describe a sample of known source taken for comparison purposes.

Example- An elimination sample is one of known source taken from a person who had lawful access to the crime scene (e.g. blood or cheek [buccal] swabs for DNA analysis, fingerprints from occupants, tire tread impressions from police vehicles, footwear impressions from emergency medical personnel) to be used for comparison with evidence of the same type.

A reference sample is material of a verifiable/documented source which, when compared with evidence of an unknown source, shows an association or linkage between an offender, crime scene and/or victim (e.g., a carpet cutting taken from a location suspected as the point of transfer for comparison with the fibers recovered from the suspect's shoes, a sample of paint removed from a suspect's vehicle to be compared with paint found on a victim's vehicle following an accident, or a sample of the suspect's and/or victim's blood submitted for comparison with a bloodstained shirt recovered as evidence).

Evidence - Something that can help identify the responsible persons, establish an element of crime, reconstruct crime events or link crimes.

Evidentiary samples - A generic term used to describe physical material/evidence discovered at crime scenes that may be compared with samples from persons, tools, and physical locations.

Excluded - Two samples cannot have come from the same source.

Exclusion - A DNA test result indicating that an individual is excluded as the source of the DNA evidence. In a criminal case, "exclusion" does not necessarily equate to "innocence."

Exclusion - The elimination of an individual as the source of a biological sample. This occurs when one or more types from a specific location in the DNA of a known individual are not present in the type(s) for that specific location in the DNA obtained from an evidence sample.

Exogenous DNA - DNA originating outside an organism that has been introduced into the organism.

Expert System - A software program or set of software programs designed to rapidly process data without human intervention.

External testing - An external test is one that is created and administered by an outside agency.

F

First responding law enforcement officer - The initial responding law enforcement officer and/or other public safety official or service provider arriving at the scene prior to the arrival of the investigators in charge.

Forensic Hit - A CODIS match between two or more crime scene profiles.

Forensic Index - DNA profiles developed from crime scene evidence and uploaded into CODIS are maintained in the forensic index of the database.

Forensic Science - The application of science to analyze evidence involved in criminal and civil litigation.

Forensic unknowns - DNA profiles obtained from crime scene evidence samples that are unmatched to a known individual.

Fractions - The result of the differential extraction; separating sperm cells from all other DNA material.

Fragile evidence - Evidence that will lose its evidentiary value if not preserved and protected, either because of its nature or the conditions at the scene (e.g., blood in the rain).

G

Gene - The basic unit of heredity; a functional sequence of DNA in a chromosome.

Genetic loci - places in the genetic material of an organism where specific DNA sequences can be found.

Genetics - The study of the patterns of inheritance of specific traits.

Genome - All the genetic material in the chromosomes of a particular organism; its size is generally given as its total number of base pairs.

Genotype - The genetic constitution of an organism, as distinguished from its physical appearance (its phenotype). The designation of two alleles at a particular locus is a genotype.

H

Haplotype - A way of denoting the collective genotype of a number of closely linked loci on a chromosome.

Hardy-Weinberg (Equilibrium) - In a large random intrabreeding population, not subjected to excessive selection or mutation, the gene and genotype frequencies will remain constant overt time. The sum of $p^2+2pq+q^2$ applies at equilibrium for a single allele pair where p is the frequency of the allele A, q is the frequency of a, p^2 is the frequency of genotype AA, q^2 is the frequency of aa, and 2pq is the frequency of Aa.

Heredity - The transmission of characteristics from one generation to the next.

Heteroplasmy - The presence of more than one mtDNA type within a single individual.

Heterozygous - If two alleles are different at one locus, the person is heterozygous at that genetic location.

HIPAA - Health Insurance Portability and Accountability Act of 1996.

HLA DQ-alpha - A polymorphic gene in the Human Leukocyte Antigen (HLA) region of chromosome 6 that has been well studied and analyzed for many purposes including paternity testing, transplantation biology, and human DNA identification testing.

Homozygous - If two alleles at a locus that are indistinguishable, the person is homozygous at that genetic location.

Hypervariable - An area on the DNA which can have many different alleles in differing sequences.

I

Included - Two samples could have come from the same source.

Inclusion (Failure to Exclude) - The inability to exclude an individual as a possible source of a biological sample. This occurs when all types from a specific location in the DNA of a known individual are also present in the types for that specific location in the DNA obtained from an evidence sample.

Inconclusive - A situation in which no conclusion can be reached regarding testing done due to one of many possible reasons (e.g., no results obtained, uninterpretable results obtained, no exemplar/standard available for testing).

Internal testing - An internal test is one that is created and administered by the laboratory itself.

Intimate Sample - An intimate sample is generally referred to a biological sample obtained from a source other than the mouth (saliva) and head (hair).

Irresolvable mixture - A DNA profile where multiple individuals have contributed biological material and no profile is more or less apparent than any other and the developed alleles cannot be isolated to a single source.

J

John Doe Warrant - a warrant used when crime scene evidence yields a DNA profile but the individual corresponding to the DNA profile is unknown. In lieu of the suspect's name, the warrant will be filed as "John Doe" and cite the DNA profile.

junk DNA - Stretches of DNA that do not code for genes; "most of the genome consists of junk DNA."

K

Known samples - A DNA sample for which the source is known. These samples are generally obtained from the victim and/or suspected perpetrator of a crime, as well as from other persons whose DNA might be reflected when samples of the evidence are analyzed (could include a boyfriend, husband, or other third-party). These samples are also referred to as reference samples, since they serve as a reference to which the unknown DNA samples are compared with the goal of identifying the source of the unknown DNA samples.

L

Latent print - A print impression that is not readily visible, made by contact with a surface.

LDIS - The Local DNA Index System of CODIS which uploads forensic and offender DNA profiles to the State DNA Index System, or SDIS.

Length heteroplasmy - The presence of mtDNA molecules that differ in length.

Likelihood ratio - The ratio of two probabilities of the same event under different hypotheses. In DNA testing often expressed as the ratio between the likelihood that a given profile came from a particular individual and the likelihood that it came from a random unrelated person. Note that in this case the likelihood of each event does not add to give 1 (100% likelihood) as it does not incorporate the possibility of error or that the profiles came from twins or other near relatives. .

Linkage Equilibrium - when two or more genetic loci appear to segregate randomly in a given population. The genotypes appear randomly with respect to each other.

Locus (pl. loci) - The specific physical location of a gene on a chromosome.

Low copy number - Refers to examination of less than 100pg (picograms) of input DNA.

M

Major contributor profile - A DNA profile where multiple individuals have contributed biologic material and one individual's DNA profile is more apparent.

Marker - Pieces of DNA sequence of known locations on chromosomes that are used to identify the specific genetic variations an individual possesses.

Match - Genetic profiles are said to 'match' when they have the same allele designations at every loci.

Measurement scale - An object showing standard units of length (e.g., ruler) used in photographic documentation of an item of evidence.

Microbial Epidemiology – microbial: relating to a microbe or microbes; epidemiology: the study or the distribution and determinants of health-related states or events in specified populations, and the application of this study to control health problems.

Mitochondrial DNA (mtDNA) - The DNA found in the many mitochondria found in each cell of a body. The sequencing of mitochondrial DNA can link individuals descended from a common female ancestor.

mtDNA types - A mtDNA type is the sequence of a region of mtDNA. Common sources of mtDNA are hairs, skeletal remains and teeth.

Multiplexed - A system for analyzing several loci at once.

N

National DNA Index System (NDIS) - Authorized by the DNA Identification Act of 1994, the FBI administers this national index. NDIS compares DNA profiles associated with a crime scene to DNA profiles collected from known convicted offenders, as well as to other crime scene profiles. When the DNA profiles are uploaded to NDIS, they are searched against the other DNA profiles submitted by other participating states.

National Research Council (NRC) - The National Research Council was convened in 1989. In 1996 the NRC filed the report The Evaluation of Forensic DNA Evidence (referred to as NRC II). This document revised and expanded the initial report written in 1992 (NRC I). These recommendations are recognized by U.S. courts.

No results - A situation in which no interpretable results are obtained from testing a DNA sample. A finding of no results can be due to the absence of DNA, insufficient DNA or substances that inhibit the PCR process, among others.

Non-conformances - Inconsistencies in laboratory practices that do not meet accreditation standards.

Nonmatch - An individual is eliminated as the source of a biological sample. This occurs when one or more types from a specific location in the DNA of a known individual are not present in the type(s) for that specific location in the DNA obtained from an evidence sample.

Nonporous Container - Packaging through which liquids or vapors cannot pass (e.g., glass jars or metal cans).

Nuclear DNA - The DNA found in the nucleus of a cell.

Nucleated - Having a nucleus or occurring in the nucleus.

Nucleus - The cellular organelle that contains most of the genetic material.

O

Objective test - A test which having been documented and validated is under control so that it can be demonstrated that all appropriately trained staff will obtain the same results within defined limits. These defined limits relate to expressions of degrees of probability as well as numerical values.

Offender Hit - A CODIS match between a crime scene profile and an offender profile.

Offender Index - DNA profiles developed from qualifying offenders and uploaded into CODIS are maintained in the offender index of the database.

P

Partial profile - DNA evidence that does not yield identifiable results in all 13 core loci.

Partially degraded DNA - Forensic DNA evidence exposed to environmental conditions that may prevent it from yielding a usable profile

Paternal inheritance - Genetic material which is inherited from one's father; for example, the possibility that mtDNA can be inherited from one's father.

PCR Inhibitors - A substance that interferes with the Polymerase Chain Reaction (PCR) process. Examples of PCR inhibitors include dyes, soil, chemicals and heme (hemoglobin).

Personal Protective Equipment (PPE) - Articles such as disposable (latex) gloves, masks, shoe covers and eye protection that are utilized to provide a barrier to keep biological or chemical hazards from contacting the skin, eyes, and mucous membranes and to avoid contamination of the crime scene.

Polymerase Chain Reaction (PCR) - A process used in DNA identification testing in which one or more specific small regions of the DNA are copied using a DNA polymerase enzyme so that a sufficient amount of DNA is generated for analysis.

Polymorphic - Variable, more than one kind.

Polymorphism - Variations in DNA sequences in a population that are detected in human DNA identification testing.

PopStats - FBI CODIS software program used to perform statistical DNA match estimates.

Probability - The chance of observing a particular future event; a simple ratio of the number of observed events divided by the total number of possible events.

Probability calculations - Predictions based on small sampling of a larger population.

Probability of Exclusion - The probability that a random individual would be excluded as the source of analyzed DNA evidence.

Probability of inclusion - The probability that a random individual would be included as a potential source of analyzed DNA evidence.

Product rule - The product rule calculates the expected chance of finding a given STR profile within a population by multiplying the frequency of occurrence of the combination of alleles (genotype) found at a single locus, by the frequency of occurrence of the genotype found at the second locus, by the frequency of occurrence, in turn, of each of the other genotypes at the remaining STR loci.

Proficiency testing - A DNA proficiency test uses biological samples to assess a lab analyst's ongoing competency and the laboratory's ability to produce accurate results.

Pull-up - Specifically related to ABI Gene Scan® software, a peak seen in one color that is not due to the presence of DNA, but to incorrect compensation for the spectral overlap of the four dyes used in detecting multiple loci in one reaction. See also: Artifact

Q

Quality Assurance (QA) - A program conducted by a laboratory to ensure accuracy and reliability of tests performed.

Quality Assurance Standards - The standards originated from the DNA Advisory Board and are maintained by the FBI; they place specific requirements on labs involved in forensic DNA analysis, both casework and convicted offender databasing.

Quantitation - Method used to determine the quantity of "x" in a given sample. In this context, it refers to the quantity of DNA in a sample and is usually reported as ng/µl.

R

Random match probability - The probability that the DNA in a random sample from the population has the same profile as the DNA in the evidence sample.

Reciprocal Discovery - Some jurisdictions enable a prosecutor by motion, to request that the defense provide specific discovery material to the prosecution.

Recombinant DNA - Altered DNA resulting from the insertion into the chain, by chemical, enzymatic, or other biological means, of a sequence (a whole or partial chain of DNA) not originally (biologically) present in that chain.

Recombination - The reversal of coupling phase I meiosis as gauged by the resulting phenotype. See also Recombinant DNA above.

Reference Samples - A standard/reference sample is material of a verifiable/documented source which, when compared with evidence of an unknown source, shows an association or linkage between an offender, crime scene, and/or victim (e.g., a carpet cutting taken from a location suspected as the point of transfer for comparison with the fibers recovered from the suspect's shoes, a sample of paint removed from a suspect vehicle to be compared with paint found on a victim's vehicle following an accident, or a sample of the suspect's and/or victim's blood submitted for comparison with a bloodstained shirt recovered as evidence).

Restriction enzyme - A protein harnessed from bacteria that recognizes specific, short nucleotide sequences and cuts DNA at those sites.

Restriction fragment length polymorphism - Variation in the length of a stretch of DNA; abbreviated RFLP.

S

SDIS - State DNA Index System containing the state-level DNA records uploaded from local laboratory sites within the state. SDIS is the state's repository of DNA identification records and is under the control of state authorities. The SDIS laboratory serves as the central point of contact for access to NDIS. The DNAUI serves as the SDIS laboratory for the FBI.

Sequence (or site) heteroplasmy - the presence of mtDNA molecules that have different nucleotides at the same address.

Sequencing - Determination of the order of base sequences in a DNA molecule.

Short Tandem Repeat (STR) typing - DNA analysis method which targets regions on the chromosome which contain multiple copies of an identical DNA sequence in succession.

Short Tandem Repeats (STR) - Multiple copies of a short identical DNA sequence arranged in direct succession in particular regions of chromosomes.

Single Nucleotide Polymorphisms (SNPs) - DNA sequence variations that occur at a single nucleotide (A,T,C,or G).

Single source profile - A DNA profile where only one individual has contributed biologic material.

Single-use Equipment - Items that will be used only once to collect evidence, such as biological samples, then discarded to minimize contamination (e.g., tweezers, scalpel blades, droppers).

Standard Operation Procedures (SOP) - A prescribed procedure to be followed routinely.

Stochastic effects - Being or having a random variable.

Stutter - A minor band or peak appearing one repeat unit smaller than a primary STR allele. Occasionally, the repeat unit is larger than the primary allele. See also: Artifact

Substrate - Any background material upon which biological sample has been deposited (e.g., clothing, glass, wood, upholstery).

SWGDAM - Scientific Working Group of DNA Analysis and Methods, formerly called TWGDAM (Technical Working Group on DNA Analysis and Methods).

T

Theta Correction - A theta adjustment is a mathematical correction applied to a frequency calculation when both alleles at a locus are the same (known as a homozygous state). It is not applied when alleles are different at a locus (known as a heterozygous state). This correction adjusts the frequency slightly upwards to account for the presence of subpopulations in a general population database that might otherwise cause the genotype frequency to be underestimated at that locus.

Third Party Defense Motion - a motion filed by the prosecution to preclude the defense from asserting that DNA evidence is derived from a third party, possibly a relative of the accused.

Threshold value - A relative fluorescent unit (RFU) value that must be exceeded to make an allele call. This value will vary among laboratories.

Trace evidence - Physical evidence that results from the transfer of small quantities of materials (e.g., hair, textile fibers, paint chips, glass fragments, gunshot residue particles).

U

Uninterpretable - Results which might be reported by the laboratory when alleles can not be interpreted.

Upper Bound Frequency Estimates - an estimate of the percentage of individuals who could be potential contributors of a mtDNA profile.

UV light source - Use of an ultraviolet light source to enhance or visualize potential items of evidence (fluids, fingerprints, clothing fibers, etc.). The light will cause possible biological stains to change color or fluoresce assisting in the location process.

V

Validation - The process of extensive and rigorous evaluation of DNA methods before acceptance for routine use.

Variable Number of Tandem Repeats (VNTRs) - Repeating units of a DNA sequence; a class of RFLPs; abbreviated VNTR.

Variant - A dissimilarity in the commonly occuring sequence of a gene.

W

Walk-through - An initial assessment conducted by carefully walking through the scene to evaluate the situation, identify potential evidence, and determine resources required. It can also be a final survey conducted to ensure the scene has been effectively and completely processed.

Y

Y-STR - short tandem repeats located on the Y chromosome.

INDEX

A

B

D

E

F

G

J

K

L

M

N

O

P

Q

R

S

T